Computerized Accounting with

Peachtree

2010

Jim Mazza PhD, MBA
DeVry University

Gary Chavez, MBA
DeVry University

St. Paul • Los Angeles • Indianapolis

Developmental Editor: Spencer Cotkin
Production Editor: Donna Mears
Cover Designer: Leslie Anderson
Composition: Ryan Hamner

Care has been taken to verify the accuracy of information presented in this book. However, the authors, editors, and publisher cannot accept responsibility for Web, e-mail, newsgroup, or chat room subject matter or content, or for consequences from application of the information in this book, and make no warranty, expressed or implied, with respect to its content.

Trademarks: Some of the product names and company names included in this book have been used for identification purposes only and may be trademarks or registered trade names of their respective manufacturers and sellers. The authors, editors, and publisher disclaim any affiliation, association, or connection with, or sponsorship or endorsement by, such owners.

Acknowledgments: The authors wish to thank Kathleen McKilligan of Chavez Accounting Concepts for her assistance in testing the exercises and verifying their accuracy.

We have made every effort to trace the ownership of all copyrighted material and to secure permission from copyright holders. In the event of any question arising as to the use of any material, we will be pleased to make the necessary corrections in future printings. Thanks are due to the aforementioned authors, publishers, and agents for permission to use the materials indicated.

ISBN 978-0-76383-795-2 (text & CD)
ISBN 978-0-76383-794-5 (text)

©2011 by Paradigm Publishing, Inc.
875 Montreal Way
St. Paul, MN 55102
E-mail: educate@emcp.com
Web site: www.emcp.com

Printed in the United States of America

19 18 17 16 15 14 13 12 11 10   1 2 3 4 5 6 7 8 9 10

Brief Contents

Contents

Preface

Computerized Accounting with Peachtree® 2010 teaches all of the key accounting software skills supported in Peachtree® Complete Accounting, Release 2010. In addition, it covers the accounting concepts associated with each chapter. Detailed step-by-step explanations followed by hands-on exercises provide students the opportunity to practice using the program features immediately after learning about them. A variety of end-of-chapter exercises help ensure mastery of the key course content.

Textbook Features

Several aspects of this text are unique and will lead to better student understanding of the material while giving the instructor the flexibility needed in the classroom.

- Learning objectives focus the instruction for each chapter.
- Each accounting concept is thoroughly explained before students begin using any of Peachtree's functions.
- All of the software instruction is presented using a step-by-step approach and illustrated by detailed screen captures.
- Definitions of key phrases and helpful hints for users are included in the margins.
- Checkpoint quizzes are located at the end of each major section in the chapter.
- Two methods of negotiating the Peachtree environment are intermittently used throughout the text. Students can use menu bar drop-down menus or navigation aids to work through the problems.
- Practice exercises specific to each objective (with selected answers) are provided at the end of each key content section.
- Two levels of comprehensive case problems test students' knowledge of the learning objectives.
- Cooperative learning problems that focus on specific chapter issues are available in each chapter.
- A writing and decision-making problem relating to the chapter's learning objectives is included at the end of each chapter.

- Comprehensive problems to be administered at the end of Chapter 7 and Chapter 13 are available in the Instructor's Guide.

Chapters at a Glance

Chapter 1 – Getting Started

Chapter 1 introduces students to accounting as the language of business and to uses of accounting information. The differences between computerized and manual accounting are stressed.

The chapter also explains how to open Peachtree 2010 and details the different navigation methods. In an effort to enhance the Peachtree experience, the Help feature is explained, and students are given instructions for exploring the Help feature. The Save and Backup features are also introduced.

Chapter 2 – Setting Up a Company

Chapter 2 explains the business organization types in detail, with charts illuminating the advantages and disadvantages of each. The chart of accounts and the general ledger are fully explained. There is an in-depth discussion of the differences between the cash and accrual methods of accounting, as well as an explanation of accounting periods. The account types that are used in Peachtree are thoroughly explained and the accounting definitions are detailed.

Students learn to set up a new company with easy-to-follow instructions and screen captures. Students create the chart of accounts, learn to create new accounts from scratch, and enter beginning balances in the accounts. Finally, students learn how to use the print filter and how to print documents.

Chapter 3 – Entering Transactions for a Cash Business

Chapter 3 introduces students to the meaning of transactions and how transactions affect the journal. Along with this, the treatment of debits and credits is explained. Subject matter is thoroughly discussed before students are expected to tackle the Peachtree functions—manual journal entries are demonstrated prior to having students do them using Peachtree.

Students create a new company and enter sample transactions using Peachtree. The sample manual transaction is presented prior to the computerized transaction so students are aware of the desired results. Edited transactions, recurring transactions, and memorized transactions are also introduced. Students then learn to print the financial transactions.

Chapter 4 – Accounts Receivable and Sales for a Service Business

In Chapter 4, the concept of accounts receivable is revisited in some detail. The concepts of subsidiary receivable ledger accounts and the controlling accounts are introduced. In addition, the concept and procedures for accounting for uncollectible accounts are introduced and explained using the direct write-off and allowance methods.

In Peachtree, students learn to create customer accounts and enter beginning balances, reviewing account terms associated with accounts receivable. They record sales on credit and record payments to the customers' accounts. Students use the journal to write off uncollectible accounts. In addition to mastering the accounts receivable transactions, students learn to use Action Items, Event Logs, and Company Alerts.

Chapter 5 – Accounts Payable and Purchases for a Service Business

Students are introduced to the concept of accounts payable. The authors explain the underlying meanings associated with accounts payable and vendors. The chapter also introduces controlling accounts and the accounts payable subsidiary.

In Peachtree, students create vendor accounts and enter their beginning balances. After the accounts are created, purchase and accounts payable transactions are demonstrated. Students use the List (Open) feature and the Action Items once again while entering accounts payable transactions. Additionally, the Peachtree Alert feature is demonstrated and practiced.

Chapter 6 – Cash Payments and Cash Receipts

Chapter 6 deals with managing cash and cash discounts. Invoices and payments to invoices are explained in detail.

In Peachtree, students learn how to process cash payments using the cash payments module. In addition, they learn how to process cash receipts using the cash receipts module and how to apply discount terms where applicable. Another Peachtree feature introduced is the bank reconciliation. The process is demonstrated for students, who then have several chances to prepare a bank reconciliation using Peachtree.

Chapter 7 – Preparing the Financial Statements

Although introduced in Chapter 2, the preparation of financial statements is covered more thoroughly in Chapter 7. This chapter discusses the different types of adjusting entries, giving examples of each. In addition, it reviews financial statements and the information contained within each.

Students practice creating adjusting journal entries and preparing financial statements using Peachtree. They learn special financial statement formatting features, including how to design unique financial statements for a given business. They work with changing the accounting period and closing the fiscal year.

Chapter 8 – Purchases of Inventory in a Merchandise Business

The two basic inventory systems and the methods for costing inventory are explained in detail. The inventory costing methods are demonstrated manually to give students a visual feel for what Peachtree will do automatically, which is to cost out inventory for a given inventory valuation method. These methods are explained using easy-to-understand examples. Additionally, there is a discussion about the results that each method provides the accountant.

In Peachtree, students create the inventory accounts and their associated subsidiary ledger accounts. Sales representatives accounts are established to allow Peachtree to track individual salespersons' inventory sales. Purchase transactions are demonstrated, and students practice the different types of transactions, including transactions involving discounts, purchase orders, and returns.

Chapter 9 – Sales of Inventory in a Merchandise Business

In this chapter students are introduced to inventory sales concepts and the perpetual inventory system. Sales tax is a part of the process of selling merchandise, so how to calculate and account for it is fully explained in this chapter. The necessary accounts and percentages are reviewed.

In Peachtree, students create the sales tax codes and accounts. After the sales tax accounts have been established, students can process sales transactions, create invoices, and add appropriate interest where applicable. Students have a chance to practice accounting for a sales return and processing a credit memo. Additionally, they have a chance to create a sales quotation and convert that quotation into a sales order.

Chapter 10 – Payroll

Chapter 10 reviews payroll concepts and introduces students to Peachtree payroll functions. Payroll concepts such as payroll periods, payroll laws and regulations, as well as the federal and state tax returns associated with payroll activities are covered. The normal payroll deductions that employees and employers are subject to are also reviewed.

In Peachtree, students use the Payroll Setup wizard to create a company's payroll system. Once the payroll system is created, students create individual employee payroll accounts. Instruction in the preparation of payroll and the printing of payroll checks follows the setup process. The payroll tax returns and payroll reports are then completed using the Print function.

Chapter 11 – Job Costing

Chapter 11 introduces students to job costing. The three basic methods for job costing—jobs only, phases, and phases with cost codes—are all demonstrated and explained.

In Peachtree, the setup for the job costing process is explored and practiced by students. This includes creating phase codes and cost codes, as well as estimating revenue and expenses. The procedures for using job costing to record and allocate purchases, payroll, and sales to specific jobs are explained and reviewed.

Chapter 12 – Fixed Assets

One feature that sets this book apart from other textbooks on computerized accounting is that fixed assets valuation and depreciation are covered. In order to work the problems in Chapter 12, students download the Peachtree Fixed Assets System (FAS) module at www.peachtree.com/fas2010download.

In this module, the most widely accepted depreciation methods are demonstrated for students with an industry accepted software application.

Using the Peachtree FAS module, students learn to create individual fixed asset accounts and to create supporting accounts, including accumulated depreciation. Transactions for the purchase, monthly depreciation, and disposal of assets are explained, demonstrated, and practiced. Additionally, transactions are viewed using both the FAS module and the main Peachtree module to see the impact one module has on another.

Chapter 13 – Partnerships and Corporations

The differences among sole proprietorships, partnerships, and corporations are revisited. The advantages of the partnership form and the corporate form are reviewed. In the case of the corporation, the chapter introduces accounting concepts associated with stock and stockholder ownership. In addition, the treatment of dividends is also covered in some length.

Students will create partnership accounts and enter partnership transactions, as well as distribute partnership gains and losses among and between the partners. Then they will create a new company as a corporation and practice several transactions.

Student Supplements

A **Student Resources CD** is packaged with this textbook. The disk includes the Education Version of Peachtree 2010 plus a self-extracting archive file (Peach10files.exe) containing the company files required for specific exercises, and instructions for downloading the Peachtree Fixed Assets System (FAS) at: www.peachtree.com/fas2010download. The other major student supplement is an **Internet Resource Center** offering both general information for succeeding in academic courses and specific information related to the text, including study aids, Web links, and additional course content. Access the Student Resource Center at www.emcp.net/peachtree2010.

Installing Peachtree 2010 from the CD

In order to successfully install and run Peachtree Complete Accounting Release 2010, Education Version, you will need at a minimum the following hardware and software:

- IBM Compatible 1 GHz Intel Pentium III computer for single and multiple users; for multiple concurrent users, 1.8 GHz Pentium 4 is recommended.
- 256 MB of RAM for a single user and 512 MB for multiple concurrent users (recommended: 512 MB for single user and 1 GB for multiple concurrent users); for Windows Vista, 512 MB for single and multiple users.
- Windows XP SP2 or Windows Vista.
- 1 GB of disk space for installation
- Internet Explorer 6.0 or higher required.
- Display settings of at least high color (16 bit) SVGA video; supports 1024 x 768 screen resolution with small fonts.
- 2x CD-ROM Drive.
- Mouse or compatible pointing device.
- 450 MB free hard disk space.
- Printers supported by Windows XP/Vista.
- Online Services require Internet access. Minimum connection speed depends on service.
- In-product demos require Macromedia® Flash™ Player.
- To use Microsoft Excel with Peachtree products, Excel 2002, 2003, or 2007 required.

Before you begin the installation process, check with your instructor to see if Peachtree Complete Accounting and/or the company files have already been loaded in a designated location for you. If you do need to install Peachtree on your workstation or you are using this book at home, simply place the Student Resources CD in your CD-ROM drive, and the Peachtree installation program will automatically appear and guide you through installing the software. The Educational Version of Peachtree Complete Accounting has the same features and functions—except for the Fixed Assets Module (needed for the Appendix)—that the commercial version does, but is not upgradeable.

Note: During installation, enter the serial number that is printed on the inside of the CD sleeve.

Extracting Company Files from the CD

If you are using a computer in a lab setting, we suggest that you create a separate folder on either your hard drive or in a designated network directory in which to save the Peachtree company files that you create, open, and add to while working

through this book. Your instructor may have already set up a designated location for your files. Once you have either created that folder or been told where your folder is, take the following steps to extract the company files from the CD to your folder:

1. Insert the Computerized Accounting with Peachtree 2010 CD into the CD-ROM drive.
2. At the Welcome to Peachtree Accounting window, click "Browse CD."
3. In the Exploring window that appears, on the right side, double-click Peach10files.exe.
4. Confirm with your instructor where your company files should be located.
5. At the WinZip Self-Extractor – Peach10files. exe dialog box, click Browse.
6. At the Browse for Folder dialog box, locate the folder where you will be storing your company files, and then click OK.
7. If the folder shown in the Unzip to folder text box is correct, click Unzip.

If you are using a computer at home, and you are the only student who is going to use that computer for the course, you can simply accept the default location in the WinZip Self-Extractor – Peach10files.exe dialog box (c:\), and click Unzip. Your files will be in a folder called Peachtree 2010 Student Data (Company Files).

Creating and Naming Company Files

As you work through the exercises in this textbook, you will create, open, and name Peachtree company files. You will learn the procedures for opening, creating, and backing up company files in Chapters 1 and 2. Company files created in Peachtree take up a lot of memory. Typically, you will save your files to a computer's hard drive or a designated network directory. You may also backup and restore to flash drives. Be aware that if you use flash drives, you will need to backup at the end of each session and restore at the beginning of each session. See your instructor to determine where exactly you should save your company files.

When you create a company file, or use one of the company files that are provided with the book, you may want to customize the name so that it is readily identifiable as your version of the company. You can do this by putting an extension at the end of the company's name. The extension could be your last name and first initial. For example, suppose you were working on the Acme Laundry Company file. When the company was first created, the file would have the name Acme Laundry Company. Everyone in the class would have the same file name; as a result, you could not tell your file from any other file. To solve this problem, you could add your name to the company name as you create the company file. If your name is John Jones, for example, the new company name and file name would be: **Acme Laundry – JONESJ**, and your file would be unique. This is only a suggestion—ask your instructor for specific instructions on how to name and save files.

To customize the name of a company as you create it, enter the customized company name in the *Company Name* field of the New Company Setup – Company Information dialog box.

To customize the names of already-created companies downloaded from the CD, take the following steps:

1. At the Peachtree Accounting-Start Window, click *Open an existing company*.
2. Find and open the company file on which you will be working.
3. Click Maintain, and then click Company Information.
4. At the Maintain Company Information window, click in the *Company Name* field, and then change the company name as needed.
5. Click the <u>O</u>K button at the top of the window. The next time you open the company, its name will reflect the changes you made.

Instructor Supplements

An Instructor's Guide CD, the Computerized Accounting Internet Resource Center, and online course management tools are available for instructors.

The **Instructor Resources CD** includes the following material:

- Overview
- Sample Syllabi
- Teaching Hints
- Solutions (Content Checks and Case Problems)
- Two Comprehensive Problems
- Objective Mid-term and Final Exams

The **Computerized Accounting Internet Resource Center** offers a password-protected Instructor site as well as a free-access Student site at www.emcp.net/peachtree2010. For instructors, a variety of tools are available, including chapter quizzes, lecture notes, and model answers, as well as the materials on the student and instructor CDs.

The **Distance Learning Course Files** is a set of files compatible with several platforms for traditional and distance learning. The course files provide supplementary content, communications via e-discussions and online group conferences, and testing resources. Content items include a syllabus, quizzes, course links, and study aids.

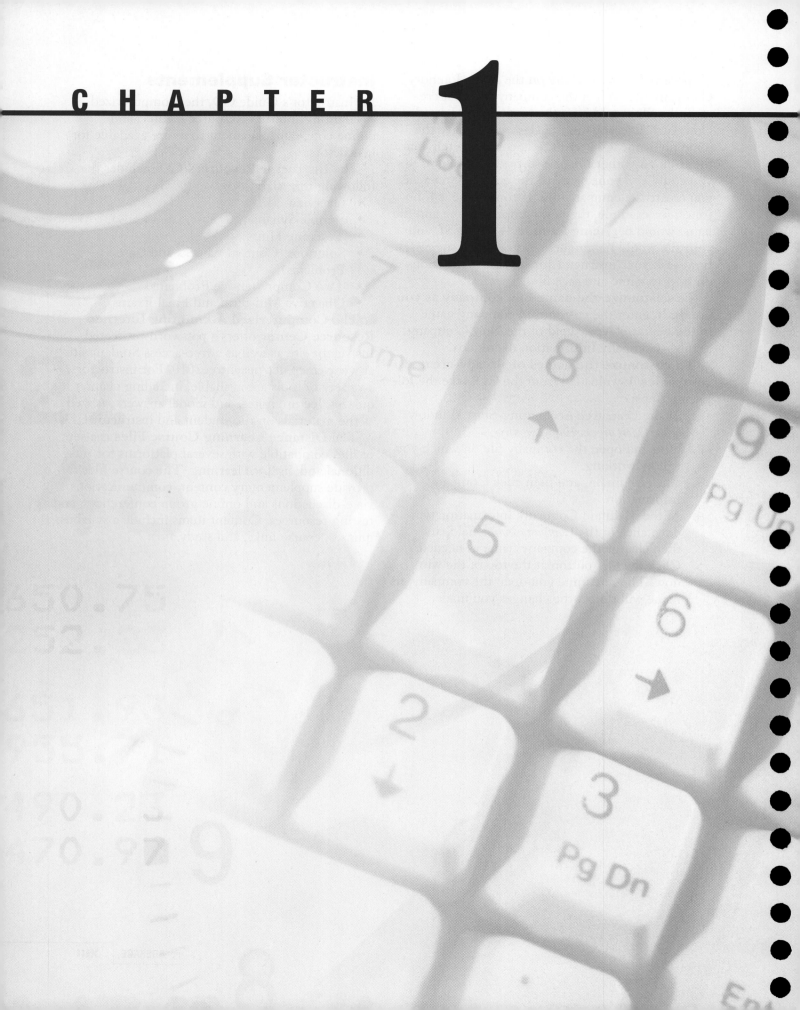

CHAPTER

1

Getting Started

Learning Objectives

1. Understand the differences between computerized and manual accounting

2. Open Peachtree Complete Accounting 2010

3. Use the basic Peachtree window, Navigation Aids toolbar, and the Menu bar

4. Use the Help feature

5. Open, back up, and restore company files

OBJECTIVE 1 — Understand the Differences between Computerized and Manual Accounting

accounting The process of recording, summarizing, analyzing, and interpreting financial activities.

Accounting is the process of recording, summarizing, analyzing, and interpreting financial activities—activities that involve money. The purpose of accounting is to provide financial information that owners, managers, and other interested parties can use to make decisions about a business.

Every accounting system—simple or complex, manual or computerized—must produce a complete, ongoing record of the financial events that take place in a business and must provide periodic reports showing the results of operations and the financial condition of the business. The steps of the accounting process are recording, summarizing, analyzing, and interpreting.

- *Recording* involves preparing a written record of financial events.
- *Summarizing* involves organizing the financial data into reports at regular intervals.
- *Analyzing* involves examining the reports to determine financial success or failure.
- *Interpreting* involves using financial data to make decisions.

Accounting is often called "the language of business" because it is used to communicate information about the financial results and financial condition of businesses. Is a firm profitable? Can it pay its debts? Does it have the resources to expand? This is the kind of information that accounting provides. Users of such information include owners, managers, current and potential investors, banks and other lending institutions, tax authorities, government agencies that regulate business activities, and potential suppliers and customers.

Manual and Computerized Accounting Systems

Whether an accounting system is manual or computerized, the underlying principles of accounting are the same. What does change when using a computerized system is the method of recording data and preparing reports. Once data about financial events is entered into a computerized accounting system, the system can be used to perform many tasks automatically: print a journal, post to the ledger accounts, prepare a trial balance, and print reports and financial statements.

Peachtree Accounting is designed for small and medium-sized businesses. One of the advantages of this software is that it produces records that are very similar to those found in a manual accounting system. For example, Peachtree allows you to work with special journals for sales, purchases, cash receipts, and cash disbursements as well as a general journal. Some other computerized accounting systems permit the use of just a single journal.

Special journals are an efficient means of recording financial data, and they make it easier to locate information that may be needed later. It is much quicker to look for a particular sale on credit in the sales journal than it is to trace through all the different transactions recorded in a single journal.

Computerized accounting systems like Peachtree save an enormous amount of time and effort for you because they do so many tasks automatically. Just as important, computerized accounting systems greatly reduce the number of errors that can occur with a manual accounting system.

A manual accounting system offers many opportunities for making errors. Data must be transferred by hand from the journals to the ledger accounts, then to the trial balance, and finally to the financial statements. Throughout this process, many calculations must be made.

With a computerized accounting system, there is still the possibility of making an error when a financial event is entered into the system. However, many computerized accounting systems have built-in checks that help you avoid errors. For example, when an entry is being made in the general journal, Peachtree alerts you if the entry contains unequal debits and credits.

Computerized accounting systems also reduce errors because they make all calculations automatically. For example, they compute the balances of the ledger accounts, the totals of the trial balance, and the subtotals and totals of the financial statements.

Note that computerized accounting systems like Peachtree do more than just the traditional tasks of journalizing, posting, preparing a trial balance, and preparing financial statements. These systems also handle many other financial activities, such as doing payroll and tax calculations, keeping records of the time and costs involved in projects, billing customers, processing credit card transactions, keeping records of fixed assets such as equipment, and keeping track of prospective customers.

Check point

1. What is the purpose of accounting?
2. What are two major advantages of computerized accounting systems over manual accounting systems?

Answers
1. *The purpose of accounting is to provide financial information that owners, managers, and other interested parties can use to make decisions about a business.*
2. *Computerized accounting systems save time and effort and reduce errors.*

OBJECTIVE 2 — Open Peachtree Complete Accounting 2010

Peachtree Complete Accounting 2010 includes two sample companies: Stone Arbor Landscaping and Bellwether Garden Supply. These sample companies are provided to help you become familiar with the basic functions of the software. In this chapter, we will work with Bellwether Garden Supply, a retail firm that sells goods and services.

Note: This text comes with a copy of Peachtree Complete Accounting 2010 (Educational Version) and assumes you will use Peachtree Complete Accounting as you work through the book. In order to be more concise, from this point on the software will be referred to as "Peachtree Accounting" or "Peachtree."

Follow the steps outlined on the following pages to begin the opening process for Peachtree Complete Accounting 2010.

Step 1:

Click the *Peachtree Complete Accounting 2010* icon from the desktop or click Start, *All Programs*, *Peachtree Complete Accounting 2010*, and again *Peachtree Complete Accounting 2010* from the Start menu lists that pop up. (See figure 1–1.)

FIGURE 1–1
Peachtree Startup Menus

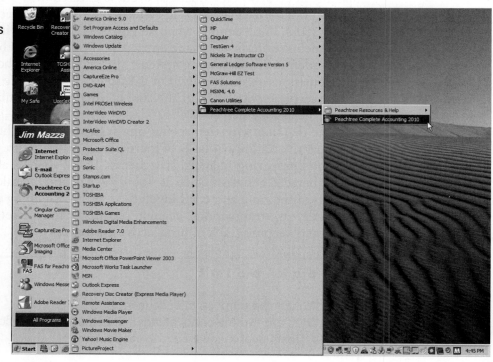

Step 2:

Click *Explore a sample company* from the Startup window, as shown in figure 1–2.

FIGURE 1–2
Peachtree Accounting
Opening Window

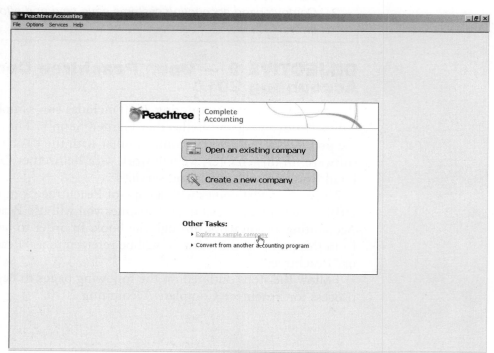

Step 3:

At the Explore a Sample Company window, click *Bellwether Garden Supply*, as shown by figure 1–3. Then click OK.

FIGURE 1–3
Bellwether Garden
Supply Selected

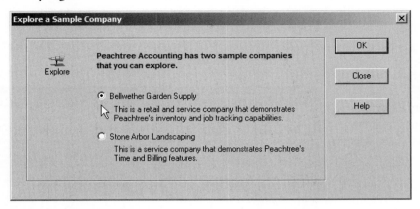

The Peachtree window which appears allows you to access many helpful options to analyze several business aspects. Through these options, you can obtain information about Peachtree and your accounts. Peachtree also offers a number of services that can be obtained by clicking the tab headings labeled Business Status, Customers & Sales, Vendors & Purchases, Inventory & Services, Employees & Payroll, Banking, and Company on the Navigation Aids toolbar.

For example, the Business Status feature provides an instant view of a firm's overall financial performance within specified areas. This section can be reached by clicking the Business Status tab that appears in the Peachtree opening window.

Step 4:

Close the *What's New in Peachtree 2010* window. Select *Do not display this message again* and click OK. Click the Business Status tab on the Navigation Aids toolbar, as shown in figure 1–4.

FIGURE 1–4
Business Status Tab
Selected

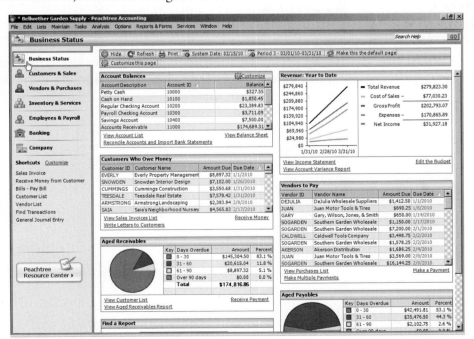

Follow steps 5 through 8 to explore a few of the valuable reports and graphs available in the Business Status section. The information shown is for Bellwether Garden Supply.

Step 5:
Scroll down to view the Aged Receivables and Aged Payables pie charts. These are shown in figure 1–5.

FIGURE 1–5
Summary Reports and Graphs from the Business Status Window

Information about any account can be reached by clicking the customer and vendor account name or any blue text line. For example, suppose that Bellwether Garden Supply wants information about the sales invoice that it issued to Armstrong Landscaping.

Step 6:
To access information about sales invoices to Armstrong Landscaping, scroll up to *Customers Who Owe Money* located in the Business Status section of the Peachtree opening window.

Step 7:

Click Armstrong in the Customer ID section, as shown in figure 1–6.

FIGURE 1–6
Armstrong Landscaping
Selected from the
Business Status Window

Step 8:

Review the latest invoice for Armstrong Landscaping in the Sales/Invoicing window. (See figure 1–7.) Then click Close on the Sales/Invoicing toolbar.

FIGURE 1–7
Armstrong Landscaping
Sales/Invoicing Window

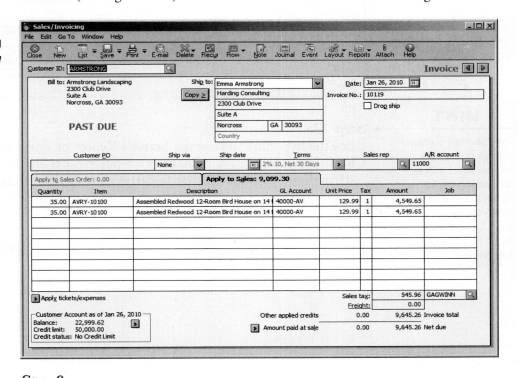

Step 9:

Click the Company tab, located below the Business Status tab. If your computer is connected to the Internet, you can click Check for Peachtree Updates located under Company Tasks to update Peachtree Complete Accounting 2010.

HINT

When you see a menu or button name with one of the letters underlined, that means you can activate that command by pressing at the same time the Alt key and the underlined letter on the keyboard.

Step 10:

Click Check <u>N</u>ow to update the program or <u>C</u>lose to proceed to the next step.

Step 11:

Scroll over the <u>View All Financial Statements</u> hyperlink in the Company window, as shown in figure 1–8. This is one example of the helpful features that are available to users through the Company section of the window.

FIGURE 1–8
View All Financial Statements Hyperlink

HINT

The Peachtree Company window or any other window listed with a tab heading can be minimized by clicking Hide from the Company Menu bar and maximized by clicking Show from the same menu.

Step 12:

Click the hyperlink to view the Select a Report or Form window. Click Close after you have reviewed the available reports and forms.

If you want to explore other features, click the hyperlinks to move between the sections of the window.

Step 13:

Exit Peachtree Complete Accounting 2010 by clicking File from the Menu bar, and then clicking *Exit*. (See figure 1–9.)

FIGURE 1–9
Exit Selected from the
File Drop-Down List

C h e c k   p o i n t

1. What is the major purpose of the Business Status window?
2. What are the seven service tabs on the Navigation Aids toolbar?

Answers

1. *The Business Status window allows you to access options that provide information about the accounts of your business.*
2. *The seven main hyperlinks are Business Status, Customers & Sales, Vendors & Purchases, Inventory & Services, Employees & Payroll, Banking, and Company.*

P r a c t i c e   O b j e c t i v e   2

1. Open Peachtree Complete Accounting 2010.
2. Click *Explore a sample company* and then *Bellwether Garden Supply*.
3. Click *Business Status* from the Peachtree opening window.
4. Access Snowden Interior Design from the Customers Who Owe Money section, review the account information, and then close the Snowden Interior Design Sales/Invoicing window.
5. Click the <u>View Income Statement</u> hyperlink from the Revenue: Year to Date section, review the financial statement, and then close the <Standard> Income Stmnt window.
6. Exit Peachtree Complete Accounting 2010.

OBJECTIVE 3 — Use the Peachtree Window and Menu Bar

Two methods can be used for navigating within Peachtree. One method involves using the opening window icons and links, and the other method involves using the traditional pull-down menus from the Menu bar. Both methods produce the same results and are accessed from the basic Peachtree window.

Basic Peachtree Window

The basic Peachtree window is made up of several parts, including the Shortcut List and the Menu bar. (See figure 1–10.)

FIGURE 1–10

Basic Peachtree Window with Business Status Tab Selected

Many of the functions located in the basic Peachtree window are general Microsoft Windows functions and are implemented using typical Windows commands. For example, the Minimize/Maximize/Close buttons function in the same way for any application of the Windows operating system.

In addition, the scroll bar, window sizing tools, and mouse pointer operate normally for Windows. There are, however, some features that are unique to the basic Peachtree window.

Opening Window Icons and Links

The opening window icons (pictures) help you move through the Peachtree accounting system. The Shortcut List, located at the left of the basic Peachtree window, accesses several functions used on a daily basis, as shown in figure 1–11.

FIGURE 1–11
View Business Status
Shortcut List

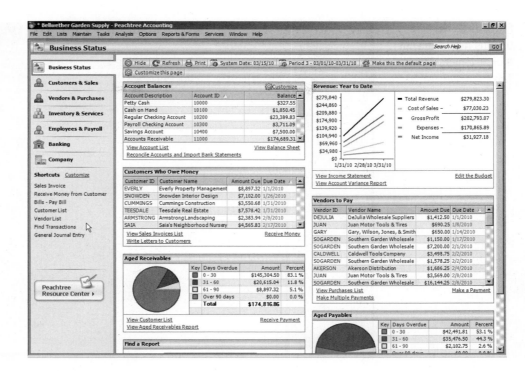

The Business Status Shortcut List is made up of seven options, providing for rapid access to vital business functions.

- Sales Invoice
- Receive Money from Customer
- Bills – Pay Bill
- Customer List
- Vendor List
- Find Transactions
- General Journal Entry

When you click any of these general business functions, Peachtree work areas, such as Sales/Invoicing, appear. To view other available icons, follow the steps outlined below.

Step 1:
Open Peachtree Accounting, and then open Bellwether Garden Supply by clicking *Explore a sample company*.

Step 2:
Click the Customers & Sales tab in the basic Peachtree window. You will now see the options available in the (Customers & Sales) folder, as shown in figure 1–12. For each tab, you will get a similar collection of icons directing you to the various parts and functions of the program.

FIGURE 1–12

Options Available with
the Customers & Sales
Tab

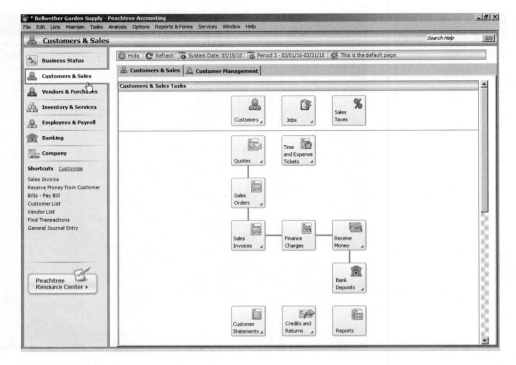

Menu Bar

The Menu bar, located at the top of the basic Peachtree window, can be used to move through Peachtree in the same way that the icons from the tabs are used. However, the Menu bar has 11 different general areas that can be accessed. These areas serve the following functions:

- File – Open, create, back up, and restore companies.
- Edit – Make changes and locate transactions.
- Lists – Create lists of various accounting aspects such as Customers & Sales, Vendors & Purchases, Chart of Accounts, and others.
- Maintain – Create and update the chart of accounts and accounts for customers, vendors, and inventory items.
- Tasks – Enter transactions of all types in the general journal and the special journals.
- Analysis – Use the cash, collection, payment, and financial management features.
- Options – Use to open, close, and customize toolbars. Use to change global options and to change the system date.
- Reports & Forms – Generate various reports.
- Services – Order checks, forms, and various customer support services.
- Window – Arrange the window.
- Help – Access help, a tutorial, technical support, and information about Peachtree products.

FIGURE 1–13
File Menu Drop-Down List

The File menu, shown in figure 1–13, is a typical main menu drop-down list. Click the screen to remove the drop-down list.

A Comparison of the Two Navigation Methods

To understand the differences between the two navigation methods, we will assume that Bellwether Garden Supply provides a service to a customer on credit.

Opening Window

Step 1:
Click the Customers & Sales tab from the left side of the basic Peachtree window.

Step 2:
Click the *Customers* icon at the top of the Customers & Sales Tasks section. (See figure 1–14.)

FIGURE 1–14

Customers Selected from
Customers & Sales Tasks
Folder

Step 3:

Click *New Customer* from the submenu list and then review the Maintain Customers/Prospects window.

Step 4:

Click the Close button from the toolbar at the top of the Maintain Customers/Prospects window.

Menu Bar

Step 1:

Now click Maintain and then *Customers/Prospects* from the Menu bar, as shown in figure 1–15.

FIGURE 1–15

Maintain Customers/
Prospects Selected from
Drop-Down List

Step 2:

Review the Maintain Customers/Prospects window. Note that it is the same window as the one you reached using the *Customers* icon.

In this example, there is no difference in the destination reached. There is only a difference in the route taken through Peachtree Complete Accounting 2010. One route involves use of the Peachtree icons, whereas the other route involves use of the Menu bar.

General Window and Screen Options

Peachtree Accounting uses certain terms in connection with its particular windows and screens. These terms are explained on the following page, using the Maintain Customers/Prospects window as a reference. (See figure 1–16.)

FIGURE 1–16
Maintain Customers/
Prospects Window with
Parts Labeled

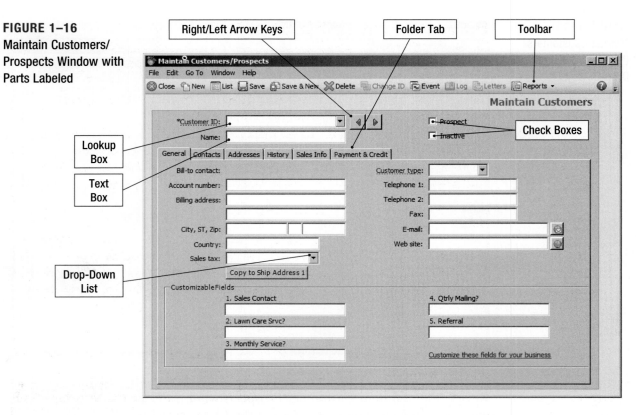

- Toolbar – Use to access the command buttons, including the Help feature.
- Lookup Box – Use the drop-down arrow in this type of field to access additional records.
- Right/Left Arrow Keys – Use to move to previous or next record.
- Check Box – Select by clicking inside the box.
- Folder Tab – Use to access the information in a file folder within the system.
- Text Box – Use to enter information.
- Drop-Down List – Click the arrow to produce a list of choices.
- Date Box – Use the *calendar* icon in this type of field to change dates (not shown).

Examine the Maintain Customers/Prospects window to see examples of a toolbar, lookup boxes, check boxes, folder tabs, text boxes, and drop-down list arrows. Then click the Close button to close the window.

Check point

1. What are the two methods of navigating through Peachtree?
2. Will the results differ when different navigation methods are used?

Answers

1. *The two methods are Peachtree icons and the Menu bar.*
2. *No, the results of the two navigation methods are the same.*

Practice Objective 3

1. Open Bellwether Garden Supply (if it is not already open).
2. Use the Shortcut List to access the General Journal Entry window. Close the window.
3. Use the Tasks drop-down menu from the Menu bar to access the General Journal Entry window. Close the window.
4. Use the Customers & Sales tab and then the *Customers* icon to access the Maintain Customers/Prospects window. Close the window.
5. Use the Maintain drop-down menu from the Menu bar to access the Maintain Customers/Prospects window. Close the window.

OBJECTIVE 4 — Use the Help Feature

Peachtree Complete Accounting 2010 provides a variety of ways for you to get help. Help is available from the Menu bar and in all other windows. The Help feature provides information that allows you to work more efficiently with Peachtree. Follow the steps outlined below to use the Help feature of Peachtree.

Step 1:
Click Help from the Menu bar as shown in figure 1–17.

FIGURE 1–17
Peachtree Accounting
Help Selected

Step 2:
Click *Peachtree Accounting Help* from the drop-down list.

Step 3:
Select and review the Contents tab of the Help window, which is shown in figure 1–18.

FIGURE 1–18
Contents Tab of Help
Window

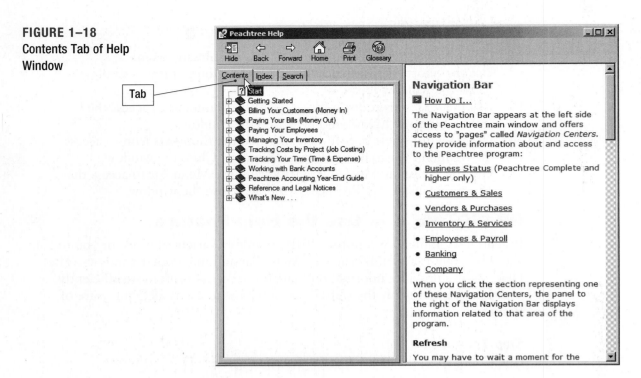

Step 4:
Click the <u>S</u>earch tab in the Peachtree Help window to view the search options, as shown in figure 1–19.

FIGURE 1–19
Search Tab Selected
from Help Window

Step 5:
Key **Accounts Receivable** in the *Type in the key<u>w</u>ord to find* text box.

Step 6:
Click <u>L</u>ist Topics to reveal a partial list of related topics, as shown in figure 1–20.

FIGURE 1–20
Accounts Receivable
Topic List

Step 7:
Select *Necessary Accounts (Getting Started)* by using the scroll bar, as shown in figure 1–21.

FIGURE 1–21
Necessary Accounts Help
Topic Selected

HINT

Select means to click a word or choice once with the mouse.

Step 8:
Double-click *Necessary Accounts* or click <u>D</u>isplay to reveal the topic information on the right side of the Peachtree Help window, as shown in figure 1–22.

FIGURE 1–22
Account Information from
Help Window

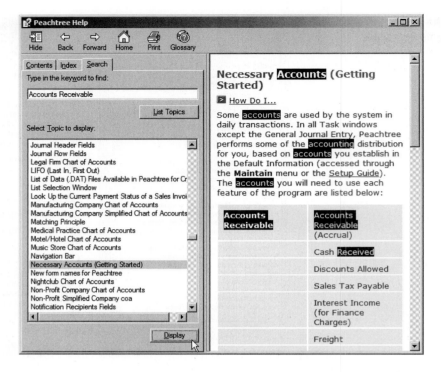

Step 9:
Scroll down the right side of the window to reveal additional topic suggestions.

Step 10:
Click *Set up your chart of accounts* to obtain information about establishing the chart of accounts.

Step 11:
Click the Index tab in the Help window.

Step 12:
Key the words **Accounts Receivable** to reveal general related topics, as shown in figure 1–23.

FIGURE 1–23
Index Topics Selected

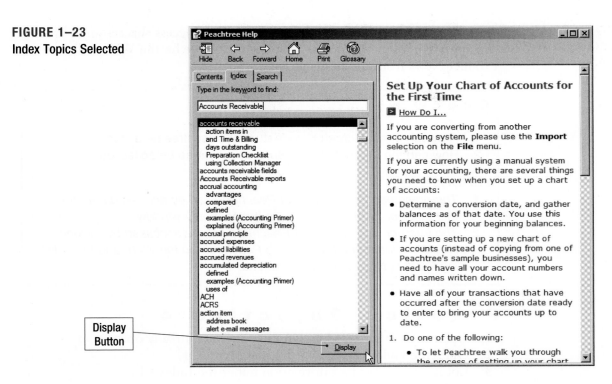

Click <u>D</u>isplay at the bottom of the Help window to reveal all of the directly related topics. This information appears in the Topics Found window, as shown in figure 1–24.

FIGURE 1–24
Accounts Receivable in
Topics Found Window

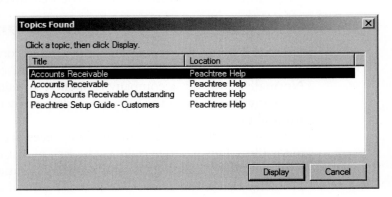

Step 14:
Click Display and view the Accounts Receivable information on the right side of the window.

Step 15:
Close the Peachtree Help window by clicking the Close button (X) in the upper right corner of the active window.

Important: Do not click the Close button (X) on the main Peachtree window because you will be closed out of Peachtree and will have to restart the program.

In addition to the Help feature on screen, there is an Internet Help feature called Peachtree on the Web. By going online, you can review product news, get answers to frequently asked questions, obtain online support, and send feedback about Peachtree features. You can access this resource by clicking Help on the Menu bar, clicking Peachtree on the Web, and then Product News from the submenu.

C h e c k   p o i n t

1. How can the on-screen Help feature of Peachtree be accessed?
2. How can the Internet Help feature of Peachtree be accessed?

Answers
1. *The on-screen Help feature of Peachtree can be accessed from the Menu bar or by clicking the Help button in any window.*
2. *The Internet Help feature of Peachtree can be accessed by clicking Help from the Menu bar, clicking Peachtree on the Web, and then clicking Product News from the submenu.*

Practice   Objective   4

1. Open Bellwether Garden Supply (if it is not already open).
2. Open the Help feature by using the Menu bar.
3. Locate the following information under the Index tab:
    a. Accounts Payable
    b. Maintain Vendors
    c. Maintain Customers
    d. Chart of Accounts
4. Close the Help window, and close Peachtree.

OBJECTIVE 5 — Open, Save, and Back Up Files

Up to this point, we have opened the sample company by using the Explore a sample company option from the Peachtree Accounting startup window. Normally, however, a company is opened by using the Open an existing company option from the startup window or by clicking File from the Menu bar and then *Open Company*.

In most working environments, it is necessary to save and back up computer files. This practice reduces the risk of lost data. Anyone who works with computers and disks is aware of the potential for data loss and the problems that it can cause. The loss of financial data can be especially troublesome. For example, suppose a computer error results in the loss of the data needed to bill customers for goods sold to them. This can result in the loss of thousands of dollars of potential cash receipts. Because so much of the data you enter into an accounting system is vital, it is important that you save and back up data.

Fortunately, Peachtree makes it easy to save data. Once posted, all transactions are saved. Data that does not require posting is automatically saved when you exit Peachtree.

The backup process saves a copy of the company data that can be used to restore a company to a previous condition. This procedure usually requires saving to a hard disk, flash drive, or CD-ROM. Floppy disks can also be used for backup purposes. However, a tremendous amount of disk space is required, and several diskettes would be needed to accomplish this task.

Opening an Existing Company

Follow the steps outlined below to open an existing company.

Step 1:
Start Peachtree Accounting.

Step 2:
Click *Open an existing company* from the Peachtree Accounting startup window, as shown in figure 1–25.

FIGURE 1–25
Startup Window with Open an Existing Company Option Selected

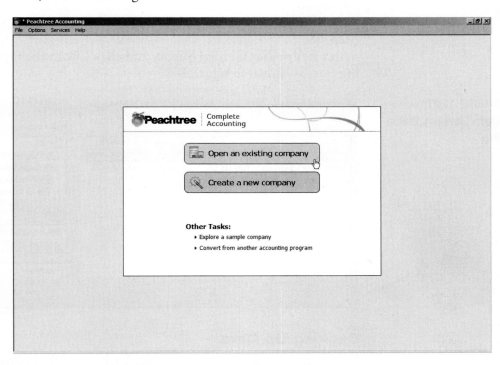

Step 3:
Click OK at the Open an Existing Company dialog box to open Bellwether Garden Supply, as shown in figure 1–26.

FIGURE 1–26
Open an Existing Company Dialog Box

HINT

If a company has recently been opened, it will appear on the list. The company can then be opened by highlighting its name and clicking OK. The dialog box may also have other companies listed.

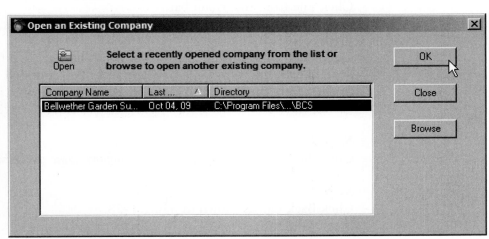

To open an existing company through the File option of the Menu bar, use the following steps.

Step 4:
Click File from the Menu bar.

HINT

Peachtree 2010 allows the user to keep several companies open at one time.

Step 5:
Click *Open Company* from the drop-down list and then click No at the Peachtree Accounting message "Do you want to keep Bellwether Garden Supply open?"

Step 6:
Select Bellwether Garden Supply and click OK in the Open Company dialog box, as shown in figure 1–27.

FIGURE 1–27
Open Company Dialog Box

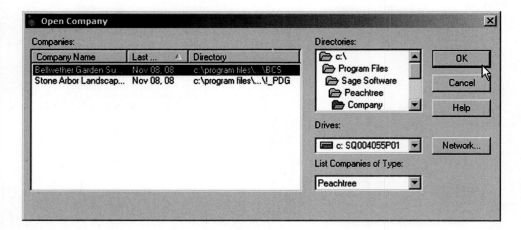

Backing Up Data

Frequently a user of Peachtree must back up work. Follow the steps outlined below to back up data.

Step 1:
Click File from the Menu bar.

Step 2:
Click *Back Up* from the drop-down list. The Back Up Company dialog box appears, and offers you the option to be reminded to back up data. It also offers the option to include the company name in the name of the backup files.

Step 3:
Click the check box next to *Include company name in the backup file name.*

Step 4:
Click Back Up, as shown in figure 1–28.

FIGURE 1–28
Back Up Company
Window

Step 5:
The Save Backup for Bellwether Garden Supply as dialog box will appear as shown in figure 1–29. If you will be backing up your company files on a flash drive, insert the flash drive into the appropriate drive. (For most computers this is the E drive.)

FIGURE 1–29
Save Backup for
Bellwether Garden
Supply as Dialog Box

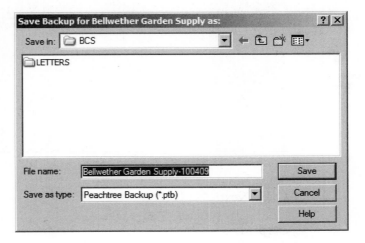

Click the down arrow next to the *Save in* box to select the destination where the backup is to be stored. The file name has already been entered. It consists of the company name and the date the file is being saved.

Step 6:
Click Save to save the company to the destination.

Step 7:
Click OK at the Peachtree Accounting window that indicates the file size. The progress of the backup is displayed until it is complete.

Restoring Data to Its Original Condition

If it is necessary to restore data you have backed up, the process is not difficult. It can be accomplished by completing the following steps.

Step 1:
Click File from the Menu bar.

Step 2:
Click *Restore*.

Step 3:
At the Restore Wizard – Select Backup File dialog box, select the location of where the file was backed up by clicking the Browse button.

Step 4:
Select *Bellwether Garden Supply*. (Various dates will appear as part of the file name.) Click Open. The company will now appear in the *Location* text box as shown in figure 1–30.

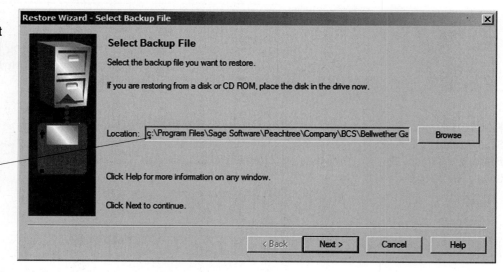

Notice the full path.

Step 5:
Click Next.

Step 6:
At the Restore Wizard – Select Company dialog box, click An Existing Company and then Browse to select the company to restore to a previous condition. Click Next.

Step 7:
At the Restore Wizard – Restore Options dialog box, select *Company Data* as shown in figure 1–31, and click Next.

FIGURE 1–31
Company Data Selected
from the Restore Wizard
– Restore Options
Window

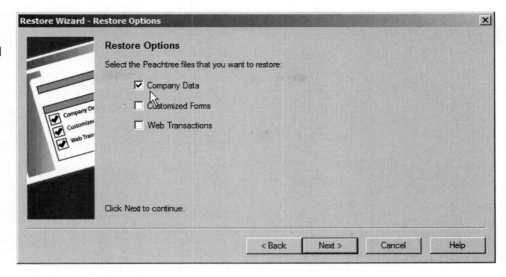

Step 8:
At the Restore Wizard – Confirmation dialog box, click Finish.

C h e c k   p o i n t

1. How is data saved in Peachtree?
2. What is the purpose of the restore process?

Answers
1. *Peachtree saves all transactions that are posted. Data that does not require posting is saved when you exit Peachtree.*
2. *The restore process will overwrite the current company data with previous saved data.*

P r a c t i c e   O b j e c t i v e   5

1. Open Bellwether Garden Supply using each of the two methods for opening a company file.
2. Practice the Back Up feature. (However, do not save any work unless you are instructed to do so.)
3. Close Bellwether Garden Supply.

End of Chapter Review

Software Command Summary

Open Start Window	Start, All Programs, Peachtree Complete Accounting 2010, Peachtree Complete Accounting 2010
Open Company	File, Open Company or Open an Existing Company, "Company Name," OK
Help	The Help button from any menu toolbar
Back up	File, Back Up
Restore	File, Restore

Projects and Problems

Content Check

Multiple Choice: Choose only one response for each question.

1. Peachtree Complete Accounting _____ is discussed in this book.
   A. 8.0
   B. 2009
   C. 2010
   D. 6.0
   E. None of the above

2. Accounting is the process of
   A. recording, summarizing, analyzing, and interpreting financial activities.
   B. journalizing, posting, and preparing financial statements.
   C. recording adjusting and closing entries.
   D. transferring data to the computer.
   E. None of the above

3. The users of accounting information include
   A. managers.
   B. investors.
   C. lenders.
   D. government agencies.
   E. All of the above

4. Peachtree allows users to record financial events in
    A. just a general journal.
    B. just special journals.
    C. special journals and a general journal.
    D. a single combined journal.
    E. None of the above

5. Computerized accounting systems
    A. improve accuracy and efficiency.
    B. save time and effort.
    C. do many tasks automatically.
    D. handle many different types of financial activities.
    E. All of the above

Short Essay Response: Provide a detailed answer for each question.

1. What is the difference between manual and computerized accounting systems?
2. Name some of the various tasks and financial activities that Peachtree Complete Accounting can perform. Explain how these might help you in operating a business.
3. Explain two ways of opening Peachtree.
4. Describe the processes of back up and restore.
5. Explain the two generally accepted methods of navigating through Peachtree. Is one superior to the other?
6. What benefits do you see from the Help feature of Peachtree?

Case Problems

Problem 1A
- Start Peachtree Complete Accounting.
- Open Bellwether Garden Supply.
- Click the Customers & Sales tab.
- Click the *Sales Invoices* icon and then New Sales Invoice.
- List the names of the buttons on the toolbar of the Sales/Invoicing window. Then close the window.
- Click Tasks from the Menu bar.
- Click *General Journal Entry* from the drop-down list.
- List the names of the buttons on the toolbar of the General Journal Entry window. Then close the window.

Problem 2A
- Using Bellwether Garden Supply, open the Help feature by using the Menu bar.
- Click *Peachtree Accounting Help* from the drop-down list.
- Click the Index tab and key **Accounts Receivable**.
- Click the Display button.
- Click the Display button again, and note the definition of *Accounts Receivable*.
- Click the Search tab.
- Key **Payroll**.
- Click List Topics.
- Scroll down and double-click *Payroll Setup Wizard – Overview*.
- List the payroll items that the Payroll Setup Wizard establishes.
- Close the Peachtree Help window.

Problem 1B
- Open Stone Arbor Landscaping.
- Click the Company tab.
- Click the *Chart of Accounts* icon and then New Account.
- List the names of the buttons on the toolbar of the Maintain Chart of Accounts window. Then close the window.
- Click Reports & Forms from the Menu bar.
- Click *Financial Statements* from the drop-down list.
- List the names of the buttons on the toolbar of the Select a Report or Form window. Then close the window.

Problem 2B
- Using Stone Arbor Landscaping, open the Help feature by using the Menu bar.
- Click *Peachtree Accounting Help* from the drop-down list.
- Click the Index tab and key **Payroll**.
- Click the Display button.
- Click the Display button again, and note the information regarding Fringe Benefits.
- Click the Search tab.
- Key **General Journal**.
- Click List Topics.
- Scroll down and double-click *Record a General Journal Entry*.
- List the reasons why the general journal might be used.
- Close the Peachtree Help window.

Cooperative Learning

1. Form into pairs and write a one-page paper comparing and contrasting manual and computerized accounting systems. Indicate which type of system you would prefer to use and why.
2. In groups of three or four students, visit some local businesses that use computerized accounting programs. List the names of the programs. How are the programs used in the daily operation of the business?
3. In groups of three or four students, visit two or three software retailers. List the names and prices of the most popular accounting software packages. Also list the main features of each package.

Writing and Decision Making

Your employer has announced that the company will be switching from a manual accounting system to a computerized accounting system. Peachtree is considered to be the favored accounting software due to all of its accounting and financial capabilities. However, the owner would still like to know what type of services would be available once the decision has been made to switch. Therefore, you have been asked to visit the Peachtree Web site at www.Peachtree.com and prepare a summary of services available.

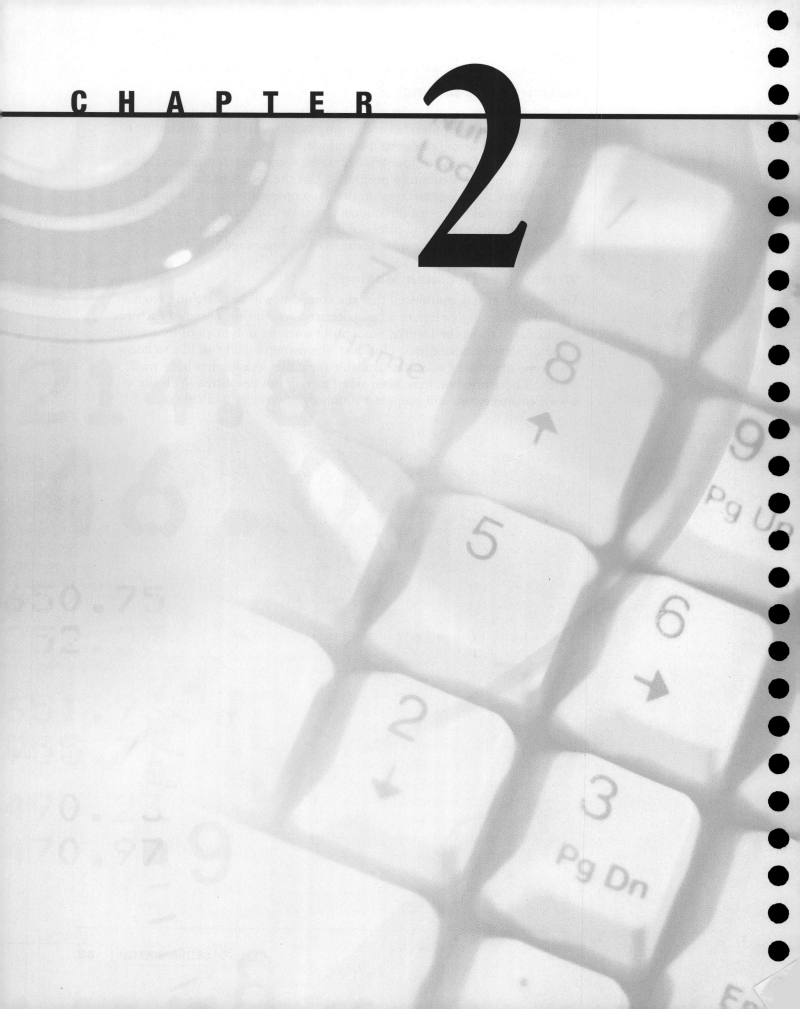

CHAPTER 2

Setting Up a Company

Learning Objectives

1. Set up a new company in Peachtree

2. Create a chart of accounts

3. Enter beginning account balances

Software Features

- Create function

- Edit function

- Print function for the chart of accounts and general ledger

An individual company must set up its books before any transactions can be entered. Regardless of whether the company uses a manual or computerized accounting system, the procedure is basically the same. The business setup process involves several steps—

- Enter company information
- Select a business organization type
- Create a chart of accounts
- Select an accounting method
- Select a posting method
- Select an accounting period

Organization Types and Company Information

Businesses can operate as merchandising, service, or manufacturing organizations. **Merchandising businesses** purchase goods from wholesalers and resell them to consumers for a profit. Examples include department stores, grocery stores, and sporting goods stores.

Service businesses, including law offices, medical offices, and accounting firms, provide services to consumers for a profit. Note, however, that some service businesses also sell merchandise. A beauty shop, for example, might sell hair care products. However, its main business of styling hair generates the vast majority of its revenue.

Manufacturing businesses produce products from raw materials and sell those products to consumers for a profit. Their customers might be wholesalers or end-users. Airplane manufacturers, construction companies, and furniture makers would be considered manufacturing businesses.

Some companies are difficult to classify because of their mix of revenue from service, merchandising, and manufacturing activities. For example, restaurants provide a service, sell products, and manufacture products using raw materials. So, what type of business is a restaurant?

Each business takes on one of three basic organization types: sole proprietorship, partnership, or corporation. The organization type, or structure, that a business decides on is a result of various factors. How many owners the company will have, for example, is one factor. Another factor is expertise. Will one owner have the knowledge required to run a specific business? If yes, then the sole proprietorship form of business might be sufficient. If, however, more expertise is needed to own and operate the company, then perhaps a partnership will provide better results.

Before an owner decides on a business organization type, liability, capital formation, and tax issues must be considered. For example, some business types provide less liability protection for their owners than do others. Sole proprietorships and partnerships, for example, have unlimited liability. This means that the owners are personally liable for the debts of the business. The owners can lose their personal as well as their business assets if the business does poorly or is the guilty party in a lawsuit. Liability is just one of the important issues to consider in determining which type of organization is best for a specific business.

Sole Proprietorships

A **sole proprietorship** is a business owned by one person who makes the decisions, takes all the risks, and earns all the profits. Unfortunately, the sole proprietor suffers all the losses, too. A sole proprietorship is very easy to form. One owner with a limited amount of capital can open a business. In most states, all that is needed is a business license and a mailing address. The sole proprietor is free to make all the management decisions. Small local businesses such as barbershops, hardware stores, and dry cleaning stores are examples of firms that might be sole proprietorships. In recent years, many individuals have set up small sole proprietorship firms that provide computer consulting and management consulting services.

One drawback to the sole proprietorship type of organization is that a single owner often does not have all the expertise needed to run a particular business. Individuals with specific technical skills open businesses and then realize later that those skills are not sufficient. For example, suppose a ski instructor decides to open a ski equipment shop. The ski instructor may know all about skiing and can discuss skiing with potential buyers. In other words, the ski instructor has a lot of technical knowledge about skiing and ski equipment. However, what does the ski instructor know about advertising, accounting, or finance? Frequently, a sole proprietor knows very little about basic business procedures.

Financing and capital formation also may be difficult for the sole proprietor. Because the asset base and creditworthiness of the business rests with one individual, banks and other potential lenders might be leery of lending to that person. This can be especially true in the early years of a business when there is very little credit history for potential lenders to evaluate.

The freedom to make all the decisions that a sole proprietor enjoys comes with a price—unlimited liability for the debts of the business. The owner's personal and business assets are accessible to creditors in the case of a business failure. Table 2–1 lists the advantages and disadvantages of the sole proprietorship type of business.

TABLE 2–1
Sole Proprietorships

Advantages	Disadvantages
1. Complete management control by owner	1. Limited level of expertise
2. Ease of formation	2. Limited amount of capital
3. Few government restrictions	3. Unlimited liability

Partnerships

partnership A business owned by two or more people.

A **partnership** is a group of two or more people who enter into a business arrangement for the purpose of making a profit. The benefits of a partnership can be great. Because there are more people involved as owners, the amount of expertise brought to the business is increased. This can lead to a synergistic relationship that can help the business grow. In the United States today, 10 percent of all businesses are partnerships. These businesses include small local firms as well as large national firms. In fact, some large multinational accounting firms are partnerships.

Because a partnership has more than one owner, it usually has more capital and capital formation potential than a sole proprietorship. Often, businesses do not start with enough capital to succeed. The owners must borrow money so that the firm can survive and grow. Generally, the more partners involved in a business, the easier it is to borrow money.

As with a sole proprietorship, in a partnership the owners are subject to unlimited liability. Creditors can go after the personal and business assets of all partners to satisfy the debts of the firm. This can be costly if a business experiences financial difficulties.

One of the biggest drawbacks to the partnership business type is the mutual agency rule. This rule provides that each partner can bind all the other partners to an agreement. For example, suppose partner X goes to a car dealer to buy a new car in the name of the partnership and, prior to the purchase, does not tell the other partners about the purchase. The result is that all partners are liable for the purchase even though they had no prior knowledge of it. Also, even if partner X leaves the business, the remaining partners are still required to pay for the car.

Partnerships have a limited life. Any time an old partner leaves or a new partner is added, a new partnership must be formed. This creates accounting as well as relationship problems. Assets, for example, must be revalued when a new partner is added or an old partner leaves. Table 2–2 lists advantages and disadvantages of partnerships.

TABLE 2–2
Partnerships

Advantages	Disadvantages
1. Ease of formation	1. Unlimited liability
2. Greater amount of expertise	2. Possible disagreements about management decisions
3. Greater potential for raising capital	3. Mutual agency rule
4. Synergistic relationship	4. Limited life

Corporations

The ownership of a corporation is divided into shares of stock. Therefore, a **corporation** is a business owned by stockholders or shareholders. A large corporation usually has many stockholders. A small corporation may have just a few stockholders. Unlike a sole proprietorship or a partnership, a corporation is considered a legal entity in and of itself. It acts as its own "person" when it comes to business transactions and holdings. In other words, the corporation acts on its own behalf. Large, well-known companies such as Ford, Sears, IBM, and Microsoft are examples of corporations that operate in the United States. The corporation type is so dominant in our economy that even though corporations make up only 20 percent of the businesses in the country, they receive more than 90 percent of the revenue.

The stockholders, or owners, of a corporation are not personally liable for its actions or debts. Stockholders can only lose what they have invested in the corporation's stock. This is known as limited liability. By issuing or selling stock, a corporation can raise needed capital more easily than can a sole proprietorship or partnership.

Stockholders elect a board of directors for a corporation, which in turn hires the management. Ordinary stockholders are not directly involved in the day-to-day operations of the business. They must rely on management to work in their best interest. However, one of the duties of the board of directors is to periodically evaluate the performance of management and make changes if necessary. Management must also consult with the board of directors about financial policies.

corporation A business owned by stockholders or shareholders.

Because a corporation is considered a separate legal entity, it is taxed like an individual. This tax reduces the amount of income available for stockholders, who are, after all, owners. Stockholders share in the earnings of the corporation by receiving dividends or by selling their stock for a profit, or capital gain. The stockholders then pay personal income tax on these dividends and capital gains. The result is double taxation: the earnings of the corporation are taxed once at the corporate level and again at the individual level when stockholders receive dividends or realize capital gains. Table 2–3 lists the advantages and disadvantages of a corporation.

TABLE 2–3
Corporations

Advantages	Disadvantages
1. Ease of raising capital	1. More difficult and expensive to form
2. Limited liability	2. Subject to more government regulation
3. Continuous life	3. Double taxation
4. No mutual agency rule	

C h e c k   p o i n t

1. What are the three main types of business organizations?
2. In what two types of business organizations do the owners have unlimited liability?

Answers
1. *Sole proprietorships, partnerships, and corporations.*
2. *Sole proprietorships and partnerships.*

OBJECTIVE 1 — Set Up a New Company in Peachtree

Several steps are necessary when setting up a new company in Peachtree. Each step must be read carefully and evaluated before you select a particular system, date, or accounting method. Follow the steps below to begin the business setup process for Wildwood Medical Services.

Step 1:
Start Peachtree Complete Accounting 2010.

Step 2:

At the Peachtree Accounting dialog box, click *Create a new company*. (See figure 2–1.)

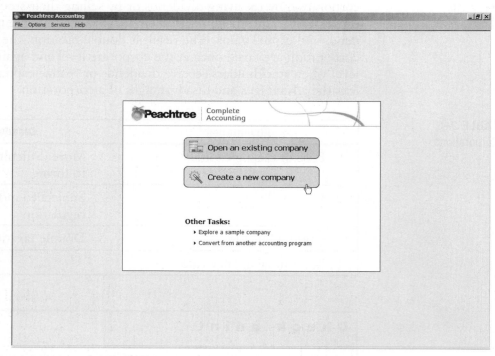

Step 3:

After reading the screen, click Next at the Create a New Company – Introduction dialog box. (See figure 2–2.)

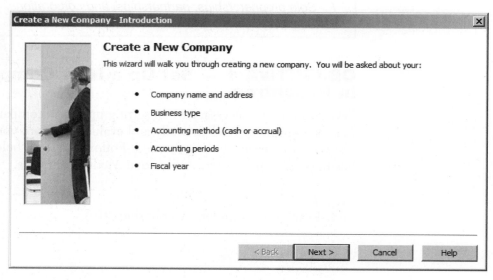

The Create a New Company – Company Information dialog box appears as shown in figure 2–3.

FIGURE 2–3
Create a New Company
– Company Information
Dialog Box

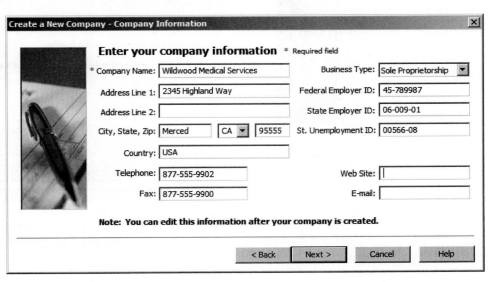

Step 4:

Complete the Create a New Company – Company Information dialog box using the following information:

Company Name:	**Wildwood Medical Services**
Address Line 1:	**2345 Highland Way**
Address Line 2:	
City, State, Zip:	**Merced, CA 95555**
Country:	**USA**
Telephone:	**877-555-9902**
Fax:	**877-555-9900**
Business Type:	**Sole Proprietorship**
Federal Employer ID:	**45-789987**
State Employer ID:	**06-009-01**
St. Unemployment ID:	**00566-08**

Press the Tab or Enter key after you complete each entry. Compare your entries with figure 2–4, and correct any errors before continuing. Click Next at the bottom of the dialog box when all entries are correct.

FIGURE 2–4
Completed Create a New
Company – Company
Information Dialog Box

The Chart of Accounts

chart of accounts
A listing of all the accounts used by a business.

The **chart of accounts** is a listing of all the accounts a business uses. Accounts provide a record of transactions in which each account groups all transactions of a similar type. For example, an account labeled Office Supplies would be used to classify purchases of file folders, staples, floppy disks, and rubber bands. These purchases could all be listed separately, but that would make it necessary to trace through hundreds or thousands of transactions to determine the firm's total purchases of office supplies in any period.

ledger A group of related accounts.

general ledger The main ledger of a business.

On the chart of accounts, all accounts are listed and numbered in the order in which they appear in the firm's general ledger. A **ledger** is simply a group of related accounts. The **general ledger** is the main ledger of a business. It contains the information that is used to prepare financial statements for the business.

Peachtree provides you with several methods for setting up a chart of accounts. You can—

- Use the chart of accounts of a sample company from the list provided. Several companies are included in the list. Once a particular company's chart of accounts is selected, accounts can be added, edited, or deleted.
- Copy a chart of accounts from an existing Peachtree Accounting company.
- Import a company's chart of accounts from another accounting program. QuickBooks files, for example, convert easily.
- Build the chart of accounts from scratch.

Step 5:
Click the *Use a sample business type that closely matches your company* option in the Create a New Company – Setup dialog box (figure 2–5), and then click Next.

FIGURE 2–5
Create a New Company – Setup Dialog Box

A Create a New Company – Business Type dialog box appears. Within the *Select a business type* text box, Service Company is highlighted (figure 2–6).

Step 6:
Click the *View details about a business type* link below the dialog box to view the help area.

Step 7:
Select Service Company (Simplified Version) after scrolling down in the Contents box. This area provides a brief overview of the service industry (figure 2–7).

FIGURE 2–7
Service Company
(Simplified Version)
Overview and Related
Topics

Explore the related topics listed in the Peachtree Help for Your Business window by selecting the desired topic.

Step 8:

After reviewing the related topics for the service industry, close the window by clicking the Close button (X) in the upper right corner of the window.

Step 9:

Now view the chart of accounts in the Create a New Company – Business Type Chart of Accounts dialog box. Scroll up and down to see the accounts that will be established for the newly created Wildwood Medical Services. Figure 2–8 illustrates a portion of the chart of accounts.

FIGURE 2–8
Service Business (Partial) Chart of Accounts

The chart of accounts selected from the sample company list will be incorporated into the accounting system being set up for Wildwood Medical Services. Some of the accounts will not be used, and some will be renamed. However, modifying an existing chart of accounts saves time and effort. If you want to build all new accounts, you would click the *Build your own chart of accounts* option in the previous Create a New Company – Setup dialog box (figure 2–9).

FIGURE 2–9
Build Your Own Company Option Selected

Step 10:

Click Next in the Create a New Company – Business Type dialog box with Service Company (Simplified Types) selected to establish the chart of accounts and move to the next step in the company setup process.

Accounting Methods

Every business must decide on an accounting method. Some firms use the cash basis, others use the accrual basis, and still others use a hybrid of cash and accrual accounting. Peachtree allows businesses to use either cash or accrual accounting.

The **cash basis** requires a business to recognize (record) revenue when the related cash is received and recognize (record) expenses when the related cash is paid. Small companies with no inventory, no accounts receivable, and no accounts payable can use the cash basis. Thus, this basis is limited to small service businesses such as law offices, consulting firms, and bookkeeping firms.

Generally accepted accounting principles (GAAP) require the use of the accrual basis by merchandising and manufacturing businesses. Under the **accrual basis**, a firm recognizes (records) revenue when it is earned, even if the related cash has not yet been received. Similarly, the firm recognizes (records) expenses when they are incurred, even if the related cash has not yet been paid. For example, if a customer purchases merchandise or receives services on account, generally, this transaction would be recorded using an accrual accounting method. Similarly, if a business purchases supplies on account, it would use an accrual accounting method. In addition to merchandising and manufacturing businesses, service businesses that make sales on credit must use the accrual basis.

Step 11:

At the Create a New Company – Accounting Method dialog box (figure 2–10), click *Cash*. This is the accounting method that Wildwood Medical Services will use. Caution: After you choose an accounting method, you CANNOT change it. Click Next.

cash basis An accounting method in which a firm recognizes revenue when cash is received and recognizes expenses when cash is paid.

accrual basis An accounting method in which a firm recognizes revenue when it is earned and recognizes expenses when they are incurred.

FIGURE 2–10
Create a New Company – Accounting Method Dialog Box with Cash Selected

Create a New Company - Accounting Method

Choose an accounting method

The accounting method defines when you record income and expenses on your books.

○ Accrual   **(Most companies choose this)**

Income is recorded when a sale occurs, regardless of when you actually receive the money. Expenses are recorded when you receive goods or services, even though you may not pay the bills for them until a later date.

● Cash

Income is recorded when you receive the money. Expenses are recorded when you pay the bills.

Note: This cannot be changed after your company is created.

[< Back] [Next >] [Cancel] [Help]

Posting Methods: Real Time or Batch Processing

posting The transfer of information about transactions to ledger accounts.

After entries are made for transactions, the information must be transferred to the appropriate ledger accounts. This process is known as **posting**. Peachtree offers two alternative posting methods: real time and batch processing.

Real-time processing results in instant account updates. For example, when a customer in a bank makes a deposit, the teller enters the transaction and the customer generally has immediate access to those funds. However, suppose a customer sends a check to a department store, and the department store waits until the end of the day to post that payment; this would be an example of batch posting.

Step 12:

Most companies select real time as their posting method so that their accounts will be updated as each transaction is entered and saved. Click *Real Time* at the Create a New Company – Posting Method dialog box (figure 2–11). Then click Next.

FIGURE 2–11

Create a New Company – Posting Method Dialog Box with Real Time Selected

The Accounting Periods

accounting period The period of time covered by a firm's financial statements.

An **accounting period** is the time covered by a firm's financial statements. It is the period for which the firm reports its operating results—its net income or net loss. Most businesses have a yearly accounting period but prepare interim statements on a monthly or quarterly basis.

An accounting period cannot exceed one year. Many firms use the calendar year (January 1–December 31) as their accounting period. However, it is not necessary to do so. Some firms have legitimate business reasons for using an accounting period other than the calendar year. For example, many department stores end their yearly accounting period on January 31. Because so much of their yearly business occurs in December, it would be an accounting nightmare to compile all the information needed for the financial statements by December 31.

fiscal year An accounting period of one year.

A yearly accounting period is often referred to as a **fiscal year**. Peachtree uses this term as well.

Step 13:

Wildwood Medical Services will use the calendar year as its accounting period. Therefore, click *12 monthly accounting periods per year* at the Create a New Company – Accounting Periods dialog box (figure 2–12), and then click Next.

FIGURE 2–12
Create a New Company
– Accounting Periods
Dialog Box

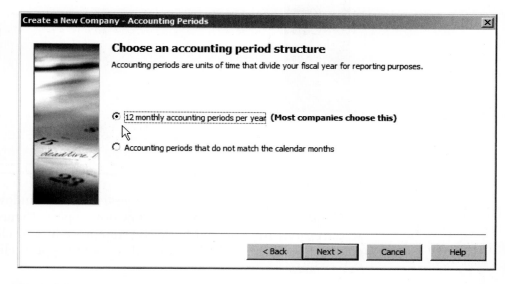

Step 14:

At the Create a New Company – Fiscal Year dialog box, follow the procedures listed below.

- Select January from the drop-down list.
- Select 2010 from the drop-down list.

Compare your entries with figure 2–13 before continuing, and then click Next.

FIGURE 2–13
Create a New Company –
Fiscal Year Dialog Box

Step 15:

The Create a New Company – Finish dialog box (figure 2–14) indicates that your setup of Wildwood Medical Services is complete. Click Finish.

FIGURE 2–14

Create a New Company
– Finish Dialog Box

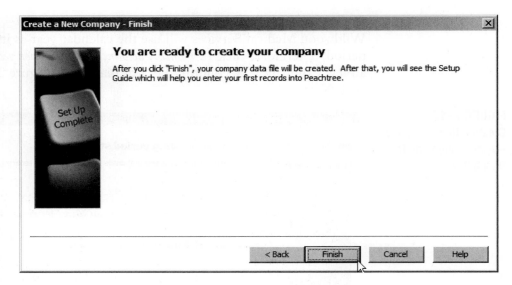

Close the *Sign Up for Peachtree Payment Solutions* window.

The Peachtree Setup Guide window now appears (figure 2–15). You can access various areas of your business setup procedure by clicking one of the areas below. **Note:** If the Setup Guide does not appear, click File and then *Setup Guide*.

FIGURE 2–15

Peachtree Setup Guide
Window

To review a specific area of the window, follow these steps:

- Click the item you want to view, for example, *Chart of Accounts*.
- Click the *general ledger* link to get more detailed information about the general ledger.
- Click the Close button (X) in the upper right corner of the Peachtree Setup Guide – Chart of Accounts window.
- Close the Peachtree Setup Guide window.

Important: Peachtree automatically creates the new company in the program folder on the hard drive. You may therefore open, work on, and save the company from and to the hard drive. However, in the unique circumstance you are unable to save any data to the hard drive because of your institution's policy, simply use the back up feature to save a copy of the company to an external drive such as a flash drive. When you need to open the company from the external drive, use the restore feature and it will place a copy of the company back on the hard drive. In this unique situation, you will need to back up at the end of each session and restore at the beginning of each session. The only difference with the restore process given in chapter 1 is that you will click *A New Company* option at the Restore Wizard – Select Company window.

An alternative method is available if you are unable to save to the hard drive because of your institution's policy. This process requires the cutting and pasting of the newly created company folder from the hard drive to the flash drive. For example, the company folder for Wildwood Medical Services will most likely be located under the following directory: C:\Program Files\Sage Software\Peachtree\Company\wilmedse. After locating the company folder, cut and paste it to the flash drive. This will allow you to open and close directly from the flash drive without having to use the back up and restore features.

C h e c k   p o i n t

1. Name one aspect of the company setup process that cannot be changed after it is selected.
2. When does posting occur if you select the real-time posting process?

Answers
1. *The accounting method, either cash or accrual, cannot be changed after its selection.*
2. *Posting occurs immediately when each transaction is entered and saved.*

Practice Objective 1

Set up the following company using the procedures outlined in Objective 1. Note that Maslow's Financial Services will use the accrual accounting method and will build its own chart of accounts.

Company Name:	**Maslow's Financial Services**
Address Line 1:	**329 Smith Ave.**
Address Line 2:	
City, State, Zip:	**Ceres, CA 95101**
Country:	**USA**
Telephone:	**209-555-2222**
Fax:	**209-555-6666**
Business Type:	**Sole Proprietorship**
Federal Employer ID:	**95-343434**
State Employer ID:	**06-3333-01**
St. Unemployment ID:	**00221-78**
Chart of Accounts:	**Build your own chart of accounts**
Accounting Method:	**Accrual**
Posting Method:	**Real Time**
Accounting Periods:	**12 monthly accounting periods**
Fiscal Year to Start:	**January 2010**

Close the Peachtree Setup Guide and click OK on the Peachtree Setup Guide dialog box.

OBJECTIVE 2 — Create a Chart of Accounts

In Objective 1, you learned the company setup process. Now you will review the setup process and explore some variations to it. For example, you set up Wildwood Medical Services with the cash basis as its accounting method. The company setup you will do in this section will use the accrual basis as the accounting method. Follow the steps below to set up a new company.

Step 1:
Click File from the main Menu bar.

Step 2:
Select *New Company* from the drop-down list (figure 2–16).

FIGURE 2–16
New Company Selected
from the File Drop-Down
List

Step 3:

Click Next at the Create a New Company – Introduction window. Then carefully enter the information shown below in the Create a New Company – Company Information dialog box. Compare your entries with figure 2–17 before continuing.

Company Name:	**Tile Installation by Ramirez**
Address Line 1:	**2110 West Avenue**
Address Line 2:	
City, State, Zip:	**Fremont, CA 95700**
Country:	**USA**
Telephone:	**209-555-1111**
Fax:	**209-555-5555**
Business Type:	**Sole Proprietorship**
Federal Employer ID:	**95-3458767**
State Employer ID:	**06-3363-01**
St. Unemployment ID:	**00321-78**

FIGURE 2–17 Completed Create a New Company – Company Information Dialog Box

Step 4:

Click Next. Enter the following information in the remaining dialog boxes to complete the Create a New Company Setup process, and then click Finish:

Chart of Accounts:	**Build your own chart of accounts**
Accounting Method:	**Accrual**
Posting Method:	**Real Time**
Accounting Periods:	**12 monthly accounting periods**
Fiscal Year to Start:	**January 2010**

Step 5:

After waiting for the software to create the company data files, close the Action Items and *Sign Up for Peachtree Payment Solutions* windows and the Peachtree Setup Guide window.

You have completed the setup process for Tile Installation by Ramirez. Now you must create a new chart of accounts for the business because you selected the *Build your own chart of accounts* option at the Chart of Accounts setup dialog box. You will need to create all of the accounts using information that includes account ID, account description, and account type.

Account ID

Every general ledger account must have a separate number for identification purposes. In Peachtree, this number is called the account ID. Peachtree specifies a numeric range for each account classification. For example, all asset accounts must fall within the range of 100–199, 1000–1999, or 10000–19999. The starting point for each numeric range is shown in table 2–4.

TABLE 2–4
Peachtree Numeric
Ranges for Account
Classification

TABLE 2–4 Peachtree Numeric Ranges for Account Classification

Account Classification	Starting Number for Account ID
Assets	100, 1000, 10000
Liabilities	200, 2000, 20000
Equity	300, 3000, 30000
Revenue	400, 4000, 40000
Expenses	500, 5000, 50000

A small business might use 100 for its Cash account and 102 for its Petty Cash account. A larger business that needs many accounts might assign 1000 or 10000 to Cash and 1020 or 10200 to Petty Cash.

All of the general ledger accounts used in Peachtree fall into the five broad classifications listed in table 2–4. The meaning of these classifications is as follows:

- *Assets* are the things a business owns.
- *Liabilities* are the debts a business owes.
- *Equity* is the difference between what a business owns and what it owes.
- *Revenue* is what a business earns when it sells goods or provides a service.
- *Expenses* are the costs a business incurs to produce revenue.

Account Description

In Peachtree, every general ledger account must have an account description as well as an account ID. The account description indicates the nature of the transactions that will be recorded in the account. For example, Cash is the account description for the account that will be used to record all transactions involving the receipt and payment of cash. Other examples of account descriptions are Office Supplies, Accounts Receivable, Office Equipment, and Accounts Payable.

Account Type

When creating a chart of accounts in Peachtree, it is necessary to assign an account type to each general ledger account as well as an ID and a description. The account type indicates to which group of accounts on the financial statements a particular account belongs. Having this information in the chart of accounts makes it possible for Peachtree to prepare automated financial statements at the end of each accounting period.

Peachtree uses the following 16 account types:

- *Cash.* This account type is used for any accounts that involve cash. In business, cash consists of funds on hand in the firm and funds on deposit in banks. The funds on hand include not only currency and coin but also cash equivalents such as checks and money orders received from customers. Some firms maintain just one cash account, but others have a variety of cash accounts such as Cash on Hand, Petty Cash, Regular Checking Account, Payroll Checking Account, and Money Market Savings.
- *Accounts Receivable.* The **accounts receivable** of a business are the amounts owed by its customers for goods or services sold to them on credit or on account.
- *Inventory.* Inventory is the stock of goods on hand. In a merchandising business, inventory is the stock of goods that the firm has purchased for resale to customers. A manufacturing business has three kinds of inventory—raw materials, work in process, and finished goods. The inventory accounts that a business uses depend on its operations.
- *Other Current Assets.* Accounts receivable and inventory are considered **current assets**—that is, assets that will be used up or turned into cash within one year. There are also other kinds of current assets that involve much smaller amounts of money, such as office supplies and

accounts receivable The amounts owed to a business by its customers for goods or services sold on credit.

current assets Assets that will be used up or turned into cash within one year.

prepaid insurance. In Peachtree, any current assets besides cash, accounts receivable, and inventory are classified as other current assets.

- *Fixed Assets.* Physical assets that will be used by a business for more than a year are called **fixed assets**. Examples of fixed assets are equipment, trucks, buildings, and land. Fixed assets are also known as plant assets, long-term assets, and property, plant, and equipment.

- *Accumulated Depreciation.* Part of the cost of a fixed asset is allocated, or expensed, to operations during each accounting period of its useful life. This process is known as depreciation. Depreciation allows a business to match the cost of fixed assets against the revenue those assets help to produce. The accumulated depreciation represents the total depreciation expense taken in past accounting periods.

- *Other Assets.* In Peachtree, assets that are not current assets or fixed assets are classified as other assets. This category includes intangible assets such as goodwill, patents, trademarks, copyrights, and franchises. Intangible assets are assets that have no physical substance.

- *Accounts Payable.* The **accounts payable** of a business are the amounts that it owes to creditors for goods and services that it purchased on credit.

- *Other Current Liabilities.* **Current liabilities** are debts that are due within one year. Accounts payable are one type of current liability. In Peachtree, all current liabilities besides accounts payable are classified as Other Current Liabilities. This category includes items such as salaries payable, taxes payable, short-term notes payable, and interest payable.

- *Long-Term Liabilities.* **Long-term liabilities** are debts that extend for more than one year. This category includes mortgages payable and long-term notes payable.

- *Equity—Doesn't Close.* In Peachtree, there are three types of equity accounts. The first type consists of accounts that do not close. These are the capital accounts of a sole proprietorship and a partnership and the capital stock accounts of a corporation.

- *Equity—Retained Earnings.* This category consists of the Retained Earnings account. At the end of each accounting period, the revenue and expense accounts are closed into Retained Earnings. The difference between the balances of the revenue and expense accounts is the net income or net loss for the period.

- *Equity—Gets Closed.* The last category of equity accounts contains the accounts that are used to record owner contributions and distributions of earnings to owners (drawings in sole proprietorships and partnerships and dividends in corporations). These equity accounts are closed at the end of the accounting period.

- *Income.* In Peachtree, the income accounts include all accounts used to record the revenue from sales of goods or services and all accounts used to record other types of revenue such as interest income.

- *Cost of Sales.* The accounts in this category apply to merchandising and manufacturing businesses but not to service businesses. The cost of sales is the cost of purchasing or making the goods that were sold during an accounting period. Cost of sales is also known as cost of goods sold. In a merchandising business, accounts for purchases, purchase returns and allowance, purchase discounts, and transportation charges would be categorized as cost of sales.

fixed assets Physical assets that will be used by a business for more than a year.

accounts payable The amounts that a business owes to its creditors for goods or services purchased on credit.

current liabilities Debts due for payment within one year.

long-term liabilities Debts that extend for more than one year.

- *Expenses.* In Peachtree, the expense accounts include all operating expenses incurred to earn revenue such as rent and salaries and other expenses such as interest.

Step 6:

Click Maintain from the Menu bar and then click *Chart of Accounts*.

For the following steps, use Tile Installation by Ramirez's chart of accounts shown in table 2–5. Complete the account ID, account description, and account type for all of Ramirez's accounts.

Account ID	Description	Account Type
100	Cash	Cash
102	Petty Cash	Cash
104	Accounts Receivable	Accounts Receivable
106	Office Supplies	Other Current Assets
108	Equipment	Fixed Assets
108.5	Accum. Depreciation-Equipment	Accumulated Depreciation
200	Accounts Payable	Accounts Payable
300	J. Ramirez, Capital	Equity-doesn't close
301	J. Ramirez, Equity	Equity-Retained Earnings
301.5	J. Ramirez, Drawing	Equity-gets closed
400	Revenue	Income
500	Rent Expense	Expenses
502	Utilities Expense	Expenses
504	Telephone Expense	Expenses
506	Office Supplies Expense	Expenses
508	Repairs Expense	Expenses
510	Depreciation Expense-Equipment	Expenses
512	Wages and Salaries Expense	Expenses
514	Miscellaneous Expense	Expenses

Step 7:

Enter **100** in the *Account ID* field of the Maintain Chart of Accounts window to create Tile Installation by Ramirez's first account, the Cash account. As the numbers are entered, a drop-down lookup box appears as shown in figure 2–18.

FIGURE 2–18

Account ID Lookup Box

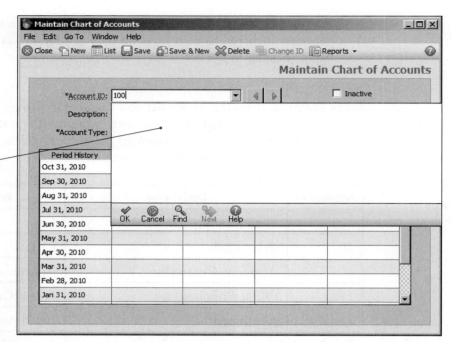

HINT

Press the Tab or Enter key to move from one box to the next. Holding down the Shift and Tab key at the same time moves the cursor to the previous box.

Step 8:
Click the OK button to accept 100 as the Account ID.

Step 9:
Key **Cash** in the *Description* field.

Step 10:
Click *Cash* from the Account Type drop-down list if it is not already showing.

Step 11:
Click the Save button on the toolbar to save the account if the information is accurate. Compare the newly created account with figure 2–19.

FIGURE 2–19

Completed Cash Account

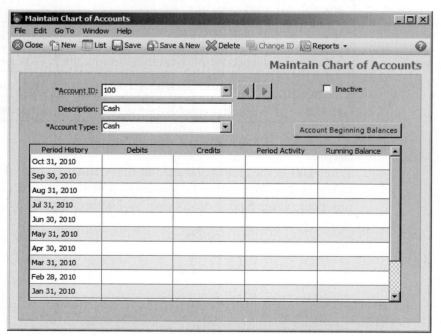

FIGURE 2–20

Account ID Drop-Down List with Revenue Selected

Step 12:

Repeat steps 7 through 11 until you have created all the accounts listed on Tile Installation by Ramirez's chart of accounts shown in table 2–5 (page 55).

Step 13:

Click the drop-down arrow or the Previous Record or Next Record buttons (left and right pointing arrows) next to the *Account ID* field to view a list of the accounts created. Use the scroll bar to view all the accounts.

Editing Accounts

In Peachtree, an account can be viewed, edited, or deleted at any time.

Step 1:

At the Maintain Chart of Accounts window, click the drop-down arrow next to the *Account ID* field, use the down arrow on the keyboard to highlight *Revenue* (ID# 400), and then click the OK button on the toolbar at the bottom of the drop-down list, as shown in figure 2–20.

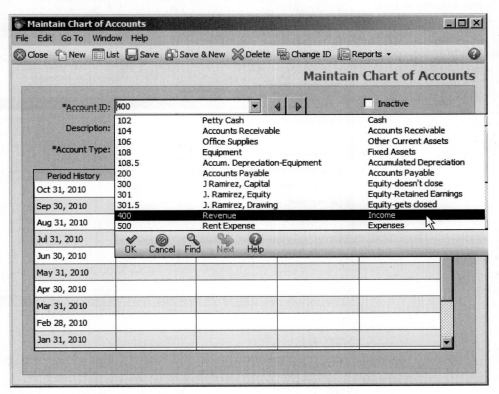

Step 2:

Any necessary changes can be made to an account by entering those changes and then clicking the Save button on the toolbar. Change the account description to *Installation Fees Earned* and then click Save. You can also delete an account by clicking the account and then clicking the Delete button on the toolbar.

Step 3:

Review and edit any accounts as necessary, and then click the Close button on the toolbar.

Printing the Chart of Accounts

It may be necessary to review the chart of accounts. If a company's chart of accounts is extensive, it may be impractical to view all of it on the screen. To print a chart of accounts, follow these steps.

Step 1:
Open Wildwood Medical Services. Close the Action Items and Setup Guide windows, if open.

Step 2:
Click Reports & Forms from the main Menu bar and then click *General Ledger*.

Step 3:
Click the Reports tab and select *Chart of Accounts* as shown in figure 2–21.

FIGURE 2–21
Select a Report or Form
– Chart of Accounts

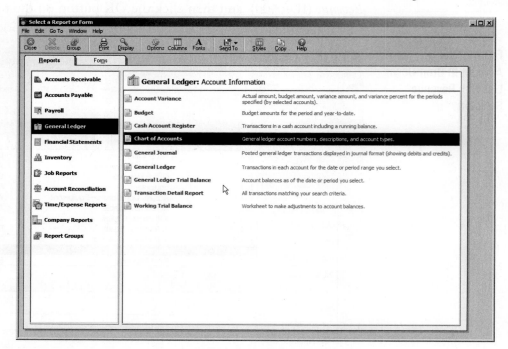

Step 4:
Click the Print button on the Select a Report or Form toolbar.

Step 5:
Select *Specific Period* from the Date drop-down list and *Period 1, (1/31/10)* from the As of drop-down list.

Step 6:
Click *GL Account ID* from the Sort by drop-down list (it may already be selected by default).

Step 7:
Enter a check mark in the box next to *Include accounts with zero amounts* by clicking it. Compare your entries with figure 2–22. If they are correct, click OK.

FIGURE 2–22
Modify Report –
Chart of Accounts

Step 8:

At the Print dialog box, click *All* in the Print range section. (Any pages, or combination of pages, may be printed by clicking the Pages option and entering the desired page range.) Click the number of copies desired from the *Number of copies* box, and then click OK.

Step 9:

Compare your printed chart of accounts with figure 2–23.

FIGURE 2–23
Wildwood Medical
Services Chart of
Accounts

Wildwood Medical Services
Chart of Accounts
As of Jan 31, 2010

Page: 1

Filter Criteria includes: Report order is by ID. Report is printed with Accounts having Zero Amounts and in Detail Format.

Account ID	Account Description	Active?	Account Type
1010	Cash on Hand	Yes	Cash
1020	Checking Account	Yes	Cash
1100	Accounts Receivable	Yes	Accounts Receivable
1150	Allowance for Doubtful Acc	Yes	Accounts Receivable
1200	Inventory	Yes	Inventory
1400	Prepaid Expenses	Yes	Other Current Assets
1500	Property and Equipment	Yes	Fixed Assets
1900	Accum. Depreciation - Pro	Yes	Accumulated Depreciation
2000	Accounts Payable	Yes	Accounts Payable
2310	Sales Tax Payable	Yes	Other Current Liabilities
2320	Deductions Payable	Yes	Other Current Liabilities
2330	Federal Payroll Taxes Paya	Yes	Other Current Liabilities
2340	FUTA Payable	Yes	Other Current Liabilities
2350	State Payroll Taxes Payabl	Yes	Other Current Liabilities
2360	SUTA Payable	Yes	Other Current Liabilities
2370	Local Taxes Payable	Yes	Other Current Liabilities
2380	Income Taxes Payable	Yes	Other Current Liabilities
2400	Customer Deposits	Yes	Other Current Liabilities
2500	Current Portion Long-Term	Yes	Other Current Liabilities
2700	Long Term Debt-Noncurren	Yes	Long Term Liabilities
3904	James, Capital	Yes	Equity-doesn't close
3910	Retained Earnings	Yes	Equity-Retained Earnings
3920	Owner's Contribution	Yes	Equity-gets closed
3930	Owner's Draw	Yes	Equity-gets closed
4000	Medical Services	Yes	Income
4050	Sales of Materials	Yes	Income
4100	Interest Income	Yes	Income
4200	Finance Charge Income	Yes	Income
4300	Other Income	Yes	Income
4900	Sales/Fees Discounts	Yes	Income
5000	Cost of Sales	Yes	Cost of Sales
5400	Cost of Sales-Salary & Wa	Yes	Cost of Sales
5900	Inventory Adjustments	Yes	Cost of Sales
6000	Wages Expense	Yes	Expenses
6050	Employee Benefit Program	Yes	Expenses
6100	Payroll Tax Expense	Yes	Expenses
6150	Bad Debt Expense	Yes	Expenses
6200	Income Tax Expense	Yes	Expenses
6250	Other Taxes Expense	Yes	Expenses
6300	Rent or Lease Expense	Yes	Expenses
6350	Maintenance & Repairs Ex	Yes	Expenses
6400	Utilities Expense	Yes	Expenses
6450	Office Supplies Expense	Yes	Expenses
6500	Telephone Expense	Yes	Expenses
6550	Other Office Expense	Yes	Expenses
6600	Advertising Expense	Yes	Expenses
6650	Commissions and Fees Ex	Yes	Expenses
6800	Freight Expense	Yes	Expenses
6850	Service Charge Expense	Yes	Expenses
6900	Purchase Disc-Expense Ite	Yes	Expenses
6950	Insurance Expense	Yes	Expenses
7050	Depreciation Expense	Yes	Expenses
7100	Gain/Loss - Sale of Assets	Yes	Expenses

Step 10:
Click the Close button to close the Select a Report or Form window.

Step 11:
Open Tile Installation by Ramirez and close the Action Items & Peachtree
Setup Guide windows.

Step 12:
Print a copy of the chart of accounts for Tile Installation by Ramirez by
repeating steps 2 through 8. Compare your chart of accounts to the one
shown in figure 2–24.

FIGURE 2–24
Tile Installation by
Ramirez Chart of
Accounts

Page: 1

Tile Installation by Ramirez
Chart of Accounts
As of Jan 31, 2010
Filter Criteria includes: Report order is by ID. Report is printed with Accounts having Zero Amounts and in Detail Format.

Account ID	Account Description	Active?	Account Type
100	Cash	Yes	Cash
102	Petty Cash	Yes	Cash
104	Accounts Receivable	Yes	Accounts Receivable
106	Office Supplies	Yes	Other Current Assets
108	Equipment	Yes	Fixed Assets
108.5	Accum. Depreciation-Equip	Yes	Accumulated Depreciation
200	Accounts Payable	Yes	Accounts Payable
300	J. Ramirez, Capital	Yes	Equity-doesn't close
301	J. Ramirez, Equity	Yes	Equity-Retained Earnings
301.5	J. Ramirez, Drawing	Yes	Equity-gets closed
400	Installation Fees Earned	Yes	Income
500	Rent Expense	Yes	Expenses
502	Utilities Expense	Yes	Expenses
504	Telephone Expense	Yes	Expenses
506	Office Supplies Expense	Yes	Expenses
508	Repairs Expense	Yes	Expenses
510	Depreciation Expense-Equi	Yes	Expenses
512	Wages and Salaries Expen	Yes	Expenses
514	Miscellaneous Expense	Yes	Expenses

Step 13:
Click the Close button to close the Select a Report or Form window.

C h e c k   p o i n t

1. What are the three pieces of information needed to create an account in Peachtree?
2. How many account types does Peachtree support?

Answers
1. *The account ID, account description, and account type are required.*
2. *Peachtree supports 16 account types.*

Practice Objective 2

Open Maslow's Financial Services and create the accounts listed in table 2–6.

TABLE 2–6
Maslow's Financial
Services Chart of
Accounts

Account ID	Description	Account Type
100	Cash	Cash
102	Petty Cash	Cash
104	Accounts Receivable	Accounts Receivable
106	Maintenance Supplies	Other Current Assets
108	Office Supplies	Other Current Assets
110	Prepaid Insurance	Other Current Assets
112	Equipment	Fixed Assets
112.5	Accum. Depreciation-Equipment	Accumulated Depreciation
200	Accounts Payable	Accounts Payable
300	H. Maslow, Capital	Equity-doesn't close
301	H. Maslow, Equity	Equity-Retained Earnings
301.5	H. Maslow, Drawing	Equity-gets closed
400	Revenue	Income
500	Rent Expense	Expenses
502	Utilities Expense	Expenses
504	Maintenance Supplies Expense	Expenses
506	Office Supplies Expense	Expenses
508	Insurance Expense	Expenses
510	Depreciation Expense-Equipment	Expenses
512	Wages and Salaries Expense	Expenses
514	Miscellaneous Expense	Expenses

Your chart of accounts should look like figure 2–25. Print and then close the chart of accounts.

FIGURE 2–25
Maslow's Financial
Services Chart of
Accounts

Page: 1

Maslow's Financial Services
Chart of Accounts
As of Jan 31, 2010

Filter Criteria includes: Report order is by ID. Report is printed with Accounts having Zero Amounts and in Detail Format.

Account ID	Account Description	Active?	Account Type
100	Cash	Yes	Cash
102	Petty Cash	Yes	Cash
104	Accounts Receivable	Yes	Accounts Receivable
106	Maintenance Supplies	Yes	Other Current Assets
108	Office Supplies	Yes	Other Current Assets
110	Prepaid Insurance	Yes	Other Current Assets
112	Equipment	Yes	Fixed Assets
112.5	Accum. Depreciation-Equip	Yes	Accumulated Depreciation
200	Accounts Payable	Yes	Accounts Payable
300	H. Maslow, Capital	Yes	Equity-doesn't close
301	H. Maslow, Equity	Yes	Equity-Retained Earnings
301.5	H. Maslow, Drawing	Yes	Equity-gets closed
400	Revenue	Yes	Income
500	Rent Expense	Yes	Expenses
502	Utiliteis Expense	Yes	Expenses
504	Maintenance Supplies Exp	Yes	Expenses
506	Office Supplies Expense	Yes	Expenses
508	Insurance Expense	Yes	Expenses
510	Depreciation Expense-Equi	Yes	Expenses
512	Wagese and Salaries Expe	Yes	Expenses
514	Miscellaneous Expense	Yes	Expenses

OBJECTIVE 3 — Enter Beginning Account Balances

Once you have created the general ledger accounts for your company,
it is time to enter the beginning balances. If a company is converting to
Peachtree from a manual accounting system, the normal practice is to use
the ending balances from the previous month, which appear on the trial balance. For example, if a company wants to convert to Peachtree on July 1, the
balances from the June 30 trial balance are used. Thus, the ending balances
of the general ledger accounts as of June 30 become the beginning balances
as of July 1. The **trial balance** is a listing of the general ledger accounts and
their balances. It is used to prove that the general ledger is in balance.

trial balance A proof
that the general ledger
is in balance.

Entering the Beginning Account Balances

To enter beginning balances, follow these steps:

Step 1:
Open Tile Installation by Ramirez

Step 2:
Click Maintain and then click *Chart of Accounts*.

Step 3:
Click the Account Beginning Balances button in the Maintain Chart of
Accounts window (figure 2–26).

FIGURE 2–26
Maintain Chart of
Accounts Window

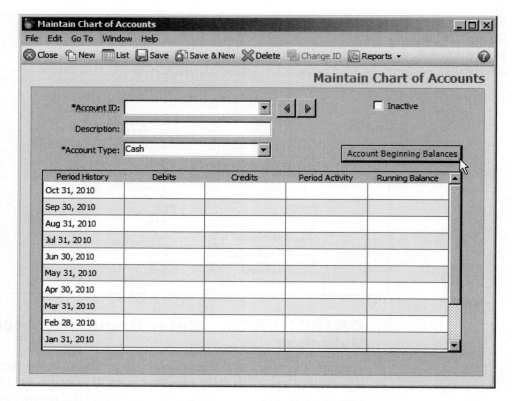

Step 4:
Use the scroll bar on the right side of the Select Period dialog box, click *From 1/1/10 through 1/31/10* (figure 2–27), and then click OK. Tile Installation by Ramirez - Ch 1 will now start its fiscal year on January 1, 2010.

FIGURE 2–27
Select Period Dialog Box

Step 5:
Enter the beginning balances, as indicated in table 2–7, in the Chart of Accounts Beginning Balances window (figure 2–28). Press the Enter or Tab key to move between accounts. Remember to enter the decimal points as needed.

Account ID	Account Description	Account Type	Assets, Expenses	Liabilities, Equity, Income
100	Cash	Cash	$12,000.00	
102	Petty Cash	Cash	250.00	
104	Accounts Receivable	Accounts Receivable	13,000.00	
106	Office Supplies	Other Current Assets	590.00	
108	Equipment	Fixed Assets	112,000.00	
108.5	Accum. Depreciation Equipment	Accumulated Depreciation		$12,000.00
200	Accounts Payable	Accounts Payable		2,300.00
300	J. Ramirez, Capital	Equity-doesn't close		123,540.00
301	J. Ramirez, Equity	Equity-Retained Earnings		
301.5	J. Ramirez, Drawing	Equity-gets closed		
400	Installation Fees Earned	Income		
500	Rent Expense	Expenses		
502	Utilities Expense	Expenses		
504	Telephone Expense	Expenses		
506	Office Supplies Expense	Expenses		
508	Repairs Expense	Expenses		
510	Depreciation Expense-Eq.	Expenses		
512	Wages and Salaries Expense	Expenses		
514	Miscellaneous Expense	Expenses		

FIGURE 2-28
Chart of Accounts
Beginning Balances
Window

Chart of Accounts Beginning Balances

Beginning Balances as of January 31, 2010

Account ID	Account Description	Account Type	Assets, Expenses	Liabilities, Equity, Income
100	Cash	Cash		
102	Petty Cash	Cash		
104	Accounts Receivable	Accounts Receivable		
106	Office Supplies	Other Current Assets		
108	Equipment	Fixed Assets		
108.5	Accum. Depreciation-Equipme	Accumulated Deprecia		
200	Accounts Payable	Accounts Payable		

The Trial Balance is made up of the balances of all accounts. In order for the Trial Balance to be in balance, the sum of Assets and Expenses should equal the sum of Liabilities, Equity, and Income.

Total: 12,000.00   0.00
Trial Balance: 12,000.00
(Difference posts to Beg Bal Equity)

Net Income is the difference of Income and Expense account values. The Income and Expense values making up Net Income are already included in the total.

Income - Expenses: 0.00   0.00
Net Income: 0.00

> **HINT**
>
> A new account may be added at any time while entering beginning balances by clicking the New button at the top of the Chart of Accounts Beginning Balances window.

> **HINT**
>
> Peachtree will not allow the Beginning Balances window to close unless the general ledger accounts are in balance. The trial balance at the bottom of the Chart of Accounts Beginning Balances window must show a zero (0) difference.

Step 6:
When you have finished entering the balances, click the OK button to save the entries and return to the Maintain Chart of Accounts window.

Step 7:
Close the Maintain Chart of Accounts window.

Printing the General Ledger with the Beginning Balances

The best way to check the accuracy of the general ledger is to print a copy. You can then check the newly created accounts and their balances. Follow these steps to print a copy of the general ledger:

Step 1:
Click the Business Status tab on the Peachtree opening window to reveal the Find a Report access area (bottom of the screen).

Step 2:
Select *General Ledger* from the Category drop-down list and *General Ledger* from the Report drop-down list (figure 2–29).

Step 3:
Click Print at the bottom of the window to display the Modify Report – General Ledger window.

Step 4:
Select *This Year* from the Time Frame drop-down list, click OK and then OK again to print the report.

The *General Ledger* report will include all transactions that occurred between January 1 and January 31, 2010. Compare your printout of the general ledger with figure 2–30.

FIGURE 2–30
Tile Installation by
Ramirez General
Ledger Report

Tile Installation by Ramirez
General Ledger
For the Period From Jan 1, 2010 to Jan 31, 2010

Page: 1

Filter Criteria includes: Report order is by ID. Report is printed with shortened descriptions and in Detail Format.

Account ID Account Description	Date	Reference	Jrnl	Trans Description	Debit Amt	Credit Amt	Balance
100 Cash	1/1/10 1/1/10	BEGBAL	GEN	Beginning Balance Current Period Cha	12,000.00 12,000.00		12,000.00
	1/31/10			Ending Balance			**12,000.00**
102 Petty Cash	1/1/10 1/1/10	BEGBAL	GEN	Beginning Balance Current Period Cha	250.00 250.00		250.00
	1/31/10			Ending Balance			**250.00**
104 Accounts Receivable	1/1/10 1/1/10	BEGBAL	GEN	Beginning Balance Current Period Cha	13,000.00 13,000.00		13,000.00
	1/31/10			Ending Balance			**13,000.00**
106 Office Supplies	1/1/10 1/1/10	BEGBAL	GEN	Beginning Balance Current Period Cha	590.00 590.00		590.00
	1/31/10			Ending Balance			**590.00**
108 Equipment	1/1/10 1/1/10	BEGBAL	GEN	Beginning Balance Current Period Cha	112,000.00 112,000.00		112,000.00
	1/31/10			Ending Balance			**112,000.00**
108.5 Accum. Depreciation-	1/1/10 1/1/10	BEGBAL	GEN	Beginning Balance Current Period Cha		12,000.00 12,000.00	-12,000.00
	1/31/10			Ending Balance			**-12,000.00**
200 Accounts Payable	1/1/10 1/1/10	BEGBAL	GEN	Beginning Balance Current Period Cha		2,300.00 2,300.00	-2,300.00
	1/31/10			Ending Balance			**-2,300.00**
300 J. Ramirez, Capital	1/1/10 1/1/10	BEGBAL	GEN	Beginning Balance Current Period Cha		123,540.00 123,540.00	-123,540.00
	1/31/10			Ending Balance			**-123,540.00**

Check point

1. What accounting period is usually used to enter beginning balances?
2. As with any accounting system, the trial balance must be in balance. What does Peachtree do to ensure the trial balance is in balance?

Answers
1. Either the current period or the period prior to the first period in which transactions will be entered.
2. Peachtree will not allow the trial balance to be saved unless it balances.

Practice Objective 3

Open Maslow's Financial Services and enter the beginning balances of the general ledger accounts. Use the information given in table 2–8. Use the period 1/1/10 through 1/31/10 for beginning balances.

Your general ledger should look like figure 2–31.

TABLE 2–8
Maslow's Financial Services Beginning Balances, January 1, 2010

Account ID	Account Description	Account Type	Assets, Expenses	Liabilities, Equity, Income
100	Cash	Cash	$14,400	
102	Petty Cash	Cash	100	
104	Accounts Receivable	Accounts Receivable		
106	Maintenance Supplies	Other Current Assets	2,300	
108	Office Supplies	Other Current Assets	490	
110	Prepaid Insurance	Other Current Assets	1,000	
112	Equipment	Fixed Assets	42,000	
112.5	Accum. Depr.-Equipment	Accumulated Depreciation		$10,000
200	Accounts Payable	Accounts Payable		
300	H. Maslow, Capital	Equity-doesn't close		50,290
301	H. Maslow, Equity	Equity-Retained Earnings		
301.5	H. Maslow, Drawing	Equity-gets closed		
400	Revenue	Income		
500	Rent Expense	Expenses		
502	Utilities Expense	Expenses		
504	Maintenance Supplies Expense	Expenses		
508	Insurance Expense	Expenses		
510	Depreciation Expense-Eq.	Expenses		
512	Wages and Salaries Expense	Expenses		
514	Miscellaneous Expense	Expenses		

FIGURE 2–31
Maslow's Financial
Services General
Ledger

Maslow's Financial Services
General Ledger
For the Period From Jan 1, 2010 to Jan 31, 2010

Page: 1

Filter Criteria includes: Report order is by ID. Report is printed with shortened descriptions and in Detail Format.

Account ID / Account Description	Date	Reference	Jrnl	Trans Description	Debit Amt	Credit Amt	Balance
100 Cash	1/1/10			Beginning Balance			
	1/1/10	BEGBAL	GEN		14,400.00		
				Current Period Cha	14,400.00		14,400.00
	1/31/10			**Ending Balance**			**14,400.00**
102 Petty Cash	1/1/10			Beginning Balance			
	1/1/10	BEGBAL	GEN		100.00		
				Current Period Cha	100.00		100.00
	1/31/10			**Ending Balance**			**100.00**
106 Maintenance Supplies	1/1/10			Beginning Balance			
	1/1/10	BEGBAL	GEN		2,300.00		
				Current Period Cha	2,300.00		2,300.00
	1/31/10			**Ending Balance**			**2,300.00**
108 Office Supplies	1/1/10			Beginning Balance			
	1/1/10	BEGBAL	GEN		490.00		
				Current Period Cha	490.00		490.00
	1/31/10			**Ending Balance**			**490.00**
110 Prepaid Insurance	1/1/10			Beginning Balance			
	1/1/10	BEGBAL	GEN		1,000.00		
				Current Period Cha	1,000.00		1,000.00
	1/31/10			**Ending Balance**			**1,000.00**
112 Equipment	1/1/10			Beginning Balance			
	1/1/10	BEGBAL	GEN		42,000.00		
				Current Period Cha	42,000.00		42,000.00
	1/31/10			**Ending Balance**			**42,000.00**
112.5 Accum. Depreciation-	1/1/10			Beginning Balance			
	1/1/10	BEGBAL	GEN			10,000.00	
				Current Period Cha		10,000.00	-10,000.00
	1/31/10			**Ending Balance**			**-10,000.00**
300 H. Maslow, Capital	1/1/10			Beginning Balance			
	1/1/10	BEGBAL	GEN			50,290.00	
				Current Period Cha		50,290.00	-50,290.00
	1/31/10			**Ending Balance**			**-50,290.00**

End of Chapter Review

Software Command Summary

Set Up Company	Create a New Company or File, New Company, Enter Company Information, Select Chart of Accounts Option, Select Accounting Method, Select Posting Method, Set Accounting Periods, Finish
Create Chart of Accounts	Maintain, Chart of Accounts, Account ID, Description, Account Type
Enter Account Balances	Maintain, Chart of Accounts, Account Beginning Balances, Select Period, Enter Balances

Projects and Problems

Content Check

Multiple Choice: Choose only one response for each question.

1. After graduating from college, a fellow student started a payroll processing business. He handles payroll work for small firms in your area. This is an example of what type of business?
   A. manufacturing business
   B. merchandising business
   C. service business
   D. a combined merchandising and service business
   E. None of the above

2. Which of the following is *not* an advantage of a sole proprietorship?
   A. complete management control by owner
   B. ease of formation
   C. few government restrictions
   D. unlimited liability
   E. None of the above

3. Revenue accounts would use which set of account IDs in Peachtree?
   A. 100, 1000, 10000
   B. 200, 2000, 20000
   C. 300, 3000, 30000
   D. 400, 4000, 40000
   E. 500, 5000, 50000

4. The amounts owed to a business by its customers for goods or services sold to them on credit are called
   A. accounts payable.
   B. accounts receivable.
   C. equity – retained earnings.
   D. notes payable.
   E. None of the above

5. The financial report that lists all of a company's accounts and their balances is the
   A. general journal.
   B. general ledger.
   C. chart of accounts.
   D. account ID.
   E. None of the above

Short Essay Response: Provide a detailed answer for each question.

1. Describe the three basic forms of business organizations. List the advantages and disadvantages of each.
2. What is the difference between the cash basis and accrual basis of accounting?
3. What are the steps required for entering beginning balances in Peachtree?
4. When setting up a new business in Peachtree, what are the six main steps in the setup process?
5. What is the difference between the two posting methods in Peachtree—real time and batch?
6. What are the three items necessary to create a new account in Peachtree? Define each.

Case Problems

Problem 1A

1. Set up a new company for GJ Professional Accounting. Use the information given below.

Company Name:	**GJ Professional Accounting**
Address Line 1:	**1506 East March Lane**
Address Line 2:	
City, State, Zip:	**Stockton, CA 95207**
Country:	**USA**
Telephone:	**209-555-2112**
Fax:	**209-555-1221**
Business Type:	**Sole Proprietorship**
Federal Employer ID:	**95-2962962**
State Employer ID:	**06-556-02**
St. Unemployment ID:	**00546-76**
Chart of Accounts:	**Use a sample business type that closely matches your company**
Available Charts of Accounts:	**Accounting Agency**
Accounting Method:	**Accrual**
Posting Method:	**Real Time**
Accounting Periods:	**12 monthly accounting periods**
Fiscal Year to Start:	**January 2010**

2. Edit the following accounts to reflect the information given:

Account ID	Account Description	Account Type
12000	Office Supplies	Other Current Assets
15100	Computer Equipment	Fixed Assets
39006	Garret Johnson, Capital	Equity-doesn't close
39007	Garret Johnson, Drawing	Equity-gets closed
40200	Tax Preparation Fees	Income
67500	Office Cleaning Expense	Expenses
75500	Equipment Repair Expense	Expenses

3. Enter the following beginning balances for the period from 1/1/10 through 1/31/10:

Account ID	Account Description	Account Type	Assets, Expenses	Liabilities, Equity, Income
10200	Regular Checking Account	Cash	$23,000	
11000	Accounts Receivable	Accounts Receivable	5,600	
12000	Office Supplies	Other Current Assets	1,120	
15100	Computer Equipment	Fixed Assets	4,700	
20000	Accounts Payable	Accounts Payable		$4,920
39006	Garret Johnson, Capital	Equity-doesn't close		29,500

4. Delete the following accounts:

Account ID	Account Description	Account Type
10000	Petty Cash	Cash
10500	Special Account	Cash
14100	Employee Advances	Other Current Assets
48000	Fee Refunds	Income
63000	Commissions and Fees Exp	Expenses

5. Print a *Chart of Accounts* report and a *General Ledger* report for the period 1/1/10 to 1/31/10.

Problem 2A

1. Set up a new company for the Olsen Construction Company. Use the information given below.

Company Name:	**Olsen Construction Company**
Address Line 1:	**1308 Madison Avenue**
Address Line 2:	
City, State, Zip:	**Tracy, CA 95376**
Country:	**USA**
Telephone:	**209-555-7695**
Fax:	**209-555-7698**
Business Type:	**Sole Proprietorship**
Federal Employer ID:	**95-2862978**
State Employer ID:	**06-556-05**
St. Unemployment ID:	**00546-79**
Chart of Accounts:	**Build your own chart of accounts**
Accounting Method:	**Accrual**
Posting Method:	**Real Time**
Accounting Periods:	**12 monthly accounting periods**
Fiscal Year to Start:	**January 2010**

2. Create the following chart of accounts, and then enter the beginning balances for the period from 1/1/10 through 1/31/10:

Olsen Construction Company Chart of Accounts

Account ID	Account Description	Account Type	Assets, Expenses	Liabilities, Equity, Income
100	Cash	Cash	$27,340	
104	Accounts Receivable	Accounts Receivable	13,250	
106	Office Supplies	Other Current Assets	365	
108	Construction Equipment	Fixed Assets	11,300	
108.5	Accum. Depr.- Equipment	Accumulated Depreciation		$1,800
200	Accounts Payable	Accounts Payable		2,455
300	Dave Olsen, Capital	Equity-doesn't close		48,000
301	Dave Olsen, Equity	Equity-Retained Earnings		
301.5	Dave Olsen, Drawing	Equity-gets closed		

Account ID	Account Description	Account Type	Assets, Expenses	Liabilities, Equity, Income
400	Revenue	Income		
500	Rent Expense	Expenses		
502	Utilities Expense	Expenses		
504	Telephone Expense	Expenses		
506	Office Supplies Expense	Expenses		
508	Repairs Expense	Expenses		
510	Depreciation Expense-Eq.	Expenses		
512	Wages and Salaries Expense	Expenses		
514	Miscellaneous Expense	Expenses		

3. Print a *Chart of Accounts* report and a *General Ledger* report for the period 1/1/10 to 1/31/10.

Problem 1B

1. Set up a new company for Finite Graphics. Use the information given below.

Company Name:	**Finite Graphics**
Address Line 1:	**6051 East Sycamore Avenue**
Address Line 2:	
City, State, Zip:	**Stockton, CA 95207**
Country:	**USA**
Telephone:	**209-555-3113**
Fax:	**209-555-1331**
Business Type:	**Sole Proprietorship**
Federal Employer ID:	**95-2962984**
State Employer ID:	**06-557-03**
St. Unemployment ID:	**00546-68**
Chart of Accounts:	**Use a sample business type that closely matches your company**
Available Charts of Accounts:	**Graphic Artist**
Accounting Method:	**Accrual**
Posting Method:	**Real Time**
Accounting Periods:	**12 monthly accounting periods**
Fiscal Year to Start:	**January 2010**

2. Edit the following accounts to reflect the information given:

Account ID	Account Description	Account Type
12000	Graphing Supplies	Other Current Assets
15100	Graphing Equipment	Fixed Assets
39006	Ana Rosario, Capital	Equity-doesn't close
39007	Ana Rosario, Drawing	Equity-gets closed

3. Enter the following beginning balances for the period from 1/1/10 through 1/31/10:

Account ID	Account Description	Account Type	Assets, Expenses	Liabilities, Equity, Income
10200	Regular Checking Account	Cash	$13,000	
11000	Accounts Receivable	Accounts Receivable	2,600	
12000	Graphing Supplies	Other Current Assets	750	
15100	Graphing Equipment	Fixed Assets	7,700	
20000	Accounts Payable	Accounts Payable		$3,290
39006	Ana Rosario, Capital	Equity-doesn't close		20,760

4. Delete the following accounts:

Account ID	Account Description	Account Type
10000	Petty Cash	Cash
15500	Building	Fixed Assets
15600	Building Improvements	Fixed Assets
19100	Organization Costs	Other Assets
58500	Inventory Adjustments	Cost of Sales

5. Print a *Chart of Accounts* report and a *General Ledger* report for the period 1/1/10 to 1/31/10.

Problem 2B

1. Set up a new company for Robinson Brothers Builders. Use the information given below.

Company Name:	**Robinson Brothers Builders**
Address Line 1:	**732 Alhambra Way**
Address Line 2:	
City, State, Zip:	**Tracy, CA 95376**
Country:	**USA**
Telephone:	**209-555-9567**
Fax:	**209-555-5679**
Business Type:	**Sole Proprietorship**
Federal Employer ID:	**95-2862879**
State Employer ID:	**06-566-15**
St. Unemployment ID:	**00564-97**
Chart of Accounts:	**Build your own chart of accounts**
Accounting Method:	**Accrual**
Posting Method:	**Real Time**
Accounting Periods:	**12 monthly accounting periods**
Fiscal Year to Start:	**January 2010**

2. Create the following chart of accounts, and then enter the beginning balances for the period from 1/1/10 through 1/31/10:

Robinson Brothers Builders Chart of Accounts

Account ID	Account Description	Account Type	Assets, Expenses	Liabilities, Equity, Income
100	Cash	Cash	$18,470	
104	Accounts Receivable	Accounts Receivable	4,320	
106	Construction Supplies	Other Current Assets	3,560	
108	Construction Equipment	Fixed Assets	5,300	
108.5	Accum. Depr.-Equipment	Accumulated Depreciation		$2,400
200	Accounts Payable	Accounts Payable		2,350
300	Randy Robinson, Capital	Equity-doesn't close		26,900
301	Randy Robinson, Equity	Equity-Retained Earnings		
301.5	Randy Robinson, Drawing	Equity-gets closed		
400	Revenue	Income		
500	Rent Expense	Expenses		

Account ID	Account Description	Account Type	Assets, Expenses	Liabilities, Equity, Income
502	Utilities Expense	Expenses		
504	Telephone Expense	Expenses		
506	Construction Supplies Expense	Expenses		
508	Repairs Expense	Expenses		
510	Depreciation Expense-Eq.	Expenses		
512	Wages and Salaries Expense	Expenses		
514	Miscellaneous Expense	Expenses		

3. Print a *Chart of Accounts* report and a *General Ledger* report for the period 1/1/10 to 1/31/10.

Cooperative Learning

1. Form into groups of three or four students, and create your own hypothetical service business. Decide on the information needed for the business setup. Summarize your ideas on paper.
2. Using the newly formed company from Cooperative Learning Exercise 1, create the chart of accounts that will be needed. Print the chart of accounts.
3. Using the newly created accounts from Cooperative Learning Exercise 2, enter beginning balances that you consider reasonable for the new business. Print the general ledger.

Writing and Decision Making

Assume that the owner of the company for which you work, Maria Richardson, believes in the cross training of employees. Therefore, she has informed you that next week an employee from the purchasing department will spend a day with you and observe some of the reports you work with in the accounting department. She especially wants you to explain to this employee the significance of both the chart of accounts and the general ledger and how they relate to each other. Ms. Richardson would like you to give her a memo with the information that you plan to share with the employee from the purchasing department.

CHAPTER 3

Entering Transactions for a Cash Business

Learning Objectives

1. Create new accounts and enter beginning balances for a simple cash business

2. Record transactions in the general journal

3. Edit selected transactions in the general journal

4. Print the general journal and financial statements

Software Features

- General journal toolbar buttons

- General journal edit function

- General journal delete function

- General journal recurring transaction function

- General journal memorized transaction function

- Report filter and print procedures

Transactions are financial events that change a firm's assets, liabilities, or owner's equity. Examples of transactions are selling goods on credit, purchasing office supplies for cash, paying salaries to employees, and paying an amount owed to a creditor. Every firm must record the financial effects of its transactions. Generally, the first record of a business transaction is entered in a journal.

Transactions and the General Journal

A **journal** is simply a chronological record of transactions—a listing of transactions in order by date. There are various types of journals, but the most basic type is the **general journal**, which can be used to record all kinds of financial transactions.

Peachtree's General Journal Entry window, shown in figure 3–1, is very similar to a manual general journal. In both manual and computerized accounting systems, the information needed for general journal entries normally comes from business papers such as invoices, check stubs, cash register tapes, bills, and receipts, which provide evidence of the transactions. These business papers are known as **source documents**.

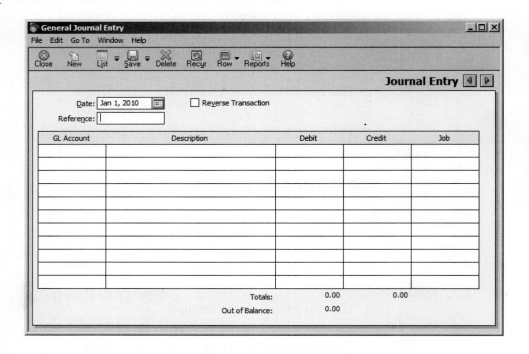

Debits and Credits

Debits and credits are at the heart of **double-entry accounting**. Every transaction is recorded by debiting one or more accounts and crediting one or more accounts. The total of the debits and the total of the credits recorded for the transaction must be equal.

Using source documents, the accountant analyzes each transaction to determine what accounts must be debited and credited and the amounts involved. The accountant follows the rules of debit and credit, which can be summarized as follows:

- *Asset, drawing, dividend, and expense accounts:* Record increases as debits and decreases as credits.

- *Liability, capital, and revenue accounts:* Record increases as credits and decreases as debits.

One of the great advantages of a computerized accounting system like Peachtree is that it has features that alert the accountant to unbalanced journal entries and prevent the posting of such entries to the general ledger. In a manual accounting system, entries with unequal debits and credits often go unnoticed in the general journal and are posted to the general ledger. The presence of errors is not revealed until the trial balance is prepared at the end of the accounting period. At this point, much time and effort must be spent tracing the individual errors through the journal and ledger and recording correcting entries.

Figure 3–2 illustrates a general journal entry in Peachtree that has unequal debits and credits. A notice at the bottom of the screen indicates that the journal is out of balance and shows the difference between the debit and credit totals ($90). Peachtree will not allow an unbalanced entry such as this one to be posted.

HINT

To learn more about the general ledger, select Help from the main Menu bar and *Peachtree Accounting Help* from the drop-down list. Key "General Ledger" at the prompt.

FIGURE 3–2
General Journal Entry with Unequal Debits and Credits

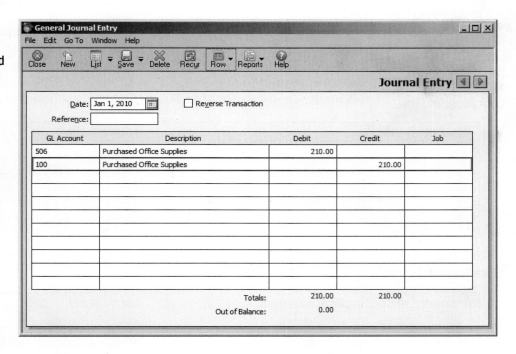

Check point

1. Each journal entry for a transaction must be in balance. What does that mean?
2. How does Peachtree treat a general journal entry that is not in balance?

Answers
1. *The total of the debits must equal the total of the credits.*
2. *Peachtree will not allow an unbalanced general journal entry to be posted.*

Journalizing and Posting a Sample Transaction

Suppose that a business purchases office supplies for $250 in cash. The accountant's analysis of this transaction reveals that an expense (Office Supplies Expense) has increased by $250 and an asset (Cash) has decreased by $250. The accountant records this transaction by debiting Office Supplies Expense for $250 and crediting Cash for $250. (In this example, the business operates on a pure cash basis and therefore treats purchases of supplies as an expense.)

If the business has a manual accounting system, the accountant will make the necessary entry in the general journal as shown in figure 3–3.

FIGURE 3–3
General Journal Entry

	Date		Account Title	P.R.	Debit	Credit
	General Journal					Page 1
1	Feb.	1	Office Supplies Expense	508	250 00	
2			Cash	100		250 00
3			Purchased office supplies.			

NOTE

It is a good practice to provide a brief explanation.

After the general journal entry is made, the accountant posts to the appropriate general ledger accounts and records the account numbers in the posting reference (P.R.) column of the general journal. See figures 3–4 and 3–5. In the Cash account (figure 3–4), the credit entry of $250 is subtracted from the beginning debit balance of $6,500 to find the new debit balance of $6,250.

FIGURE 3–4
Cash Account

	Date		Item	P.R.	Debit	Credit	Debit	Credit
Account Cash							**Account No. 100**	
							Balance	
1	Feb.	1	Beginning balance	✔			6500 00	
2		1		GJ1	250 00		6250 00	
3								

FIGURE 3–5
Office Supplies Expense

	Date		Item	P.R.	Debit	Credit	Debit	Credit
Account Office Supplies Expense							**Account No. 508**	
							Balance	
1	Feb.	1		GJ1	250 00		250 00	
2								
3								

Once an entry is posted to the ledger accounts, a posting reference (P.R.) is recorded in the accounts to identify the source of the entry. In this example, the source of the entry is page 1 of the general journal. Therefore, GJ1 is recorded in the P.R. column of each account.

In computerized accounting systems like Peachtree, posting is done automatically by the system. Once the chart of accounts has been set up, as described in chapter 2, Peachtree can automatically transfer information from journal entries to the general ledger accounts. This feature eliminates much repetitive work and prevents many of the errors that occur in manual posting.

The General Journal and Special Journals

special journal A journal that is used to record a single type of transaction.

A very small business may record all of its transactions in the general journal, but a larger business would probably use special journals as well as the general journal. A **special journal** is a journal that is used to record a single type of transaction. Peachtree allows you to use special journals for sales, purchases, cash receipts, and cash payments. These journals increase efficiency by grouping like transactions in their own journals.

The sales journal is used to record sales of goods or services on credit. The purchases journal is used to record purchases of goods or services on credit. The cash receipts journal is used to record all cash receipts. The cash disbursements journal is used to record all cash payments.

The use of special journals does not eliminate the need for a general journal. Some transactions still require a general journal entry. For example, in Peachtree, it is necessary to use the general journal for correcting entries and adjusting entries.

In the rest of this chapter, you will establish an accounting system for a small business in Peachtree and then use the general journal functions of Peachtree. The business that you will work with—Forward Thinking Graphic Design—is a small service business that operates on a cash basis.

Check point

1. What is the advantage of using the special journals provided by Peachtree?
2. What are the four basic types of special journals?

Answers
1. *The special journals increase efficiency by grouping similar transactions.*
2. *Sales journal, purchases journal, cash receipts journal, and cash disbursements journal.*

OBJECTIVE 1 — Create New Accounts and Enter Beginning Balances for a Simple Cash Business

In chapter 2, you learned how to set up a company in Peachtree, create a chart of accounts, and enter the beginning balances of the general ledger accounts. You will now use this knowledge to establish a computerized accounting system for Forward Thinking Graphic Design.

Setting Up a Simple Cash Business in Peachtree

Follow the steps outlined below to begin the setup process.

Step 1:
Start Peachtree Accounting.

Step 2:
At the Peachtree Accounting opening window, click *Create a new company*.

Step 3:
Click Next at the bottom of the Create a New Company – Introduction dialog box.

Step 4:
Enter the information for Forward Thinking Graphic Design in the Create a New Company – Company Information dialog box. Use the information shown in figure 3–6.

FIGURE 3–6
Create a New Company –
Company Information
Dialog Box

Step 5:
Click Next to reveal the Create a New Company – Setup dialog box. Click the *Build your own chart of accounts* option.

Step 6:
Click Next to move to the Create a New Company – Accounting Method dialog box, and then click **Cash.**

Step 7:
Click Next to move to the Create a New Company – Posting Method dialog box, and then click Real Time.

Step 8:
Click Next to move to the Create a New Company – Accounting Periods dialog box, click the *12 monthly accounting periods per year* option.

Step 9:
Click Next to move to the Create a New Company – Fiscal Year dialog box. Forward Thinking Graphic Design will use the calendar year as its fiscal year. Choose *January 2010* as the starting date of the fiscal year. (See figure 3–7.)

FIGURE 3–7
Create a New Company –
Fiscal Year Dialog Box

Step 10:
Click Next to move to the Create a New Company – Finish dialog box.

Step 11:
Click Finish. Wait for Peachtree to finish creating files. Then close the Action Items and Peachtree Setup Guide windows.

Creating New Accounts and Entering Beginning Balances

In chapter 2, you learned about the procedures for creating general ledger accounts and entering their beginning balances. You will now use these procedures for Forward Thinking Graphic Design. Follow the steps outlined below to create new accounts and enter the beginning balances for Forward Thinking Graphic Design.

Step 1:
Click Maintain from the main Menu bar and then click *Chart of Accounts*.

Step 2:
Create the Cash account by keying **100** in the *Account ID* field.

Step 3:
Click OK to accept account number 100. Then key **Cash** in the *Description* field.

Step 4:
At the Account Type drop-down list, click *Cash* (if it is not already selected). Compare your entries with those shown in figure 3–8. Then click Save.

FIGURE 3–8
Completed Cash Account

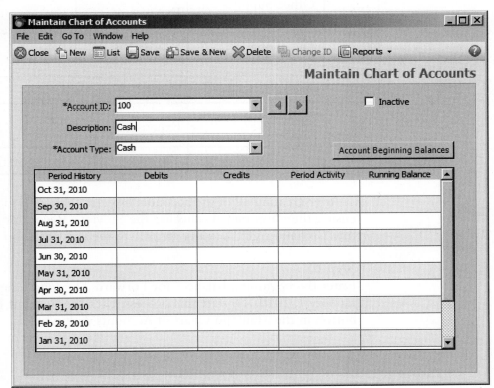

Step 5:

Click New to set up another account. Create the remainder of the general ledger accounts for Forward Thinking Graphic Design. Use the account IDs, account descriptions, and account types shown in table 3–1.

TABLE 3–1

Forward Thinking Graphic Design Accounts and Beginning Balances as of January 1, 2010

Account ID	Account Description	Account Type	Assets, Expenses	Liabilities, Equity, Income
100	Cash	Cash	$107,650.00	
102	Petty Cash	Cash	400.00	
300	Y. Lopez, Capital	Equity-doesn't close		$108,050.00
301	Y. Lopez, Equity	Equity-Retained Earnings		
301.5	Y. Lopez, Drawing	Equity-gets closed		
400	Design Fees	Income		
500	Independent Contractor Expense	Expenses		
502	Rent Expense	Expenses		
504	Utilities Expense	Expenses		
506	Office Supplies Expense	Expenses		
508	Telephone Expense	Expenses		
510	Design Expense	Expenses		
512	Professional Expense	Expenses		
		TOTALS	$108,050.00	$108,050.00

After creating all of the accounts listed in table 3–1, view your accounts to ensure their accuracy by clicking the Previous Record or Next Record buttons (left and right pointing arrows) to the right of the *Account ID* field.

Step 6:

Enter the beginning balances for Forward Thinking Graphic Design as of January 1, 2010. To start this process, click the Account Beginning Balances button in the Maintain Chart of Accounts dialog box.

Step 7:

Click *From 1/1/10 through 1/31/10* from the Select Period dialog box, as shown in figure 3–9, and then click OK.

FIGURE 3–9
Select Period Dialog Box

Step 8:

Enter the balances for Forward Thinking Graphic Design from table 3–1. The completed Chart of Accounts Beginning Balances window is shown in figure 3–10. Press the Tab key to move from account to account.

FIGURE 3–10
Completed Chart of Accounts Beginning Balances Window

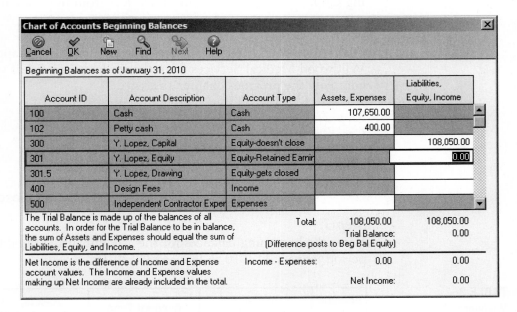

Step 9:

The totals at the bottom of the window should be equal, and the trial balance difference should be zero. This indicates that the general ledger accounts are in balance. Click the OK button after reviewing the Chart of Accounts Beginning Balances window.

Step 10:

Close the Maintain Chart of Accounts window.

Check point

1. After you enter beginning balances in Peachtree, how can you be sure that the general ledger accounts are in balance?
2. In Peachtree, the completed chart of accounts contains what four items of information for each account?

Answers

1. *If the totals of the balances are equal and the trial balance difference is zero, the general ledger accounts are in balance.*
2. *The account ID, description, account type, and balance for each account appear in the completed chart of accounts.*

Practice Objective 1

Create a new account and enter beginning balances for Wildwood Medical Services.

Note: Wildwood Medical Services was created in chapter 2. If you did not complete chapter 2, you may still complete this chapter's tasks by opening Chp. 3 – Wildwood Medical Services from the student data disk.

Step 1:

Open Wildwood Medical Services from the previous chapter or Chp. 3 – Wildwood Medical Services from the student data disk if you failed to complete the previous chapter's tasks.

Step 2:

Create the following account:

Account ID:	**3904**
Description:	**James, Capital**
Account Type:	**Equity-doesn't close**

Step 3:

Enter the beginning balances for the accounts listed in table 3–2 for the period January 1, 2010 to January 31, 2010.

TABLE 3–2
Wildwood Medical Services, January 1, 2010

Account ID	Account Description	Account Type	Assets, Expenses	Liabilities, Equity, Income
1010	Cash on Hand	Cash	$250.00	
1020	Checking Account	Cash	15,000.00	
3904	James, Capital	Equity-doesn't close		$15,250.00

Step 4:
Preview the general ledger for the period January 1, 2010 to January 31, 2010 and compare it with figure 3–11.

Page: 1

Chp. 3 - Wildwood Medical Services
General Ledger
For the Period From Jan 1, 2010 to Jan 31, 2010
Filter Criteria includes: Report order is by ID. Report is printed with shortened descriptions and in Detail Format.

Account ID Account Description	Date	Reference	Jrnl	Trans Description	Debit Amt	Credit Amt	Balance
1010 Cash on Hand	1/1/10 1/1/10 1/31/10	BEGBAL	GEN	Beginning Balance Current Period Cha Ending Balance	250.00 250.00		 250.00 **250.00**
1020 Checking Account	1/1/10 1/1/10 1/31/10	BEGBAL	GEN	Beginning Balance Current Period Cha Ending Balance	15,000.00 15,000.00		 15,000.00 **15,000.00**
3904 James, Capital	1/1/10 1/1/10 1/31/10	BEGBAL	GEN	Beginning Balance Current Period Cha Ending Balance		15,250.00 15,250.00	 -15,250.00 **-15,250.00**

OBJECTIVE 2 — Record Transactions in the General Journal

Once you have established the general ledger accounts and their balances, you can enter transactions. The transactions presented in this section are for Forward Thinking Graphic Design, a simple cash business. The company has no accounts receivable or accounts payable and owns no fixed assets. It rents a furnished office suite.

You will use the general journal entry function of Peachtree to record these transactions. Follow the steps listed below to journalize the January transactions of Forward Thinking Graphic Design.

Step 1:
Open Forward Thinking Graphic Design which you created previously in the chapter. Close the Action Items and Setup Guide windows.

Step 2:
Analyze the following transaction:

- On January 4, 2010, Forward Thinking Graphic Design purchased office supplies for $1,200 in cash from a local store.

  Analysis: An expense (Office Supplies Expense) has increased by $1,200 and an asset (Cash) has decreased by $1,200. Therefore, debit Office Supplies Expense for $1,200 and credit Cash for $1,200.

The manual general journal entry needed to record this transaction is shown in figure 3–12.

FIGURE 3–12
General Journal Entry

General Journal					Page 1	
	Date	Account Title	P.R.	Debit	Credit	
1	Jan. 4	Office Supplies Expense	506	1 2 0 0 00		
2		Cash	100		1 2 0 0 00	
3		Purchased office supplies.				

Step 3:
Use Peachtree to record the above transaction in the general journal of Forward Thinking Graphic Design. Click Tasks, and then click *General Journal Entry*.

You can also access the general journal by clicking the General Journal Entry shortcut at the lower left of the Peachtree screen, as shown in figure 3–13. The general journal entry window appears.

FIGURE 3–13
General Journal Entry
Shortcut

Step 4:
Enter the date of the transaction, January 4, 2010, by clicking the *calendar* icon to the right of the *Date* field. Choose *January* as the month, *4* as the day, and *2010* as the year.

Step 5:
Enter the account to be debited. Click the cell under *GL Account* and then click the *magnifying glass* icon to the right of the *GL Account* field. Highlight the account *506, Office Supplies Expense* by scrolling down to it. Compare your screen with figure 3–14 and then click OK.

FIGURE 3–14
Account Drop-Down
List with Account 506
Selected

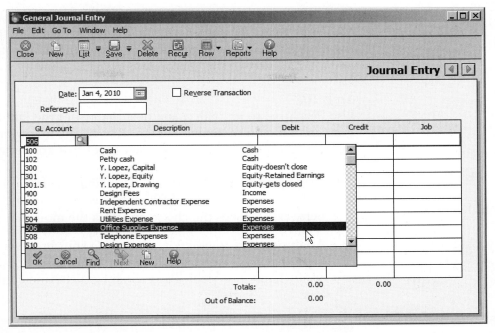

Step 6:
Key **Purchased Office Supplies** in the *Description* field. Press the Tab key and key **1,200.00** in the *Debit* field. Then tab down to the second row.

Step 7:
Enter the account to be credited. Click the *magnifying glass* icon to the right of the *GL Account* field in the second row, highlight or click the account *100*, *Cash*, and then click OK.

Step 8:
Peachtree will automatically enter the same description, *Purchased Office Supplies*, in the *Description* field. Press the Tab key and key **1,200.00** in the *Credit* field. Compare your completed general journal entry with figure 3–15.

FIGURE 3–15
Completed General
Journal Entry – Office
Supplies

General Journal Entry

File   Edit   Go To   Window   Help

Close   New   List   Save   Delete   Recur   Row   Reports   Help

Journal Entry

Date: Jan 4, 2010   ☐ Reverse Transaction
Reference:

GL Account	Description	Debit	Credit	Job
506	Purchased Office Supplies	1,200.00		
100	Purchased Office Supplies		1,200.00	

Totals: 1,200.00   1,200.00
Out of Balance: 0.00

Step 9:

Complete the recording of the transaction by clicking the Save button from the toolbar. Peachtree then transfers (posts) the information from the general journal entry to the appropriate ledger accounts.

Step 10:

Use Peachtree to journalize and post the rest of the January transactions for Forward Thinking Graphic Design. Review the following analysis of these transactions and the general journal entries that are shown.

- On January 5, 2010, Forward Thinking decided to increase the petty cash fund from $400 to $500. The owner writes a check for $100 to petty cash, cashes the check, and puts the money in the petty cash box.

  Analysis: This transaction produces a shift in assets. One asset (Petty Cash) has increased by $100, and another asset (Cash) has decreased by $100. Therefore, debit Petty Cash for $100 and credit Cash for $100. (See figure 3–16.)

FIGURE 3–16
Completed General
Journal Entry – Petty
Cash

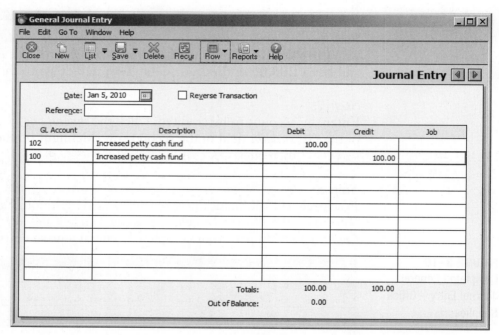

- On January 7, 2010, Forward Thinking collected fees of $9,200 for a completed design job.

  Analysis: Revenue (Design Fees) has increased by $9,200, and an asset (Cash) has increased by $9,200. Therefore, debit Cash for $9,200 and credit Design Fees for $9,200. (See figure 3–17.)

FIGURE 3–17
Completed General
Journal Entry – Design
Fees

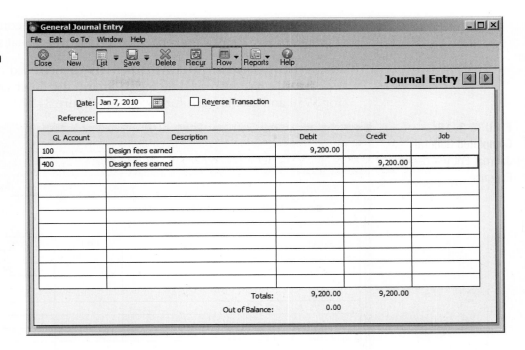

- On January 9, 2010, Forward Thinking paid the electric bill of $675.

  Analysis: An expense (Utilities Expense) has increased by $675, and an asset (Cash) has decreased by $675. Therefore, debit Utilities Expense for $675 and credit Cash for $675. (See figure 3–18.)

FIGURE 3–18
Completed General
Journal Entry – Electric
Bill

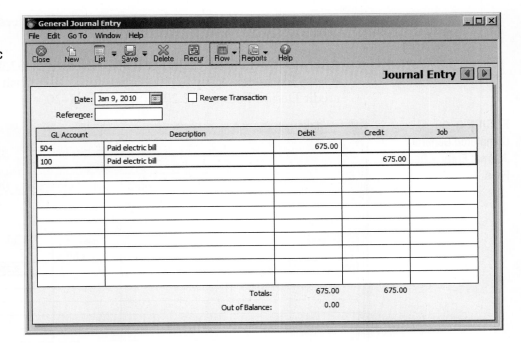

- On January 12, 2010, Forward Thinking utilized the consulting services of a design expert about a potential client. The fee for that service was $950.

  Analysis: An expense (Design Expense) has increased by $950, and an asset (Cash) has decreased by $950. Therefore, debit Design Expense for $950 and credit Cash for $950. (See figure 3–19.)

FIGURE 3–19
Completed General Journal Entry – Design Expense

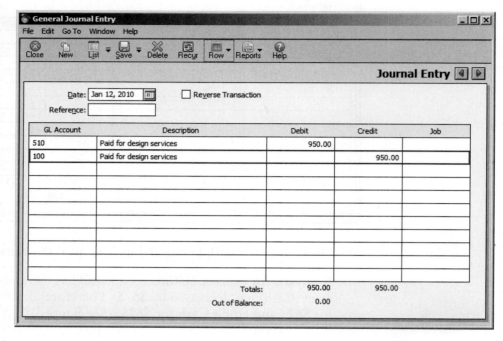

- On January 20, 2010, Forward Thinking collected fees of $2,200 after completing the first stage of a job.

  Analysis: Revenue (Design Fees) has increased by $2,200, and an asset (Cash) has increased by $2,200. Therefore, debit Cash for $2,200 and credit Design Fees for $2,200. (See figure 3–20.)

FIGURE 3–20
Completed General Journal Entry – Design Fees

• On January 23, 2010, Forward Thinking paid $2,600 to an independent contractor who did work for the business. (An independent contractor is someone who is not an employee and does not receive a salary. Instead, this person works for a fee on a project-by-project basis.)

Analysis: An expense (Independent Contractor Expense) has increased by $2,600, and an asset (Cash) has decreased by $2,600. Therefore, debit Independent Contractor Expense for $2,600 and credit Cash for $2,600. (See figure 3–21.)

FIGURE 3–21
Completed General Journal Entry – Contractor's Fee

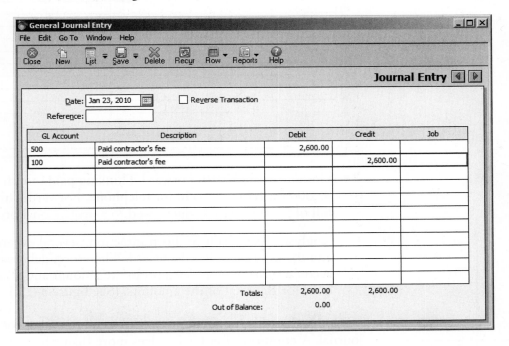

• On January 24, 2010, Forward Thinking paid $850 to a local newspaper for advertising.

Analysis: An expense (Advertising Expense) has increased by $850, and an asset (Cash) has decreased by $850. Therefore, debit Advertising Expense for $850 and credit Cash for $850. (See figure 3–22.) Forward Thinking has no Advertising Expense account, and you must create one. Use the following information to create the account:

Account ID:	**514**
Description:	**Advertising Expense**
Account Type:	**Expenses**

HINT

For a detailed review of the procedure for creating an account, refer to Objective 2 in chapter 2.

FIGURE 3–22
Completed General
Journal Entry –
Newspaper Ads

FIGURE 3–22
Completed General Journal Entry – Newspaper Ads

- On January 31, 2010, Forward Thinking paid month-end bills of $1,200 for rent and $350 for telephone. Forward Thinking also paid a bill of $230 for yearly dues owed to a professional organization.

  Analysis: As a result of this transaction, several expenses have increased, and the asset Cash has decreased. Therefore, debit each of the expense accounts affected for the appropriate amount and then credit Cash all at once for the total of the amounts. (See figure 3–23.)

  Notice that this transaction requires a compound entry in the general journal. A **compound entry** involves more than two accounts. In Peachtree, such entries can be tracked most easily if the word *Compound* is recorded in either the Reference or Description section of the General Journal Entry window. In the Reference section of this entry, key the word **Compound**.

compound entry
A journal entry that involves more than two accounts.

FIGURE 3–23
Completed General
Journal Entry –
Month-End Bills

FIGURE 3–23
Completed General Journal Entry – Month-End Bills

Step 11:
Click Save. Then close the General Journal Entry window.

C h e c k   p o i n t

1. What are two methods for accessing the general journal in Peachtree?
2. Why is it necessary to analyze a transaction before journalizing it?

Answers
1. *The general journal can be accessed by using the Menu bar or the Shortcut List.*
2. *It is necessary to analyze a transaction to determine the appropriate accounts and amounts to debit and credit in the journal entry for that transaction.*

P r a c t i c e   O b j e c t i v e   2

Several transactions for Wildwood Medical Services are listed below. Record these transactions in the general journal for the month of January 2010.

HINT

Remember that Wildwood Medical Services uses the cash basis accounting method and will not use Accounts Receivable, Other Current Assets, Fixed Assets, and Accounts Payable type accounts.

Step 1:
Open Wildwood Medical Services (Chp. 3 – Wildwood Medical Services if data disk is used).

Step 2:
Change the description of Account 4000 from Professional Fees to Medical Services.

Step 3:
Journalize the following transactions.*

- On January 2, Wildwood purchased $2,400 of office supplies. (Because Wildwood uses the cash basis, it records purchases of supplies in an expense account.) Use Account 6450, Office Supplies Expense.
- On January 4, Wildwood provided medical services for $5,200 in cash.
- On January 12, Wildwood paid $1,235 for maintenance and repair services.
- On January 20, Wildwood paid for an employee's retirement dinner (Account 6550) for $450.
- On January 24, Wildwood paid advertising costs of $750. Use Account 6600, Advertising Expense.
- On January 31, Wildwood paid the following month-end bills (compound entry):

Utilities	$300
Telephone	$245

* For all cash transactions, use Account 1020, Checking Account.

Step 4:
Review your journal entries for accuracy.

Step 5:
Close the General Journal Entry window.

OBJECTIVE 3 — Edit Selected Transactions in the General Journal

Occasionally it is necessary to alter a general journal entry that contains an error. For example, if you have used the wrong date or selected a wrong account, the entry must be corrected. Peachtree has an edit function that can be used to accomplish this task. The steps outlined below illustrate the procedures for editing a general journal entry.

Step 1:
Open Forward Thinking Graphic Design. Close the Setup Guide and Action Items windows.

Step 2:
Click Tasks, and then click *General Journal Entry*.

Step 3:
Click the List button at the top of the General Journal Entry toolbar. The General Journal List window will appear.

Step 4:
Click the entry from the General Journal List window which shows the purchase of office supplies for $1,200. Compare your screen with figure 3–24. Click Open when the correct journal entry is highlighted.

FIGURE 3–24
General Journal List Window

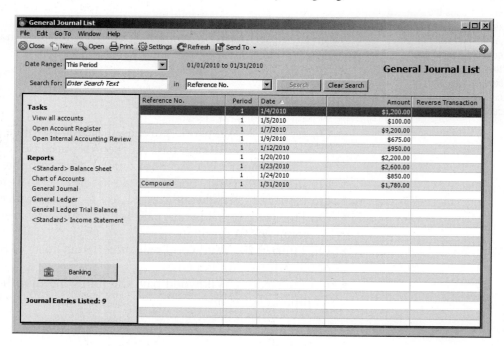

The general journal entry selected for editing is now in the active window, as shown in figure 3–25, and can be changed.

FIGURE 3–25
Selected General Journal
Entry

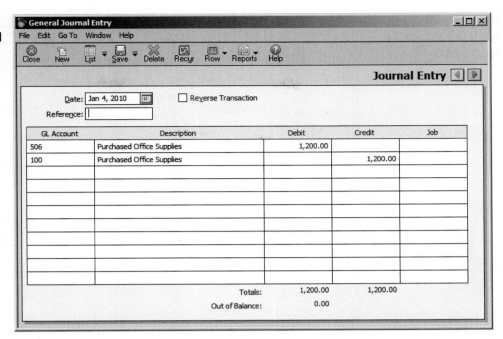

Step 5:

Assume that the accountant for Forward Thinking Graphic Design has entered the wrong date for the purchase of office supplies. Change the date from January 4, 2010, to January 5, 2010. Click the *calendar* icon, and then click 5 from the drop-down calendar.

Step 6:

Click Save and then Close to complete the editing process.

Step 7:

Use the List function or the Previous Transaction or Next Transaction buttons (left and right pointing arrows) at the top-right of the General Journal Entry window to review the other transactions you posted for Objective 2. Make any necessary changes.

Deleting a General Journal Entry

It may be necessary to delete an entire general journal entry. Peachtree has a function that makes this process simple.

Step 1:

Open Forward Thinking Graphic Design, if it is not currently open.

Step 2:

Create the following general journal entry for Forward Thinking Graphic Design:

- On January 23, 2010, purchased office supplies for $230 in cash. Compare the newly completed general journal entry with figure 3–26.

FIGURE 3–26
Newly Created General
Journal Entry

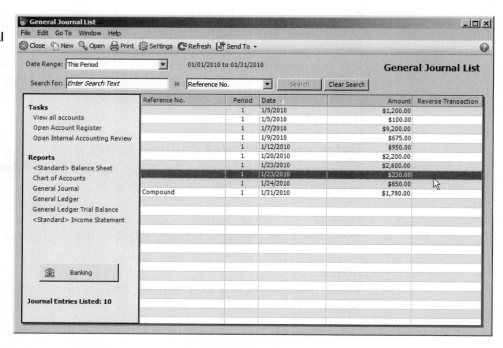

Step 3:
Click Save.

Step 4:
Retrieve the general journal entry just posted by clicking the List button on the toolbar and highlighting the desired entry as shown in figure 3–27. Then click Open (top of General Journal List toolbar).

FIGURE 3–27
Selected General Journal
Entry Highlighted

Step 5:
Assume that the accountant for Forward Thinking Graphic Design wants to delete the entire general journal entry created in step 2. Click the Delete

button in the General Journal Entry toolbar. Peachtree will ask, "Are you sure you want to delete this transaction?" Click Yes and the general journal entry is deleted. Close the General Journal List window.

Adding a Recurring Transaction

Most businesses have certain transactions that recur on a regular basis. For example, payment of rent may be due on a specified day each month. Peachtree has a recurring transaction function that makes it possible to journalize and post such transactions automatically on a predetermined schedule. This feature of Peachtree greatly increases efficiency and reduces errors. The following steps demonstrate how to establish a recurring transaction.

Step 1:
Create the following general journal entry for Forward Thinking Graphic Design:

- On January 31, 2010, paid the monthly rent of $1,200. (See figure 3–28.)

FIGURE 3–28
Completed General Journal Entry

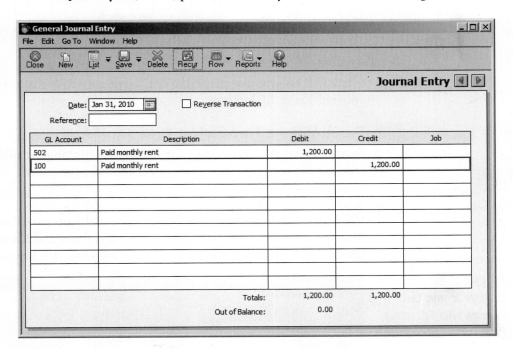

Step 2:
Because the rent payment occurs at the same time and for the same amount each month, the transaction can be saved and automatically recalled at specific intervals by Peachtree. Click the Recur button at the top of the General Journal Entry window to access the Create Recurring Journal Entries dialog box.

Step 3:
You can now save the journal entry for the payment of rent and designate how often it should recur. Select *Monthly* to answer "How often do you want to recur this transaction?"

Step 4:

Select *Jan 31, 2010* as "First transaction date." Select *End after* and key **12** for occurrences, as shown in figure 3–29.

FIGURE 3–29
Create Recurring Journal
Entries Dialog Box

Step 5:

Click OK to save the recurring transaction and return to the General Journal Entry dialog box.

Removing a Recurring Transaction

Suppose that the accountant for Forward Thinking Graphic Design wants to remove the recurring transaction for the rent payment.

Step 1:

Click the List button on the General Journal Entry toolbar. Click *All Transactions* from the Date Range drop-down list and then click the entry for the monthly rent, as shown in figure 3–30, and click Open.

FIGURE 3–30
General Journal List
Window with Recurring
Rent Transaction Chosen

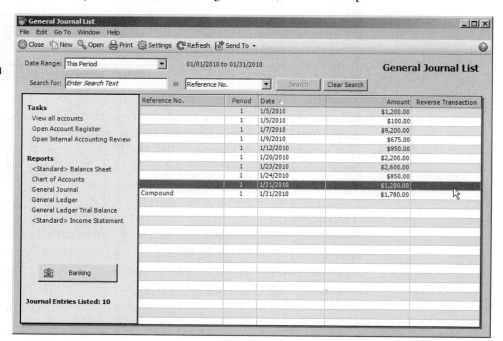

Step 2:
Click the Delete button on the General Journal Entry toolbar.

Step 3:
In the Delete Recurring Journal Entries dialog box, click the button next to *This transaction and all remaining*, as shown in figure 3–31, and click OK. This selection eliminates both the current journal entry for the rent payment and all recurring entries.

FIGURE 3–31
Delete Recurring Journal Entries Dialog Box

Step 4:
Close the General Journal List.

Adding a Memorized Transaction

Peachtree allows users to store in its memory transactions that occur often and recalls such transactions as they are needed. These transactions are known as memorized transactions.

Memorized transactions differ from recurring transactions because you must recall memorized transactions, whereas Peachtree makes recurring transactions automatically once they are established. The following steps demonstrate how to create, edit, and delete a memorized transaction.

Step 1:
Open Forward Thinking Graphic Design, if it is not already open.

Step 2:
Click Maintain, and then select *Memorized Transactions*.

Step 3:
At the Memorized Transactions submenu, click *General Journal Entries*.

Create a general journal entry for the following transaction, which Forward Thinking Graphic Design wants to establish as a memorized transaction. The actual date of this transaction will vary from month to month.

- Paid a monthly fee of $250 to the bookkeeper, who is an independent contractor.

Step 4:
Every memorized transaction requires an identification name or number. Key **BOOKKEEPER** in the *Transaction ID* lookup box, as shown in figure 3–32. Then click OK.

FIGURE 3–32
Transaction ID Lookup
Box with Bookkeeper
Entered

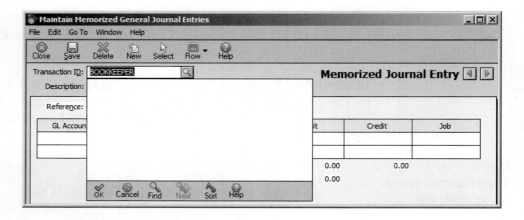

Step 5:
Key **Bookkeeper's Fee** in the *Description* field.

Step 6:
Record the remaining data as you would a regular general journal entry. Debit Independent Contractor Expense (Account 500) for $250 and credit Cash (Account 100) for $250. The completed entry for the memorized transaction is shown in figure 3–33.

FIGURE 3–33
Completed Memorized
General Journal Entry

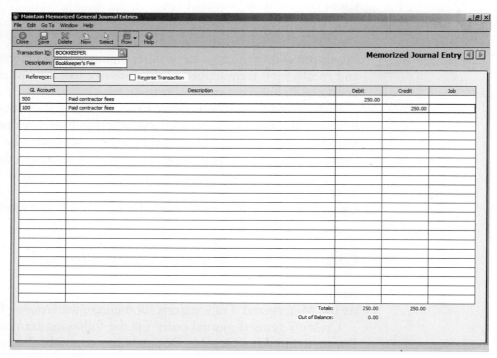

Step 7:
Click Save and Close. The memorized transaction is now available for recall whenever it is needed.

HINT

Transactions can be memorized and saved directly from the General Journal Entry window by selecting the down arrow key to the right of the *Save* icon and selecting the Memorize option.

Recalling a Memorized Transaction

Suppose that Forward Thinking Graphic Design pays the bookkeeper's fee on January 31, 2010, and wants to recall the memorized transaction.

Step 1:
Click Maintain, and then select *Memorized Transactions*.

Step 2:
At the Memorized Transactions submenu, click *General Journal Entries*.

Step 3:
Click the *magnifying glass* icon next to the *Transaction ID* lookup box, and then click *BOOKKEEPER*. The general journal entry for the memorized transaction appears.

Step 4:
Click the Select button from the Maintain Memorized General Journal Entries toolbar. This places the memorized transaction in the general journal entry window.

HINT

The date of the transaction is not memorized. It is necessary to enter the date each time the memorized transaction is used.

Step 5:
Key **1/31/10** in the *Date* field and press the Enter key. *Jan 31, 2010* will appear as the date. Save the completed entry, and close the general journal entry window. Close the Maintain Memorized General Journal Entries window.

Editing or Deleting a Memorized Transaction

It is possible to edit or delete existing memorized transactions.

Step 1:
Click Maintain, select *Memorized Transactions*, and then click *General Journal Entries*.

Step 2:
Click *BOOKKEEPER* from the *Transaction ID* lookup box and edit it as desired. For example, the description could be changed and then saved.

Step 3:
To delete an entire memorized transaction, click Delete and click <u>Y</u>es when prompted with the "Are you sure you want to delete this record?" message.

Step 4:
Close the active window.

Practice Objective 3

Use the general journal entries that you previously recorded for Wildwood Medical Services to practice the edit function. Then record recurring and memorized transactions for Wildwood.

Step 1:
Open Wildwood Medical Services (Chp. 3 – Wildwood Medical Services if data disk is used).

Step 2:
Edit the journal entry for the January 4, 2010, transaction. Change the date to January 5, 2010.

Step 3:
Create a recurring transaction for the payment of rent on January 31, 2010, for $900. (Use Account 6300, Rent or Lease Expense.) This transaction should recur monthly for 12 months.

Step 4:
Create a memorized transaction for maintenance costs of $750 and name it MAINTENANCE EXPENSE. (Use Account 6350, Maintenance and Repairs Expense.)

Step 5:
Review your work for accuracy. If any changes are necessary, use the edit function.

Step 6:
Close the active window.

OBJECTIVE 4 — Print the General Journal and Financial Statements

Peachtree allows you to review and print the general journal and financial statements by using the Reports option. There are two methods for accessing the Reports & Forms menu. The first method is by clicking Reports & Forms and then *General Ledger* from the Menu bar. The second method for accessing the Select a Report or Form menu is found by selecting the Business Status tab from the side toolbar and then *General Ledger* from the Category drop-down list and *General Journal* from the Report drop-down list, as shown in figure 3–34.

FIGURE 3–34
Find a Report with General Journal Selected

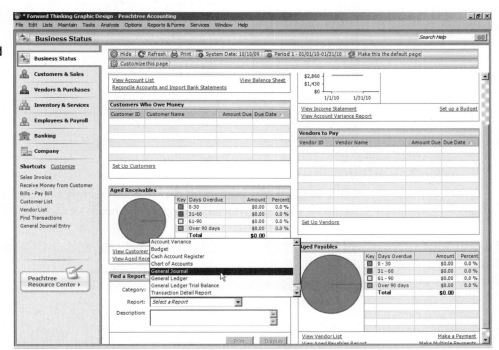

Viewing the General Journal

Follow the steps outlined below to view and print the general journal.

Step 1:
Open Forward Thinking Graphic Design.

Step 2:
Click Reports & Forms from the main Menu bar and then *General Ledger*, and then click *General Journal* from the General Ledger: Account Information section, as shown in figure 3–35.

FIGURE 3–35
Select a Report or Form
Dialog Box with General
Ledger and General
Journal Chosen

Step 3:
Click the Options button on the Select a Report or Form toolbar. The Modify Report – General Journal dialog box appears as shown in figure 3–36.

FIGURE 3–36
Modify Report – General
Journal Dialog Box

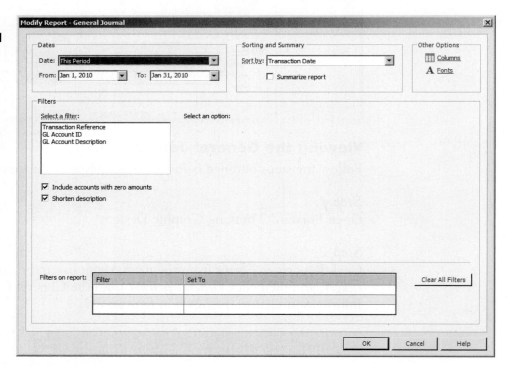

Step 4:
Click *Range* from the Date drop-down list. In addition to the current monthly period, several other options are available including quarterly and annual periods.

Step 5:
Select the first date of the period when transactions were entered, *Jan. 1, 2010*, in the From drop-down list and *Jan. 31, 2010*, in the To drop-down list.

Step 6:
Deselect (or uncheck) the check mark in the box next to *Include accounts with zero amounts*. This feature is a toggle function. It is like an on/off switch. The check mark in this box indicates that all accounts, even those with zero balances, will be listed in the report. Also, deselect the *Shorten description* box.

Step 7:
Review your selections with figure 3–37. Then click OK.

FIGURE 3–37
Completed Modify Report – General Journal Dialog Box

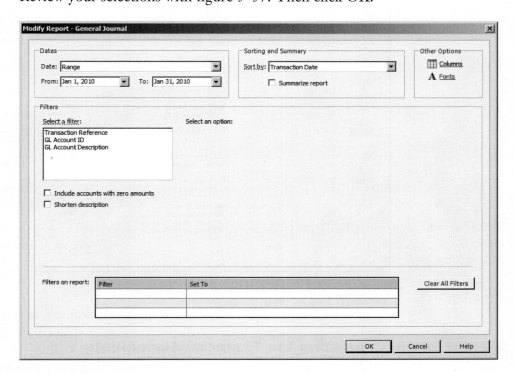

Step 8:
Review the general journal entries of Forward Thinking Graphic Design. Then click Close.

Printing the General Journal

To print the general journal, follow the same procedure as you did to view the journal entries, but in step 3, click the Print button on the toolbar. Remember to use the same selection criteria in the Modify Report – General Journal dialog box. This will result in a printed copy. However, also take the following additional steps.

Step 1:
Make sure that the printer is on. Then click OK.

Step 2:

Compare your printout with the one shown in figure 3–38. If you find any errors, correct them by using the edit function as described in Objective 3.

FIGURE 3–38
Printout of
General Journal
Entries

Forward Thinking Graphic Design
General Journal
For the Period From Jan 1, 2010 to Jan 31, 2010

Page: 1

Filter Criteria includes: Report order is by Date. Report is printed in Detail Format.

Date	Account ID	Reference	Trans Description	Debit Amt	Credit Amt
1/1/10	100	BEGBAL		107,650.00	
	102			400.00	
	300				108,050.00
1/5/10	506		Purchased Office Supplies	1,200.00	
	100		Purchased Office Supplies		1,200.00
	102		Increased petty cash fund	100.00	
	100		Increased petty cash fund		100.00
1/7/10	100		Design fees earned	9,200.00	
	400		Design fees earned		9,200.00
1/9/10	504		Paid electric bill	675.00	
	100		Paid electric bill		675.00
1/12/10	510		Paid for design services	950.00	
	100		Paid for design services		950.00
1/20/10	100		Design fees earned	2,200.00	
	400		Design fees earned		2,200.00
1/23/10	500		Paid contractor's fee	2,600.00	
	100		Paid contractor's fee		2,600.00
1/24/10	514		Paid for newspaper ads	850.00	
	100		Paid for newspaper ads		850.00
1/31/10	500		Paid contractor fees	250.00	
	100		Paid contractor fees		250.00
1/31/10	502	Compound	Paid monthly rent	1,200.00	
	508		Paid telephone bill	350.00	
	512		Paid yearly dues	230.00	
	100		Paid month-end bills		1,780.00
		Total		127,855.00	127,855.00

Step 3:

Click Close to exit the Select a Report or Form dialog box.

Printing the Financial Statements

After all transactions for the period have been journalized and posted, the next step in the accounting process for a small cash business like Forward Thinking Graphic Design is to produce financial statements. For example, on January 31, 2010, the accountant for Forward Thinking used Peachtree to print an income statement, a statement of changes in financial position, and a balance sheet.

An **income statement** reports the results of operations for the period—the revenue, expenses, and net income or net loss. The **net income** or **net loss** is the difference between the revenue and expenses.

income statement
A report of a firm's revenue, expenses, and net income or net loss for a period.

net income or net loss The difference between revenue and expenses.

A **statement of changes in financial position** shows the sources and uses of working capital for the period. **Working capital** is the excess of current assets over current liabilities.

A **balance sheet** reports the financial condition of a business on a specific date. It shows the assets, liabilities, and owner's equity of the business. A cash firm like Forward Thinking Graphic Design has a very simple balance sheet because it has no accounts receivable and accounts payable and no fixed assets (property and equipment).

You can print the financial statements for any given period by using the Reports & Forms function of Peachtree, as outlined below.

Step 1:
Click Reports & Forms.

Step 2:
Click *Financial Statements*.

Step 3:
Click *<Standard> Income Stmnt* from the Financial Statements: Balance Sheets and Income Statements section as shown in figure 3–39.

FIGURE 3–39

<Standard> Income Stmnt Chosen from Select a Report or Form Dialog Box

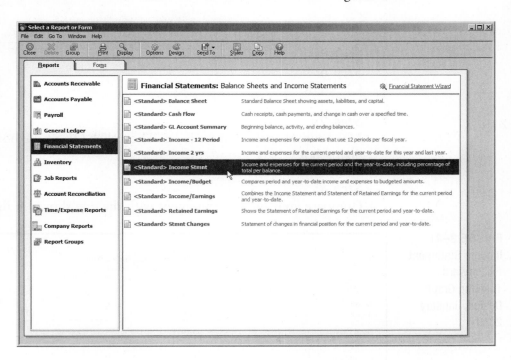

Step 4:
Click the Print button on the Select a Report or Form toolbar.

Step 5:

Select the following in the Options folder tab for the predefined income statement:

- *Range* in the *Time Frame* field.
- *Period 1, (1/1/10)* in the *From* field and *Period 1, (1/31/10)* in the *To* field. (Only one month will be covered.)
- No check mark in the box next to *Show Zero Amounts.*

Compare your screen to the Options dialog box shown in figure 3–40.

FIGURE 3–40
Completed Options Folder Tab for <Standard> Income Stmnt

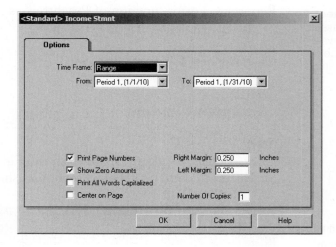

Step 6:

Click OK.

Step 7:

Make sure that the printer is on. Then click OK at the bottom of the Print dialog box.

Step 8:

Compare your income statement with the one shown in figure 3–41.

FIGURE 3–41
Income Statement for Forward Thinking Graphic Design, January 2010

Page: 1

Forward Thinking Graphic Design
Income Statement
For the One Month Ending January 31, 2010

	Current Month			Year to Date	
Revenues					
Design Fees	$	11,400.00	100.00	$	11,400.00	100.00
Total Revenues		11,400.00	100.00		11,400.00	100.00
Cost of Sales					
Total Cost of Sales		0.00	0.00		0.00	0.00
Gross Profit		11,400.00	100.00		11,400.00	100.00
Expenses					
Independent Contractor Expense		2,850.00	25.00		2,850.00	25.00
Rent Expense		1,200.00	10.53		1,200.00	10.53
Utilities Expense		675.00	5.92		675.00	5.92
Office Supplies Expense		1,200.00	10.53		1,200.00	10.53
Telephone Expenses		350.00	3.07		350.00	3.07
Design Expenses		950.00	8.33		950.00	8.33
Professional Expense		230.00	2.02		230.00	2.02
Advertising Expense		850.00	7.46		850.00	7.46
Total Expenses		8,305.00	72.85		8,305.00	72.85
Net Income	$	3,095.00	27.15	$	3,095.00	27.15

Step 9:

Click *<Standard> Stmnt Changes* from the Financial Statements: Balance Sheets and Income Statements section as shown in figure 3–42.

Step 10:

Click the Print button, then repeat the procedures from step 5 to complete the Options folder tab for the predefined statement of changes in financial position.

Step 11:

Click OK when the Options folder tab for the predefined statement of changes in financial position is complete.

Step 12:

Click OK at the Print dialog box.

Step 13:

Compare your statement of changes in financial position with the one shown in figure 3–43.

FIGURE 3–43
Statement of Changes in Financial Position for Forward Thinking Graphic Design, January 2010

Forward Thinking Graphic Design
Statement of Changes in Financial Position
For the one month ended January 31, 2010

Page: 1

	Current Month	Year To Date
Sources of Working Capital		
Net Income	$ 3,095.00	$ 3,095.00
Add back items not requiring working capital		
Working capital from operations	3,095.00	3,095.00
Other sources		
Y. Lopez, Capital	108,050.00	108,050.00
Total sources	111,145.00	111,145.00
Uses of working capital		
Y. Lopez, Capital	0.00	0.00
Total uses	0.00	0.00
Net change	$ 111,145.00	$ 111,145.00
Analysis of componants of changes		
Increase <Decrease> in Current Assets		
Cash	$ 110,645.00	$ 110,645.00
Petty Cash	500.00	500.00
<Increase> Decrease in Current Liabilities		
Net change	$ 111,145.00	$ 111,145.00

Step 14:

Click <*Standard*> *Balance Sheet* from the Financial Statements: Balance Sheets and Income Statements section.

Step 15:

Click the Print button, and then repeat the procedures from step 5 to complete the Options folder tab for the predefined balance sheet.

Step 16:

Click OK when the Options folder tab for the predefined balance sheet is complete.

Step 17:

Click OK at the Print dialog box.

Step 18:

Compare your balance sheet with the one shown in figure 3–44.

Forward Thinking Graphic Design
Balance Sheet
January 31, 2010

ASSETS

Current Assets		
Cash	$ 110,645.00	
Petty Cash	500.00	
Total Current Assets		111,145.00
Property and Equipment		
Total Property and Equipment		0.00
Other Assets		
Total Other Assets		0.00
Total Assets		$ 111,145.00

LIABILITIES AND CAPITAL

Current Liabilities		
Total Current Liabilities		0.00
Long-Term Liabilities		
Total Long-Term Liabilities		0.00
Total Liabilities		0.00
Capital		
Y. Lopez, Capital	$ 108,050.00	
Net Income	3,095.00	
Total Capital		111,145.00
Total Liabilities & Capital		$ 111,145.00

Step 19:

Click the Close button on the Select a Report or Form toolbar.

Check point

1. What are the two methods used to access the *General Ledger* report from the Reports menu?
2. What three financial statements were prepared for Forward Thinking Graphic Design?

Answers

1. *The first method is to click Reports & Forms and then General Ledger from the Menu bar. The second method is to select General Ledger from both the Category and Report drop-down lists from the Business Status Find a Report section.*
2. *The financial statements prepared were the income statement, the statement of changes in financial position, and the balance sheet.*

Practice Objective 4

Print the general journal and the financial statements for Wildwood Medical Services.

Step 1:

Open Wildwood Medical Services (Chp. 3 – Wildwood Medical Services if data disk is used).

Step 2:

Print the general journal entries for January 1–31, 2010. Compare your printout to figure 3–45.

FIGURE 3–45
General Journal
for Wildwood
Medical Services

Chp. 3 - Wildwood Medical Services
General Journal
For the Period From Jan 1, 2010 to Jan 31, 2010

Page: 1

Filter Criteria includes: Report order is by Date. Report is printed with Accounts having Zero Amounts and with shortened descriptions and in Detail Format.

Date	Account ID	Reference	Trans Description	Debit Amt	Credit Amt
1/1/10	1010	BEGBAL		250.00	
	1020			15,000.00	
	3904				15,250.00
	3910				
1/2/10	6450		Purchased office supplies	2,400.00	
	1020		Purchased office supplies		2,400.00
1/5/10	1020		Provided medical services	5,200.00	
	4000		Provided medical services		5,200.00
1/12/10	6350		Paid maintenance and repair service	1,235.00	
	1020		Paid maintenance and repair service		1,235.00
1/20/10	6550		Paid employee's retirement dinner	450.00	
	1020		Paid employee's retirement dinner		450.00
1/24/10	6600		Paid advertising expense	750.00	
	1020		Paid advertising expense		750.00
1/31/10	6300		Paid monthly rent	900.00	
	1020		Paid monthly rent		900.00
1/31/10	6400	Compound	Paid monthly utility bills	300.00	
	6500		Paid monthly telephone bills	245.00	
	1020		Paid monthly bills		545.00
		Total		26,730.00	26,730.00

Step 3:

Print the income statement for the month of January 2010. Compare your printout to figure 3–46.

FIGURE 3–46
Income Statement
for Wildwood
Medical Services

Chp. 3 - Wildwood Medical Services
Income Statement
For the One Month Ending January 31, 2010

	Current Month		Year to Date	
Revenues				
Medical Services	$ 5,200.00	100.00	$ 5,200.00	100.00
Total Revenues	5,200.00	100.00	5,200.00	100.00
Cost of Sales				
Total Cost of Sales	0.00	0.00	0.00	0.00
Gross Profit	5,200.00	100.00	5,200.00	100.00
Expenses				
Rent or Lease Expense	900.00	17.31	900.00	17.31
Maintenance & Repairs Expense	1,235.00	23.75	1,235.00	23.75
Utilities Expense	300.00	5.77	300.00	5.77
Office Supplies Expense	2,400.00	46.15	2,400.00	46.15
Telephone Expense	245.00	4.71	245.00	4.71
Other Office Expense	450.00	8.65	450.00	8.65
Advertising Expense	750.00	14.42	750.00	14.42
Total Expenses	6,280.00	120.77	6,280.00	120.77
Net Income	$ (1,080.00)	(20.77)	$ (1,080.00)	(20.77)

Step 4:

Print the statement of changes in financial position for the month of January 2010. Compare your printout to figure 3–47.

Chp. 3 - Wildwood Medical Services
Statement of Changes in Financial Position
For the one month ended January 31, 2010

	Current Month	Year To Date
Sources of Working Capital		
Net Income	$ (1,080.00)	$ (1,080.00)
Add back items not requiring working capital		
Working capital from operations	(1,080.00)	(1,080.00)
Other sources		
James, Capital	15,250.00	15,250.00
Total sources	14,170.00	14,170.00
Uses of working capital		
Total uses	0.00	0.00
Net change	$ 14,170.00	$ 14,170.00
Analysis of componants of changes		
Increase <Decrease> in Current Assets		
Cash on Hand	$ 250.00	$ 250.00
Checking Account	13,920.00	13,920.00
<Increase> Decrease in Current Liabilities		
Net change	$ 14,170.00	$ 14,170.00

Step 5:

Print the balance sheet for January 31, 2010. Compare your printout to figure 3–48.

FIGURE 3–48
Balance Sheet for
Wildwood Medical
Services

Chp. 3 - Wildwood Medical Services
Balance Sheet
January 31, 2010

ASSETS

Current Assets		
Cash on Hand	$ 250.00	
Checking Account	13,920.00	
Total Current Assets		14,170.00
Property and Equipment		
Total Property and Equipment		0.00
Other Assets		
Total Other Assets		0.00
Total Assets		$ 14,170.00

LIABILITIES AND CAPITAL

Current Liabilities		
Total Current Liabilities		0.00
Long-Term Liabilities		
Total Long-Term Liabilities		0.00
Total Liabilities		0.00
Capital		
James, Capital	$ 15,250.00	
Net Income	(1,080.00)	
Total Capital		14,170.00
Total Liabilities & Capital		$ 14,170.00

Step 6:

Review the general journal and financial statements for accuracy.

Step 7:

Close the Select a Report or Form dialog box.

End of Chapter Review

Software Command Summary

Create New Account	Maintain, Chart of Accounts, Account ID, Description, Account Type
Enter Beginning Balances	Maintain, Chart of Accounts, Account Beginning Balances, Select Period, Enter Balances
Journalize	Tasks, General Journal Entry, Save
Edit a Selected Transaction	Tasks, General Journal Entry, List, Select Desired Transaction, Open, Make Necessary Changes, Save
Delete a Selected Transaction	Tasks, General Journal Entry, List, Select Desired Transaction, Open, Delete
Print or Preview Reports	Reports & Forms, Select Category of Reports, Highlight Specific Report, Print or Options Screen

Projects and Problems
Content Check

Multiple Choice: Choose only one response for each question.

1. A record in which transactions are listed in order by date is a
   A. chart of accounts.
   B. journal.
   C. ledger.
   D. trial balance.
   E. None of the above

2. The financial statement that reports assets, liabilities, and owner's equity as of a specific date is the
   A. statement of changes in financial position.
   B. chart of accounts.
   C. balance sheet.
   D. income statement.
   E. None of the above

3. The financial statement that shows the revenues, expenses, and net income or net loss for a period of time is known as the
   A. balance sheet.
   B. general journal.
   C. general ledger.
   D. income statement.
   E. None of the above

4. Suppose that an accountant has recorded the wrong date in a journal entry. In Peachtree, the best way to correct the error is to
   A. use the delete function and then record the entire entry again.
   B. use the list and then open function.
   C. use the memorized transaction function.
   D. use the recurring transaction function.
   E. None of the above

5. Which of the following functions is used to set up a journal entry that will automatically repeat in future accounting periods?
   A. add a row function
   B. open function
   C. memorized transaction function
   D. recurring transaction function
   E. None of the above

Short Essay Response: Provide a detailed answer for each question.

1. What is the purpose of the general journal?
2. What are the steps necessary to add a new account to the chart of accounts?
3. What steps are necessary to ensure accurate posting of journal entries?
4. Under what circumstances can a business use the cash basis of accounting?
5. What is the purpose of the general ledger?
6. What information must be recorded in the general journal entry window before a transaction can be posted?

Case Problems

Problem 1A

Open Johnson & Associates Accounting from the student data disk.
The following transactions occurred during the month of January 2010.

Date	Transaction
Jan. 4	Paid rent of $2,500 for January. Because this payment must be made each month, set it up as a recurring transaction. Use 12 as the number of times the transaction will recur.
4	Purchased computer equipment for $3,500 in cash. (Because this business is using the accrual basis of accounting, it records purchases of equipment in an Asset account.)
4	Purchased office supplies for $375 in cash. (Because this business is on the accrual basis, it records purchases of supplies in an Asset account.)
5	Paid a $240 insurance premium for the month. This is also a recurring monthly transaction. Use 12 as the number of times that it will recur. (Because this insurance covers just one month, treat it as an expense.)
6	Purchased furniture and fixtures for $3,100 on account. (*Use Account 20000, Accounts Payable.*)
10	Paid $600 for a newspaper ad that will run during the month of January. The business may run more ads in the future. Thus, create this transaction using the memorization feature. You will need to create a new account for this transaction: *60200, Advertising Expense, Expenses.*
12	Performed accounting services for Monroe Construction and received $2,400 in cash.
14	Performed accounting services for Ramirez Consultants and received $2,250 in cash.
18	The owner withdrew $500 for his personal use. (Use *Account 39007, Richard Johnson, Drawing.*)
24	Performed accounting services for Steve's Landscaping and received $1,575 in cash.
28	Paid automobile expenses of $350 in cash.
29	Paid utilities of $325.
29	Paid the telephone bill of $135.
30	Performed accounting services for Mary's Daycare for $160 in cash.

1. Enter each of the transactions for January in the general journal. Create new accounts as needed. For all cash transactions, use *Account 10200, Regular Checking Account.*

2. Print the following reports for the month of January: *General Journal, Income Statement,* and *Balance Sheet.*

Problem 2A

1. Set up a new company for Ruben's Auto Detailing. Use the information given below:

Company Name:	**Ruben's Auto Detailing**
Address Line 1:	**1480 East Madison Avenue**
Address Line 2:	
City, State, Zip:	**Stockton, CA 95207**
Country:	**USA**
Telephone:	**209-555-4358**
Fax:	**209-555-2332**
Business Type:	**Sole Proprietorship**
Federal Employer ID:	**09-6776754**
State Employer ID:	**098-8743-09**
St. Unemployment ID:	**00441-98**
Chart of Accounts:	**Build your own chart of accounts**
Accounting Method:	**Cash**
Posting Method:	**Real Time**
Accounting Periods:	**12 monthly accounting periods**
Fiscal Year to Start:	**January 2010**

2. Enter the following in the chart of accounts:

Account ID	Description	Account Type
10200	Regular Checking Account	Cash
39004	Ruben Sanchez, Capital	Equity-doesn't close
39005	Ruben Sanchez, Equity	Equity-Retained Earnings
39006	Ruben Sanchez, Drawing	Equity-gets closed
40000	Detailing Fees	Income
60000	Advertising Expense	Expenses
60010	Laundry Expense	Expenses
60020	Telephone Expense	Expenses
60030	Utilities Expense	Expenses
60040	Rent Expense	Expenses
60050	Detailing Supplies Expense	Expenses

3. The following transactions occurred during the month of January 2010. Enter each of the transactions in the general journal. Create new accounts as needed.

Date	Transaction
Jan. 3	The owner invested $12,500 of his personal funds in the business. (*Ruben Sanchez, Capital*)
3	Paid rent of $1,250 for January. Because this payment must be made each month, set it up as a recurring transaction. Use 12 as the number of times the transaction will recur.
3	Purchased detailing supplies for $850 in cash.
5	Set up a petty cash fund of $200. You will need to create a new account for this transaction: *10100, Petty Cash, Cash*.
5	Detailed a fleet of cars for Mavis Car Rentals and received $725 in cash. This is a recurring biweekly transaction. The number of times it will recur is 26.
11	Paid $180 for advertising flyers. Create this transaction using the memorization feature.
15	Detailing fees for the week amounted to $1,220 in cash.
19	The owner withdrew $525 for his personal use. (Use *Ruben Sanchez, Drawing*.)
19	Detailed a fleet of trucks for Blackmun Trucking and received $625 in cash. This is a recurring monthly transaction. The number of times it will recur is 12.
20	Paid a telephone bill of $145.
23	Detailing fees for the week amounted to $860 in cash.
25	Paid automobile expenses of $475 in cash. You will need to create a new account for this transaction: *60060, Automobile Expense, Expenses*.
25	Paid utilities bill of $320.
31	Detailing fees for the week amounted to $760 in cash.

4. Print the following reports for the month of January: *General Ledger Trial Balance, General Journal, Income Statement,* and *Balance Sheet.*

Problem 1B

Open Katie's Graphic Designs from the student data disk. The following transactions occurred during the month of January 2010.

Date	Transaction
Jan. 3	Paid office rent of $650 for January. Because this payment must be made each month, set it up as a recurring transaction. Use 12 as the number of times the transaction will recur.
4	Purchased graphing equipment for $2,750 on account. (Because this business is using the accrual basis of accounting, it records purchases of equipment in an Asset account. Use *Account 20000, Accounts Payable.*)
4	Purchased graphing supplies for $265 in cash. (Because this business is using the accrual basis of accounting, it records purchases of supplies in an Asset account.)
5	Paid a $110 insurance premium for the month. This is also a recurring monthly transaction. Use 12 as the number of times that it will recur. (Because this insurance covers just one month, treat it as an expense.)
6	Purchased furniture and fixtures for $2,210 on account.
11	Paid $195 for a newspaper ad that will run during the month of January. The business may run more ads in the future. Thus, create this transaction using the memorization feature.
12	Created a business logo (*Graphic Design Income*) for the ABC Nursery School and received $420 in cash.
13	Performed printing services for Gomez Consultants and received $2,100 in cash.
15	The owner withdrew $300 for her personal use. (*Katie Rosario, Drawing*)
18	Retouched photos for an advertising campaign and received $1,800 in cash.
26	Performed photo services for the *Daily News* and received $1,090 in cash.
28	Paid automobile expenses of $328 in cash.
28	Paid utilities bill of $183.
29	Paid a telephone bill of $122.
30	Performed illustration services for J and K Architects and received $1,725 in cash.

1. Enter each of the transactions for January in the general journal. Create new accounts as needed. For all cash transactions, use *Account 10200, Regular Checking Account.*

2. Print the following reports for the month of January: *General Journal, Income Statement*, and *Balance Sheet*.

Problem 2B

1. Set up a new company for Cindy's Office Cleaning. Use the information given below:

Company Name:	**Cindy's Office Cleaning**
Address Line 1:	**64 West Bessie Avenue**
Address Line 2:	
City, State, Zip:	**Stockton, CA 95207**
Country:	**USA**
Telephone:	**209-555-3536**
Fax:	**209-555-3537**
Business Type:	**Sole Proprietorship**
Federal Employer ID:	**09-6776457**
State Employer ID:	**098-8734-08**
St. Unemployment ID:	**00221-87**
Chart of Accounts:	**Build your own chart of accounts**
Accounting Method:	**Cash**
Posting Method:	**Real Time**
Accounting Periods:	**12 monthly accounting periods**
Fiscal Year to Start:	**January 2010**

2. Enter the following in the chart of accounts:

Account ID	Description	Account Type
10200	Regular Checking Account	Cash
39004	Cindy Robinson, Capital	Equity-doesn't close
39005	Cindy Robinson, Equity	Equity-Retained Earnings
39006	Cindy Robinson, Drawing	Equity-gets closed
40000	Cleaning Fees	Income
60000	Advertising Expense	Expenses
60010	Laundry Expense	Expenses
60020	Telephone Expense	Expenses
60030	Utilities Expense	Expenses
60040	Rent Expense	Expenses
60050	Cleaning Supplies Expense	Expenses

3. The following transactions occurred during the month of January 2010. Enter each of the transactions in the general journal. Create new accounts as needed.

Date	Transaction
Jan. 3	The owner invested $3,400 of her personal funds in the business. (*Cindy Robinson, Capital*)
3	Paid $250 in cash for a bonding fee. You will need to create a new account for this transaction: *60060, Bond Fee Expense, Expenses*.
3	Purchased cleaning supplies for $375 in cash.
4	Established a petty cash fund of $125. You will need to create a new account for this transaction: *10100, Petty Cash, Cash*.
4	Cleaned the offices of O'Brien Car Rentals and received $420 in cash. Set this up as a recurring biweekly transaction. The number of times it will recur is 26.
5	Purchased an ad in the local newspaper for $120.
7	Performed cleaning services for the Delta Insurance Agency and received $145 in cash. Set this up as a recurring weekly transaction. The number of times it will recur is 52.
15	Cleaning fees for the week amounted to $760 in cash.
19	The owner withdrew $450 for her personal use.
21	Cleaned the offices of Baxter Trucking and received $200 in cash. Set this up as a recurring monthly transaction. The number of times it will recur is 12.
24	Paid utilities bill of $158.
27	Paid automobile expenses of $650 in cash. You will need to create a new account for this transaction: *60070, Auto Expense, Expenses*.
28	Paid a telephone bill of $110.
30	Cleaning fees for the week amounted to $1,290 in cash.

4. Print the following reports for the month of January: *General Ledger Trial Balance, General Journal, Income Statement,* and *Balance Sheet.*

Cooperative Learning

1. Form groups of three or four students and create your own retail business. Decide on the business setup criteria.
2. Create 10 transactions for the newly formed business from Cooperative Learning Exercise 1. Use Peachtree to enter the transactions in the general journal. Create any new accounts as needed. Print the general ledger, general journal, chart of accounts, and balance sheet.

Writing and Decision Making

The company for which you work, MH Design Consulting, is converting from a manual accounting system to a computerized system. You are responsible for the conversion. The owner of the company, Maria Holtzman, wants to know how you plan to use Peachtree to ensure that an accurate conversion to a computerized accounting system occurs. Therefore, in memo format, list in detail what information is needed and what decisions must be made for each screen of the New Company Setup procedure.

CHAPTER 4

Accounts Receivable and Sales for a Business

Learning Objectives

1. Create subsidiary ledger accounts for customers and enter the beginning balances

2. Process accounts receivable and sales transactions

3. Create action items and event logs

4. Adjust the accounts receivable for uncollectible accounts and print reports

Software Features

- Maintain Customer Prospects toolbar buttons

- Customer defaults

- Sales and Invoicing toolbar

- Action items

- Alerts

- Accounting Behind the Screens function

Many firms sell goods and services on credit. In fact, it is often said that credit is the lifeblood of American business. Credit makes it possible for customers to obtain goods and services immediately and pay for them in the future. This arrangement is convenient for customers and usually produces higher sales for the firms that offer credit.

Recording Accounts Receivable

The amounts owed by customers to a business for goods or services sold to them on credit are called **accounts receivable**. Firms that sell on credit set up an asset account called Accounts Receivable in their general ledger.

When these firms make a sale on credit, they debit the amount to Accounts Receivable and credit the appropriate revenue account. Later, when they collect the amount owed by the customer, they debit (increase) Cash and credit (decrease) Accounts Receivable.

The Accounts Receivable Subsidiary Ledger

In addition to the Accounts Receivable account in the general ledger, most businesses that sell on credit maintain a subsidiary ledger with individual accounts for their customers. This subsidiary ledger is known as the **accounts receivable ledger** or customer ledger.

A **subsidiary ledger** contains detailed information for a single general ledger account. Remember that the general ledger is a firm's main ledger. It includes the accounts that are used to prepare the financial statements. Subsidiary ledgers supplement the information in the general ledger.

The advantage of having an accounts receivable subsidiary ledger is that it provides detailed information about the transactions with credit customers and shows the balances they owe. Peachtree updates these accounts automatically when transactions are recorded and posted. As a result, management can closely monitor the status of the firm's accounts receivable.

Being able to collect its accounts receivable on time is critical to the success of a business that sells on credit. The cash from accounts receivable is needed to pay debts and operating expenses such as rent and salaries. A business may have rising sales but experience cash flow problems if it does not manage its accounts receivable properly.

Peachtree improves the efficiency of accounts receivable procedures because it allows for—

- Quick preparation of invoices (bills)
- Automatic posting of accounts receivable transactions, which eliminates the time and effort required by manual posting
- Quick preparation of a wide variety of reports, which show management the current status of the accounts receivable
- An action item feature that can be programmed to alert users to high balances, past-due amounts, and other problems with a specific customer account
- Quick preparation of contact letters and past-due notices

accounts receivable The amounts owed to a business by its customers for goods or services sold on credit.

accounts receivable ledger A subsidiary ledger that contains accounts for credit customers.

subsidiary ledger A ledger that contains detailed information for a single general ledger account.

The Controlling Account in the General Ledger

controlling account
A general ledger account that summarizes the balances of all the accounts in a subsidiary ledger.

When there is an accounts receivable subsidiary ledger, the Accounts Receivable account in the general ledger becomes a **controlling account**. It provides a link between the general ledger and the accounts receivable subsidiary ledger because its balance is equal to the total of all the balances of the individual accounts in the subsidiary ledger.

Every subsidiary ledger must have a controlling account in the general ledger.

Handling Uncollectible Accounts

No matter how careful management is in granting credit to customers, monitoring the status of the accounts receivable, and making efforts to collect overdue balances, some accounts will become uncollectible. Events occur that are beyond the control of the seller. For example, companies may go bankrupt or have disasters occur that prevent them from paying their accounts. In those cases, the accounts must be written off or discharged. When accounts are written off, it is considered an expense of doing business.

Two methods are used to account for uncollectible accounts: the allowance method and the direct write-off method. Both will be discussed later in this chapter.

OBJECTIVE 1 — Create Subsidiary Ledger Accounts for Customers and Enter the Beginning Balances

In chapters 2 and 3, you learned how to set up general ledger accounts and enter the beginning balances. The procedure for establishing customer accounts in the accounts receivable ledger is very similar. In this chapter, you will use Peachtree to handle the accounts receivable of Superior Carpet and Tile.

The Maintain Customers/Prospects Window

In Peachtree, certain information is needed to create an account for each customer in the accounts receivable subsidiary ledger. This information is entered into the following fields of the Maintain Customers/Prospects window. To view this window, open Chp. 4 – Superior Carpet and Tile, click Maintain and then *Customers/Prospects*. Review the following fields:

- **Customer ID**
  Peachtree requires an alphanumeric identifier for each customer's account. For example, Superior Carpet and Tile uses Norman-01 as the identifier for the first account in its accounts receivable subsidiary ledger. This account is for Norman Construction Company.
- **Name**
  The name given to a customer's account may be the name of the business, such as Norman Construction Company, or the name of an individual.
- **Prospect**
  Peachtree allows a firm to open accounts for potential customers as well as current customers. This feature helps salespeople keep track of potential customers. When an order is placed, Peachtree automatically

activates the account of the potential customer and changes it to a current customer. A check mark is entered in the *Prospect* box to indicate a potential customer.

- **Inactive**

  Sometimes customers stop doing business with a company. A check mark is entered in the *Inactive* box to indicate this type of customer. Peachtree automatically removes the accounts of inactive customers when the fiscal year closes.

General Tab

- **Account Number**

  Enter the customer's identifying account number.

- **Billing Address**

  Peachtree permits the entry of separate billing and shipping addresses for a customer. In fact, Peachtree allows for several shipping addresses. If a customer has a single address for both billing and shipping, you need only enter the billing address.

- **Sales Tax**

  Retail businesses in most states and some cities and counties must charge their customers a sales tax on goods. In some areas, this tax is also levied on services. Wholesale businesses that sell to retailers do not charge sales tax because the retailers have resale certificates that exempt them from paying sales tax. If sales tax does apply, you enter the type when creating each customer's account.

- **Customer Type**

  Peachtree allows you to classify customers by type. For example, some companies have both retail and wholesale customers.

- **Telephone/Fax Numbers and E-Mail Addresses**

  Peachtree provides space for recording two telephone numbers, a fax number, and an e-mail address in each customer's account. You can e-mail a customer directly by clicking on the E-mail button to the right of the *E-mail address* field.

- **Web Site**

  Enter the customer's Web site address. The customer's Web site can be displayed by clicking the Internet button to the right of the *Web Site* field.

- **Customizable Fields**

  Peachtree provides additional space for second contact information, references, and other customized business related fields.

Contact Tab

- **Contact**

  The contact is the person whom the business calls or writes in connection with questions about orders.

Addresses Tab

- **Copy Billing Address to**

  This allows the Peachtree user to select different billing addresses to be setup for any individual client. The default address is Address 1.

History Tab

- **Customer Since**
  Some businesses enter the date of the customer's first order in the customer's account.
- **Last Invoice Date**
  Some businesses enter the date of the last invoice sent to the customer.
- **Last Invoice Amount**
  Some businesses enter the amount of the last invoice sent to the customer.
- **Last Payment Date**
  Some businesses enter the date of the last payment the customer made.
- **Last Payment Amount**
  Some businesses enter the amount of the last payment the customer made.
- **Last Statement Date**
  Some businesses enter the date of the last statement sent to the customer.
- **Customer Beginning Balances**
  When a business creates accounts for its customers, there may be some outstanding (unpaid) invoices. Information about these invoices is needed in order to enter the beginning balances in the accounts.

Sales Info Tab

- **Sales Rep**
  Some businesses assign a sales representative to each customer. The name of the sales representative is entered in the customer's account. (Peachtree's accounts receivable procedures allow a business to organize information about its sales staff and to maintain an up-to-date list of sales representatives.)
- **GL Sales Account**
  GL Sales Acct refers to the revenue account in the general ledger that is credited when a sale is made to the customer. The number of the appropriate general ledger account is entered in the customer's account.
- **Open PO Number**
  When a customer's account is created, it may have an open purchase order. The number of this purchase order is entered in the account.
- **Ship Via**
  Some businesses allow their customers to select a shipping method. The method chosen is entered in the customer's account.
- **Resale Number**
  Sales tax authorities issue certificates to retailers that exempt them from paying sales tax on goods they buy for resale. If a customer is a retailer, the resale certificate number must be entered here.
- **Pricing Level**
  Some businesses have several different pricing levels for merchandise. For example, if a firm sells to both retailers and wholesalers, it will charge them different prices. The pricing level is entered in the customer's account.
- **Form Options**
  Businesses today use differing methods for delivering invoices. This option allows the user to check for delivery via Paper Form or E-mail, including a choice to forward invoices or statements to the sales representative when sending customers e-mails.

Payment & Credit Tab

- **Cardholder's Name and Address**
  A business may want to create account information for credit card users. The cardholder's information is entered in this section.
- **City, State, Zip and Country**
  The customer's/prospect's city, state, zip, and country information are entered here.
- **Credit Card Number and Expiration Date**
  The credit card information is entered and stored here.
- **Receipt Settings**
  The payment method and the account to be debited are selected in this section. All major credit cards, as well as cash, are supported. The system's default settings are used by Peachtree if *Use payment method and cash account from last saved receipt* setting is check marked.
- **Terms and Credit Tab**
  Many companies use Default (Standard) credit terms and this is an option that can be selected. Other terms as well as specifying discount periods, credit periods, discount percents, credit limits, credit status, and finance changes can be selected.

Click the Close button when you have finished reviewing the fields of the Maintain Customers/Prospects window.

Creating Subsidiary Ledger Accounts for Customers

In this section, you will create subsidiary ledger accounts for four customers of Superior Carpet and Tile.

Follow the steps outlined below to create subsidiary ledger accounts for the customers.

Step 1:
Open Superior Carpet and Tile (Chp. 4 – Superior Carpet and Tile if student data disk is used).

Step 2:
Click Maintain, and then click *Customers/Prospects*.

Step 3:
Click the General folder tab, if it is not already selected. (See figure 4–1.)

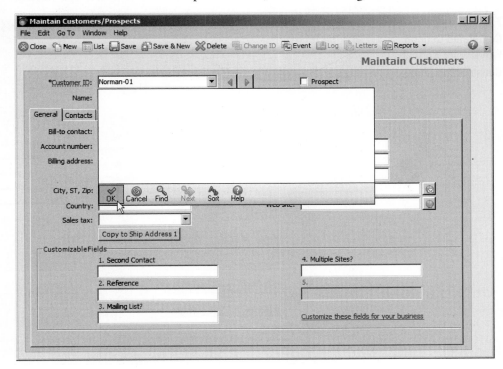

Set up the account information listed below for Norman Construction Company, the first customer of Superior Carpet and Tile.

Step 4:

Key **Norman-01** in the *Customer ID* field. Click the OK button at the bottom of the Customer ID drop-down list, as shown in figure 4–2.

FIGURE 4–2
Customer ID Field with
Norman-01 Entered

Step 5:

Key **Norman Construction Company** in the *Name* field.

Step 6:
Key **120201** in the *Account Number* field.

Step 7:
Key **2890 Washington Blvd.** in the *Billing Address* field.

Step 8:
Key **Kelsey, CA** and **95556** in the *City, ST, Zip* field.

Step 9:
Key **USA** in the *Country* field and select "Copy to Ship Address 1".

Step 10:
Key **General** in the *Customer Type* field.

Step 11:
Key **916-555-1947** in the *Telephone 1* field.

Step 12:
Key **916-555-4653** in the *Fax* field.

Step 13:
Click the Contact tab and key **John Norman** in the *Contact* field.

Step 14:
Compare your completed window with figure 4–3. Make any necessary corrections by selecting the erroneous items and reentering the information.

FIGURE 4–3
Completed General
Window for Norman
Construction Company

Sales Info Tab

Whenever you create a customer's account, you need to establish sales defaults.

Step 1:
Click the Sales Info tab as shown in figure 4–4.

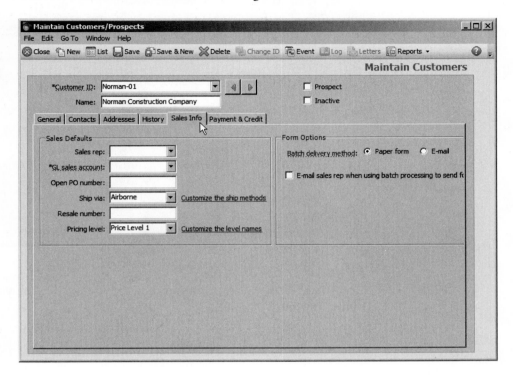

Step 2:
Click the drop-down arrow next to GL Sales Account, and then click *Account 400, Installation Services* (Income).

Step 3:
Click *Fed-EX* in the Ship Via drop-down list.

Step 4:
Accept the default (Price Level 1) in the Pricing Level drop-down list.

Step 5:
Accept the default in the Form Options box. Compare your entries for Norman Construction Company with the entries shown in figure 4–5. Make any necessary changes.

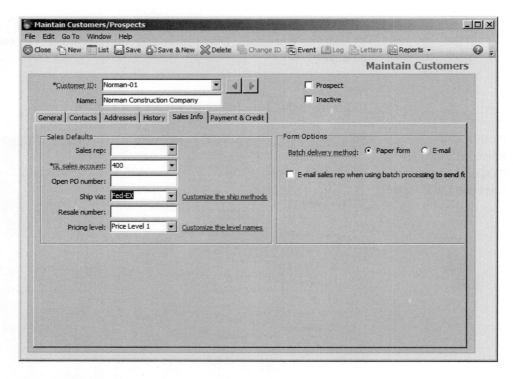

Payment & Credit Tab

Credit and discount information must be included when you create a customer's account.

Step 1:

Click the Payment & Credit tab as shown in figure 4–6.

FIGURE 4–6
Payment & Credit
Window for Norman
Construction Company

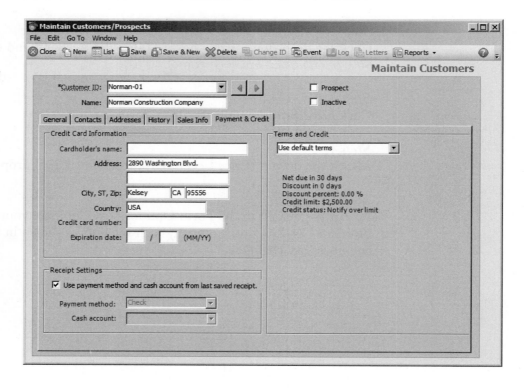

The default for the credit terms is currently set at Net 30 Days. Superior offers terms set at 2% 10, net 30 days. These terms mean that the customer can pay in 10 days and receive a 2% discount or pay the net (full) amount in 30 days.

The pricing level and the credit terms relate mostly to merchandising businesses and will be explained in future chapters. The credit terms can be changed by selecting *Customize terms for this customer* from the Terms and Credit drop-down box. Make the following changes to reflect Superior's credit terms.

Step 2:
Select *Customize terms for this customer* from the Terms and Credit drop-down list.

Step 3:
Select *Due in number of days* and key **30** in the Net due in days box.

Step 4:
Select *Use discounts* and key **10** in the Discount in days box.

Step 5:
Key **2.00** in the Discount Percent box.

There is also a default for a credit limit, which is currently set at $2,500. Whenever the recording of a sale takes a customer's balance over this limit, Peachtree sends a warning message.

Step 6:
Click the Save button at the top of the Maintain Customers/Prospects window.

Beginning Balances
The final phase in creating the customer account involves the entry of the beginning balances.

Step 1:
Click the History folder tab in the Maintain Customers/Prospects window.

Step 2:
Click the *Customer Beginning Balances* button at the bottom of the window.

Step 3:
Key **Beginning Balance** in the *Invoice Number* field.

Step 4:
Key **01/01/10** in the *Date* field. (Peachtree will convert this to *Jan 1, 2010.*)

Step 5:
Key **5,000.00** in the *Amount* field.

Step 6:
Click *Account 104 (Accounts Receivable)* from the A/R Account drop-down list.

Step 7:
Click the Save button and then the Close button.

Create the remaining three customer accounts for Superior Carpet and Tile by clicking the Save & New button at the top of the Maintain Customers/Prospects window and enter the beginning balances as of 01/01/10 using the information listed below. Use the steps that you followed for the Norman Construction Company account. When you complete your work, close and exit Superior Carpet and Tile.

Customer

Customer ID:	**Calif-02**
Name:	**State of California**

General Tab

Account Number:	**120202**
Billing Address:	**2356 State Street**
City, ST, Zip:	**Sacramento, CA 95670**
Country:	**USA**
Customer Type:	**General**
Telephone 1:	**916-555-2122**
Fax:	**916-555-2887**

Contact Tab

Contact:	**Lisa Jones**

Sales Info Tab

GL Sales Account:	**400**
Ship Via:	**Fed-Ex**
Pricing Level:	**Default**
Form Delivery Options:	**Default**

Payment & Credit Tab

Terms and Credit:	**2% 10 Days, Net 30 Days**

History Tab

Beginning Balance:	**4,000.00**

Customer

Customer ID:	**Parker-03**
Name:	**Parker's Construction**

General Tab

Account Number:	**120203**
Billing Address:	**326 Henry Ave.**
City, ST, Zip:	**Sacramento, CA 95665**
Country:	**USA**
Customer Type:	**General**
Telephone 1:	**916-555-9147**
Fax:	**916-555-5536**

Contact Tab

Contact:	**George Parker**

Sales Info Tab
GL Sales Account:	**400**
Ship Via:	**Fed-Ex**
Pricing Level:	**Default**
Form Delivery Options:	**Default**

Payment & Credit Tab
Terms and Credit:	**2% 10 Days, Net 30 Days**

History Tab
Beginning Balance:	**2,000.00**

Customer
Customer ID:	**Running-04**
Name:	**Running Water Tile**

General Tab
Account Number:	**120204**
Billing Address:	**3234 Flying Spur Road**
City, ST, Zip:	**Roseville, CA 95660**
Country:	**USA**
Customer Type:	**General**
Telephone 1:	**916-555-2556**
Fax:	**916-555-9998**

Contact Tab
Contact:	**Joyce Holman**

Sales Info Tab
GL Sales Account:	**400**
Ship Via:	**Fed-Ex**
Pricing Level:	**Default**
Form Delivery Options:	**Default**

Payment & Credit Tab
Terms and Credit:	**2% 10 Days, Net 30 Days**

History Tab
Beginning Balance:	**4,000.00**

Check point

1. What is the purpose of the customer accounts in the accounts receivable subsidiary ledger?
2. Why is the Accounts Receivable account in the general ledger known as a controlling account?

Answers
1. *The accounts in the subsidiary ledger provide detailed information about transactions with customers and show the current balances owed by the individual customers.*
2. *The Accounts Receivable controlling account is a link between the general ledger and the subsidiary ledger because its balance is equal to the total of the balances in the subsidiary ledger.*

Practice Objective 1

Create subsidiary ledger accounts for the customers of Meadowland Healthcare Services.

Step 1:
Open Chp. 4 – Meadowland Healthcare Services from the student data disk. This company has been created for you.

Step 2:
Create the following customer accounts. There are no beginning balances.

Customer

Customer ID:	**Doctor's-10**
Name:	**Doctor's Medical Center**

General Tab

Account Number:	**120210**
Billing Address:	**2122 Mercy Street**
City, ST, Zip:	**Sacramento, CA 95661**
Country:	**USA**
Customer Type:	**General**
Telephone 1:	**916-555-4934**
Fax:	**916-555-3122**

Contact Tab

Contact:	**Jim Conway, MD**

Sales Info Tab

GL Sales Account:	**40000**
Ship Via:	**Fed-Ex**
Pricing Level:	**Default**
Form Delivery Options:	**Default**

Payments & Credit Tab

Terms and Credit:	**2% 10 Days, Net 30 Days**

History Tab

Beginning Balance:	**0**

Customer

Customer ID:	**Good-20**
Name:	**Good Samaritan Hospital**

General Tab

Account Number:	**120220**
Billing Address:	**2415 10th Street**
City, ST, Zip:	**Sacramento, CA 95671**
Country:	**USA**
Customer Type:	**General**
Telephone 1:	**916-555-6780**
Fax:	**916-555-8987**

Contact Tab

Contact:	**Jane Campbell, RN**

Sales Info Tab

GL Sales Account:	**40000**
Ship Via:	**Fed-Ex**
Pricing Level:	**Default**
Form Delivery Options:	**Default**

Payments & Credit Tab

Terms and Credit:	**2% 10 Days, Net 30 Days**

History Tab

Beginning Balance:	**0**

Customer

Customer ID:	**Rapid-30**
Name:	**Rapid Medical Response**

General Tab

Account Number:	**120230**
Billing Address:	**2516 Main Street**
City, ST, Zip:	**Sacramento, CA 95671**
Country:	**USA**
Customer Type:	**General**
Telephone 1:	**916-555-4719**
Fax:	**916-555-2166**

Contact Tab

Contact:	**Kim Smith, RN**

Sales Info Tab

GL Sales Account:	**40000**
Ship Via:	**Fed-Ex**
Pricing Level:	**Default**
Form Delivery Options:	**Default**

Payments & Credit Tab

Terms and Credit:	**2% 10 Days, Net 30 Days**

History Tab

Beginning Balance:	**0**

Customer

Customer ID:	**Valley-40**
Name:	**Valley Response**

General Tab

Account Number:	**120240**
Billing Address:	**3211 Main Street**
City, ST, Zip:	**Sacramento, CA 95761**
Country:	**USA**
Customer Type:	**General**
Telephone 1:	**916-555-5678**
Fax:	**916-555-7812**

Contact Tab

    Contact: **Robert Romero, PA**

Sales Info Tab

    GL Sales Account: **40000**
    Ship Via: **Fed-Ex**
    Pricing Level: **Default**
    Form Delivery Options: **Default**

Payments & Credit Tab

    Terms and Credit: **2% 10 Days, Net 30 Days**

History Tab

    Beginning Balances: **0**

Step 3:

Close the Maintain Customers/Prospects window.

OBJECTIVE 2 — Process Accounts Receivable and Sales Transactions

Once the customer accounts have been established, you can use Peachtree to record transactions with credit customers and post them automatically to the accounts receivable subsidiary ledger. Remember that you record a sale on credit by debiting Accounts Receivable and crediting the appropriate revenue account. You record cash collected from a credit customer by debiting Cash and crediting Accounts Receivable.

When there is an accounts receivable ledger, each sale on credit requires a debit to both the Accounts Receivable controlling account in the general ledger and the customer's account in the subsidiary ledger. Similarly, each collection of cash from a credit customer requires a credit to both the Accounts Receivable controlling account in the general ledger and the customer's account in the subsidiary ledger.

In chapter 3, you recorded all transactions in the general journal. However, the general journal function of Peachtree does not permit the automatic posting of entries to the customer accounts. Therefore, in this chapter, you will use the sales and invoicing function of Peachtree to record credit sales and cash received on account. The sales and invoicing function, which is part of the accounts receivable module of Peachtree, permits automatic posting to both the general ledger and the accounts receivable subsidiary ledger.

Recording Sales on Credit

A sale on credit may involve goods or services. Superior Carpet and Tile is a small firm that provides construction services to local businesses and individuals. Almost all of its sales to businesses are made on credit.

On January 4, 2010, Superior Carpet and Tile did a small job for Norman Construction Company. The job involved 10 hours of installation work at $125 per hour. Norman issued a purchase order (PO 4567) before the job began. After it was completed, Superior issued Invoice 1001 to bill Norman Construction Company for $1,250. Superior's invoice has default terms of 2% 10 days, net 30 Days.

An analysis of this transaction reveals that an asset (Accounts Receivable) has increased by $1,250 and revenue has increased by $1,250. The account for Norman Construction Company has also increased by $1,250. The accountant records this transaction by debiting Accounts Receivable for $1,250 and crediting Revenue for $1,250.

When this transaction is posted, the debit part of the entry must be posted to both the Accounts Receivable controlling account in the general ledger and the Norman Construction Company account in the accounts receivable subsidiary ledger.

Use the steps outlined below to record the sale on credit that Superior Carpet and Tile made to Norman Construction Company.

Step 1:
Open Chp. 4 – Superior Carpet and Tile from the student data disk.

Step 2:
Click Tasks, and then click *Sales/Invoicing*.

Step 3:
The Sales/Invoicing window will appear, as shown in figure 4–7. Enter the information for the sale on credit that occurred on January 4, 2010, using the steps outlined below.

FIGURE 4–7
Sales/Invoicing Window

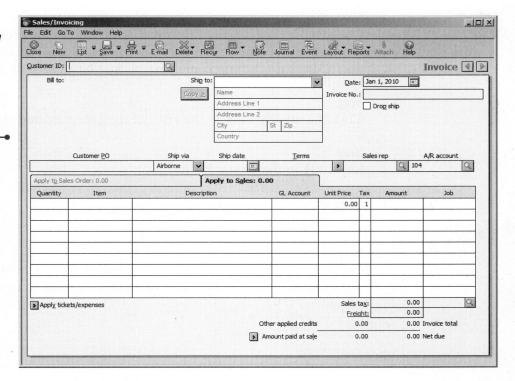

HINT

If the *GL Account* field does not display as shown in figure 4-7, click Options, and then click *Global*. The Maintain Global Options dialog box will appear. Deselect the box that is check marked next to Accounts Receivable (Quotes, Sales Orders, Invoicing, Credit Memos, Receipts). Click OK. Then close and reopen the Sales/Invoicing window.

Step 4:
Click the *magnifying glass* icon next to the Customer ID drop-down list.

Step 5:
Highlight *Norman-01* from the drop-down list of customers, as shown in figure 4–8.

FIGURE 4–8
Customer ID Drop-Down
List with Norman-01
Selected

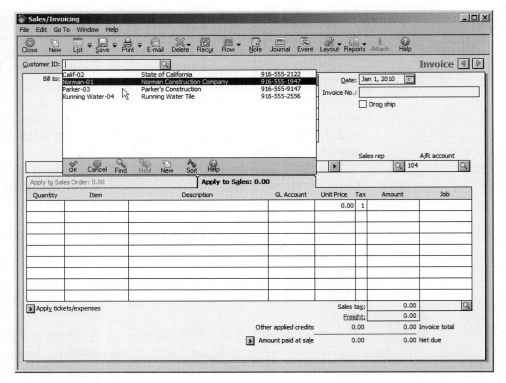

Step 6:
Click OK at the bottom of the drop-down list of customers to accept Norman-01. Peachtree automatically enters the address and billing information. (Alternatively, you could have clicked Norman-01.)

Step 7:
Click the *calendar* icon to the right of the *Date* field and choose *Jan 4, 2010*.

Step 8:
Key **1001** in the *Invoice No.* field.

Step 9:
Key **4567** in the *Customer PO* field.

Step 10:
Click *Hand Deliver* from the Ship Via drop down-list, as shown in figure 4–9. It is Superior's custom to hand deliver invoices to customers whenever possible.

FIGURE 4–9
Ship Via Drop-Down
List with Hand Deliver
Selected

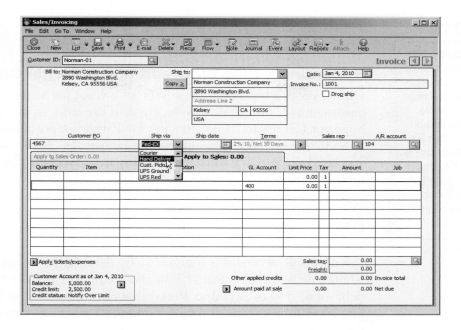

HINT

In some cases, you
may want to omit the
quantity and unit price
and enter only a total
amount.

Step 11:
Key **10.00** (10 hours) in the *Quantity* field.

Step 12:
Key **10 Hours of installation services** in the *Description* field.

Step 13:
Key **125.00** in the *Unit Price* field. The total of $1,250 is automatically
calculated. Leave the *Tax code* field at 1.

Step 14:
Review the completed Sales/Invoicing window for Norman Construction
Company, as shown in figure 4–10. If your entries contain any errors,
correct them.

FIGURE 4–10
Completed Sales/Invoicing
Window for Norman
Construction Company

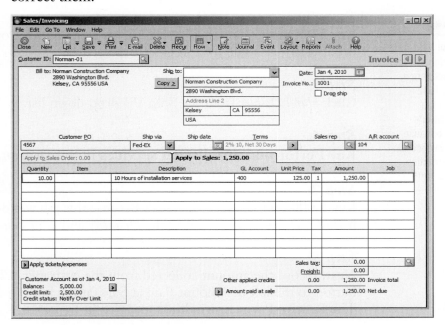

Step 15:
Click the Save button to save the entry of the sale on credit.

Recording a Sale on Credit and a Partial Collection

On occasion, a business will present an invoice for a sale on credit to a customer and immediately collect part of the amount owed. For example, Superior Carpet and Tile did a job for Parker's Construction for a fixed fee of $5,000. The job was completed on January 14, 2010, and Invoice 1002 was hand delivered. Parker immediately issued a check for one-half of the total due ($2,500).

The analysis of this transaction reveals that revenue has increased by $5,000, the asset Accounts Receivable has increased by $2,500, and the asset Cash has increased by $2,500. The account for Parker's Construction has also increased by $2,500.

You would record this transaction by debiting Accounts Receivable for $2,500, debiting Cash for $2,500, and crediting Revenue for $5,000. The debit of $2,500 to Accounts Receivable must be posted to both the controlling account in the general ledger and the Parker's Construction account in the accounts receivable subsidiary ledger.

Use the steps outlined below to record the sale on credit and the partial collection involving Parker's Construction.

Step 1:
Click the *magnifying glass* icon next to the *Customer ID* field of the Sales/Invoicing window.

Step 2:
Click *Parker-03* from the drop-down list of customers.

Step 3:
Select *Bill To* from the Ship To drop-down list and use the *calendar* icon next to the *Date* field and choose *Jan 14, 2010*.

Step 4:
Key **2356** in the *Customer PO* field. This is the number of the purchase order that was issued by Parker's Construction.

Step 5:
Click *Hand Deliver* from the Ship Via drop-down list.

Step 6:
Key **Performed installation services** in the *Description* field.

Step 7:
Key **5,000.00** in the *Amount* field. Because this job was done for a fixed fee, it is not necessary to complete the *Quantity* and *Unit Price* fields.

Step 8:
Next, record the amount collected from the customer. Click the right arrow button to the left of Amount Paid at Sale (at the bottom of the window). The Receive Payment window appears as in figure 4–11.

FIGURE 4–11
Receive Payment
Window

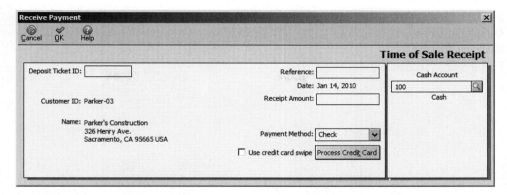

Step 9:
Key **01/14/10** in the *Deposit Ticket ID* field. This is the date of the probable bank deposit.

Step 10:
Key **1002** in the *Reference* field. This is the invoice number.

Step 11:
Key **2,500.00** in the *Receipt Amount* field.

Step 12:
At the Payment Method drop-down list, click *Check*. (It should be already selected as a default.)

Step 13:
At the Cash Account drop-down list, double-click *100* if not already selected.

Step 14:
Compare your work with the completed Receive Payment window, shown in figure 4–12.

FIGURE 4–12
Completed Receive
Payment Window

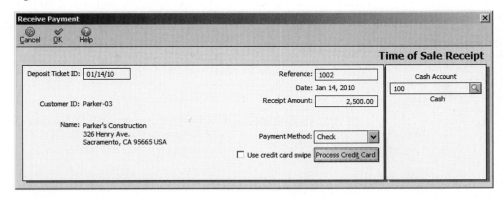

Step 15:
Click OK. Peachtree will automatically transfer the information about the amount collected to the Sales/Invoicing window and will calculate the net amount that is now due.

Step 16:
Review the completed Sales/Invoicing window for Parker's Construction, as shown in figure 4–13.

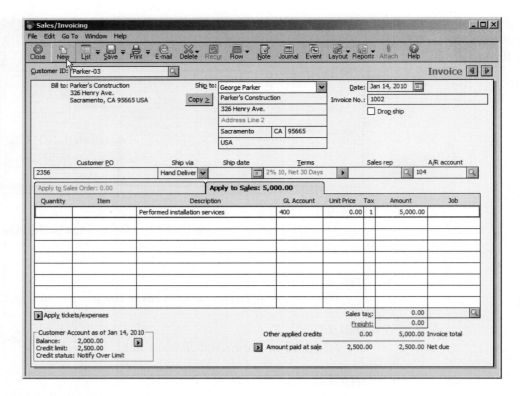

Step 17:
Click Save, and then Yes (at the credit warning message) to save the transaction, then close the Sales/Invoicing window.

Printing Customer Ledger Reports

Peachtree produces a wide variety of accounts receivable reports. The *Customer Ledgers* report is probably the most important of the accounts receivable reports. This report shows all transactions with credit customers and the balances they owe. Use the following steps to view and print the *Customer Ledgers* report.

Step 1:
Click Reports & Forms, and then click *Accounts Receivable*.

Step 2:
At the Accounts Receivable: Customers and Sales section, click *Customer Ledgers*, as shown in figure 4–14.

FIGURE 4–14

Accounts Receivable Report List with Customer Ledgers Selected

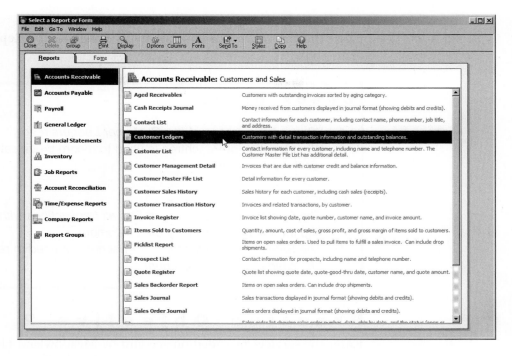

Step 3:

Click the Print button on the Select a Report or Form toolbar.

Step 4:

At the Modify Report – Customer Ledgers window, click *Range* from the Date drop-down list, and then *Jan. 1, 2010 to Jan. 31, 2010* as the range date. Then click OK.

Step 5:

Click OK at the Print dialog box. Examine the *Customer Ledgers* report shown in figure 4–15. (The abbreviation *SJ* in the report stands for sales journal. The abbreviation *CRJ* stands for cash receipts journal.)

FIGURE 4–15

Customer Ledgers Report

Page: 1

Chp. 4 - Superior Carpet and Tile
Customer Ledgers
For the Period From Jan 1, 2010 to Jan 31, 2010
Filter Criteria includes: Report order is by ID. Report is printed in Detail Format.

Customer ID Customer	Date	Trans No	Type	Debit Amt	Credit Amt	Balance
Calif-02 State of California	1/1/10	Beginning Bala	SJ	4,000.00		4,000.00
Norman-01 Norman Construction Co	1/1/10 1/4/10	Beginning Bala 1001	SJ SJ	5,000.00 1,250.00		5,000.00 6,250.00
Parker-03 Parker's Construction	1/1/10 1/14/10 1/14/10	Beginning Bala 1002 1002	SJ SJ CRJ	2,000.00 5,000.00	2,500.00	2,000.00 7,000.00 4,500.00
Running Water-04 Running Water Tile	1/1/10	Beginning Bala	SJ	4,000.00		4,000.00
Report Total				**21,250.00**	**2,500.00**	**18,750.00**

Step 6:
Close the Customer Ledgers window and the Select a Report or Form dialog box.

C h e c k   p o i n t

1. What is the purpose of the *Customer Ledgers* report?
2. What function of Peachtree is used to record credit sales and cash received on account?

Answers
1. *The Customer Ledgers report lists all transactions with credit customers and the balances owed by the customers.*
2. *The Sales/Invoicing function of Peachtree is used to record credit sales and cash received on account.*

P r a c t i c e   O b j e c t i v e   2

Enter the services provided on account by Meadowland Healthcare Services. You previously created customer accounts for this firm.

Step 1:
Open Chp. 4 – Meadowland Healthcare Services, which you updated previously with customer accounts.

Step 2:
Record the following transactions using the Sales/Invoicing window. All cash must be entered into the Regular Checking Account (10200) account.

*   On January 2, 2010, Meadowland Healthcare Services issued Invoice 1101 to Doctor's Medical Center for 100 hours of professional fees at a rate of $120 per hour. The invoice was sent by regular mail.
*   On January 8, 2010, Meadowland Healthcare Services issued Invoice 1102 to Good Samaritan Hospital for a fixed professional fee of $2,420, which covers monthly services. The invoice was hand delivered.
*   On January 19, 2010, Meadowland Healthcare Services issued Invoice 1103 to Rapid Medical Response for 48 hours of professional fees at a rate of $120 per hour. The invoice was sent by regular mail.
*   On January 29, 2010, Meadowland Healthcare Services issued Invoice 1104 to Valley Response for a fixed fee of $1,650, which covers monthly professional fees and services. The invoice was hand delivered, and the customer immediately wrote a check for one-half of the amount due.

Step 3:
Print the *Customer Ledgers* report. Check the accuracy of your work by comparing your report with figure 4–16.

FIGURE 4–16

Meadowland
Healthcare
Services
Customer
Ledgers Report

					Page: 1

Chp. 4 - Meadowland Healthcare Services
Customer Ledgers
For the Period From Jan 1, 2010 to Jan 31, 2010

Filter Criteria includes: Report order is by ID. Report is printed in Detail Format.

Customer ID Customer	Date	Trans No	Type	Debit Amt	Credit Amt	Balance
Doctor's-10 Doctor's Medical Center	1/2/10	1101	SJ	12,000.00		12,000.00
Good-20 Good Samiritan Hospital	1/8/10	1102	SJ	2,420.00		2,420.00
Rapid-30 Rapid Medical Response	1/19/10	1103	SJ	5,760.00		5,760.00
Valley-40 Valley Response	1/29/10 1/29/10	1104 1104	SJ CRJ	1,650.00	825.00	1,650.00 825.00
Report Total				**21,830.00**	**825.00**	**21,005.00**

Step 4:
Close the Customer Ledgers window and the Select a Report or Form dialog box.

OBJECTIVE 3 — Create Action Items and Event Logs

Having reliable, up-to-date information about customer accounts is one of the keys to collecting balances on time and minimizing losses from bad debts. Management must keep a close watch on the status of customer accounts and take prompt action to collect overdue amounts. The longer an amount remains overdue, the more likely it is that the account will eventually become uncollectible.

Peachtree has certain features that help management track problem customer accounts. One of these features has already been mentioned: the warning message that the system produces whenever a customer's balance exceeds the credit limit. Other features provided by Peachtree are action items and event logs.

Action items and event logs allow you to create a list of actions to be taken and program the system to display alerts on your screen before these events occur. For example, you might want to schedule meetings, telephone calls, or letters in connection with overdue balances and might want to be alerted to these events two days ahead of time. Action items and event logs can be used for other purposes besides managing customer accounts. They can also be used to schedule actions related to the vendor (creditor) accounts and to employees.

Follow the steps listed below to access the Action Items/Event Log Options.

Step 1:
Open Chp. 4 – Superior Carpet and Tile.

Step 2:
Click Tasks from the main Menu bar and then *Action Items* from the drop-down list.

Step 3:
Click Options from the Action Items toolbar. The Action Items and Event Log Options window appears.

Using the Activities and Transactions Tabs

Events can be set up as defaults so that they can later be displayed as action items. For example, the managers of Superior Carpet and Tile want to be advised two days before any meeting and one day before any telephone call is to be made. Use the following steps to establish the necessary defaults.

Step 1:
Click the Activities tab in the Action Items and Event Log Options window.

Step 2:
Place a check mark for *Call To* in the *Display in Action Items* field. Key **1** in the *# of Days* field. Then place a check mark for *Meeting* in the *Display in Action Items* field. Key **2** in the *# of Days* field if not already entered. Compare the window with figure 4–17.

FIGURE 4–17
Activities Tab

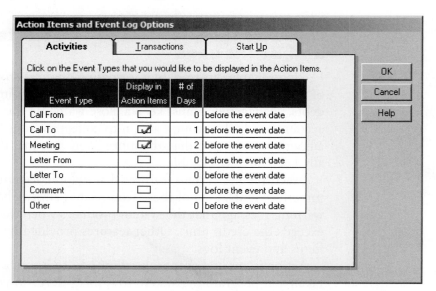

Peachtree can be programmed to generate alerts for a variety of events. For example, Superior Carpet and Tile wants to create events for all possible event types specified by Peachtree. Superior also wants an advance warning for customer invoices that are due for payment. They want this warning to appear as an action item two days before payment due dates. Use the following steps to generate an alert to Superior two days before a customer's invoice is due.

Step 1:
Click the Transactions tab in the Action Items and Event Log Options window.

Step 2:
For *Customer Invoices Due,* key **2** in the *# of Days* field, as shown in figure 4–18.

FIGURE 4–18
Transactions Tab

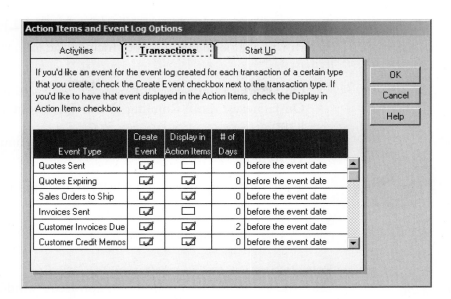

Using the Start Up Tab

You can have the action items displayed whenever you open a new company or you can have the items displayed on top of the screen.

Step 1:
Click the Start Up tab in the Action Items and Event Log Options window.

Step 2:
Place a check mark next to *Display Action Items each time a new company is opened* if not already checked. (See figure 4–19.)

FIGURE 4–19
Start Up Tab

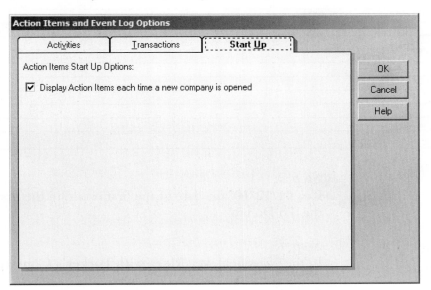

Step 3:
Click OK to accept all of the defaults that you have established and then close Action Items.

Because the process of setting up the defaults is complete, you can now create and access events that are action items.

Recording Action Items on the To Do List

Superior Carpet and Tile wants to include the following events as action items:

- On January 12, meet with Parker's Construction at 2:00 p.m.
- On January 13, call Running Water Tile about an increase in its credit limit.
- On January 13, meet with Norman Construction Company for lunch at 12:30 p.m.

Use the following steps to establish these events as action items.

Step 1:
Click Tasks, and then click *Action Items*.

Step 2:
Click the To Do folder tab in the Action Items window, as shown in figure 4–20.

FIGURE 4–20
To Do Tab Selected from Action Items Window

Step 3:
Key **01/12/10**, the date of the first event, in the first cell of the *Date* field in the To Do tab.

Step 4:
In the *Notes* field, key **Meet with Parker's Construction at 2:00 p.m.**

Step 5:
Key **01/13/10**, the date of the second event, in the second cell of the *Date* field in the To Do tab.

Step 6:
In the *Notes* field, key **Call Running Water Tile about an increase in its credit limit.**

Step 7:
Key **01/13/10**, the date of the third event, in the next cell of the *Date* field.

Step 8:
In the *Notes* field, key **Meet with Norman Construction Company for lunch at 12:30 p.m.**

Step 9:
Compare your completed To Do list with the one shown in figure 4–21.

FIGURE 4–21
Completed To Do List

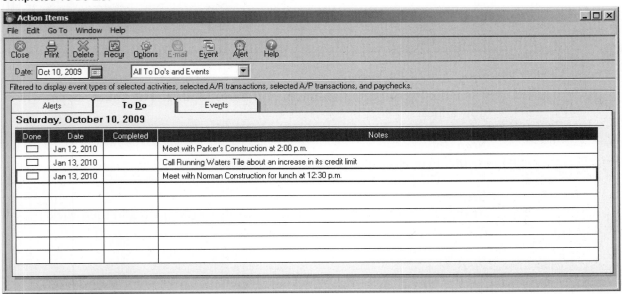

Recording Events on the Action List

Some events have been programmed to appear as action items. For example, customer invoices that are due for payment will be listed as action items two days prior to their due dates. The programming of this item was accomplished when the defaults were set up. However, a business might want to add other events to its action list.

Assume that Superior Carpet and Tile wants to place the following additional event on its action list: Set up a meeting with Parker's Construction for January 18, 2010. Advise two days ahead of time.

Step 1:
Click the Events tab as shown in figure 4–22.

FIGURE 4–22
Events Tab Selected from
Action Items Window

Step 2:
Click the Event button on the Action Items toolbar. The Create Event window appears.

Step 3:
At the Type drop-down list, click *Customer/Prospect*.

Step 4:
At the ID drop-down list, click the *magnifying glass* icon and then click *Parker-03*.

Step 5:
To the right of the *Date* field, click the *calendar* icon and choose *Jan 18, 2010*.

Step 6:
At the Event Type section, click *Meeting*.

Step 7:
In the *Note* field, key **Set up meeting.**

Step 8:
Place a check mark next to *Display in Action Items*.

Step 9:
Key **2** as the number of days. Then click *Before* in the "_____ the event date" drop-down list. (These may already be selected by default.)

Step 10:
Compare your work with the completed Create Event window shown in figure 4–23.

FIGURE 4–23
Completed Create Event
Window

Step 11:
Click the Save button on the Create Event window toolbar, and then click Close.

Step 12:
Superior Carpet and Tile wants to add the following two events to its action list. Add them using steps 1 through 11:

- Call Norman Construction Company three days before a meeting set for January 19, 2010.
- Send a letter to Running Water Tile advising it of a change in credit terms that will take effect on January 31, 2010. Send the letter five days before (on January 26).

Step 13:
Click the Close button, and then close the Action Items window.

Displaying the Events

Each of the events placed on the action list is scheduled to appear according to the number of days set before the event. For example, the first event for Superior Carpet and Tile—the meeting with Parker's Construction on January 18—will automatically appear two days before the event in the Action Items window as the system date changes to January 16. Follow the steps outlined below to check the events listed for any date. In this case, the date to be checked is January 16, 2010.

Step 1:
Click Tasks, and then *Action Items*.

Step 2:
Click the Events tab.

FIGURE 4–24
Action Items Window
with Date Field Showing
Jan 16, 2010

Step 3:
At the Action Items window, in the *Date* field, click the *calendar* icon to choose *Jan 16, 2010*. (See figure 4–24.)

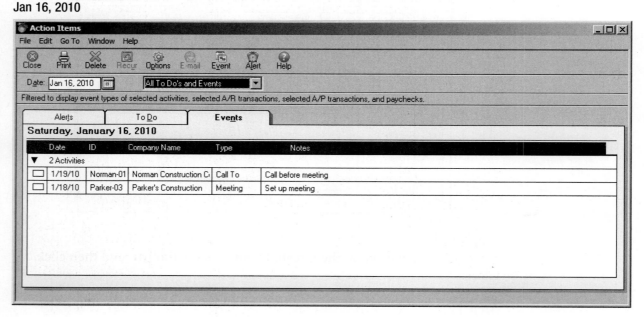

The events that are scheduled will appear in the Action Items window when Peachtree is started on January 16, 2010.

Setting Alerts

The Action Items window has an Alerts tab that allows you to select certain conditions for notification. For example, an alert can be set to notify you when a particular customer's balance is too high. Assume that Superior Carpet and Tile wants to be notified when the balance owed by Norman Construction Company, the State of California, or Parker's Construction reaches $4,000. Follow the steps outlined below to set the alert.

Step 1:
Click the Alerts tab in the Action Items window.

Step 2:
Click the Alert button on the Action Items toolbar. The Set Company Alerts window appears, as shown in figure 4–25.

FIGURE 4–25
Set Company Alerts
Window

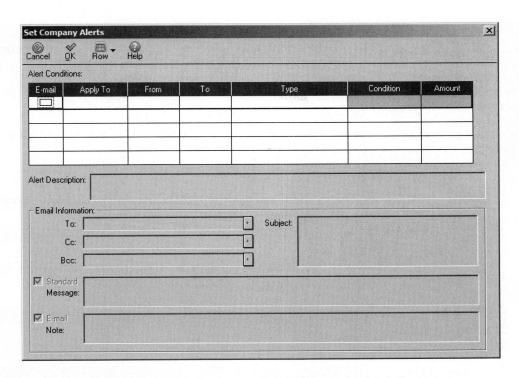

Setting an alert requires entry of information using the following steps:

Step 3:
Click inside the *Apply To* field, click the down-pointing arrow that appears, and then click *Customer*.

Step 4:
Click in the *From* field, click the *magnifying glass* icon, and then click *Calif-02*. (See figure 4–26.)

FIGURE 4–26
Set Company Alerts
Window – From Field

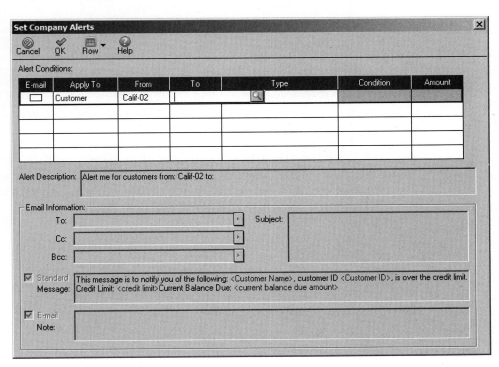

Step 5:

In the *To* field, click the *magnifying glass* icon, and then click *Parker-03*. Steps 4 and 5 establish a filter for the customer who is the subject of the alert.

Step 6:

In the *Type* field, click the down-pointing arrow, and then click *Current Balance*.

Step 7:

Click in the *Condition* field, click the down-pointing arrow, and then click >= *(if necessary)*.

Step 8:

Key **4,000.00** in the *Amount* field. Compare your work with the completed window shown in figure 4–27.

FIGURE 4–27
Completed Set Company Alerts Window

Step 9:

Click the <u>O</u>K button to save the alert. Change the date to January 1, 2010 in the Action Items window and the alerts that were set up for Norman Construction Company, the State of California, and Parker's Construction will now appear in the Aler<u>t</u>s tab. (See figure 4–28.)

FIGURE 4–28
Alerts Tab with Alerts for
Customers' Balances

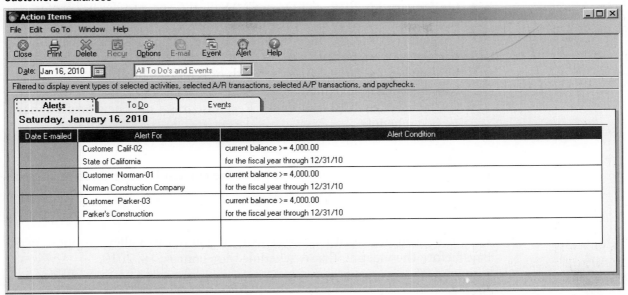

Step 10:
Close the Action Items window.

C h e c k   p o i n t

1. What is the purpose of the action items and event log options of Peachtree?
2. What is the purpose of the alert function of Peachtree?

Answers
1. *The action item and event log options allow you to create a list of actions to be taken and program the system to display alerts before these events occur.*
2. *The alert function allows you to select certain conditions for notification.*

P r a c t i c e   O b j e c t i v e   3

You previously established customer accounts for Meadowland Healthcare Services. Now you will set up action items and alerts for this firm.

Step 1:
Open Chp. 4 – Meadowland Healthcare Services.

Step 2:
Use the Start Up tab from the Action Items and Event Log Options window to check mark the *Display Action Items each time a new company is opened* box.

Step 3:

Record the following events as action items on the To Do list.

- On January 12, 2010, call Doctor's Medical Center to discuss professional monthly services for its new facility.
- On January 18, 2010, meet with Good Samaritan Hospital to explain our new pricing policy.
- On January 23, 2010, call Kim Smith of Rapid Medical Response to wish her a happy birthday.
- On January 24, 2010, call Valley Response to set up a new professional service schedule.

Step 4:

Create an alert that will notify you when the current balance owed by any of the customers reaches or exceeds $1,500.

Step 5:

Create an event in which Peachtree will tell you to call Valley Response two days before the meeting that is scheduled for January 18, 2010.

Step 6:

Close the Action Items window.

OBJECTIVE 4 — Adjust the Accounts Receivable for Uncollectible Accounts and Print Reports

A well-run business is careful about extending credit, closely monitors the status of its customer accounts, and makes strong efforts to collect overdue balances. However, no matter how diligent a business is in managing its accounts receivable, some customer accounts will become uncollectible. Bad economic conditions in an area, bad management decisions, or new competition may cause a previously sound customer to go bankrupt.

Methods for Recording Uncollectible Accounts

direct write-off method A method in which the expense from uncollectible accounts is recorded when the accounts actually become bad debts.

allowance method A method in which the expense from uncollectible accounts is estimated at the end of each accounting period and recorded by means of an adjusting entry.

Two methods are available for recording uncollectible accounts. The first and simpler approach is the **direct write-off method**. With this method, the expense from an uncollectible account is recorded when the customer's account actually becomes a bad debt. At that time, you debit the loss to Uncollectible Accounts Expense and credit it to Accounts Receivable. The credit part of this entry is posted to both the Accounts Receivable controlling account in the general ledger and the customer's account in the subsidiary ledger.

The second approach to recording uncollectible accounts is the **allowance method**. At the end of each accounting period, the accountant makes an estimate of the bad debts loss that will result from the period's sales. This amount is recorded by means of an adjusting entry. You debit Uncollectible Accounts Expense and credit Allowance for Doubtful Accounts. Figure 4–29 illustrates the adjusting entry for an estimated bad debts loss of $45,000.

FIGURE 4–29
Initial Adjustment for Estimation of Bad Debt Loss Using the Allowance Method

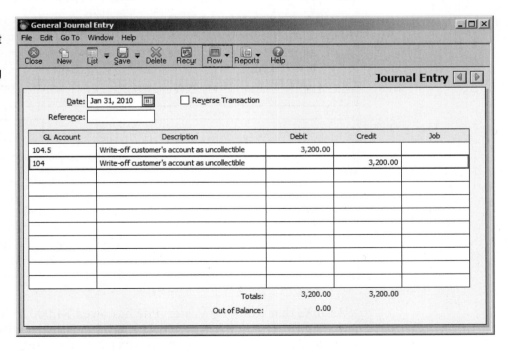

GL Account	Description	Debit	Credit	Job
515	Adjustment for bad debt loss	45,000.00		
104.5	Adjustment for bad debt loss		45,000.00	

Totals: 45,000.00   45,000.00
Out of Balance: 0.00

With the allowance method, when a customer's account actually becomes uncollectible, you write it off by debiting Allowance for Doubtful Accounts and crediting Accounts Receivable, as shown in figure 4–30. The credit part of this entry is posted to both the Accounts Receivable controlling account in the general ledger and the customer's account in the subsidiary ledger.

FIGURE 4–30
Adjustment for Bad Debt Loss against a Specific Customer Account Using the Allowance Method

GL Account	Description	Debit	Credit	Job
104.5	Write-off customer's account as uncollectible	3,200.00		
104	Write-off customer's account as uncollectible		3,200.00	

Totals: 3,200.00   3,200.00
Out of Balance: 0.00

When financial statements are prepared at the end of an accounting period, Uncollectible Accounts Expense appears as an operating expense on

contra asset account An account with a balance opposite to the normal balance of an asset account.

the income statement. Allowance for Doubtful Accounts is a **contra asset account**—an account with a balance opposite to the normal balance of an asset account. If the allowance method is used, the balance sheet will show the credit balance of Allowance for Doubtful Accounts deducted from the debit balance of Accounts Receivable.

The allowance method is the approach required by generally accepted accounting principles (GAAP). However, the direct write-off method will be used in this chapter to adjust for bad debt loss because this chapter deals with small businesses. The direct write-off method is used by many small businesses because it is simple compared with the allowance method.

Using the Direct Write-Off Method to Record the Write-Off of a Customer's Account

In a manual accounting system, the write-off of a customer's account is recorded in the general journal. However, in Peachtree, it is necessary to use the accounts receivable module so that the credit part of the entry can be posted automatically to the accounts receivable subsidiary ledger as well as to the general ledger.

A simple journal entry is used to write off a specific accounts receivable when it is deemed uncollectible. Therefore, no end-of-the-period adjusting entry is required. Figure 4–31 gives an example of a general journal entry needed to write off a bad debt loss.

FIGURE 4–31
Adjustment for Bad Debt Loss Using the Direct Write-Off Method

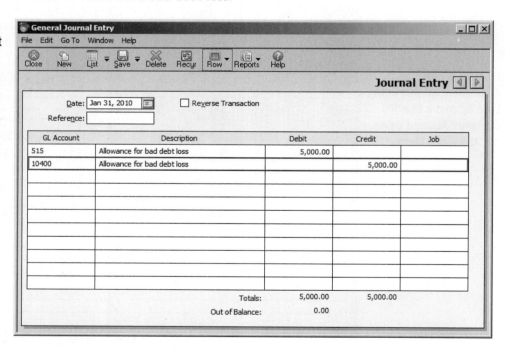

Assume that Running Water Tile has owed $4,000 to Superior Carpet and Tile for six months. Superior has been unsuccessful in its efforts to collect this overdue balance. On January 31, 2010, Superior receives a legal notice that Running Water Tile has gone bankrupt.

Superior uses the direct write-off method for recording uncollectible accounts. Therefore, on January 31, 2010, its accountant made a journal entry to record the bad debt loss for the sale that occurred in 2009. Now you must write off the account of Running Water Tile as of January 31, 2010.

Step 1:
Open Chp. 4 – Superior Carpet and Tile.

Step 2:
Open the Chart of Accounts, add the account *Uncollectible Accounts Expense* to it using the information below, and then click Save and Close.

Account ID:	**515**
Description:	**Uncollectible Accounts Expense**
Account Type:	**Expenses**

Step 3:
Click Tasks, and then click *Receipts*. The Receipts window will appear. (See figure 4–32.)

FIGURE 4–32
Receipts Window

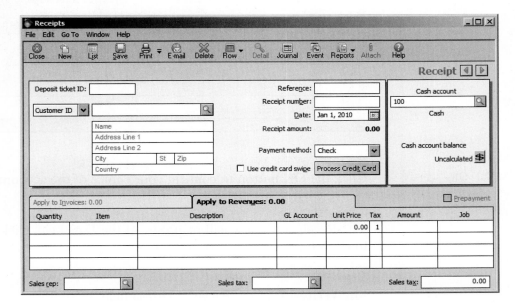

Step 4:
Key **01/31/10** in the *Deposit Ticket ID* field.

Step 5:
Click the *magnifying glass* icon and then click *Running Water Tile* from the drop-down list of customer IDs.

Step 6:
Key **Bankruptcy** in the *Reference* field.

Step 7:
Click the Journal button from the Receipts window toolbar. You will now see the Accounting Behind the Screens window.

Step 8:
Click the *magnifying glass* icon in the *Account No.* field and then click *515 Uncollectible Accounts Expense* from the drop-down list of accounts. Normally, there is a default to Cash in the Receipts window because Cash is the account debited to record an amount received from a customer. However,

because a customer's account is being written off, you must go "behind the screens" to ensure that Uncollectible Accounts Expense will be debited. See figure 4–33.

FIGURE 4–33
Uncollectible Accounts
Expense Selected

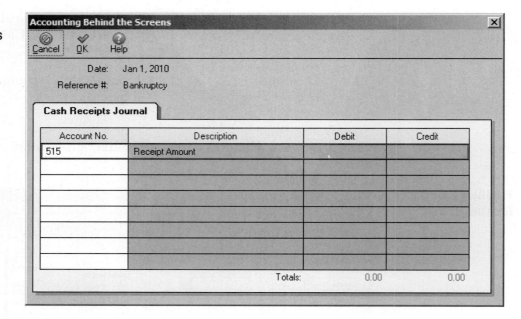

Step 9:
Click the <u>O</u>K button to confirm your choice of the account to be debited.

Step 10:
The Receipts window will reappear. At the *Date* field, click the *calendar* icon to choose *Jan 31, 2010,* as the date.

Step 11:
Key **Write-off** in the *Payment Method* field.

Step 12:
Click the Apply to I<u>n</u>voices tab.

Step 13:
Key **Bad debt loss** in the *Description* field.

Step 14:
Key **4,000.00** in the *Amount Paid* field.

Step 15:
Tab to the *Pay* field and notice that a check mark appears there.

Step 16:
Click the Journal button from the Receipts window toolbar. Compare the Accounting Behind the Screens window with figure 4–34, and then click the <u>O</u>K button.

FIGURE 4–34
Accounting Behind the Screens Window

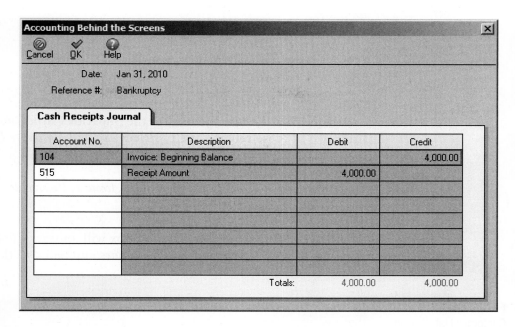

Step 17:
Compare your entries for the write-off with the completed Receipts window shown in figure 4–35.

FIGURE 4–35
Completed Receipts Window with Write-off

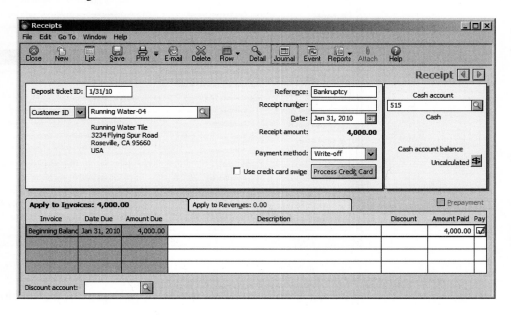

Step 18:
Click the Save button and then the Close button. Select Yes if the Cash Account Warning appears.

Printing Accounts Receivable Reports

Peachtree can produce several accounts receivable reports, including:

- *Aged Receivables*
- *Cash Receipts Journal*
- *Customer Ledgers*
- *Customer List*

- *Customer Management Detail*
- *Customer Master File List*
- *Customer Transaction History*
- *Invoice Register*
- *Items Sold to Customers*

Assume that the management of the Superior Carpet and Tile wants to print two of these reports: the *Customer List* and *Customer Ledgers*.

Step 1:
Click Reports & Forms, and then click *Accounts Receivable*.

Step 2:
The Select a Report or Form dialog box will appear. Click *Customer List* from the Accounts Receivable: Customers and Sales section, as shown in figure 4–36.

FIGURE 4–36
Customer List Chosen from Select a Report or Form Dialog Box

Step 3:
Click the Print button on the Select a Report or Form toolbar.

Step 4:
Click *Customer ID*, if it is not already selected, from the *Select a filter* scroll-down list and select the *All* radio button from the *Select an option* section, as shown in figure 4–37.

FIGURE 4–37
Customer ID Selected
from Select a Filter
Scroll-Down List

Step 5:
Click OK.

Step 6:
Complete the Print window, and click OK to print.

Step 7:
Compare your *Customer List* report with the one shown in figure 4–38.

FIGURE 4–38
Customer List for
Superior Carpet
and Tile

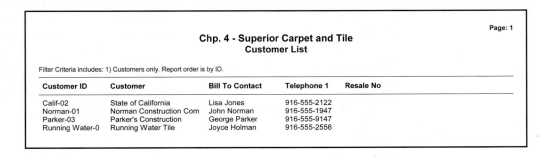

Step 8:
Use steps 2–6 to print a copy of the *Customer Ledgers*. (In step 2, select *Customer Ledgers* from the Accounts Receivable: Customers and Sales section and select *Jan. 1, 2010* to *Jan. 31, 2010* as the range date.) Compare your printed report with the one shown in figure 4–39.

FIGURE 4–39
Customer Ledgers
for Superior Carpet
and Tile

Chp. 4 - Superior Carpet and Tile
Customer Ledgers
For the Period From Jan 1, 2010 to Jan 31, 2010

Page: 1

Filter Criteria includes: Report order is by ID. Report is printed in Detail Format.

Customer ID Customer	Date	Trans No	Type	Debit Amt	Credit Amt	Balance
Calif-02 State of California	1/1/10	Beginning Bala	SJ	4,000.00		4,000.00
Norman-01 Norman Construction Co	1/1/10 1/4/10	Beginning Bala 1001	SJ SJ	5,000.00 1,250.00		5,000.00 6,250.00
Parker-03 Parker's Construction	1/1/10 1/14/10 1/14/10	Beginning Bala 1002 1002	SJ SJ CRJ	2,000.00 5,000.00	2,500.00	2,000.00 7,000.00 4,500.00
Running Water-04 Running Water Tile	1/1/10 1/31/10	Beginning Bala Bankruptcy	SJ CRJ	4,000.00	4,000.00	4,000.00 0.00
Report Total				**21,250.00**	**6,500.00**	**14,750.00**

Step 9:
Close the Select a Report dialog box.

Check point

1. What two methods are used to record uncollectible accounts?
2. When a customer's balance is written off under the direct write-off method, what accounts are debited and credited?

Answers
1. *The two methods used to record uncollectible accounts are the direct write-off method and the allowance method.*
2. *When a customer's balance is written off under the direct write-off, it is necessary to debit Uncollectible Accounts Expense and credit Accounts Receivable in the general ledger. It is also necessary to credit the customer's account in the subsidiary ledger.*

Practice Objective 4

Step 1:
Open Chp. 4 – Meadowland Healthcare Services.

Step 2:
Write off the Doctor's Medical Center account as of January 31, 2010. Doctor's Medical Center has gone bankrupt. It owes $12,000 for Invoice 1101.

Step 3:

Print a copy of the *Customer List* report. Compare your report to the report shown in figure 4–40.

Chp. 4 - Meadowland Healthcare Services
Customer List

Page: 1

Filter Criteria includes: 1) Customers only. Report order is by ID.

Customer ID	Customer	Bill To Contact	Telephone 1	Resale No
Doctor's-10	Doctor's Medical Center	Dr. Jim Conway	916-555-4834	
Good-20	Good Samiritan Hospital	Jane Campbell, RN	916-555-6780	
Rapid-30	Rapid Medical Response	Kim Smith, RN	916-555-4719	
Valley-40	Valley Response	Robert Romero, PA	916-555-5678	

Step 4:

Print a copy of the *Customer Ledgers* report. Compare your report to the report shown in figure 4–41.

Chp. 4 - Meadowland Healthcare Services
Customer Ledgers
For the Period From Jan 1, 2010 to Jan 31, 2010

Page: 1

Filter Criteria includes: Report order is by ID. Report is printed in Detail Format.

Customer ID / Customer	Date	Trans No	Type	Debit Amt	Credit Amt	Balance
Doctor's-10	1/2/10	1101	SJ	12,000.00		12,000.00
Doctor's Medical Center	1/31/10	Bankruptcy	CRJ		12,000.00	0.00
Good-20	1/8/10	1102	SJ	2,420.00		2,420.00
Good Samiritan Hospital						
Rapid-30	1/19/10	1103	SJ	5,760.00		5,760.00
Rapid Medical Response						
Valley-40	1/29/10	1104	SJ	1,650.00		1,650.00
Valley Response	1/29/10	1104	CRJ		825.00	825.00
Report Total				**21,830.00**	**12,825.00**	**9,005.00**

Step 5:

Close the Select a Report or Form dialog box.

End of Chapter Review

Software Command Summary

Create Customer Accounts	Maintain, Customers/Prospects, General Tab, Sales Info Tab, Payment & Credit Tab, Enter Beginning Balances
Accounts Receivable and Sales Transactions	Tasks, Sales/Invoicing
Adjusting Accounts Receivables	Tasks, Receipts
Action Items and Event Log Options	Tasks, Action Items, Options, Action Items and Event Log Options
Create Action Items/Alerts	Tasks, Action Items, To Do, Event Toolbar Icon, Alert Toolbar Icon

Projects and Problems

Content Check

Multiple Choice: Choose only one response for each question.

1. When a business sells goods or services on credit, it records the amounts owed by the customers as
   A. accounts receivable.
   B. accounts payable.
   C. prepaid expenses.
   D. unearned revenue.
   E. None of the above

2. From a seller's perspective, sales on credit to customers affect
   A. assets and expenses.
   B. assets and revenue.
   C. liabilities and expenses.
   D. liabilities and revenue.
   E. None of the above

3. When a business makes a sale on credit, what function of Peachtree is used to record the transaction?
   A. Action Items
   B. Purchases/Receive Inventory
   C. Receipts
   D. Sales/Invoicing
   E. None of the above

4. Which accounts receivable report shows the beginning balances of the customer accounts, all transactions with the customers during a period, and the ending balances?
   A. *Aged Receivables*
   B. *Customer Ledgers*
   C. *Invoice Register*
   D. *Sales Journal*
   E. None of the above

5. Which general ledger accounts are involved in the direct write-off of a specific customer's account?
   A. Accounts Receivable and Sales
   B. Uncollectible Accounts Expense and Accounts Receivable
   C. Allowance for Doubtful Accounts and Accounts Receivable
   D. Uncollectible Accounts Expense and Allowance for Doubtful Accounts
   E. None of the above

Short Essay Response: Provide a detailed answer for each question.

1. What are the advantages and disadvantages to a business when it sells on credit?
2. What is the purpose of the accounts receivable subsidiary ledger?
3. Under what circumstance will a resale number be required when an account is set up for a new customer?
4. Why is a default for a credit limit established when customer accounts are set up?
5. How can the Alert function be used to aid a business in collecting its accounts receivable?
6. Explain the difference between the direct write-off method and the allowance method of recording uncollectible accounts.

Case Problems

Problem 1A

Open Tracy Accounting Solutions from the student data disk.

The following are customers who purchase services on credit.

Customer

Customer ID:	**JM-1**
Name:	**Johnson Manufacturing**

General Tab

Account Number:	**120501**
Billing Address:	**4731 Eaton Avenue**
City, ST, Zip:	**Stockton, CA 95210**
Country:	**USA**
Customer Type:	**General**
Telephone 1:	**209-555-4178**
Fax:	**209-555-4180**

Contact Tab

Contact:	**Randy Johnson**

Sales Info Tab

GL Sales Account:	**40000**
Ship Via:	**Fed-Ex**
Pricing Level:	**Default**
Form Delivery Options:	**Default**

Payment & Credit Tab

Terms and Credit:	**Default**

History Tab

Beginning Balance:	**400**

Customer

Customer ID:	**CE-2**
Name:	**Computer Expertise**

General Tab

Account Number:	**120502**
Billing Address:	**475 West Lincoln Boulevard**
City, ST, Zip:	**Tracy, CA 95376**
Country:	**USA**
Customer Type:	**General**
Telephone 1:	**209-555-3820**
Fax:	**209-555-3840**

Contact Tab

Contact:	**Marie Jameson**

Sales Info Tab

GL Sales Account:	**40000**
Ship Via:	**Fed-Ex**
Pricing Level:	**Default**
Form Delivery Options:	**Default**

Payment & Credit Tab

Terms and Credit:	**Default**

History Tab

Beginning Balance:	**320**

Customer

Customer ID:	**SC-3**
Name:	**Stephanie's Catering**

General Tab

Account Number:	**120503**
Billing Address:	**4837 6th Street**
City, ST, Zip:	**Watsonville, CA 95760**

Country:	**USA**
Customer Type:	**General**
Telephone 1:	**209-555-2864**
Fax:	**209-555-2875**

Contact Tab

Contact:	**Stephanie Barron**

Sales Info Tab

GL Sales Account:	**40000**
Ship Via:	**Fed-Ex**
Pricing Level:	**Default**
Form Delivery Options:	**Default**

Payment & Credit Tab

Terms and Credit:	**Default**

History Tab

Beginning Balance:	**180.00**

The following cash sales and credit sales occurred during January 2010.

Date	Transaction
Jan. 3	Performed accounting services for $1,400 on credit for Johnson Manufacturing. Issued Invoice 1001.
4	Performed tax preparation services for $850 in cash.
6	Performed accounting services for $650 on credit for Computer Expertise. Issued Invoice 1002.
14	Performed accounting services for $350 on credit for Stephanie's Catering. Issued Invoice 1003. Received a check for $100 from the customer.
15	Performed consulting services for $220 in cash.
24	Performed consulting services for $725 on credit for Johnson Manufacturing. Issued Invoice 1004. Received a check for $200 from the customer.
27	Performed accounting services for $245 on credit for Computer Expertise. Issued Invoice 1005. Received a check for $120 from the customer.

> **HINT**
>
> Enter all performances of service on credit using the Sales/Invoicing function. Enter cash sales and all other transactions using the General Journal Entry function. Use Account 10200, Regular Checking Account for all cash sales transactions.

1. Create a subsidiary ledger account for each credit customer and enter their beginning balance as of January 1, 2010.

2. Enter each of the transactions for January. Use the appropriate option on the Tasks menu: Sales/Invoicing or General Journal Entry. Note that this business has three different types of revenue: accounting fees, tax preparation fees, and consulting fees. Therefore, be sure that you select the number of the correct revenue account in the GL Sales Account section of the Sales/Invoicing window. (The customer accounts have been set up with a GL Sales Account default to Account 40000, Accounting Fees.)

3. Print the following reports for January: *Customer Ledgers, Sales Journal, General Journal,* and *Income Statement.*

Problem 2A
Open Tracy Accounting Solutions.

1. Record the following events as action items on the To Do list.

   - On January 3, 2010, call Computer Expertise to discuss accounting services schedule.
   - On January 15, 2010, meet with a graphic design company, Infinite Graphics, to discuss company logo.
   - On January 17, 2010, call Johnson Manufacturing to discuss pricing policy.
   - On January 24, 2010, meet with Stephanie's Catering to set up a new accounting services schedule.

2. Create the following alert.

   - Notify you when the current balance owed by any of its customers reaches or exceeds $2,500.

Problem 1B
Open Infinite Graphics from the student data disk.

The following are customers who purchase services on credit.

Customer

Customer ID:	**JP-1**
Name:	**Jackson Photography**

General Tab

Account Number:	**510**
Billing Address:	**1374 West Bessie Avenue**
City, ST, Zip:	**Stockton, CA 95210**
Country:	**USA**
Customer Type:	**General**
Telephone 1:	**209-555-1478**
Fax:	**209-555-1485**

Contact Tab

Contact:	**Sarah Bautista**

Sales Info Tab

GL Sales Account:	**40000**
Ship Via:	**Fed-Ex**
Pricing Level:	**Default**
Form Delivery Options:	**Default**

Payment & Credit Tab

Terms and Credit:	**Default**

History Tab

Beginning Balance:	**400.00**

Customer

Customer ID:	CC-2
Name:	Computer Creations

General Tab

Account Number:	520
Billing Address:	733 Madison Boulevard
City, ST, Zip:	Tracy, CA 95376
Country:	USA
Customer Type:	General
Telephone 1:	209-555-4710
Fax:	209-555-4730

Contact Tab

Contact:	Lee Chang

Sales Info Tab

GL Sales Account:	40000
Ship Via:	Fed-Ex
Pricing Level:	Default
Form Delivery Options:	Default

Payment & Credit Tab

Terms and Credit:	Default

History Tab

Beginning Balance:	0

Customer

Customer ID:	FD-3
Name:	First Design

General Tab

Account Number:	530
Billing Address:	1385 12th Street
City, ST, Zip:	Stockton, CA 95210
Country:	USA
Customer Type:	General
Telephone 1:	209-555-6842
Fax:	209-555-6846

Contact Tab

Contact:	Richard Thompson

Sales Info Tab

GL Sales Account:	40000
Ship Via:	Fed-Ex
Pricing Level:	Default
Form Delivery Options:	Default

Payment & Credit Tab
    Terms and Credit: **Default**

History Tab
    Beginning Balance: **1,000.00**

The following cash sales and credit sales occurred during January 2010:

Date	Transaction
Jan. 3	Performed graphic design services for $875 on credit for Jackson Photography. Issued Invoice 1001.
4	Performed graphic design services for $950 in cash.
6	Performed graphic design services for $560 on credit for Computer Creations. Issued Invoice 1002.
12	Performed retouching services for $1,050 in cash.
15	Performed graphic design services for $1,350 on credit for Jackson Photography. Issued Invoice 1003. Received a check for $350 from the customer.
15	Performed drafting services for $320 in cash.
20	Purchased graphing supplies for $120 in cash. (Because this business is on the accrual basis, it records purchases of supplies in an asset account.)
25	Performed graphic design services for $1,325 on credit for First Design. Issued Invoice 1004. Received a check for $725 from the customer.
26	Performed retouching services for $460 on credit for Jackson Photography. Issued Invoice 1005. Received a check for $360 from the customer.
27	Performed graphic design services for $750 on credit for Computer Creations. Issued Invoice 1006.

> **HINT**
>
> Enter all performances of service on credit using the Sales/Invoicing function. Enter cash sales and all other transactions using the General Journal Entry function. Use Account 10200, Regular Checking Account for all cash sales transactions.

1. Create a subsidiary ledger account for each credit customer and enter their beginning balances as of January 1, 2010.

2. Enter each of the transactions for January. Use the appropriate option on the Tasks menu: Sales/Invoicing or General Journal Entry. Note that this business has three different types of revenue: graphic design fees, retouching fees, and drafting fees. Therefore, be sure that you select the number of the correct revenue account in the GL Sales Account section of the Sales/Invoicing window. (The customer accounts have been set up with a GL Sales Account default to Account 40000, Graphic Design Fees.)

3. Print the following reports for January: *Customer Ledgers*, *Sales Journal*, *General Journal*, and *Income Statement*.

Problem 2B
Open Infinite Graphics from the student data disk.

1. Record the following events as action items on the To Do list.

   - On January 4, 2010, call Computer Creations to discuss pricing policy.
   - On January 13, 2010, meet with Jackson Photography to discuss graphic design work.
   - On January 20, 2010, meet with First Design to discuss subcontracting work.
   - On January 27, 2010, call GJ Professional Accounting to discuss accounting services offered.

2. Create the following alert.

   - Notify you when the current balance owed by any of its customers reaches or exceeds $2,300.

Cooperative Learning

1. Form groups of three or four students, and assume that you are the managers of a business that sells on credit. Discuss the criteria necessary to decide whether to grant credit to a new customer.
2. As a group, prepare a list of Peachtree features that help a business to monitor its accounts receivable and locate problems that may lead to uncollectible accounts.

Writing and Decision Making

Assume that the company for which you work has always had a policy of selling for cash. The owner, Susan Nicholson, is now considering whether to provide credit to customers. She has asked you to suggest measures that the company can take to organize, manage, and collect its accounts receivable. She has also asked that you explain to her how the controlling account in the general ledger relates to the customer accounts in the subsidiary ledger. Prepare a memo that provides Ms. Nicholson with the information she has requested.

CHAPTER 5

Accounts Payable and Purchases for a Service Business

Learning Objectives

1. Create subsidiary ledger accounts for vendors and enter the beginning balances

2. Process accounts payable and purchase transactions

3. Print accounts payable reports

Software Features

- Maintain Vendor toolbar buttons

- Vendor defaults

- Purchases/Receive Inventory toolbar

Most businesses make use of credit to buy the goods and services they need in their operations. Credit helps a firm to grow and to handle its resources efficiently. Paying cash for all purchases would make it much more difficult to expand operations and take advantage of new opportunities.

Recording Accounts Payable

The amounts that a firm owes for goods or services purchased on credit are called **accounts payable**. The businesses or individuals to whom these amounts are owed are known as **vendors**, creditors, or suppliers.

Accounts payable are short-term debts that usually extend for 30 or 60 days, depending on the credit terms offered by the vendor. Many vendors also allow a discount if payment is made within a specified short discount period. For example, a vendor might offer terms of 2% 10 days, net 30 days. This means that the buyer can pay in 10 days and receive a 2% discount from the total due or pay the full amount in 30 days.

As you learned in chapter 2, businesses that buy on credit set up a liability account called Accounts Payable in the general ledger. This account is credited for purchases of goods or services. The account debited depends on the nature of the purchase. A purchase of an asset such as office supplies or equipment is debited to the appropriate asset account. A purchase of a service is usually debited to an expense account. For example, a bill for electricity would be debited to Utilities Expense. A purchase of merchandise for resale is debited to a cost account called Purchases or debited to the Inventory account directly.

When a bill for a purchase on credit becomes due, a check is issued to the vendor. The payment is debited to Accounts Payable and credited to Cash.

The Accounts Payable Subsidiary Ledger

In addition to the Accounts Payable account in the general ledger, most businesses that buy on credit maintain a subsidiary ledger with individual accounts for their vendors. This subsidiary ledger is known as the **accounts payable ledger** or vendors ledger.

Remember that subsidiary ledgers supplement the information in the general ledger. For example, the accounts payable ledger provides detailed information about all transactions with vendors and shows the balances owed to them. Peachtree updates the vendor accounts automatically when accounts payable transactions are recorded and posted.

The Controlling Account in the General Ledger

When an accounts payable subsidiary ledger is used, the Accounts Payable account in the general ledger becomes a controlling account. It provides a link between the general ledger and the accounts payable ledger because its balance is equal to the total of all the balances of the individual accounts in the subsidiary ledger. This is similar in function to how the accounts receivable subsidiary ledger is used as described earlier (in chapter 4).

Managing Accounts Payable

If credit is used properly, it can be very helpful to a business. However, credit can also present a danger. Some firms take on too much debt, find that their cash flow is not adequate to pay bills as they become due, and eventually go bankrupt.

accounts payable Amounts that a firm owes for goods or services purchased on credit.

vendors The businesses or individuals to whom accounts payable are owed. Also called creditors or suppliers.

accounts payable ledger A subsidiary ledger that contains accounts for vendors. Also called the vendors ledger.

Every firm that buys on credit should have procedures in place to ensure that it—

- Pays vendors on time in order to maintain a good credit reputation.
- Takes advantage of discounts whenever they are offered.
- Keeps the total amount owed to vendors from becoming too high in relation to the firm's resources.

Peachtree assists firms in managing their accounts payable by providing a means of quickly and efficiently recording purchases and cash payments and by generating a wide variety of accounts payable reports. Peachtree produces 16 reports that can be used to closely monitor the status of the accounts payable. Another helpful feature of Peachtree is the Action Items function, which can be programmed to alert you to actions that must be taken in connection with vendor accounts.

OBJECTIVE 1 — Create Subsidiary Ledger Accounts for Vendors and Enter the Beginning Balances

In chapters 2 and 3, you learned how to set up general ledger accounts and enter the beginning balances. The procedure for establishing vendor accounts in the accounts payable ledger is very similar. In this chapter, you will use Peachtree to handle the accounts payable of Superior Carpet and Tile.

Superior is a small service business that operates on the accrual basis. In chapter 4, you established customer accounts for this firm and recorded its credit sales.

Information Needed to Create the Vendor Accounts

In Peachtree, certain information is needed to create an account for each vendor in the accounts payable subsidiary ledger. This information, which is entered in the Maintain Vendors window (see figure 5–1), is outlined below.

FIGURE 5–1

Maintain Vendors Blank Window with General Folder Tab Selected

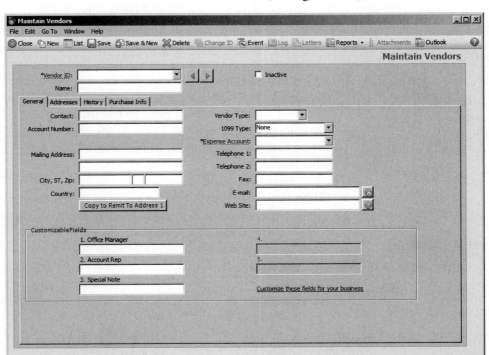

- **Vendor ID**

  Peachtree requires an alphanumeric identifier for each vendor's account. For example, Superior Carpet and Tile uses JCM-001 as the identifier for the first account in its accounts payable subsidiary ledger. This account is for John Charles Management.
- **Name**

  The name given to a vendor's account may be the name of a business, such as John Charles Management, or the name of an individual.
- **Inactive**

  Sometimes a company stops doing business with a vendor. A check mark is entered in the *Inactive* box to indicate this type of vendor. Peachtree automatically removes the accounts of inactive vendors when the fiscal year is closed.

General Tab

- **Contact**

  The contact is the person whom the business calls or writes in connection with questions about orders.
- **Account Number**

  The account number is the numeric identifier the vendor has issued to the company.
- **Mailing Address**

  The address entered in the account is the one where the vendor receives checks and correspondence.
- **Vendor Type**

  Peachtree allows you to classify vendors by type. For example, many companies have vendors that provide services and vendors that provide goods. Superior uses Expense as the type for vendors that provide services and Supplier as the type for vendors that provide goods and supplies.
- **1099 Type**

  It is necessary to issue Form 1099, a tax form, to certain types of vendors. For example, some vendors are individuals who provide their services on a project-by-project basis. These individuals are considered independent contractors rather than part-time employees. By January 31 of each year, the Internal Revenue Service requires that a company issue a Form 1099 to each independent contractor for tax reasons. This form shows the amount paid to the independent contractor during the previous year. A copy of Form 1099 goes to the IRS. (If the company pays less than $600 to an independent contractor, it need not issue a Form 1099.)
- **Expense Account**

  The Expense Account is the account in the general ledger that is debited when a purchase is made from a particular vendor. As noted previously, a purchase of a service such as electricity is debited to an expense account. A purchase of an asset such as office supplies is debited to an asset account. A purchase of goods for resale is debited to a cost account called Purchases or debited directly to an Inventory account. The number of the appropriate general ledger account is entered in each vendor's account.

- **Telephone/Fax Numbers**
  Peachtree provides space for recording two telephone numbers and a fax number in each vendor's account.
- **E-mail**
  Enter the customer's e-mail address in this field for correspondence. E-mail can be sent by clicking the E-mail button to the right of the *E-mail* field.
- **Web Site**
  Enter the customer's Web site address in this field. The customer's Web site can be displayed by clicking the Internet button to the right of the *Web Site* field.

Custom Fields

- **Office Manager**
  In some cases, a business will want to enter the name of the vendor's office manager as a second contact person.
- **Account Rep**
  Some vendors assign a sales representative to each of their customers. The name of the sales representative is entered in the vendor's account.
- **Special Note**
  Any additional information about the vendor that is needed can be entered in the *Special Note* field.

Addresses Tab

- Default addresses are selected using the Address Defaults drop-down boxes. Specific addresses can be selected for Payments, Purchase Orders, and Shipments.

History Tab

- **Vendor Since**
  Some businesses enter the date of the first order issued to the vendor.
- **Last Invoice Date**
  Some businesses enter the date of the last invoice received from the vendor.
- **Last Invoice Amt**
  Some businesses enter the amount of the last invoice received from the vendor.
- **Last Payment Date**
  Some businesses enter the date of the last payment made to the vendor.
- **Last Payment Amt**
  Some businesses enter the amount of the last payment made to the vendor.
- **Period, Payments, Purchases Grid**
  This section gives the user running totals of purchases and payments.
- **Vendor Beginning Balances**
  When a business creates accounts for its vendors, there may be some outstanding (unpaid) invoices. Information about these invoices is needed to enter the beginning balances in the accounts.

Purchase Info Tab

- **Purchase Rep**
  The Purchase Rep is used to select the purchaser's representative to the vendor.
- **Tax ID Number**
  The tax identification number is the number of the resale certificate (the sales tax exemption certificate) that the vendor may have. This number is entered in the vendor's account. It is also the number used to identify a vendor on a Form 1099.
- **Ship Via**
  The vendor may have a preferred method of shipping. The method chosen should be entered in the vendor's account.
- **Terms and Credit**
  Each vendor specifies certain credit terms. For example, one vendor might offer terms of 2% 10 days, net 30 days. Another vendor might offer terms of net EOM, which means that the full amount of a bill is due at the end of the month in which the bill is issued. The terms are entered in the vendor's account. (Standard vendor terms can be established as a default when a company is set up in Peachtree. These terms can be changed as necessary for individual vendors.)
- **Form Options**
  The Form Option allows the user to deliver paper or e-mail forms. E-mail can be carbon copied (CC) to the purchase rep.

Creating Subsidiary Ledger Accounts for Vendors

In this section, you will create subsidiary ledger accounts for four vendors of Superior Carpet and Tile. Start Peachtree and then open Superior Carpet and Tile (Chp. 5 - Superior Carpet and Tile if student data disk is used). Then follow the steps outlined below to create a subsidiary ledger account for John Charles Management.

Step 1:
Click Maintain, and then click *Vendors*.

Step 2:
Click the General folder tab in the Maintain Vendors window. Set up the account information for John Charles Management, the first vendor of Superior Carpet and Tile, by taking the following steps:

Step 3:
Key **JCM-001** in the *Vendor ID* field.

Step 4:
Click the OK button at the bottom of the Vendor ID drop-down list, as shown in figure 5–2.

FIGURE 5–2
Vendor ID Drop-Down
List with JCM-001
Entered

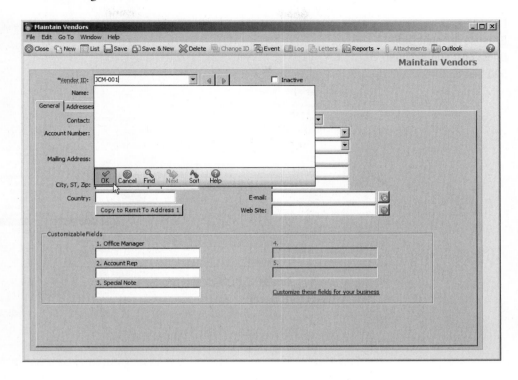

Step 5:
Key **John Charles Management** in the *Name* field.

Step 6:
If there is a check mark in the *Inactive* box, remove it because John Charles Management is an active vendor.

Step 7:
Key **John Charles** in the *Contact* field.

Step 8:
Key **2800** in the *Account Number* field.

Step 9:
Key **1320 Washington Street** in the *Mailing Address* field.

Step 10:
Key **Sacramento, CA 95760** in the *City, ST, Zip* field, **USA** in the *Country* field, and select "Copy to Remit to Address 1."

Step 11:
Key **Expense** in the *Vendor Type* field.

Step 12:
At the 1099 Type drop-down list, click *None*.

Step 13:
At the Expense Account drop-down list, select *Account 500, Rent Expense*, as shown in figure 5–3.

FIGURE 5–3
Expense Account Drop-Down List with Account 500 Selected

Step 14:
Key **916-555-2456** in the *Telephone 1* field.

Step 15:
Key **916-555-7890** in the *Telephone 2* field.

Step 16:
Key **916-555-3846** in the *Fax* field.

Step 17:
Compare your completed window with figure 5–4. Make any necessary corrections by selecting the erroneous items and reentering the information.

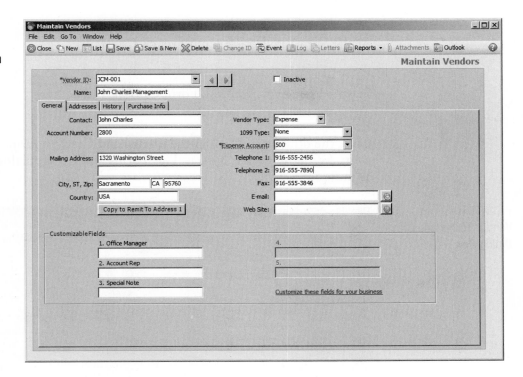

Purchase Info Tab
The purchase defaults must be established whenever a vendor's account is created.

Step 1:
Click the Purchase Info folder tab, as shown in figure 5–5.

FIGURE 5–5
Maintain Vendors
Window with Purchase
Info Tab Selected

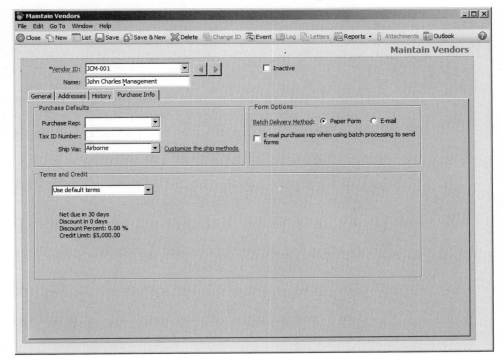

Step 2:
Leave the *Purchase Rep* and *Tax ID Number* fields blank.

Step 3:
At the Ship Via drop-down list, click *US Mail.*

Step 4:
Select *Paper Form* from the Form Options box.

Step 5:
Click the down arrow key in the Terms and Credit box and then select *Customize terms for this vendor.* The Terms and Credit dialog box will appear as in figure 5–6.

FIGURE 5–6
Vendor Terms and Credit Dialog Box

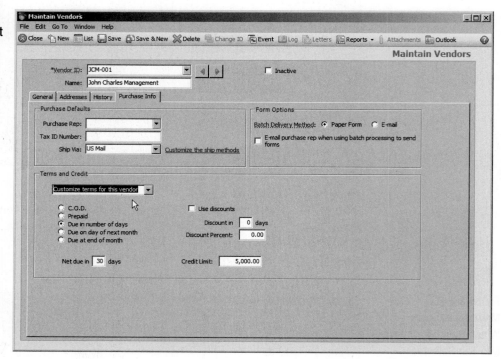

As noted previously, credit terms may vary from vendor to vendor. In addition, each vendor may set a credit limit. The Terms and Credit dialog box is used to change the credit terms and credit limit whenever necessary.

Step 6:
Click the radio button next to *Due at end of month.* These are the terms offered by John Charles Management.

Step 7:
Deselect *Use discounts* if checked. Generally, only vendors of supplies or other goods allow a discount.

Step 8:
Compare your entry with the completed Terms and Credit dialog box as in figure 5–7.

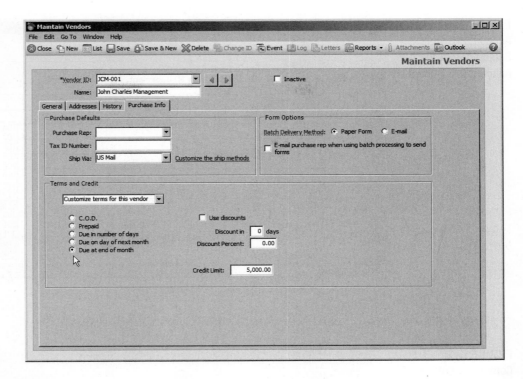

Step 9:
Click the Save button to accept the changes in the vendor terms.

Beginning Balances

Step 1:
Click the History folder tab in the Maintain Vendors window.

Step 2:
Click the Vendor Beginning Balances button at the bottom of the window.

Step 3:
Click the Purchases from: JCM-001 John Charles Management folder tab.
Then key **Beginning Balance** in the *Invoice Number* field.

Step 4:
Key **01/01/10** in the *Date* field.

Step 5:
Key **900.00** in the *Amount* field.

Step 6:
Click *Accounts Payable (200)* from the A/P Account drop-down list, as shown
in figure 5–8.

Step 7:
Compare your entries with those in figure 5–9.

FIGURE 5-9
Completed Entries
in Vendor Beginning
Balances Window

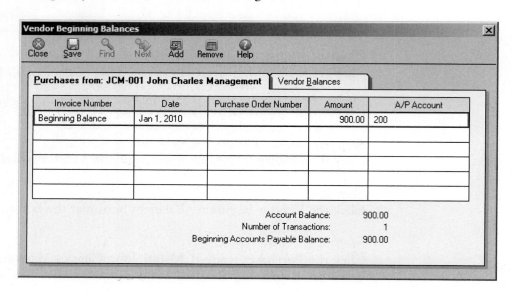

Step 8:
Click the Save button, and then click the Close button.

Step 9:
Click the History folder tab to view the current balance for the selected vendor, as shown in figure 5–10.

FIGURE 5–10
History Window

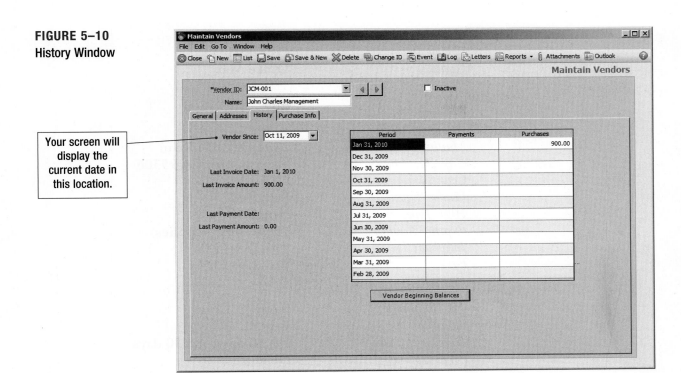

Your screen will display the current date in this location.

Create the following three vendor accounts for Superior Carpet and Tile using the information given below and enter their beginning balances as of January 1, 2010. Use the steps that you followed for the account of John Charles Management. When you complete your work, close the Maintain Vendors window.

Vendor

Vendor ID:	**MID-002**
Name:	**MID Midtown Irrigation District**

General Tab

Contact:	**Harvey Bliss**
Account Number:	**3548**
Mailing Address:	**2356 Orangethorpe Street**
City, ST, Zip:	**Sacramento, CA 95506**
Country:	**USA**
Vendor Type:	**Expense**
1099 Type:	**None**
Expense Account:	**502 (Utilities Expense)**
Telephone 1:	**916-555-6675**
Fax:	**916-555-9008**

Purchase Info Tab

Tax ID Number:	**None**
Ship Via:	**US Mail**
Terms and Credit:	**Net 30 Days (Use default terms)**
Form Options:	**Default**

History Tab

Beginning Balance:	**450.00**

Vendor

Vendor ID:	**OFF-003**
Name:	**Office Max**

General Tab

Contact:	**Bill Baker**
Account Number:	**2778**
Mailing Address:	**2532 Oakdale Road**
City, ST, Zip:	**Sacramento, CA 95306**
Country:	**USA**
Vendor Type:	**Supplier**
1099 Type:	**None**
Expense Account:	**108 (Office Supplies)**
Telephone 1:	**916-555-1978**
Fax:	**916-555-2334**

Purchase Info Tab

Tax ID Number:	**None**
Ship Via:	**Fed-Ex**
Terms and Credit:	**2% 10 days, net 30 days**
Form Options:	**Default**

History Tab

Beginning Balance:	**450.00**

Vendor

Vendor ID:	**PAC-004**
Name:	**Pacific Bell**

General Tab

Contact:	**Customer Service**
Account Number:	**2379**
Mailing Address:	**3234 Airport Road**
City, ST, Zip:	**Sacramento, CA 95670**
Country:	**USA**
Vendor Type:	**Expense**
1099 Type:	**None**
Expense Account:	**514 (Miscellaneous Expense)**
Telephone 1:	**916-555-2556**
Fax:	**916-555-9998**

Purchase Info Tab

Tax ID Number:	**None**
Ship Via:	**US Mail**
Terms and Credit:	**Net 30 Days (Use default terms)**
Form Options:	**Default**

History Tab

Beginning Balance:	**500.00**

Practice Objective 1

Create subsidiary ledger accounts for the vendors of Meadowland Healthcare Services.

Step 1:
Open Meadowland Healthcare Services (Chp. 5 – Meadowland Healthcare Services if student data disk is used).

Step 2:
Create the vendor accounts, and enter the beginning balances.

Vendor

Vendor ID:	**ALT-001**
Name:	**Alta Vista Business Park**

General Tab

Contact:	**Alicia Marquez**
Account Number:	**3900**
Mailing Address:	**1325 Smith Road**
City, ST, Zip:	**Lodi, CA 95355**
Country:	**USA**
Vendor Type:	**Expense**
1099 Type:	**None**
Expense Account:	**50000 (Rent Expense)** *Create the account.*
Telephone 1:	**209-555-4256**
Fax:	**209-555-8346**

Purchase Info Tab

Tax ID Number:	**None**
Ship Via:	**US Mail**
Terms and Credit:	**Net 30 Days (Use default terms)**
Form Options:	**Default**

History Tab

Beginning Balance:	**0**

Vendor

Vendor ID:	**PGE-002**
Name:	**Pacific Gas & Electric**

General Tab

Contact:	**George House**
Account Number:	**345566**
Mailing Address:	**3423 Mission Street**
City, ST, Zip:	**Sacramento, CA 95655**
Country:	**USA**
Vendor Type:	**Expense**
1099 Type:	**None**
Expense Account:	**50200 (Utilities Expense)**
Telephone 1:	**916-555-9905**
Fax:	**916-555-0008**

Purchase Info Tab

Tax ID Number:	**None**
Ship Via:	**US Mail**
Terms and Credit:	**Net 30 Days (Use default terms)**
Form Options:	**Default**

History Tab

Beginning Balance:	**0**

Vendor

Vendor ID:	**OFD-003**
Name:	**Office Depot**

General Tab

Contact:	**Jim Nielson**
Account Number:	**3465**
Mailing Address:	**125 Oak Road**
City, ST, Zip:	**Sacramento, CA 95655**
Country:	**USA**
Vendor Type:	**Supplier**
1099 Type:	**None**
Expense Account:	**10800 (Office Supplies)**
Telephone 1:	**916-555-9178**
Fax:	**916-555-3234**

Purchase Info Tab

Tax ID Number:	**None**
Ship Via:	**Fed-Ex**
Terms and Credit:	**2% 10 days, net 30 Days**
Form Options:	**Default**

History Tab

Beginning Balance:	**0**

Vendor

Vendor ID:	**GTE-004**
Name:	**General Telephone**

General Tab

Contact:	**Customer Service**
Account Number:	**391345**
Mailing Address:	**32133 Tuolumne Road**
City, ST, Zip:	**Sacramento, CA 95655**
Country:	**USA**
Vendor Type:	**Expense**
1099 Type:	**None**
Expense Account:	**50200 (Utilities Expense)**
Telephone 1:	**916-555-2545**
Fax:	**916-555-9945**

Purchase Info Tab

Tax ID Number:	**None**
Ship Via:	**US Mail**
Terms and Credit:	**Net 30 Days (Use default terms)**
Form Options:	**Default**

History Tab

Beginning Balance:	**0**

Step 3:
Close the Maintain Vendors window.

OBJECTIVE 2 — Process Accounts Payable and Purchase Transactions

Once the vendor accounts have been established, Peachtree can be used to record purchases on credit and post them automatically to the accounts payable subsidiary ledger. Remember that each purchase is credited to Accounts Payable. The account debited may be an asset account, an expense account, or a cost account, depending on the nature of the purchase. When the bill for a purchase becomes due, the payment is debited to Accounts Payable and credited to Cash.

If there is an accounts payable ledger, each purchase requires a credit to both the Accounts Payable controlling account in the general ledger and the vendor's account in the subsidiary ledger. Similarly, each payment to a vendor requires a debit to both the Accounts Payable controlling account in the general ledger and the vendor's account in the subsidiary ledger.

It is possible to record purchases of goods and services on credit in the general journal. However, the general journal function of Peachtree does not permit the automatic posting of entries to the vendor accounts. Therefore, in this chapter, you will use the purchases function of Peachtree to record purchases of goods and services. This function, which is called Purchases/ Receive Inventory, allows automatic posting to both the general ledger and the accounts payable subsidiary ledger.

Recording Purchases on Credit

During January 2010, Superior Carpet and Tile conducted three transactions that involved the purchase of services and one transaction that involved the purchase of supplies.

- On January 3, 2010, Superior received a bill (Invoice 2621) from John Charles Management for its monthly rent of $2,100. The bill is payable at the end of the month.

The accountant's analysis of this transaction reveals that an expense (Rent Expense) has increased by $2,100 and a liability (Accounts Payable) has increased by $2,100. The account for John Charles Management has also increased by $2,100. The accountant records this transaction by debiting Rent Expense for $2,100 and crediting Accounts Payable for $2,100.

When you post this transaction, you must post the credit part of the entry to both the Accounts Payable controlling account in the general ledger and the vendor's account in the accounts payable subsidiary ledger.

Use the steps outlined below to record this purchase on credit made by Superior Carpet and Tile during January 2010.

Step 1:
Open Chp. 5 – Superior Carpet and Tile which you updated previously in the chapter and close the Action Items window, if open.

Step 2:
Click Tasks, and then click *Purchases/Receive Inventory*.

The Purchases/Receive Inventory window will appear, as shown in figure 5–11. Enter the data for the purchase on credit that occurred on January 3, 2010.

FIGURE 5–11
Blank Purchases/Receive
Inventory Window

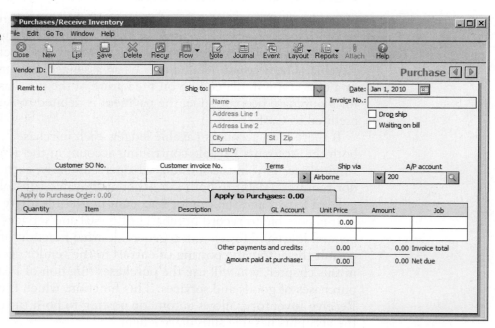

Step 3:
Click the *magnifying glass* icon next to the *Vendor ID* field.

Step 4:

Highlight *JCM-001* from the drop-down list of vendors, as shown in figure 5–12.

FIGURE 5–12
Drop-Down List of
Vendors with JCM-001
Highlighted

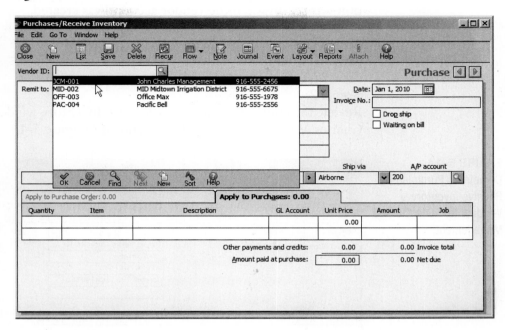

Step 5:

Click OK at the bottom of the drop-down list of vendors to accept JCM-001. Peachtree enters the name and address automatically.

Step 6:

Click the *calendar* icon to the right of the *Date* field and select *Jan 3, 2010*.

Step 7:

Key **2621** in the *Invoice No.* field.

Step 8:

The credit terms are selected when the vendor accounts are originally created. To view the terms for John Charles Management, click the right arrow key in the *Terms* field. You will then see the Terms Information dialog box, as shown in figure 5–13. Click OK after viewing the terms.

FIGURE 5–13
Terms Information
Dialog Box

Step 9:

Key **Monthly Rent** in the *Description* field.

Step 10:

Click *500 (Rent Expense)* from the drop-down list of general ledger accounts. The GL Account information should already be completed. This information was set up when the vendor account was created.

Step 11:

Key **2,100.00** in the *Amount* field.

Step 12:

Review the completed Purchases/Receive Inventory window for John Charles Management, JCM-001 as shown in figure 5–14.

FIGURE 5–14
Completed Purchases/ Receive Inventory Window for John Charles Management

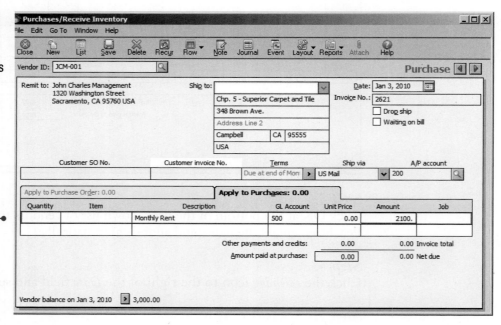

HINT

When there is no quantity and unit price, leave those fields blank and simply enter the total of the vendor's bill in the *Amount* field.

Step 13:

Click the <u>S</u>ave button to save the entry of the purchase on credit.

Step 14:

Repeat steps 3–13 to enter the following three purchases that Superior Carpet and Tile had during January 2010.

• On January 10, 2010, Superior received a bill (Invoice 4763) of $226.65 from MID Midtown Irrigation District for its monthly usage of electricity. The bill is payable net 30 days.

The accountant's analysis of this transaction reveals that an expense (Utilities Expense) has increased by $226.65 and a liability (Accounts Payable) has increased by $226.65. The account for MID Midtown Irrigation District has also increased by $226.65. The accountant records this transaction by debiting Utilities Expense for $226.65 and crediting Accounts Payable for $226.65.

• On January 12, 2010, Superior received a bill (Invoice 2867) of $265.39 from Pacific Bell for special repair services. The bill is payable net 30 days.

The accountant's analysis of this transaction reveals that an expense (Miscellaneous Expense) has increased by $265.39 and a liability (Accounts Payable) has increased by $265.39. The account for Pacific Bell has also increased by $265.39. The accountant records this transaction by debiting Miscellaneous Expense for $265.39 and crediting Accounts Payable for $265.39.

- On January 29, 2010, Superior received a bill (Invoice 3556) from Office Max for $1,400 of office supplies. The bill has terms of 2% 10 days, net 30 days.

The accountant's analysis of this transaction reveals that an asset (Office Supplies) has increased by $1,400 and a liability (Accounts Payable) has increased by $1,400. The account for Office Max has also increased by $1,400. The accountant records this transaction by debiting Office Supplies for $1,400 and crediting Accounts Payable for $1,400.

Editing Accounts Payable Transactions

Accounts payable transactions can be edited as necessary after they are entered. Follow the steps outlined below to edit a particular transaction.

Step 1:
Click List from the toolbar at the top of the Purchases/Receive Inventory window.

Step 2:
At the Date Range drop-down list, click *All Transactions*.

Step 3:
Select the entry for John Charles Management as shown in figure 5–15. (Notice that its window contains a *Status* section, which shows that the four bills recorded in January are unpaid.) Click Open from the top of the Purchase List toolbar.

FIGURE 5–15
Purchase List (Edit) Window with John Charles Management Selected

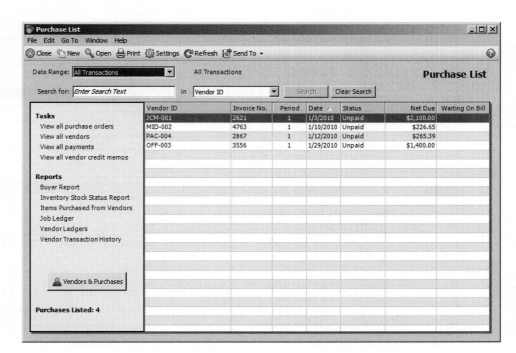

Step 4:

The entry appears in the Purchases/Receive Inventory window and can be edited if necessary. For example, if there is an error in the date, invoice number, or amount, you can change it now. When your work is complete, click Save. Then close the Purchases/Receive Inventory window.

Step 5:

Close the Purchase List window.

Printing the Vendor Ledgers Report

Peachtree produces a wide variety of accounts payable reports. All of these reports will be covered to some extent throughout this text. The *Vendor Ledgers* report is probably the most important of the accounts payable reports. This report shows all transactions with the vendors and the balances owed to them. Use the following steps to view and print the *Vendor Ledgers* report.

Step 1:

Click Reports & Forms, and then click *Accounts Payable*.

Step 2:

At the Select a Report or Form dialog box, in the Accounts Payable: Vendor and Purchases section, click *Vendor Ledgers*, as shown in figure 5–16.

FIGURE 5–16
Accounts Payable:
Vendors and Purchases
Report List with Vendor
Ledgers Selected

Step 3:

Click the Options button so that you can view the *Vendor Ledgers* report.

Step 4:

At the Modify Report – Vendor Ledgers window, in the *Date* field, click *Range* and then *Jan 1, 2010* to *Jan 31, 2010* as the period to be covered. Click OK (figure 5–17).

FIGURE 5–17
Modify Report – Vendor
Ledgers Window

Step 5:

Examine the *Vendor Ledgers* report, as shown in figure 5–18. Use the scroll bar to make sure that the four purchases recorded in January appear in the report. (The abbreviation *PJ* in the report stands for purchases journal.)

FIGURE 5–18
Vendor Ledgers
Report

Page: 1

Chp. 5 - Superior Carpet and Tile
Vendor Ledgers
For the Period From Jan 1, 2010 to Jan 31, 2010

Filter Criteria includes: Report order is by ID.

Vendor ID Vendor	Date	Trans No	Type	Paid	Debit Amt	Credit Amt	Balance
JCM-001	1/1/10	Beginning Bala	PJ			900.00	900.00
John Charles Manageme	1/3/10	2621	PJ			2,100.00	3,000.00
MID-002	1/1/10	Beginning Bala	PJ			450.00	450.00
MID Midtown Irrigation Di	1/10/10	4763	PJ			226.65	676.65
OFF-003	1/1/10	Beginning Bala	PJ			450.00	450.00
Office Max	1/29/10	3556	PJ			1,400.00	1,850.00
PAC-004	1/1/10	Beginning Bala	PJ			500.00	500.00
Pacific Bell	1/12/10	2867	PJ			265.39	765.39
Report Total						**6,292.04**	**6,292.04**

Step 6:

Click <u>P</u>rint to print a copy of the *Vendor Ledgers* report.

Practice Objective 2

You previously created vendor accounts for Meadowland Healthcare Services. Now you will record purchases on credit for this firm.

Step 1:
Open Chp. 5 – Meadowland Healthcare Services which you updated previously in the chapter.

Step 2:
Record the following transactions:
- On January 2, 2010, Meadowland Healthcare Services received a bill (Invoice 012301) from Alta Vista Business Park for its monthly rent of $1,200.
- On January 10, 2010, Meadowland received a bill (Invoice 98345) of $345.89 from Pacific Gas & Electric for its monthly usage of electricity.
- On January 18, 2010, Meadowland received a bill (Invoice 55665) from Office Depot for $890 of office supplies.
- On January 27, 2010, Meadowland Healthcare Services received a bill (Invoice 645935) of $265.98 from General Telephone for its monthly usage of telephone service (Utilities Expense).

Step 3:
Print the *Vendor Ledgers* report for the month of January 2010. Check the accuracy of your work by comparing your report to the report shown in figure 5–19.

FIGURE 5–19
Vendor Ledgers
Report for
Meadowland
Healthcare Services

Chp. 5 - Meadowland Healthcare Services
Vendor Ledgers
For the Period From Jan 1, 2010 to Jan 31, 2010
Page: 1

Filter Criteria includes: Report order is by ID.

Vendor ID Vendor	Date	Trans No	Type	Paid	Debit Amt	Credit Amt	Balance
ALT-001 Alta Vista Business Park	1/2/10	012301	PJ			1,200.00	1,200.00
GTE-004 General Telephone	1/27/10	645935	PJ			265.98	265.98
OFD-003 Office Depot	1/18/10	55665	PJ			890.00	890.00
PGE-002 Pacific Gas & Electric	1/10/10	98345	PJ			345.89	345.89
Report Total						**2,701.87**	**2,701.87**

Step 4:
Close the Select a Report dialog box.

OBJECTIVE 3 — Printing Accounts Payable Reports

Peachtree can produce the following accounts payable reports and many others.

- Vendor List
- Vendor Master File List
- Vendor Ledgers
- Purchase Order Report

- Purchase Journal
- Aged Payables
- 1099 Vendor Report

Assume that the management of Superior Carpet and Tile wants to print two of these reports: the *Vendor List* and the *Vendor Ledgers*.

Step 1:
Click Reports & Forms, and then click *Accounts Payable*.

Step 2:
The Select a Report or Form dialog box will appear. At the Accounts Payable: Vendors and Purchases section, click *Vendor List*, as shown in figure 5–20.

FIGURE 5–20

Accounts Payable: Vendors and Purchases List with Vendor List Selected

Step 3:
Click the <u>P</u>rint button on the Select a Report or Form toolbar.

Step 4:
At the Modify Report – Vendor List window, in the Select a filter scroll-down list, click *Vendor ID*, as shown in figure 5–21, and then click OK.

FIGURE 5–21

Vendor ID Selected
from Select a Filter
Scroll-Down List

Step 5:

Complete the Print window, and then click OK to print. Compare your *Vendor List* report with the one shown in figure 5–22.

FIGURE 5–22

Vendor List Report
for Superior Carpet
and Tile

Page: 1

Chp. 5 - Superior Carpet and Tile
Vendor List

Filter Criteria includes: Report order is by ID.

Vendor ID	Vendor	Contact	Telephone 1	Tax Id No
JCM-001	John Charles Management	John Charles	916-555-2456	
MID-002	MID Midtown Irrigation Dist	Harvey Bliss	916-555-6675	
OFF-003	Office Max	Bill Baker	916-555-1978	
PAC-004	Pacific Bell	Customer Service	916-555-2556	

Step 6:

Repeat steps 1–5 to print a copy of the *Vendor Ledgers* report. In step 2, click *Vendor Ledgers* and then select *Jan 1, 2010* to *Jan 31, 2010* as the range. Compare your printed report with the one shown in figure 5–23.

FIGURE 5–23

Vendor Ledgers
Report for Superior
Carpet and Tile

Page: 1

Chp. 5 - Superior Carpet and Tile
Vendor Ledgers
For the Period From Jan 1, 2010 to Jan 31, 2010

Filter Criteria includes: Report order is by ID.

Vendor ID Vendor	Date	Trans No	Type	Paid	Debit Amt	Credit Amt	Balance
JCM-001	1/1/10	Beginning Bala	PJ			900.00	900.00
John Charles Manageme	1/3/10	2621	PJ			2,100.00	3,000.00
MID-002	1/1/10	Beginning Bala	PJ			450.00	450.00
MID Midtown Irrigation Di	1/10/10	4763	PJ			226.65	676.65
OFF-003	1/1/10	Beginning Bala	PJ			450.00	450.00
Office Max	1/29/10	3556	PJ			1,400.00	1,850.00
PAC-004	1/1/10	Beginning Bala	PJ			500.00	500.00
Pacific Bell	1/12/10	2867	PJ			265.39	765.39
Report Total						**6,292.04**	**6,292.04**

Step 7:
Close the Select a Report or Form dialog box.

C h e c k   p o i n t

1. What is the purpose of the Vendor List?
2. What is the purpose of the Vendor Ledgers report?

Answers
1. *The Vendor List lists all active and inactive vendors.*
2. *The Vendor Ledgers reports payment and balance information for each vendor.*

P r a c t i c e   O b j e c t i v e   3

You previously established vendor accounts for Meadowland Healthcare Services and recorded purchases. Now you will print reports.

Step 1:
Open Chp. 5 – Meadowland Healthcare Services and enter the following action items related to vendors:

- On January 14, 2010, call General Telephone about its new rate plan.
- On January 15, 2010, call to set up a meeting with Alicia Marquez of Alta Vista Business Park.
- On January 18, 2010, call Office Depot to check the price of a new computer.

Step 2:
Print the *Vendor List* report. (See figure 5–24.)

FIGURE 5–24
Vendor List Report for Meadowland Healthcare Services

Page: 1

Chp. 5 - Meadowland Healthcare Services
Vendor List

Filter Criteria includes: Report order is by ID.

Vendor ID	Vendor	Contact	Telephone 1	Tax Id No
ALT-001	Alta Vista Business Park	Alicia Marquez	916-555-4256	
GTE-004	General Telephone	Customer Service	916-555-2545	
OFD-003	Office Depot	Jim Nielson	916-555-9178	
PGE-002	Pacific Gas & Electric	George House	916-555-9905	

Step 3:

Print the *Vendor Ledgers* report. (See figure 5–25.)

FIGURE 5–25
Vendor Ledgers
Report for
Meadowland
Healthcare Services

Page: 1

Chp. 5 - Meadowland Healthcare Services
Vendor Ledgers
For the Period From Jan 1, 2010 to Jan 31, 2010

Filter Criteria includes: Report order is by ID.

Vendor ID Vendor	Date	Trans No	Type	Paid	Debit Amt	Credit Amt	Balance
ALT-001 Alta Vista Business Park	1/2/10	012301	PJ			1,200.00	1,200.00
GTE-004 General Telephone	1/27/10	645935	PJ			265.98	265.98
OFD-003 Office Depot	1/18/10	55665	PJ			890.00	890.00
PGE-002 Pacific Gas & Electric	1/10/10	98345	PJ			345.89	345.89
Report Total						**2,701.87**	**2,701.87**

Step 4:

Close the Select a Report or Form dialog box.

End of Chapter Review

Software Command Summary

Create Vendor Accounts	Maintain, Vendors, General Tab, Purchase Info Tab, History Tab, Enter Beginning Balances
Accounts Payable and Purchases Transactions	Tasks, Purchases/Receive Inventory

Projects And Problems

Content Check

Multiple Choice: Choose only one response for each question.

1. Purchases made on credit are entered in the accounting records as
   A. accounts receivable.
   B. accounts payable.
   C. prepaid expense.
   D. unearned revenue.
   E. None of the above

2. When a business purchases a service such as electricity on credit, the two types of accounts affected from the buyer's perspective are
   A. an asset account and an expense account.
   B. an asset account and a revenue account.
   C. a liability account and an expense account.
   D. a liability account and a revenue account.
   E. None of the above

3. What function of Peachtree is used when a business buys goods or services on credit and must enter the transaction?
   A. Action Items
   B. Purchases/Receive Inventory
   C. Receipts
   D. Sales/Invoicing
   E. None of the above

4. Which accounts payable report contains information about all transactions with vendors and the balances owed to them?
   A. *Vendor List*
   B. *Check Register*
   C. *Customer Ledgers*
   D. *Vendor Ledgers*
   E. None of the above

5. Which general ledger account is credited to record a company's purchases on credit?
   A. Cash
   B. Accounts Payable
   C. Accounts Receivable
   D. Purchases
   E. None of the above

Short Essay Response: Provide a detailed answer for each question.

1. What are the advantages and disadvantages to a business when it purchases goods and services on credit?
2. What is the purpose of the accounts payable subsidiary ledger?
3. How does the Accounts Payable controlling account in the general ledger relate to the accounts payable subsidiary ledger?
4. Why should a business closely monitor its accounts payable?
5. Briefly explain how a purchase can be edited after it has been posted.

Case Problems

Problem 1A

Open Professional Accounting Concepts from the student data disk. The owner has decided to set up vendor accounts and purchase goods and services on credit.

1. Create a subsidiary ledger account for the following vendors dated 01/01/10.

Vendor
Vendor ID:	**JMC-01**
Name:	**JMC Management Group**

General Tab
Contact:	**Annette Bradley**
Account Number:	**1178**
Mailing Address:	**41374 Lincoln Boulevard**
City, ST, Zip:	**Stockton, CA 95210**
Country:	**USA**
Vendor Type:	**Expense**
1099 Type:	**None**
Expense Account:	**75000 (Rent or Lease Expense)**
Telephone 1:	**209-555-3349**
Fax:	**209-555-3352**

Purchase Info Tab
Tax ID Number:	**None**
Ship Via:	**US Mail**
Terms and Credit:	**Net 30 Days**
Form Options:	**Default**

History Tab
Beginning Balance:	**1,100.00**

Vendor

Vendor ID:	**SW-02**
Name:	**Stockton Water District**

General Tab

Contact:	**Robert Henderson**
Account Number:	**95845**
Mailing Address:	**3159 Madison Avenue**
City, ST, Zip:	**Stockton, CA 95210**
Country:	**USA**
Vendor Type:	**Expense**
1099 Type:	**None**
Expense Account:	**78500 (Utilities Expense)**
Telephone 1:	**209-555-4738**
Fax:	**209-555-4750**

Purchase Info Tab

Tax ID Number:	**None**
Ship Via:	**US Mail**
Terms and Credit:	**Net 30 Days**
Form Options:	**Default**

History Tab

Beginning Balance:	**820.00**

Vendor

Vendor ID:	**OFFMAX-03**
Name:	**Office Max**

General Tab

Contact:	**Joshua Baker**
Account Number:	**61345**
Mailing Address:	**3915 Webber Lane**
City, ST, Zip:	**Stockton, CA 95207**
Country:	**USA**
Vendor Type:	**Supplier**
1099 Type:	**None**
Expense Account:	**12000 (Office Supplies)**
Telephone 1:	**209-555-7981**
Fax:	**209-555-7988**

Purchase Info Tab

Tax ID Number:	**None**
Ship Via:	**Fed-Ex**
Terms and Credit:	**2% 10 days, net 30 days**
Form Options:	**Default**

History Tab

Beginning Balance:	**2,400.00**

Vendor

Vendor ID:	**PACBELL-04**
Name:	**Pacific Bell**

General Tab

Contact:	**Barbara Sinclair**
Account Number:	**127648**
Mailing Address:	**6581 East Montgomery Avenue**
City, ST, Zip:	**Stockton, CA 95207**
Country:	**USA**
Vendor Type:	**Expense**
1099 Type:	**None**
Expense Account:	**79000 (Telephone Expense)**
Telephone 1:	**209-555-7890**
Fax:	**209-555-7900**

Purchase Info Tab

Tax ID Number:	**None**
Ship Via:	**US Mail**
Terms and Credit:	**Net 30 Days**
Form Options:	**Default**

History Tab

Beginning Balance:	**600.00**

HINT

To change accounting period:
- Click Tasks
- Click System
- Change Accounting Period
- Select *02-Feb 01, 2010* to *Feb 28, 2010*
- Click OK
- Select No to query

---

2. Change the accounting period to *Feb 1, 2010 to Feb 28, 2010*.

3. Enter each of the following transactions for February 2010. Note that this business has three different sources of revenue: accounting fees, tax preparation fees, and consulting fees. Therefore, be sure that you select the number of the correct revenue account in the GL Sales Account section of the Sales/Invoicing window. (The customer accounts have been set up with a GL Sales Account default to Account 40000, Accounting Fees.) Services performed on account will be entered in the Sales/Invoicing window, and purchases on account in the Purchases/ Receive Inventory window.

Date	Transaction
Feb. 3	Received a bill (Invoice 16475) of $1580 for monthly rent from JMC Management Group.
4	Received a bill (Invoice 62351) of $65 for monthly usage of water from Stockton Water District.
5	Performed accounting services for $620 on credit for Johnson Manufacturing. Issued Invoice 1006.
5	Received a bill (Invoice 51956) of $125 for monthly usage of telephone service from Pacific Bell.
8	Performed accounting services for $450 on credit for Computer Expertise. Issued Invoice 1007.
10	Purchased office supplies for $340 on credit from Office Max. Received Invoice 4891.

	Date	Transaction

Date   Transaction

Feb. 14   Performed accounting services for $650 on credit for Stephanie's Catering. Issued Invoice 1008. Received Check No. 461 for $325 from the customer.

17   Purchased office supplies for $234 on credit from Office Max. Received Invoice 5216.

24   Performed consulting services for $800 on credit, for Johnson Manufacturing. Issued Invoice 1009. Received Check No. 11964 for $350 from the customer.

27   Performed accounting services for $245 on credit for Computer Expertise. Issued Invoice 1010. Received Check No. 9865 for $100 from the customer.

4. Print the following reports for February: *Vendor Ledgers*, *Customer Ledgers*, and *Cash Receipts Journal*.

Problem 2A

Open CC Advertising, which is located on the student data disk. The owner has decided to set up vendor accounts and purchase goods and services on credit.

1. Create a subsidiary ledger account for each of the following new vendors. Enter the beginning balances as of March 1, 2010.

Vendor
Vendor ID:	**JMG-01**
Name:	**J. Madison Graphing**

General Tab
Contact:	**John Madison**
Account Number:	**2180**
Mailing Address:	**6529 West Highland Avenue**
City, ST, Zip:	**Tracy, CA 95376**
Country:	**USA**
Vendor Type:	**Expense**
1099 Type:	**None**
Expense Account:	**516 (Advertising Expense)**
Telephone 1:	**209-555-3349**
Fax:	**209-555-3352**

Purchase Info Tab
Tax ID Number:	**None**
Ship Via:	**US Mail**
Terms and Credit:	**Net 30 Days**
Form Options:	**Default**

History Tab
Beginning Balance:	**640**

Vendor
Vendor ID: **OD-02**
Name: **Office Depot**

General Tab
Contact: **Brian Gentry**
Account Number: **32181**
Mailing Address: **6529 Harding Avenue**
City, ST, Zip: **Tracy, CA 95376**
Country: **USA**
Vendor Type: **Supplier**
1099 Type: **None**
Expense Account: **108 (Office Supplies)**
Telephone 1: **209-555-6459**
Fax: **209-555-6467**

Purchase Info Tab
Tax ID Number: **None**
Ship Via: **UPS Ground**
Terms and Credit: **2% 10 days, net 30 days**
Form Options: **Default**

History Tab
Beginning Balance: **1,200**

2. Print a *Vendor List* report and a *Vendor Ledgers* report for March, 2010.

Problem 1B

Open Alpha Zeta Graphics from the student data disk. The owner has now decided to set up vendor accounts and purchase goods and services on credit.

1. Create a subsidiary ledger account for each vendor dated 01/01/10.

Vendor
Vendor ID: **JPS-01**
Name: **Johnson Photography**

General Tab
Contact: **Matthew Rosario**
Account Number: **3194**
Mailing Address: **1374 West Bessie Avenue**
City, ST, Zip: **Stockton, CA 95210**
Country: **USA**
Vendor Type: **Expense**
1099 Type: **None**
Expense Account: **76000 (Printing and Copying Expense)**
Telephone 1: **209-555-4651**
Fax: **209-555-4658**

Purchase Info Tab

Tax ID Number:	None
Ship Via:	Fed-Ex
Terms and Credit:	Net 30 Days
Form Options:	Default

History Tab

Beginning Balance:	370.00

Vendor

Vendor ID:	SD-02
Name:	Stockton Water District

General Tab

Contact:	Robert Henderson
Account Number:	40381
Mailing Address:	3159 Madison Avenue
City, ST, Zip:	Stockton, CA 95210
Country:	USA
Vendor Type:	Expense
1099 Type:	None
Expense Account:	81500 (Utilities Expense)
Telephone 1:	209-555-4738
Fax:	209-555-4750

Purchase Info Tab

Tax ID Number:	None
Ship Via:	US Mail
Terms and Credit:	Net 30 Days
Form Options:	Default

History Tab

Beginning Balance:	420.00

Vendor

Vendor ID:	OFFMAX-03
Name:	Office Max

General Tab

Contact:	Kevin Randall
Account Number:	395481
Mailing Address:	3915 Webber Lane
City, ST, Zip:	Stockton, CA 95207
Country:	USA
Vendor Type:	Supplier
1099 Type:	None
Expense Account:	12000 (Graphing Supplies)
Telephone 1:	209-555-7981
Fax:	209-555-7988

Purchase Info Tab

Tax ID Number:	**None**
Ship Via:	**Fed-Ex**
Terms and Credit:	**2% 10 days, net 30 days**
Form Options:	**Default**

History Tab

Beginning Balance:	**2,200.00**

Vendor

Vendor ID:	**SJR-04**
Name:	**San Joaquin Rentals**

General Tab

Contact:	**Peter Ramirez**
Account Number:	**94612**
Mailing Address:	**9462 Lowell Avenue**
City, ST, Zip:	**Stockton, CA 95207**
Country:	**USA**
Vendor Type:	**Expense**
1099 Type:	**None**
Expense Account:	**78500 (Rent-Office)**
Telephone 1:	**209-555-6454**
Fax:	**209-555-6460**

Purchase Info Tab

Tax ID Number:	**None**
Ship Via:	**US Mail**
Terms and Credit:	**Net 30 Days**
Form Options:	**Default**

History Tab

Beginning Balance:	**0**

Vendor

Vendor ID:	**PACBELL-05**
Name:	**Pacific Bell**

General Tab

Contact:	**Barbara Sinclair**
Account Number:	**32348**
Mailing Address:	**6581 East Montgomery Avenue**
City, ST, Zip:	**Stockton, CA 95207**
Country:	**USA**
Vendor Type:	**Expense**
1099 Type:	**None**
Expense Account:	**80000 (Telephone Expense)**
Telephone 1:	**209-555-7890**
Fax:	**209-555-7900**

Purchase Info Tab
Tax ID Number: **None**
Ship Via: **US Mail**
Terms and Credit: **Net 30 Days**
Form Options: **Default**

History Tab
Beginning Balance: **300.00**

HINT

To change accounting period:
- Click Tasks
- Click System
- Change Accounting Period
- Select *02-Feb 01, 2010* to *Feb 28, 2010*
- Click OK
- Select No to query

2. Change the accounting period to *Feb 1, 2010 to Feb 28, 2010*.

3. Enter each of the following transactions for February 2010. Note that this business has three different types of revenue: graphic design fees, retouching fees, and drafting fees. Therefore, be sure that you select the number of the correct revenue account in the GL Sales Account section of the Sales/Invoicing dialog box. (The customer accounts have been set up with a GL Sales Account default to Account 40000, Graphic Design Income.) Services performed on account will be entered in the Sales/Invoicing window, purchases on account in the Purchases/Receive Inventory window.

Date	Transaction
Feb. 2	Performed graphic design services for $575 on credit for Jackson Photography. Issued Invoice 1007.
3	Received a bill (Invoice 4952) of $695 for the monthly rent from San Joaquin Rentals.
4	Received a bill of $120 (Invoice 13795) for monthly usage of telephone service from Pacific Bell.
4	Received a bill (Invoice 65429) of $134 for monthly usage of water from Stockton Water District.
5	Purchased graphing supplies for $335 on credit from Office Max. Received Invoice 4620.
8	Performed graphic design services for $620 on credit for Computer Creations. Issued Invoice 1008.
12	Purchased printing services for $550 on credit from Johnson Photography. Received Invoice 2615.
15	Performed graphic design services for $1,250 on credit for Jackson Photography. Issued Invoice 1009. Received Check No. 4504 for $400 from the customer.
19	Purchased graphing supplies for $235 on credit from Office Max. Received Invoice 5229.
25	Performed graphic design services for $1,125 on credit for First Design. Issued Invoice 1010. Received Check No. 3271 for $350 from the customer.
26	Performed retouching services for $460 on credit for Jackson Photography. Issued Invoice 1011.
27	Performed graphic design services for $750 on credit for Computer Creations. Issued Invoice 1012.

4. Print the following reports for February: *Vendor Ledgers*, *Customer Ledgers*, and *Cash Receipts Journal*.

Problem 2B

Open Ritter Insurance, which is located on the student data disk. This firm plans to purchase goods and services on credit.

1. Create a subsidiary ledger account for each of the following new vendors. Enter the beginning balances as of March 1, 2010.

Vendor

Vendor ID:	**OFFMAX-01**
Name:	**Office Max**

General Tab

Contact:	**Kevin Randall**
Account Number:	**4150**
Mailing Address:	**3915 Webber Lane**
City, ST, Zip:	**Stockton, CA 95207**
Country:	**USA**
Vendor Type:	**Supplier**
1099 Type:	**None**
Expense Account:	**108 (Office Supplies)**
Telephone 1:	**209-555-7981**
Fax:	**209-555-7988**

Purchase Info Tab

Tax ID Number:	**None**
Ship Via:	**Fed-Ex**
Terms and Credit:	**2% 10 days, net 30 days**
Form Options:	**Default**

History Tab

Beginning Balance:	**840**

Vendor

Vendor ID:	**GJPA-02**
Name:	**GJ Professional Accounting**

General Tab

Contact:	**Jim Tyler**
Account Number:	**491502**
Mailing Address:	**1506 East March Lane**
City, ST, Zip:	**Stockton, CA 95207**
Country:	**USA**
Vendor Type:	**Expense**
1099 Type:	**None**
Expense Account:	**516 (Accounting Expense)**
Telephone 1:	**209-555-2112**
Fax:	**209-555-1221**

Purchase Info Tab

Tax ID Number:	**None**
Ship Via:	**US Mail**
Terms and Credit:	**Net 30 Days**
Form Options:	**Default**

History Tab

Beginning Balance:	**720**

2. Print a *Vendor List* report and a *Vendor Ledgers* report for March, 2010.

Cooperative Learning

1. Form into groups of three or four students, and discuss what a business can do to maintain a good credit reputation. Why is a good credit reputation important?

2. As a group, research the Small Business Administration, a government entity that helps businesses to obtain the capital they need to start or expand operations. What methods does it use to assist businesses? What are its requirements to receive assistance?

Writing and Decision Making

Assume that the company for which you work currently makes all purchases for cash. However, the owner, Susan Nicholson, has decided to obtain credit from vendors. She has therefore asked you to suggest measures that the company can take to organize and manage its accounts payable. She has also asked that you explain to her how the controlling account in the general ledger relates to the vendor accounts in the subsidiary ledger. Prepare a memo with the information that has been requested.

CHAPTER 6

Cash Payments and Cash Receipts

Learning Objectives

1. Process cash payments using the cash payments module

2. Process cash receipts using the cash receipts module

3. Prepare a reconciliation of the checking account

Software Features

- Receipts toolbar buttons

- Payments toolbar buttons

- Account reconciliation toolbar

Cash is the most essential of all assets. Without an adequate cash flow, no business can operate for long. Because cash is so important, every firm should have efficient procedures for managing its cash receipts and cash payments.

Recording and Managing Cash

Remember that **cash** consists of the funds that a business has on hand and the funds that it has on deposit in banks. The funds on hand may include not only currency and coin but also cash equivalents such as checks and money orders received from customers.

Some firms maintain a single cash account in their general ledger. Other firms have a variety of cash accounts such as Cash on Hand, Petty Cash, Regular Checking Account, Payroll Checking Account, and Money Market Savings. If there is a single account called Cash, this account is debited whenever cash is received and credited whenever cash is paid.

You may choose to record all cash transactions in the general journal as you did in chapter 3. However, many businesses prefer to use special journals for cash receipts and cash payments. Peachtree provides such journals.

Cash is the asset that is most easily stolen, lost, or misused. Therefore, accountants recommend that businesses follow certain procedures to protect their cash. Some of these procedures are outlined below:

- Make all payments by check except for small expenditures from a petty cash fund.
- Avoid keeping large amounts of cash on the premises. Make frequent bank deposits of cash receipts.
- Use a locked safe or cash drawer to protect any cash that is on hand.
- Record cash transactions promptly.
- Reconcile the monthly bank statement with the firm's internal cash records.
- Divide responsibility. If possible, have different employees handle cash, record cash, and reconcile the bank statement.

Peachtree allows you to quickly and efficiently issue checks, record cash receipts and cash payments, and carry out the bank reconciliation process.

OBJECTIVE 1 — Process Cash Payments Using the Cash Payments Module

During January 2010, Superior Carpet and Tile received several bills from vendors. In chapter 5, you learned how these purchases of goods and services were recorded. Now you will see how the business uses the cash payments module of Peachtree to issue checks to the vendors and record the payments.

Paying an Invoice with a Discount

On January 29, 2010, Superior Carpet and Tile received Invoice 3556 from Office Max for a purchase of office supplies. The total of the invoice was $1,400 and the terms were 2% 10 days, net 30 days (2/10, net 30). On January 31, Superior's accountant paid bills and issued a check to Office Max. Because the invoice is being paid within the discount period, Superior is entitled to take the 2% discount offered by the vendor.

Step 1:
Open Superior Carpet and Tile (Chp. 6 – Superior Carpet and Tile if student data disk is used).

Step 2:
Click Tasks, and then click *Payments*.

Step 3:
At the Select a Cash Account dialog box, click *Cash* from the drop-down list, as shown in figure 6–1.

FIGURE 6–1
Select a Cash Account
Dialog Box with Cash
Selected

Step 4:
Click OK. The Payments window will then appear, as shown in figure 6–2.

FIGURE 6–2
Blank Payments Window

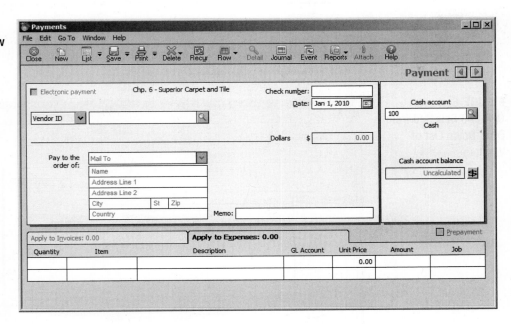

Step 5:

If it is not already selected, click the down arrow in the first box on the left, and then click *Vendor ID* from the drop-down list as shown in figure 6–3, .

FIGURE 6–3
Vendor ID Selected from Drop-Down List

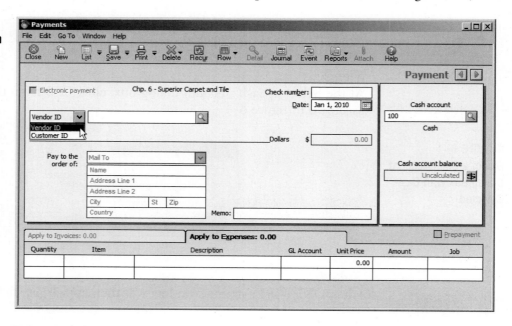

Step 6:

Click the *magnifying glass* icon and then select *OFF-003* from the drop-down list of vendors, as shown in figure 6–4.

FIGURE 6–4
OFF-003 Selected from Drop-Down List of Vendors

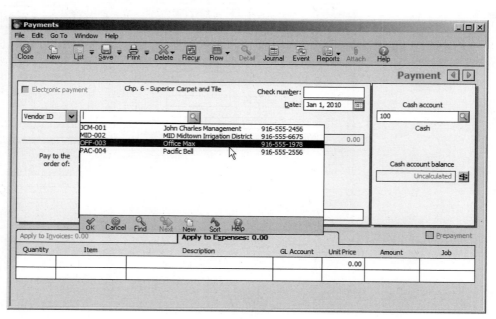

Step 7:

Click OK at the bottom of the drop-down list of vendors. Alternatively, you could simply click OFF-003. The information for Office Max appears. The beginning balance of its account and the open invoice are listed near the bottom of the window, as shown in figure 6–5.

FIGURE 6–5
Account Information for
Office Max Displayed

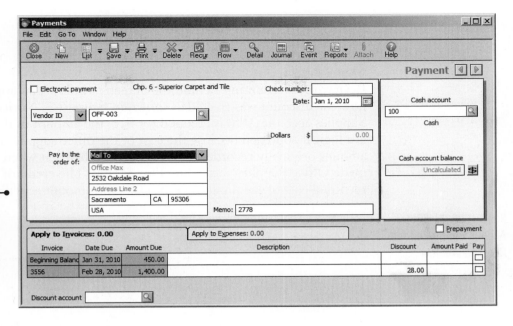

HINT

The *Apply to Invoices*
folder tab is highlighted
because there are open
(unpaid) invoices for the
selected vendor.

Step 8:
Choose *Jan 31, 2010* in the *Date* field using the *calendar* icon.

Step 9:
Click the *magnifying glass* icon at the *Discount Account* field, which is at the
lower left side of the Payments window. Click *108, Office Supplies*, and it will
appear as shown in figure 6–6.

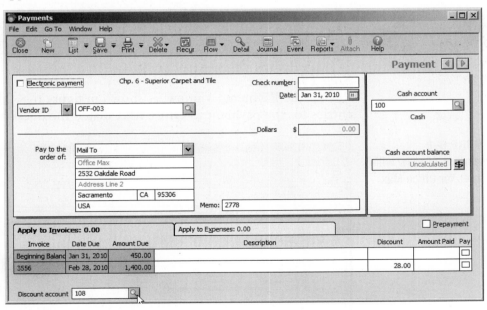

Step 10:
Click to add a check mark in the *Pay* field on the line where Invoice 3556
appears. When the check mark is entered, Peachtree will automatically
calculate the amount to be paid by deducting any discount from the total
of the invoice. For example, Invoice 3556 from Office Max is for $1,400.
However, because Superior is paying within the discount period, it can take
a 2% discount ($28), which reduces the amount it owes to $1,372.

Step 11:
Click the Journal button on the Payments toolbar.

Step 12:
Review the Accounting Behind the Screens window that appears to see how the discount was treated as shown in figure 6–7. Notice that the Office Supplies account (108) is credited for $28, the amount of the discount. This is a logical approach because the cost of the office supplies is less than the amount originally recorded ($1,400). Remember that when the purchase was made Office Supplies was debited for $1,400. The credit of $28 reduces the recorded cost of the purchase to $1,372, the amount actually paid. Click OK.

FIGURE 6–7
Accounting Behind the
Screens Window

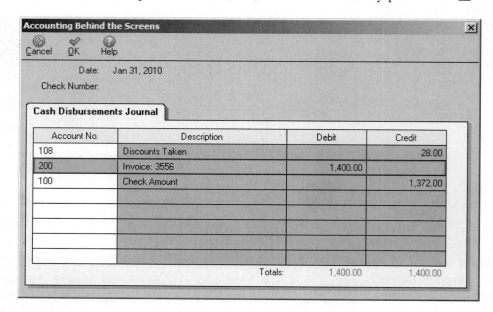

Step 13:
Review the Payments window, as shown in figure 6–8. Make sure that your entries for the payment to Office Max match the ones shown here.

FIGURE 6–8
Payments Window with
Entries for Office Max

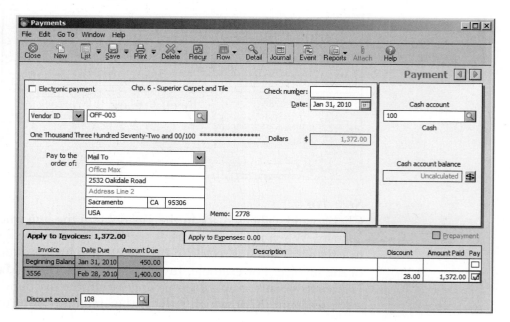

Do not key anything in the *Check Number* field. Peachtree will automatically record the check number when the check is printed. If the payment were to be made in cash rather than by check, you would key **CASH**. (In some rare circumstances, you may want to bypass the automatic check preparation feature and write a check manually. In such a case, you must key in the check number.)

Step 14:

If the number of the Cash account (100) is not already selected, click the *magnifying glass* icon next to the *Cash Account* field, and then click *100*, as shown in figure 6–9.

FIGURE 6–9
Payments Dialog Box
with Cash Account 100
Selected

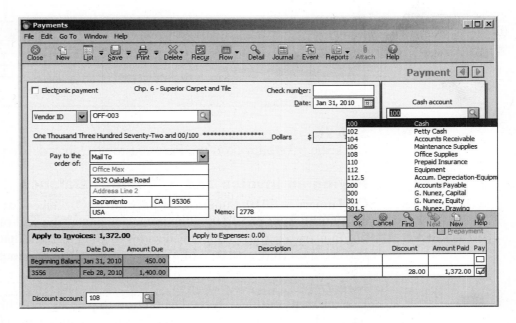

Step 15:

Peachtree maintains a running balance in the Cash account. This balance can be viewed in the *Cash Account Balance* field. However, the *Cash Account Balance* field will sometimes contain only *??????????* or *Uncalculated*. To reveal the balance, click the Recalculate button ($) next to the *Cash Account Balance* field and the updated Cash account balance will appear in the *Cash Account Balance* field, as shown in figure 6–10.

FIGURE 6–10
Cash Account Balance
Field Showing Current
Cash Balance

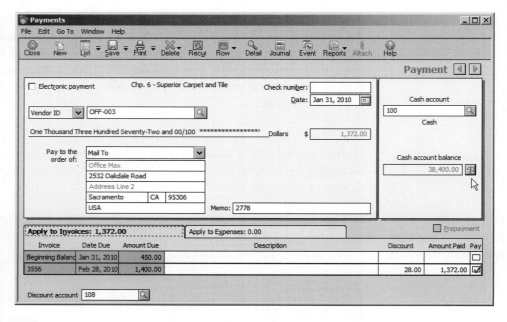

Step 16:

Click the Save button on the Payment toolbar in order to post the payment.

Paying an Invoice and a Previous Balance

On January 3, 2010, Superior Carpet and Tile received Invoice 2621 for its monthly rent of $2,100. The invoice is due at the end of the month. On January 31, the accountant decides to issue a check that will cover both Invoice 2621 and a balance of $900 owed from the previous month.

Step 1:

Use the steps outlined in the last section to pay the monthly rent and the outstanding balance owed to John Charles Management. However, in this case, key check marks in the *Pay* field on the lines for both the beginning balance and Invoice 2621. Also, keep in mind that there is no discount involved in this payment.

Step 2:

Compare your entries with those shown in figure 6–11. Then click Save.

FIGURE 6–11
Completed Payments
Window with Entries
for John Charles
Management

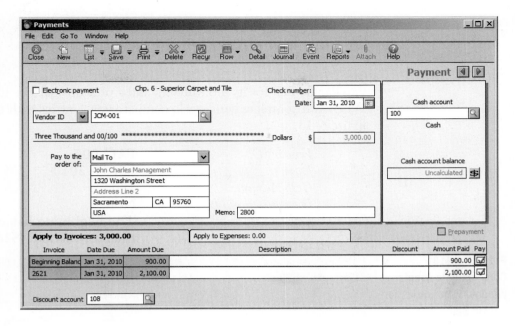

During January 2010, Superior Carpet and Tile received two bills. One came from MID Midtown Irrigation District (Invoice Number 4763), and the other came from Pacific Bell (Invoice Number 2867).

Step 3:

Pay MID Midtown Irrigation District for its monthly bill and a previous balance that Superior owes. When you complete your work, compare your entries with those shown in figure 6–12.

Vendor ID:	**MID-002**
Date:	**Jan 31, 2010**
Cash Account:	**100**
Discount Account:	**None**
Pay:	**The beginning balance ($450) and the monthly bill ($226.65)**

FIGURE 6–12
Completed Payments
Window with Entries for
MID Midtown Irrigation
District

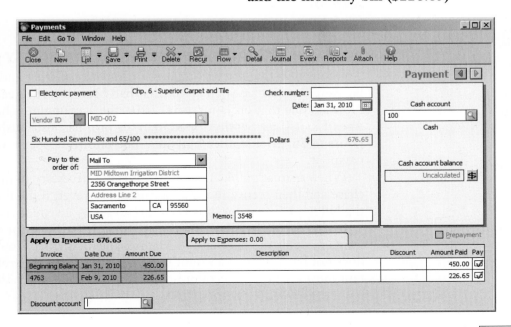

Step 4:
Click Save in order to post the payment.

Step 5:
Pay Pacific Bell for its monthly bill and a previous balance that Superior owes. When you complete your work, compare your entries with those shown in figure 6–13.

Vendor ID:	**PAC-004**
Date:	**Jan 31, 2010**
Cash Account:	**100**
Discount Account:	**None**
Pay:	**The beginning balance ($500) and the monthly bill ($265.89)**

FIGURE 6–13
Completed Payments Window with Entries for Pacific Bell

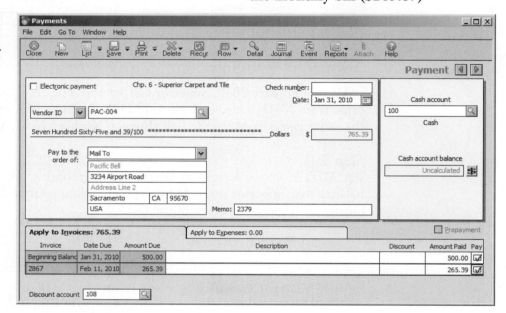

Step 6:
Click Save.

Paying a Bill for a Purchase Not Previously Recorded

The four bills that the accountant for Superior Carpet and Tile has paid so far were for purchases on credit that had been recorded earlier in the month. Now assume that on January 31, 2010, the accountant is handed a bill from Apex Floor Care Service for $250. This firm has just finished polishing the floors in Superior's office building. The bill from Apex requests immediate payment.

When a situation like this occurs, it is not necessary to first record the purchase and then record the cash payment. However, if the firm that submitted the bill is a new vendor, it is necessary to set up a vendor account for the firm.

In this particular situation, the accountant for Superior Carpet and Tile wants to debit the purchase to Maintenance Expense. However, the business does not have such an account in its general ledger. Therefore, the accountant must create this account before recording the purchase.

Use the steps outlined below to create the Maintenance Expense account, set up the vendor account, record the purchase, and record the cash payment.

Step 1:
Click Tasks from the main Menu bar and *Write Checks* from the drop-down list, as shown in figure 6–14.

FIGURE 6–14
Write Checks Selected from the Tasks Drop-Down List

Step 2:
Click the *magnifying glass* icon next to the Expense Account box located in the lower left corner of the screen. A drop-down list appears, as shown in figure 6–15.

FIGURE 6–15
GL Account Drop-Down List

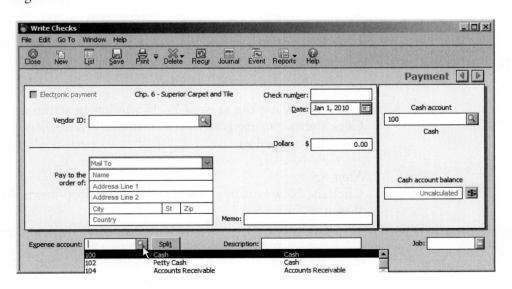

Step 3:
Click the New button at the bottom of the drop-down list of general ledger accounts.

Step 4:

At the Maintain Chart of Accounts window, key the following information to complete the setup of the new account:

Account ID:	**518**
Description:	**Maintenance Expense**
Account Type:	**Expenses**

Step 5:

Compare your entries with the ones shown in figure 6–16.

FIGURE 6–16
Completed Entries for Maintenance Expense Account

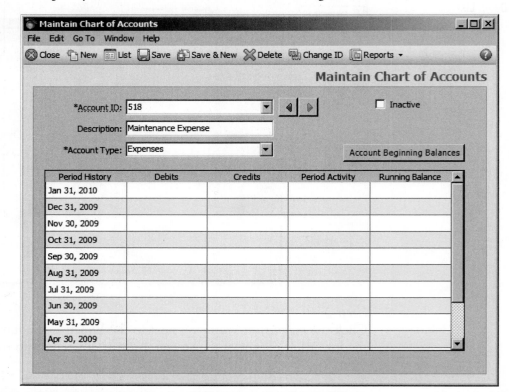

Step 6:

Click Save and then click Close to return to the Payments window.

Step 7:

We will now use the Write Checks window to set up a new vendor account. Click the *magnifying glass* icon next to the *Vendor ID* box to reveal the drop-down list of vendors.

Step 8:

Click the New button at the bottom of the drop-down list of vendors, as shown in figure 6–17.

FIGURE 6–17
New Button from Drop-
Down List of Vendors

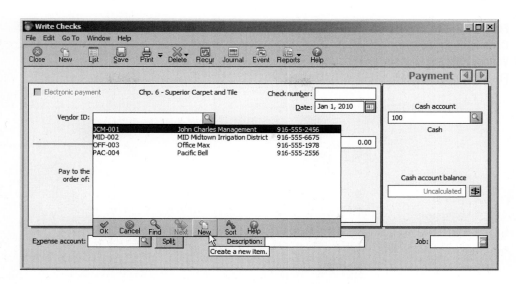

Step 9:
The Maintain Vendors window appears. Use the following information to complete the setup of a new vendor account for Apex Floor Care Service:

Vendor

Vendor ID:	**APX-005**
Name:	**Apex Floor Care Service**

General Tab

Contact:	**Tarin Land**
Account Number:	**334223**
Mailing Address:	**2310 Windham Avenue**
City, ST, Zip:	**Sacramento, CA 95670**
Country:	**USA**
Vendor Type:	**Expense**
1099 Type:	**None**
Expense Account:	**518 (Maintenance Expense)**
Telephone 1:	**408-555-5634**
Fax:	**408-555-4638**

Purchase Info Tab

Tax ID Number:	**None**
Ship Via:	**US Mail**
Terms and Credit:	**Due in 30 days, 0.00 Discount**
Form Options:	**Default**

History Tab

Beginning Balance:	**0**

Step 10:
Compare your entries with the ones shown in figure 6–18.

FIGURE 6–18
Completed Entries for
Vendor Account for Apex
Floor Care Service

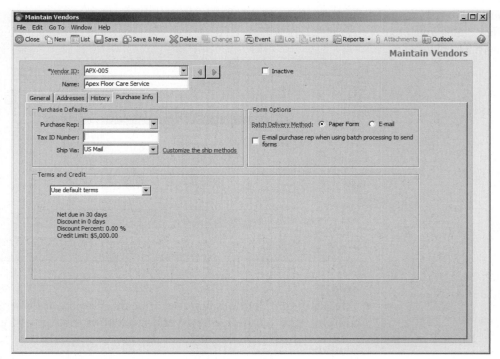

Step 11:

Click Save and then Close to return to the Write Checks window. We are now ready to actually write the check.

Step 12:

Click *APX-005* from the drop-down list of vendors. The information for Apex Floor Care Service appears as shown in figure 6–19.

FIGURE 6–19
Write Checks Window
Showing Apex Floor Care
Service Information

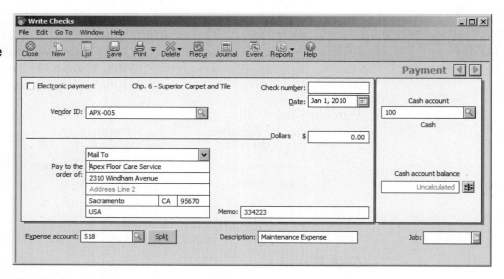

Step 13:

Click the *calendar* icon and then choose *Jan 31, 2010* in the *Date* field.

Step 14:

Key **250.00** in the *Dollars* field.

Step 15:

Click the *magnifying glass* icon and then click the number of the Cash account (*100*) in the *Cash Account* field.

Step 16:

Click account *518, Maintenance Expense* from the drop-down list of general ledger accounts in the *Expense Account* field, if not already complete.

Step 17:

Key **Floor Care** in the *Description* field.

Step 18:

Compare your entries with the ones shown in figure 6–20.

FIGURE 6–20
Completed Write Checks Window for Apex Floor Care Service

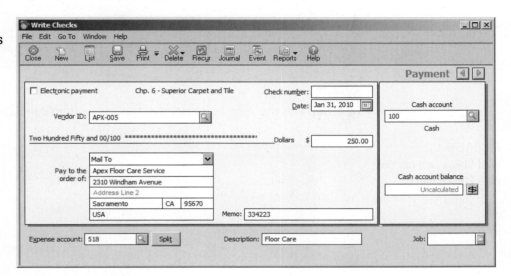

Printing Individual Checks

As noted previously, Peachtree allows you the option of either preparing checks automatically or preparing them manually. If you select automatic check preparation, the system will enter the check numbers in the *Check Number* field of the Payments window. With manual check preparation, you must key in the check numbers.

Superior Carpet and Tile uses automatic check preparation. Follow the steps outlined below to issue a check for the bill owed to the Apex Floor Care Service.

Step 1:

Click the Print button on the Write Checks toolbar. The Print Forms: Disbursement Checks dialog box appears as shown in figure 6–21.

FIGURE 6–21
Print Forms:
Disbursement Checks
Dialog Box

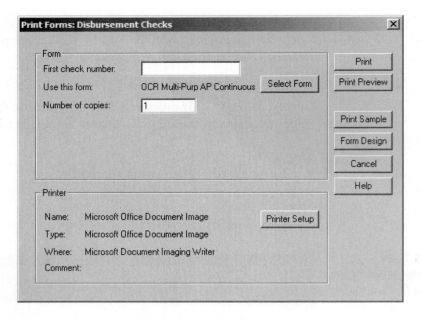

Step 2:
Key **2004** in the *First check number* box, as in figure 6–22.

FIGURE 6–22
First Check Number Box
with 2004 Entered

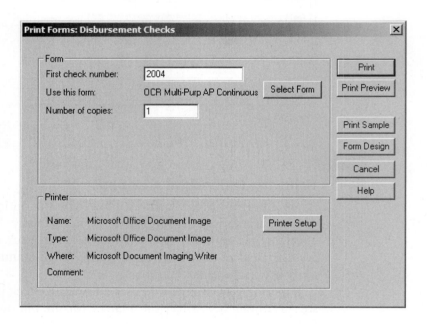

Step 3:
Select Print to print the check. The check will print out on a blank sheet of
paper because no check form was placed in the printer paper tray. Compare
your check with the one shown in figure 6–23. It is not necessary to save.
The entries are saved when the check is printed.

FIGURE 6–23
Sample of Printed Check
for Apex Floor Care
Service

Apex Floor Care Service

Check Number: 2004
Check Date: Jan 31, 2010

Item to be Paid - Description

Check Amount: $250.00
Discount Taken   Amount Paid

Floor Care   250.00

Check Number: 2004   Jan 31, 2010

Memo: 334223   250.00

Two Hundred Fifty and 00/100 Dollars

Apex Floor Care Service
2310 Windham Avenue
Sacramento, CA 95670
USA

Step 4:
Close the Write Checks window.

Printing Checks Previously Marked for Payment

Superior Carpet and Tile needs the following checks marked for payment in January. Use the Open function for this task.

- Office Max, Check 2005
- John Charles Management, Check 2006
- Pacific Bell, Check 2007
- MID Midtown Irrigation District, Check 2008

Step 1:
Select Tasks from the main Menu bar and *Payments* from the drop-down list.

Step 2:
Click the List button from the Payments toolbar.

Step 3:
Click *OFF-003(Office Max)* from the Payment List window, and then click Open.

Step 4:
Enter the check number, 2005, if not already entered.

Step 5:
Click the Print button on the Payments toolbar.

Step 6:
Click Print on the Print Forms: Disbursement Checks dialog box.

Step 7:
Follow steps 2 through 6 to print the remaining checks. Notice that the check numbers will automatically be printed in sequence after the first check number is entered. The check numbers appear in the *Check No.* field of the Payment List window, as shown in figure 6–24.

FIGURE 6–24
Payment List Window

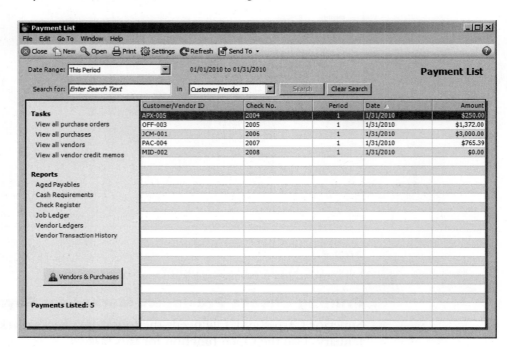

Step 8:
Close the Payment List window.

Check point

1. What is the cash payments module of Peachtree used for?
2. Why is it not necessary to key anything in the *Check Number* field when Peachtree is used to issue checks?

Answers

1. *The cash payments module of Peachtree is used to record payments to vendors and issue the necessary checks.*
2. *Peachtree automatically enters a check number for the check being printed and all subsequent checks.*

Practice Objective 1

In chapter 5, you created vendor accounts for Meadowland Healthcare Services and recorded its purchases on credit. In this chapter, you will record payments to the vendors.

Step 1:

Open Meadowland Healthcare Services (Chp. 6 – Meadowland Healthcare Services if student data disk is used).

Step 2:

Record the following payments using 10200 (Regular Checking Account) as the Cash Account:

- On January 27, 2010, paid Invoice 55665 for $890, less a discount, owed to Office Depot, Check 700. (Use Office Supplies as the Discount account.)
- On January 31, 2010, paid Invoice 012301 for $1,200 owed to Alta Vista Business Park, Check 701.
- On January 31, 2010, paid a bill of $345.89 owed to Pacific Gas & Electric, Check 702.
- On January 31, 2010, paid a bill of $265.98 owed to General Telephone, Check 703.

Step 3:

On January 31, 2010, Meadowland received Invoice 33223 for $650 from Merry Maids, a new vendor. Meadowland does not have an expense account for housekeeping services. Create the necessary general ledger account.

Account ID:	**50520**
Description:	**Housekeeping Expense**
Account Type:	**Expenses**

Step 4:

Create the necessary vendor account for Merry Maids.

Vendor

Vendor ID:	**MER-005**
Name:	**Merry Maids**

General Tab

Contact:	**David Lee**
Account Number:	**88997**
Mailing Address:	**3211 Williams Avenue**
City, ST, Zip:	**Fresno, CA 96330**
Country:	**USA**
Vendor Type:	**Expense**
1099 Type:	**None**
Expense Account:	**50520 (Housekeeping Expense)**
Telephone 1:	**209-555-6534**
Fax:	**209-555-8364**

Purchase Info Tab
    Tax ID Number: **None**
    Ship Via: **US Mail**
    Terms and Credit: **Due EOM, 0.00 Discount**
    Form Options: **Default**

History Tab
    Beginning Balance: **0**

Step 5:
Using the Write Checks feature, record the immediate payment of Invoice 33223 for $650 owed to Merry Maids, Check 704.

Step 6:
Select List from the Payments window and review the checks and check numbers for correctness against figure 6–25.

FIGURE 6–25
Payment List Window

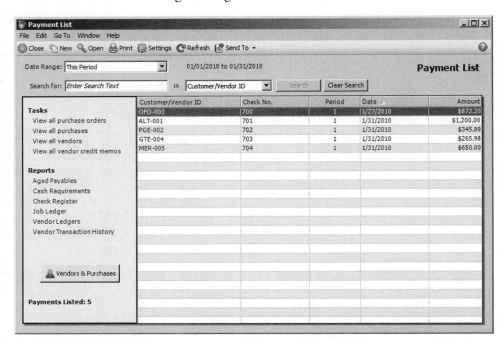

Step 7:
Close the Payment List and Payments windows.

OBJECTIVE 2 — Process Cash Receipts Using the Cash Receipts Module

During January 2010, Superior Carpet and Tile sold services on credit to several customers. In chapter 4, you learned how these sales were recorded. Now you will see how the business uses the cash receipts module of Peachtree to issue invoices and record the amounts collected from customers.

Issuing Invoices

If a business wants to collect the amounts owed by customers on time, it must issue invoices promptly. Remember that an **invoice** is a bill for the goods or services sold to a customer. The invoice shows the amount that the customer owes and the credit terms as well as other information about the sale.

invoice A bill for goods or services sold to a customer.

Peachtree allows for quick preparation of invoices. It also provides flexibility in what information is presented on invoices. For example, on January 14, 2010, Superior Carpet and Tile did a job for Parker's Construction for a fixed fee of $5,000. Parker agreed to pay one-half of the total due ($2,500) as soon as the job was completed. Therefore, when Superior issues Invoice 1002 for this job, the invoice must include both the total of $5,000 and the partial collection of $2,500.

Step 1:
Open Chp. 6 – Superior Carpet and Tile which you updated previously in the chapter. Click Tasks, and then click *Sales/Invoicing*.

Step 2:
Click the List button on the Sales/Invoicing toolbar.

Step 3:
Click *Parker's Construction* from the Sales Invoice List window, as shown in figure 6–26.

FIGURE 6–26
Parker's Construction
Selected from Sales
Invoice List Window

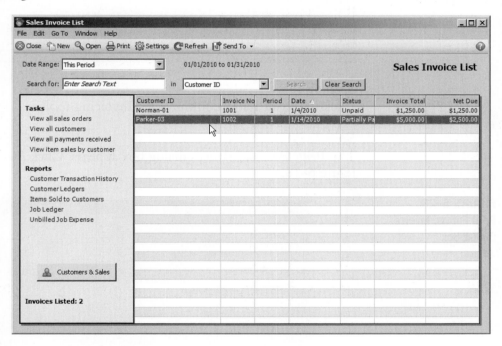

Step 4:
Click Open. The invoice for Parker's Construction appears, as shown in figure 6–27.

FIGURE 6–27

Invoice 1002 for Parker's
Construction

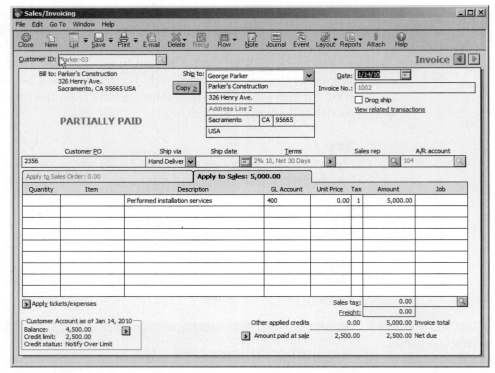

Step 5:
Click the Print button on the Sales/Invoicing toolbar.

Step 6:
The Print Forms: Invoices dialog box appears. Click *Print*, as shown in
figure 6–28.

FIGURE 6–28

Print Forms: Invoice
Dialog Box

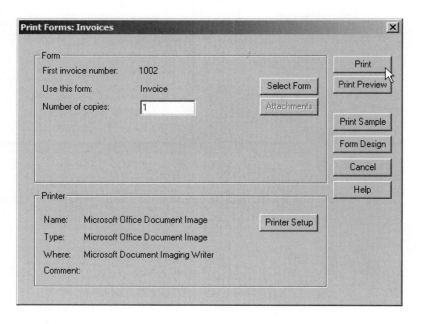

Step 7:

Compare your invoice with the one shown in figure 6–29.

FIGURE 6–29
Invoice 1002 for Parker's
Construction

FIGURE 6–29
Invoice 1002 for Parker's
Construction

Chp. 6 - Superior Carpet and Tile
348 Brown Ave.
Campbell, CA 95555
USA

Voice: 916-555-2222
Fax: 916-555-2222

INVOICE

Invoice Number: 1002
Invoice Date: Jan 14, 2010
Page: 1
Duplicate

Bill To:
Parker's Construction
326 Henry Ave.
Sacramento, CA 95665
USA

Ship to:
Parker's Construction
326 Henry Ave.
Sacramento, CA 95665
USA

Customer ID	Customer PO	Payment Terms
Parker-03	2356	2% 10, Net 30 Days

Sales Rep ID	Shipping Method	Ship Date	Due Date
	Hand Deliver		2/13/10

Quantity	Item	Description	Unit Price	Amount
		Performed installation services		5,000.00

Check/Credit Memo No: 1002

	Amount
Subtotal	5,000.00
Sales Tax	
Total Invoice Amount	5,000.00
Payment/Credit Applied	2,500.00
TOTAL	**2,500.00**

Step 8:

Close the Sales/Invoicing window.

Recording Cash Receipts

On January 23, 2010, Superior Carpet and Tile received a check for $2,400 from Parker's Construction. This check represents the balance owed on Invoice 1002 ($2,500) less a 2% discount on the total of the invoice ($5,000 × .02 = $100). Remember that Superior billed Parker for $5,000 and received $2,500 immediately. Because the invoice is dated January 14, Parker has now paid the full amount due within the 10-day discount period. Thus, it is entitled to the 2% discount on the total of the invoice.

Discounts on sales are debited to an account called Sales Discount. This account is known as a contra income account because its debit balance is contrary to the normal credit balance of an income account. Superior Carpet and Tile does not yet have such an account in its general ledger. Therefore, use the following information to create this account using Maintain, Chart of Accounts.

Account ID:	**401**
Account Description:	**Sales Discount**
Account Type:	**Income**

After you have created the new account, you will then process a receipt of cash on account using the following steps:

Step 1:
Click Tasks, and then click *Receipts.*

Step 2:
Key **01/23/10** in the *Deposit Ticket ID* field.

Step 3:
In the box below click the down arrow and then click *Customer ID* if necessary.

Step 4:
Click the *magnifying glass* icon and then click *Parker-03* from the drop-down list of customers, as shown in figure 6–30.

FIGURE 6–30
Parker-03 Selected from Drop-Down List of Customers

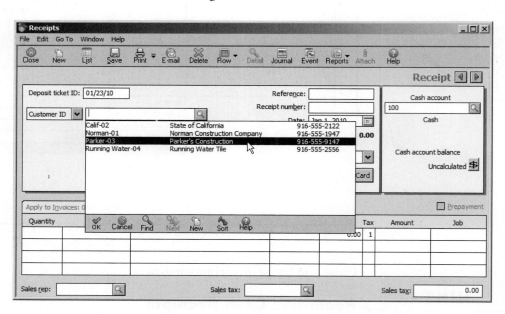

Step 5:
Key **1080** (the check number) in the *Reference* field.

Step 6:
Click the *calendar* icon and choose *Jan 23, 2010* in the *Date* field.

Step 7:

Click *Check* in the *Payment Method* field and *Cash (100)* in the *Cash Account* field.

Note: If you do not see available account numbers in the *Cash Account* field or the *Discount Account* field at the bottom of the window, select Options from the Main Menu bar, and then Global from the drop-down list. With the Accounting tab selected, remove the check mark in front of Accounts Receivable (Quotes, Sales Orders, Invoicing, Credit Memos, Receipts).

Step 8:

Key **100.00** in the *Discount* field aligned with Invoice 1002. Press Enter.

Step 9:

The amount of 2,400.00 will appear in the *Amount Paid* field. Press Enter. A check mark will appear in the *Pay* field as shown in figure 6–31.

FIGURE 6–31
Pay Field Selected for Invoice 1002

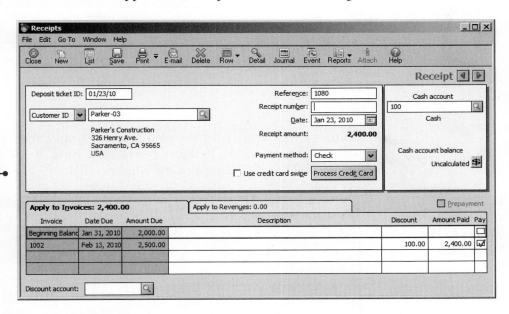

HINT

Remember that if you click the Recalculate button ($), the new cash balance will appear in the *Cash Account Balance* field.

Step 10:

Click the Journal button on the Receipts toolbar.

Step 11:

Click in the *Account No.* field, click the *magnifying glass* icon, and then click *401*. This is the account that is used for recording sales discounts. Your screen should look like figure 6–32.

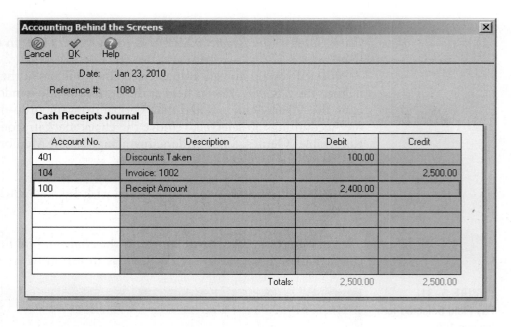

Step 12:
Click OK.

Step 13:
Compare your entries for the cash received from Parker's Construction with the entries shown in figure 6–33. Make note of *401* in the *Discount Account* field at the bottom of the window.

FIGURE 6–33
Completed Receipts
Window for Parker's
Construction

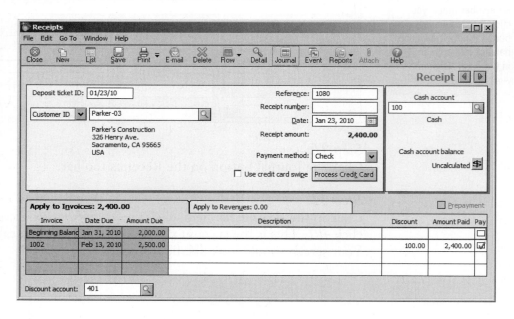

Step 14:
Click Save.

Step 15:

Click the List button on the Receipts toolbar to view the Receipt List dialog box, and then select *All Transactions* in the *Date Range* field. Compare your screen with figure 6–34. If any corrections are needed, you can now select and then edit the transaction.

FIGURE 6–34
Receipt List Dialog Box

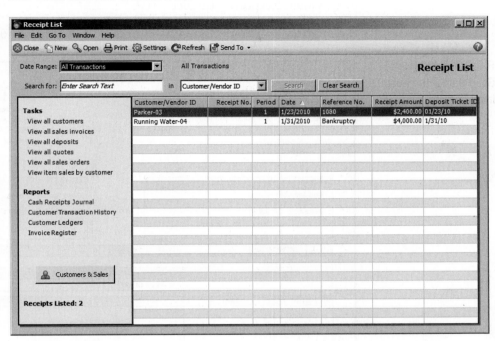

Step 16:

Click Close if no corrections are required.

Step 17:

Close the Receipts window.

C h e c k   p o i n t

1. What is an invoice?
2. The cash receipts module of Peachtree is used for what task?

Answers
1. *An invoice is a bill for goods or services sold to a customer.*
2. *The cash receipts module is used to record amounts received from customers.*

P r a c t i c e   O b j e c t i v e   2

In chapter 4, you created customer accounts for Meadowland Healthcare Services. In this chapter, you will issue invoices and record cash received from a customer.

Step 1:

Open Chp. 6 – Meadowland Healthcare Services, which you updated previously in the chapter.

Step 2:

Print invoices for the following customers:

- Good Samaritan Hospital, Invoice 1102
- Rapid Medical Response, Invoice 1103
- Valley Response, Invoice 1104

Your printouts should look like figures 6–35, 6–36, and 6–37.

FIGURE 6–35
Good Samaritan Hospital,
Invoice 1102

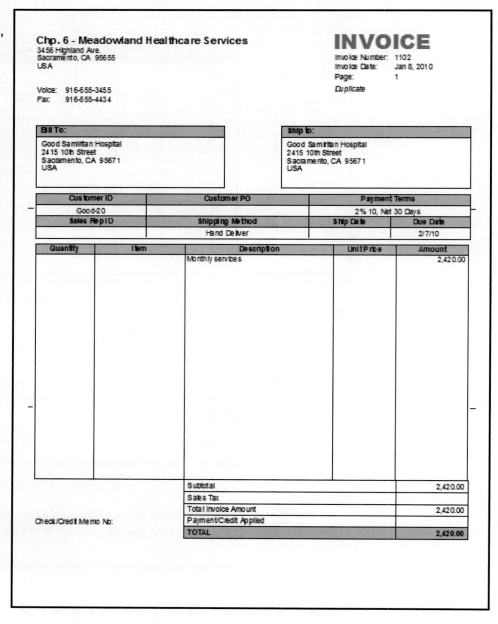

FIGURE 6–36
Rapid Medical Response,
Invoice 1103

Chp. 6 - Meadowland Healthcare Services
3456 Highland Ave.
Sacramento, CA 95655
USA

Voice: 916-655-3455
Fax: 916-655-4434

INVOICE

Invoice Number: 1103
Invoice Date: Jan 19, 2010
Page: 1
Duplicate

Bill To:	Ship to:
Rapid Medical Response 2516 main Street Sacramento, CA 95671 USA	Rapid Medical Response 2516 main Street Sacramento, CA 95671 USA

Customer ID	Customer PO	Payment Terms
Rapid-30		2% 10, Net 30 Days

Sales Rep ID	Shipping Method	Ship Date	Due Date
	US Mail		2/18/10

Quantity	Item	Description	Unit Price	Amount
48.00		Professional fees	120.00	5,760.00
			Subtotal	5,760.00
			Sales Tax	
			Total Invoice Amount	5,760.00
			Payment/Credit Applied	
			TOTAL	**5,760.00**

Check/Credit Memo No:

FIGURE 6–37
Valley Response, Invoice
1104

Chp. 6 - Meadowland Healthcare Services
3456 Highland Ave.
Sacramento, CA 95655
USA

Voice: 916-555-3455
Fax: 916-555-4434

INVOICE

Invoice Number: 1104
Invoice Date: Jan 29, 2010
Page: 1
Duplicate

Bill To:	Ship to:
Valley Response 3211 Main Street Sacramento, CA 95761 USA	Valley response 3211 Main Street Sacramento, CA 95761 USA

Customer ID	Customer PO	Payment Terms	
Valley-40		2% 10, Net 30 Days	
Sales Rep ID	**Shipping Method**	**Ship Date**	**Due Date**
	Hand Deliver		2/28/10

Quantity	Item	Description	Unit Price	Amount
		Fixed monthly fees		1,650.00

Subtotal		1,650.00
Sales Tax		
Total Invoice Amount		1,650.00
Payment/Credit Applied		825.00
TOTAL		**825.00**

Check/Credit Memo No: 1104

Step 3:

Meadowland Healthcare Services does not have a Sales Discount account. Use the following information to create this general ledger account:

Account ID:	**40100**
Description:	**Sales Discount**
Account Type:	**Income**

Step 4:

On January 28, 2010, received $5,644.80 from Rapid Medical Response, Check 3240. This check is for Invoice 1103 ($5,760) less a 2% discount ($115.20). Record the transaction. (Remember to enter the sales discount account.) Make sure that *Check* and *10200* are selected in the *Payment Method* and *Cash Account* fields, respectively.

Step 5:

Print the *Customer Ledgers* report. Your printout should look like figure 6–38.

FIGURE 6–38
Customer Ledgers
for Meadowland
Healthcare Services

						Page: 1
Chp. 6 - Meadowland Healthcare Services						
Customer Ledgers						
For the Period From Jan 1, 2010 to Jan 31, 2010						
Filter Criteria includes: Report order is by ID. Report is printed in Detail Format.						
Customer ID **Customer**	**Date**	**Trans No**	**Type**	**Debit Amt**	**Credit Amt**	**Balance**
Doctor's-10	1/2/10	1101	SJ	12,000.00		12,000.00
Doctor's Medical Center	1/31/10	Bankruptcy	CRJ		12,000.00	0.00
Good-20	1/8/10	1102	SJ	2,420.00		2,420.00
Good Samaritan Hospital						
Rapid-30	1/19/10	1103	SJ	5,760.00		5,760.00
Rapid Medical Response	1/28/10	3240	CRJ	115.20	115.20	5,760.00
	1/28/10	3240	CRJ		5,760.00	0.00
Valley-40	1/29/10	1104	SJ	1,650.00		1,650.00
Valley Response	1/29/10	1104	CRJ		825.00	825.00
Report Total				**21,945.20**	**18,700.20**	**3,245.00**

Step 6:

Close the Select a Report or Form dialog box.

OBJECTIVE 3 — Prepare a Reconciliation of the Checking Account

bank statement
A listing of all transactions that occurred in a checking account during a month and the beginning and ending balances.

Every month, a business receives a **bank statement** that shows all transactions that occurred in connection with its checking account. The bank statement lists the following information:

- The beginning balance for the period
- All deposits received by the bank and added to the balance
- Other items added to the balance such as the proceeds from promissory notes collected for the business by the bank
- All checks paid by the bank and deducted from the balance
- Other items deducted from the balance such as bank service charges
- The ending balance for the period

A business that has efficient cash control procedures will promptly reconcile the bank statement with its own cash records, known as a **bank reconciliation**.

bank reconciliation
Bringing the ending balances of the bank statement and the firm's own cash records into agreement.

The ending balance on the bank statement will almost always differ from the ending balance in the firm's checkbook and Cash account. The reconciliation process involves finding the factors that are causing the difference and bringing the balances into agreement.

Some of the factors that may cause a difference between the ending bank statement balance and the ending balance in a firm's cash records are as follows:

- Deposits in transit—deposits made by the firm and listed in its cash records that do not appear on the bank statement.
- Outstanding checks—checks issued by the firm and listed in its cash records that have not yet been paid by the bank.
- ATM deposits and withdrawals—deposits and withdrawals made by automatic teller machine that appear on the bank statement but may not yet be listed in the firm's cash records.

- Bank fees—service charges and other bank fees that appear on the bank statement but may not yet be listed in the firm's cash records.
- NSF checks—customer checks that were deposited but have been returned by the bank because of insufficient funds. (NSF means "non-sufficient funds.")
- Errors—errors made by the bank that appear on the bank statement or errors made by the firm in its cash records.

The accountant must examine the bank statement and the firm's cash records to find the factors causing the difference between the two ending balances. The accountant then prepares a bank reconciliation statement such as the one shown below.

ACME Computer Repair
Bank Reconciliation Statement

Ending Bank Statement Balance		$36,800
Add:		
Deposits in Transit	$ 2,000	
Bank Errors	100	2,100
		$38,900
Deduct:		
Outstanding Checks	$ 4,400	
Bank Errors	200	4,600
Adjusted Bank Statement Balance		$34,300
Ending Cash Account/Checkbook Balance		$31,500
Add:		
Bank Collections	$ 5,000	
ATM Deposits	1,000	
Errors	300	6,300
		$37,800
Deduct:		
NSF Checks	$ 400	
Errors	150	
ATM Withdrawals	2,900	
Bank Fees	50	3,500
Adjusted Cash Account/Checkbook Balance		$34,300

Peachtree allows you to automate this task of preparing a bank reconciliation statement. To prepare for the bank reconciliation process for Superior Carpet and Tile, use the Report function of Peachtree to obtain information about the firm's cash receipts/bank deposits and checks issued.

Reviewing/Printing the Cash Receipts Journal
Step 1:
Open Chp. 6 – Superior Carpet and Tile, which you updated previously in the chapter. Click Reports & Forms, and then click *Accounts Receivable*.

Step 2:
The Select a Report or Form dialog box will appear. At the Accounts Receivable: Customer and Sales section, click *Cash Receipts Journal*, as shown in figure 6–39.

FIGURE 6–39
Accounts Receivable: Customers and Sales Section with Cash Receipts Journal Chosen

Step 3:
Click the <u>P</u>rint button on the Select a Report or Form toolbar.

Step 4:
Click *Check Date* from the drop-down list in the *Sort by* field.

Step 5:
Select *Cash Account ID* from the *Select a filter* scroll-down list.

Step 6:
Select the *Equal to* radio button and click *100, Cash* from the drop-down list of chart of accounts.

Step 7:
Click *Range* in the *Date* field, *Jan 1, 2010* in the *From* field, and *Jan 31, 2010* in the *To* field. Compare your Modify Report – Cash Receipts Journal dialog box with figure 6–40. Make any changes if necessary.

FIGURE 6-40
Modify Report – Cash
Receipts Journal Dialog
Box

Step 8:
Click OK. Then click OK again at the Print screen.

FIGURE 6-41
Printout of Cash
Receipts Journal

Step 9:
Compare your printout of the Cash Receipts Journal for Superior Carpet and Tile with the one shown in figure 6–41.

Chp. 6 - Superior Carpet and Tile
Cash Receipts Journal
For the Period From Jan 1, 2010 to Jan 31, 2010

Filter Criteria includes: Report order is by Check Date. Report is printed in Detail Format.

Date	Account ID	Transaction Ref	Line Description	Debit Amnt	Credit Amnt
1/14/10	104	1002	Invoice: 1002		2,500.00
	100		Parker's Construction	2,500.00	
1/23/10	401	1080	Discounts Taken	100.00	
	104		Invoice: 1002		2,500.00
	100		Parker's Construction	2,400.00	
				5,000.00	5,000.00

Reviewing/Printing the Check Register

Step 1:
At the Select a Report or Form dialog box, in the Reports tab list, click *Accounts Payable*.

Step 2:
At the Accounts Payable: Vendors and Purchases section, click *Check Register*, as shown in figure 6–42.

Step 3:
Click the Options button on the Select a Report or Form toolbar.

Step 4:
From the Modify Report – Check Register window, select the following:

Sort by:	**Check Number**
Select a Filter:	**Cash Account ID**
Equal to:	**Account 100, Cash**
Date:	**Range**
From:	**Jan 1, 2010**
To:	**Jan 31, 2010**

Step 5:
Click OK. Then click Print on the Check Register toolbar.

Step 6:
Compare your printout of the Check Register for Superior Carpet and Tile with the one shown in figure 6–43.

FIGURE 6–43
Printout of Check
Register

Page: 1

Chp. 6 - Superior Carpet and Tile
Check Register
For the Period From Jan 1, 2010 to Jan 31, 2010
Filter Criteria includes: Report order is by Date.

Check #	Date	Payee	Cash Account	Amount
2005	1/31/10	Office Max	100	1,372.00
2006	1/31/10	John Charles Manag	100	3,000.00
2008	1/31/10	MID Midtown Irrigatio	100	676.65
2007	1/31/10	Pacific Bell	100	765.39
2004	1/31/10	Apex Floor Care Serv	100	250.00
Total				6,064.04

Step 7:

Close the Select a Report or Form dialog box.

Preparing the Account Reconciliation

On February 8, 2010, Superior Carpet and Tile received the bank statement shown in figure 6–44. This bank statement shows checks that the business issued in January and deposits that it made in January. The bank paid the checks early in February. Follow the steps outlined below to reconcile the bank statement with the firm's cash records.

FIGURE 6–44
Bank Statement for
Superior Carpet and Tile

Bank of California
2346 Center Way
Fresno, CA 94534

Superior Carpet and Tile
Acct: 2341121

REGULAR CHECKING

Previous Balance	$ 35,900.00	**Statement Date: January 31, 2010**
2 Deposits (+)	4,900.00	
4 Checks (-)	5,298.65	
2 Other Deductions (-)	150.00	
Service (-)	20.00	
Ending Balance	35,331.35	

DEPOSITS

January 14, 2010	$ 2,500.00				
January 23, 2010	2,400.00				

CHECKS (Asterisk* indicates break in check number sequence)

January 31, 2010	2005	$ 1,372.00			
January 31, 2010	2006	3,000.00			
January 31, 2010	2008	676.65			
January 31, 2010	2004*	250.00			
January 31, 2010	Bank Fees	20.00			

OTHER DEDUCTIONS (ATM's)

January 16, 2010	ATM	$ 50.00			
January 21, 2010	ATM	100.00			

Step 1:

Click Tasks, and then click *Account Reconciliation*.

Step 2:

Click the *magnifying glass* icon next to the *Account to Reconcile* field and then click *100* (the number of the Cash account) from the drop-down list.

Step 3:

At the *Statement Date* field, choose *Jan 31, 2010*.

Step 4:

Click in the *Status* field for each check that is listed on Superior's bank statement to display a blue check mark which designates that the check has cleared (figure 6–44). Remember to check off only the cleared checks (the checks paid by the bank).

Step 5:

Compare your work with figure 6–45. Check 2007 should not be check marked because it did not clear the bank.

FIGURE 6–45
Account Reconciliation
Window – Cleared
Checks

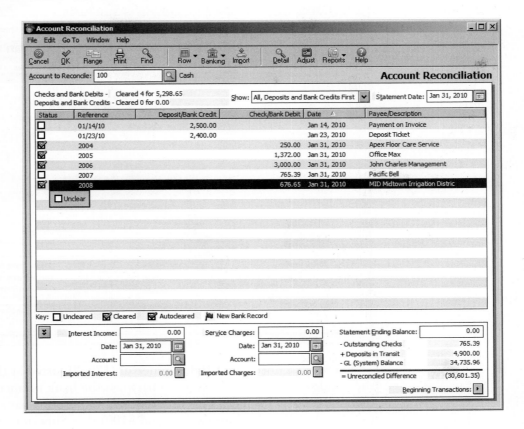

Step 6:

Click a blue check mark in the *Status* field for each of the deposits listed on the bank statement.

Step 7:

Key **35,331.35** in the *Statement Ending Balance* field at the bottom right of the screen, as shown in figure 6–46, and then press Enter.

FIGURE 6–46
Account Reconciliation
Window – Statement
Ending Balance

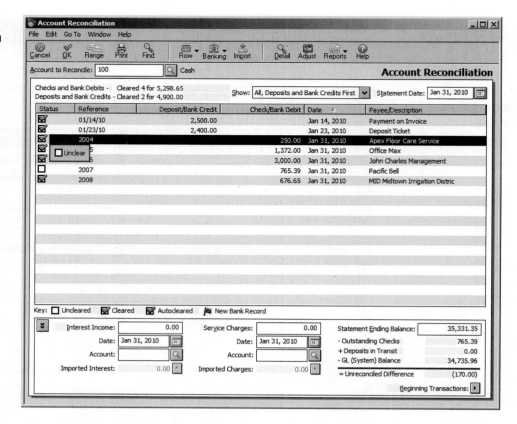

There is an unreconciled difference of (170.00) listed at the bottom of the window. This is the difference between the bank balance and the GL (general ledger) balance. This difference results from a bank service charge ($20) and ATM withdrawals ($50 and $100) that Superior has not yet recorded in its cash records.

Step 8:
Click the Adjust button on the Account Reconciliation toolbar to create the new account needed and enter the necessary transactions. Use the General Journal Entry window, as shown in figure 6–47.

FIGURE 6–47
General Journal Entry
Window

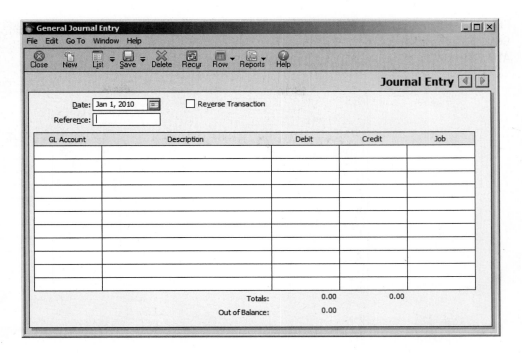

Step 9:
Key **01/16/10** in the *Date* field.

Step 10:
Key **Stmnt 1/31** in the *Reference* field.

Step 11:
Key **301.5 (Drawing)** in the *GL Account* field.

Step 12:
Key **ATM Withdrawals** in the *Description* field.

Step 13:
Key **50.00** in the *Debit* field. This represents the personal withdrawal from the ATM.

Step 14:
Key **100 (Cash)** in the next *GL Account* field. The system should automatically add "ATM Withdrawals" on each description line until the entire entry is saved.

Step 15:
Key **50.00** in the *Credit* field.

Step 16:
Compare your entries with the one shown in figure 6–48.

FIGURE 6–48

General Journal Entry for ATM Withdrawals

Step 17:
Click Save on the General Journal Entry toolbar.

Step 18:
Key **01/21/09** in the *Date* field and **Stmnt 1/31** in the *Reference* field.

Step 19:
Key **301.5 (Drawing)** in the *GL Account* field.

Step 20:
Key **ATM Withdrawals** in the *Description* field.

Step 21:
Key **100.00** in the *Debit* field. This represents the second personal withdrawal from the ATM.

Step 22:
Key **100 (Cash)** in the next *GL Account* field. The system should automatically add "ATM Withdrawals" on each description line until the entire entry is saved.

Step 23:
Key **100.00** in the *Credit* field.

Step 24:
Click Save and then close the General Journal Entry window.

Step 25:
Check the *Status* field to enter a blue check mark next to the ATM Withdrawals of $50.00 and $100.00 listed in the Account Reconciliation window.

Step 26:

Key **20.00** in the *Service Charges* field at the bottom of the screen.

Step 27:

Create the following account:

Account ID:	**520**
Description:	**Bank Fee Expense**
Account Type:	**Expenses**

Step 28:

Click *Account 520, Bank Fee Expense,* after clicking the *magnifying glass* next to the *Account* field.

Step 29:

After checking off the ATM withdrawals and entering the service charge and the account number, review figure 6–49 for accuracy.

FIGURE 6–49
Account Reconciliation
Window with
Adjustments Cleared

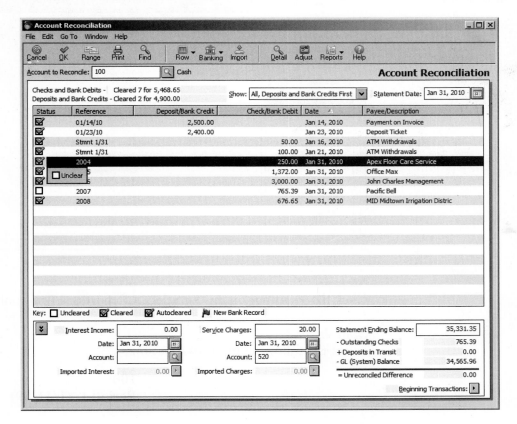

The account reconciliation is now in balance. The unreconciled difference at the bottom of the window is 0.00.

Step 30:

Click <u>O</u>K.

Printing the Account Reconciliation

It is good policy to print a copy of the account reconciliation and keep it on file with the bank statement.

Step 1:
Click Reports & Forms, and then click *Account Reconciliation*.

Step 2:
At the Select a Report or Form dialog box, at the Account Reconciliation: Banking Transactions section, click *Account Reconciliation*, as shown in figure 6–50.

FIGURE 6–50
Account Reconciliation: Banking Transactions Section with Account Reconciliation Chosen

Step 3:
Click the Print button on the Select a Report or Form toolbar.

Step 4:
Select the following filter information:

GL Account ID:	**100**
As of:	**Period 1, (1/31/09)**

Step 5:
Click OK. Then click OK again at the Print window.

Step 6:
Compare your printout with the one shown in figure 6–51.

FIGURE 6–51
Account Reconciliation
for Superior Carpet and
Tile

```
                                                                              Page: 1
                            Chp. 6 - Superior Carpet and Tile
                                Account Reconciliation
                                 As of Jan 31, 2010
                                     100 - Cash
                         Bank Statement Date: January 31, 2010
Filter Criteria includes: Report is printed in Detail Format.


Beginning GL Balance

Add: Cash Receipts                                             4,900.00

Less: Cash Disbursements                                     (6,064.04)

Add (Less) Other                                             35,730.00

Ending GL Balance                                            34,565.96

Ending Bank Balance                                          35,331.35

Add back deposits in transi

Total deposits in transit

(Less) outstanding checks
            Jan 31, 2010    2007              (765.39)

Total outstanding checks                                      (765.39)

Add (Less) Other

Total other

Unreconciled difference                              0.00

Ending GL Balance                                            34,565.96
```

Step 7:

Close the Select a Report or Form dialog box.

Check point

1. What is the purpose of the bank reconciliation process?
2. Name six factors that can cause a difference between the bank statement balance and the Cash account/checkbook balance.

Answers

1. *The purpose of the bank reconciliation process is to bring the ending bank statement balance and the ending Cash account/checkbook balance into agreement.*
2. *Six factors that can cause a difference between the balances are deposits in transit, outstanding checks, ATM deposits and withdrawals, bank fees, NSF checks, and errors.*

Practice Objective 3

Meadowland Healthcare Services received the bank statement shown in figure 6–52 for the month ended January 31, 2010. Use the following steps to prepare a bank reconciliation.

FIGURE 6–52
Bank Statement for
Meadowland Healthcare
Services

Bank of California
2121 Market Street
San Francisco, CA 95434

Meadowland Healthcare Services
  Acct: 20000897

REGULAR CHECKING

Previous Balance	$ 25,000.00	Statement Date: January 31, 2010
2 Deposits (+)	6,469.80	
3 Checks (-)	2,338.18	
2 Other Deductions (-)	150.00	
Service (-)	35.00	
Ending Balance	28,946.62	

DEPOSITS

January 28, 2010	$ 5,644.80				
January 29, 2010	825.00				

CHECKS (Asterisk* indicates break in check number sequence)

January 27, 2010	700	$ 872.20			
January 31, 2010	701	1,200.00			
January 31, 2010	703*	265.98			
January 31, 2010	Bank Fees	35.00			

OTHER DEDUCTIONS (ATM's)

January 16, 2010	ATM	$ 50.00			
January 21, 2010	ATM	100.00			

Step 1:
Open Chp. 6 – Meadowland Healthcare Services, which you updated
previously in the chapter.

Step 2:
Print the Check Register. Your printout should look like figure 6–53.

FIGURE 6–53
Check Register
for Meadowland
Healthcare Services

Chp. 6 - Meadowland Healthcare Services
Check Register
For the Period From Jan 1, 2010 to Jan 31, 2010

Filter Criteria includes: Report order is by Date.

Check #	Date	Payee	Cash Account	Amount
700	1/27/10	Office Depot	10200	872.20
702	1/31/10	Pacific Gas & Electri	10200	345.89
703	1/31/10	General Telephone	10200	265.98
701	1/31/10	Alta Vista Business P	10200	1,200.00
704	1/31/10	Merry Maids	10200	650.00
Total				3,334.07

Step 3:
Print the Cash Receipts Journal. Your printout should look like figure 6–54.

FIGURE 6–54
Cash Receipts
Journal for
Meadowland
Healthcare
Services

Chp. 6 - Meadowland Healthcare Services
Cash Receipts Journal
For the Period From Jan 1, 2010 to Jan 31, 2010
Filter Criteria includes: Report order is by Check Date. Report is printed in Detail Format.

Page: 1

Date	Account ID	Transaction Ref	Line Description	Debit Amnt	Credit Amnt
1/28/10	40100	3240	Discounts Taken	115.20	
	10400		Invoice: 1103		5,760.00
	10200		Rapid Medical Response	5,644.80	
1/29/10	10400	1104	Invoice: 1104		825.00
	10200		Valley Response	825.00	
1/31/10	10400	Bankruptcy	Invoice: 1101		12,000.00
	52000		Doctor's Medical Center	12,000.00	
				18,585.00	18,585.00

Step 4:

Use the following information to create the Bank Fee Expense account:

Account ID:	**50220**
Description:	**Bank Fee Expense**
Account Type:	**Expenses**

Step 5:

Prepare the account reconciliation of *10200 (Regular Checking Account)*. Use the information from the check register, the cash receipts journal, and the bank statement.

Step 6:

Print the *Account Reconciliation* report. Your report should look like figure 6–55.

FIGURE 6–55
Account
Reconciliation
for Meadowland
Healthcare Services

Chp. 6 - Meadowland Healthcare Services
Account Reconciliation
As of Jan 31, 2010
10200 - Regular Checking Account
Bank Statement Date: January 31, 2010
Filter Criteria includes: Report is printed in Detail Format.

Page: 1

Beginning GL Balance				
Add: Cash Receipts			6,469.80	
Less: Cash Disbursements			(3,334.07)	
Add (Less) Other			24,815.00	
Ending GL Balance			27,950.73	
Ending Bank Balance			28,946.62	
Add back deposits in transi				
Total deposits in transit				
(Less) outstanding checks				
	Jan 31, 2010	702	(345.89)	
	Jan 31, 2010	704	(650.00)	
Total outstanding checks				(995.89)
Add (Less) Other				
Total other				
Unreconciled difference			0.00	
Ending GL Balance			27,950.73	

Step 7:

Close the Select a Report or Form dialog box.

End of Chapter Review

Software Command Summary

Cash Payments on Account	Tasks, Payments, Vendor ID, Apply to Invoices
Cash Payments without Invoice	Tasks, Payments, Vendor ID, Apply to Expenses
Cash Receipts on Account	Tasks, Receipts, Customer ID, Apply to Invoices
Cash Receipts without Invoice	Tasks, Receipts, Customer ID, Apply to Revenues
Prepare an Account Reconciliation	Print Cash Receipts Journal, Print Check Register, Tasks, Account Reconciliation, Adjust

Projects and Problems

Content Check

Multiple Choice: Choose only one response for each question.

1. What button within the Receipts window is used to compute the new balance of the Cash account?
   A. Open
   B. Row
   C. Journal
   D. Recalculate
   E. Save

2. To verify that the correct accounts have been debited and credited, what toolbar button would you use to view the Accounting Behind the Screens window?
   A. Open
   B. Event
   C. Journal
   D. Row
   E. Save

3. Which of the following would provide the most useful information needed for the cash account reconciliation?
   A. Aged Payables
   B. Sales Journal
   C. Check Register
   D. Purchases Journal
   E. Vendor List

4. What toolbar button in the Account Reconciliation dialog box is used to enter withdrawals and other items that must be recorded to update the balance of the firm's Cash account?
   A. Range
   B. Adjust
   C. Row
   D. Open
   E. Recur

5. When a business provides a service on credit to a customer, what function of Peachtree is used to record the transaction?
   A. General Journal Entry
   B. Payments
   C. Purchases/Receive Inventory
   D. Receipts
   E. Sales/Invoicing

Short Essay Response: Provide a detailed answer for each question.

1. What are some of the procedures that a business should use to protect its cash?
2. What is the purpose of an account reconciliation?
3. What is the purpose of the Accounting Behind the Screens window?
4. What information appears on the bank statement?
5. Why do the ending balance of the bank statement and the ending balance in a firm's cash records usually differ?
6. What information from a firm's records is needed for the account reconciliation?

Case Problems

Problem 1A

Open Transnational Management Group (TMG), a business consulting firm, which is located on the student data disk.

1. TMG plans to make credit purchases from four new vendors. Create new vendor accounts for the businesses listed below.

Vendor

Vendor ID:	**OPS-01**
Name:	**O'Neal Payroll Services**

General Tab

Contact:	**Annette O'Neal**
Account Number:	**846357**
Mailing Address:	**7314 Sycamore Avenue**
City, ST, Zip:	**Stockton, CA 95210**
Country:	**USA**
Vendor Type:	**Expense**
1099 Type:	**None**
Expense Account:	**78500 (Payroll Service Expense)**

Telephone 1:	209-555-7821
Fax:	209-555-7823

Purchase Info Tab

Tax ID Number:	None
Ship Via:	US Mail
Terms and Credit:	Due EOM, 0.00 Discount

History Tab

Beginning Balance:	0

Vendor

Vendor ID:	GR-02
Name:	Grupe Associates

General Tab

Contact:	Gary Robertson
Account Number:	16432571
Mailing Address:	4189 Holly Lane
City, ST, Zip:	Stockton, CA 95210
Country:	USA
Vendor Type:	Expense
1099 Type:	None
Expense Account:	74000 (Rent or Lease Expense)
Telephone 1:	209-555-7321
Fax:	209-555-7325

Purchase Info Tab

Tax ID Number:	None
Ship Via:	US Mail
Terms and Credit:	Due EOM, 0.00 Discount

History Tab

Beginning Balance:	0

Vendor

Vendor ID:	OFFMAX-03
Name:	Office Max

General Tab

Contact:	Joshua Baker
Account Number:	15491326
Mailing Address:	3915 Webber Lane
City, ST, Zip:	Stockton, CA 95207
Country:	USA
Vendor Type:	Supplier
1099 Type:	None
Expense Account:	12000 (Office Supplies)
Telephone 1:	209-555-7981
Fax:	209-555-7988

Purchase Info Tab
Tax ID Number:	**None**
Ship Via:	**Fed-Ex**
Terms and Credit:	**2% 10 Days, Net 30 Days**

History Tab
Beginning Balance:	**0**

Vendor
Vendor ID:	**ATT-04**
Name:	**AT&T**

General Tab
Contact:	**George Sanchez**
Account Number:	**19852637**
Mailing Address:	**6185 West Montgomery Avenue**
City, ST, Zip:	**Stockton, CA 95207**
Country:	**USA**
Vendor Type:	**Expense**
1099 Type:	**None**
Expense Account:	**76000 (Telephone Expense)**
Telephone 1:	**209-555-5461**
Fax:	**209-555-5463**

Purchase Info Tab
Tax ID Number:	**None**
Ship Via:	**US Mail**
Terms and Credit:	**Due EOM, 0.00 Discount**

History Tab
Beginning Balance:	**0**

2. TMG plans to sell its services on credit to the following three new customers. Create new customer accounts for each.

Customer
Customer ID:	**LM-01**
Name:	**Lee Manufacturing**

General Tab
Contact:	**Robert Lee**
Account Number:	**1731**
Billing Address:	**4639 Lincoln Boulevard**
City, ST, Zip:	**Stockton, CA 95210**
Country:	**USA**
Sales Tax:	
Customer Type:	**General**
Telephone 1:	**209-555-1320**
Fax:	**209-555-1330**

Sales Info Tab
GL Sales Account:	**40000**
Ship Via:	**Fed-Ex**

Pricing Level:	**Price Level 1**
Form Options:	**Default**

Payment & Credit Tab

Terms and Credit:	**2% 10 Days, Net 30 Days**

History Tab

Beginning Balance:	**0**

Customer

Customer ID:	**CD-02**
Name:	**Computer Design**

General Tab

Contact:	**Sylvia Harrison**
Account Number:	**1450**
Billing Address:	**48195 East Powell**
City, ST, Zip:	**Tracy, CA 95376**
Country:	**USA**
Sales Tax:	
Customer Type:	**General**
Telephone 1:	**209-555-2083**
Fax:	**209-555-2085**

Sales Info Tab

GL Sales Account:	**40000**
Ship Via:	**Fed-Ex**
Pricing Level:	**Price Level 1**
Form Options:	**Default**

Payment & Credit Tab

Terms and Credit:	**2% 10 Days, Net 30 Days**

History Tab

Beginning Balance:	**0**

Customer

Customer ID:	**BAS-03**
Name:	**Barron's Accounting Services**

General Tab

Contact:	**Armando Barron**
Account Number:	**1426**
Billing Address:	**44137 21st Street**
City, ST, Zip:	**Watsonville, CA 95760**
Country:	**USA**
Sales Tax:	
Customer Type:	**General**
Telephone 1:	**209-555-3621**
Fax:	**209-555-3635**

Sales Info Tab

GL Sales Account:	**40000**
Ship Via:	**Fed-Ex**
Pricing Level:	**Price Level 1**
Form Options:	**Default**

Payment & Credit Tab

Terms and Credit:	**2% 10 Days, Net 30 Days**

History Tab

Beginning Balance:	**0**

3. Enter each of the transactions listed below for April 2010. Choose the appropriate option on the Tasks menu: Sales/Invoicing, Purchases/Receive Inventory, Receipts, or Payments. Use Account 49000, Fee Discount for any discounts taken by customers.

Date	Transaction
Apr. 4	Received a bill (Invoice 9582) of $1,780 for monthly rent from Grupe Associates.
5	Performed consulting services for $1,600 on credit for Lee Manufacturing. Issued Invoice 3001.
6	Received a bill (Invoice 12852) of $275 for monthly usage of telephone service from AT&T.
6	Purchased office supplies for $350 on credit from Office Max. Received Invoice 6640.
9	Performed consulting services for $980 on credit for Barron's Accounting Services. Issued Invoice 3002.
9	Performed consulting services for Computer Design for $1,800 in cash, Check No. 1215.
14	Received the amount due for Invoice 3001 from Lee Manufacturing, less a 2% discount, Check No. 3291.
15	Paid the amount due for Invoice 6640 to Office Max, less a 2% discount. Issued Check No. 1020. (Use Account 12000, Office Supplies as the discount account.)
18	Purchased payroll services for $650 on credit from O'Neal Payroll Services. Received Invoice 1593.
24	Received the full amount due for Invoice 3002 from Barron's Accounting Services, Check No. 3145.
25	Performed consulting services for $785 on credit for Computer Design. Issued Invoice 3003. Received check for $225 from the customer.
30	Paid $1,780 on account to Grupe Associates. Issued Check No. 1021.
30	Paid $275 on account to AT&T. Issued Check No. 1022.
30	Received the balance due (Check No. 1265) for Invoice 3003 from Computer Design less a 2% discount on the total of the invoice ($785 × 0.02 = $15.70).

4. Print the following reports for April: *Customer Ledgers, Cash Receipts Journal, Vendor Ledgers, Cash Disbursements Journal,* and *General Ledger Trial Balance.*

Problem 2A

Open Chao and Associates, an engineering company, which is located on the student data disk.

This firm received the following bank statement for the month ended June 30, 2010:

1. Prepare an account reconciliation. Bring the ending balances of the firm's bank statement and regular checking account into agreement.

2. Print an *Account Reconciliation* report.

		Bank of San Joaquin			
		2876 Main Street			
		Tracy, CA 95376			
Chao and Associates					
Account No: 87942331					
REGULAR CHECKING					
Beginning Balance	$24,900.00	**Statement Date: June 30, 2010**			
2 Deposits (+)	9,900.00				
4 Checks (-)	9,257.50				
2 Other Deductions (-)	300.00				
Service Charges(-)	40.00				
Ending Balance	25,202.50				
DEPOSITS					
June 14, 2010	$5,000.00				
June 23, 2010	4,900.00				
CHECKS AND BANK FEES (Asterisk* indicates break in check number sequence)					
June 20, 2010	2000	$2,744.00			
June 24, 2010	2001	4,200.00			
June 28, 2010	2002	1,813.50			
June 30, 2010	2004*	500.00			
June 30, 2010	Bank Fees	40.00			
OTHER DEDUCTIONS (ATMs)					
June 16, 2010	ATM	$ 100.00			
June 21, 2010	ATM	200.00			

Problem 1B

Open Abelar Designs, an architectural firm, which is located on the student data disk.

1. Create new vendor accounts for the four new vendors listed below.

   Vendor
Vendor ID:	**GPS-01**
Name:	**Gentry Payroll Services**

   General Tab
Contact:	**Greg Gentry**
Account Number:	**659412**
Mailing Address:	**9137 Corral Drive**
City, ST, Zip:	**Stockton, CA 95210**
Country:	**USA**
Vendor Type:	**Expense**
1099 Type:	**None**
Expense Account:	**78500 (Payroll Service Expense)**
Telephone 1:	**209-555-9865**
Fax:	**209-555-9890**

   Purchase Info Tab
Tax ID Number:	**None**
Ship Via:	**US Mail**
Terms and Credit:	**Due EOM, 0.00 Discount**

   History Tab
Beginning Balance:	**0**

   Vendor
Vendor ID:	**GR-02**
Name:	**Grupe Associates**

   General Tab
Contact:	**Gary Robertson**
Account Number:	**6549763**
Mailing Address:	**4189 Holly Lane**
City, ST, Zip:	**Stockton, CA 95210**
Country:	**USA**
Vendor Type:	**Expense**
1099 Type:	**None**
Expense Account:	**79000 (Rent or Lease Expense)**
Telephone 1:	**209-555-7321**
Fax:	**209-555-7325**

   Purchase Info Tab
Tax ID Number:	**None**
Ship Via:	**US Mail**
Terms and Credit:	**Due EOM, 0.00 Discount**

History Tab
    Beginning Balance: 0

Vendor
    Vendor ID: OFFMAX-03
    Name: Office Max

General Tab
    Contact: Heather Brannon
    Account Number: 496782
    Mailing Address: 3915 Webber Lane
    City, ST, Zip: Stockton, CA 95207
    Country: USA
    Vendor Type: Supplier
    1099 Type: None
    Expense Account: 12000 (Office Supplies)
    Telephone 1:   209-555-7981
    Fax: 209-555-7988

Purchase Info Tab
    Tax ID Number: None
    Ship Via: Fed-Ex
    Terms and Credit: 2% 10 Days, Net 30 Days

History Tab
    Beginning Balance: 0

Vendor
    Vendor ID: PB-04
    Name: Pacific Bell

General Tab
    Contact: Monica Volbrecht
    Account Number: 9653294
    Mailing Address: 62918 South Street
    City, ST, Zip: Stockton, CA 95207
    Country: USA
    Vendor Type: Expense
    1099 Type: None
    Expense Account: 80500 (Telephone Expense)
    Telephone 1:   209-555-7834
    Fax: 209-555-7840

Purchase Info Tab
    Tax ID Number: None
    Ship Via: US Mail
    Terms and Credit: Due EOM, 0.00 Discount

History Tab
    Beginning Balance: 0

2. Create new customer accounts for the three customers listed below.

Customer
Customer ID:	**AR-01**
Name:	**Artistic Renovations**

General Tab
Contact:	**Francisco Moreno**
Account Number:	**1465**
Billing Address:	**95517 Tracy Boulevard**
City, ST, Zip:	**Stockton, CA 95210**
Country:	**USA**
Sales Tax:	
Customer Type:	**General**
Telephone 1:	**209-555-6497**
Fax:	**209-555-6400**

Sales Info Tab
GL Sales Account:	**40600**
Ship Via:	**Fed-Ex**
Pricing Level:	**Price Level 1**
Form Options:	**Default**

Payment & Credit Tab
Terms and Credit:	**2% 10 Days, Net 30 Days**

History Tab
Beginning Balance:	**0**

Customer
Customer ID:	**KCB-02**
Name:	**Kim's Custom Builders**

General Tab
Contact:	**Paul Kim**
Account Number:	**1398**
Billing Address:	**6432 West Howard Lane**
City, ST, Zip:	**Tracy, CA 95376**
Country:	**USA**
Sales Tax:	
Customer Type:	**General**
Telephone 1:	**209-555-2265**
Fax:	**209-555-2266**

Sales Info Tab
GL Sales Account:	**40200**
Ship Via:	**Fed-Ex**
Pricing Level:	**Price Level 1**
Form Options:	**Default**

Payment & Credit Tab
Terms and Credit: **2% 10 Days, Net 30 Days**

History Tab
Beginning Balance: **0**

Customer
Customer ID: **WC-03**
Name: **Walsh Construction**

General Tab
Contact: **Martha Walsh**
Account Number: **1080**
Billing Address: **4321 23rd Street**
City, ST, Zip: **Manteca, CA 95301**
Country: **USA**
Sales Tax:
Customer Type: **General**
Telephone 1:   **209-555-2136**
Fax: **209-555-2140**

Sales Info Tab
GL Sales Account: **40600**
Ship Via: **Fed-Ex**
Pricing Level: **Price Level 1**
Form Options: **Default**

Payment & Credit Tab
Terms and Credit: **2% 10 Days, Net 30 Days**

History Tab
Beginning Balance: **0**

3. Enter each of the following transactions for May 2010. Choose the appropriate option on the Tasks menu: Sales/Invoicing, Purchases/ Receive Inventory, Receipts, or Payments. Use Account 49000, Fee Discount for any discounts taken by customers.

Date	Transaction
May 5	Received a bill (Invoice 10115) of $1,300 for monthly rent from Grupe Associates.
6	Performed architectural design services for $825 on credit for Artistic Renovations. Issued Invoice 4001.
7	Received a bill (Invoice 26591) of $170 for monthly usage of telephone service from Pacific Bell.
7	Purchased office supplies for $125 on credit from Office Max. Received Invoice 7281.
10	Performed architectural consulting services for $980 on credit for Kim's Custom Builders. Issued Invoice 4002.
15	Received the amount due for Invoice 4001 from Artistic Renovations, less a 2% discount, Check No. 4521.
16	Paid the amount due for Invoice 7281 to Office Max, less a 2% discount. Issued Check No. 231. (Use Account 12000, Office Supplies as the discount.)
18	Purchased payroll services for $450 on credit from Gentry Payroll Services. Received Invoice 8972.
25	Performed architectural design services for $2,340 on credit for Walsh Construction. Issued Invoice 4003.
25	Received the full amount due for Invoice 4002 from Kim's Custom Builders, Check No. 3238.
26	Performed architectural design services for $1,480 on credit for Artistic Renovations. Issued Invoice 4004. Received check for $480 from the customer.
30	Paid $1,300 on account to Grupe Associates. Issued Check No. 232.
30	Paid $170 on account to Pacific Bell. Issued Check No. 233.
31	Received the balance due (Check No. 4527) for Invoice 4004 from Artistic Renovations, less a 2% discount on the total of the invoice ($1,480 × 0.02 = $29.60).

4. Print the following reports for May: *Customer Ledgers, Cash Receipts Journal, Vendor Ledgers, Cash Disbursements Journal,* and *General Ledger Trial Balance.*

Problem 2B

Open Hendrick's Construction, a home building company, which is located on the student data disk.

The firm received the following bank statement for the month ended June 30, 2010:

1. Prepare an account reconciliation. Bring the ending balances of the firm's bank statement and regular checking account into agreement.

2. Print an *Account Reconciliation* report.

		Bank of Stanislaus			
		18132 West 11th Street			
		Tracy, CA 95376			
Hendricks Construction					
Account No: 649575321					
REGULAR CHECKING					
Beginning Balance	$32,800.00	**Statement Date: June 30, 2010**			
2 Deposits (+)	14,850.00				
4 Checks (-)	13,886.25				
2 Other Deductions (-)	450.00				
Service Charges(-)	60.00				
Ending Balance	33,253.75				
DEPOSITS					
June 14, 2010	$7,500.00				
June 23, 2010	$7,350.00				
CHECKS AND BANK FEES (Asterisk* indicates break in check number sequence)					
June 20, 2010	2000	$4,116.00			
June 24, 2010	2001	6,300.00			
June 28, 2010	2002	2,720.25			
June 30, 2010	2004*	750.00			
June 30, 2010	Bank Fees	60.00			
OTHER DEDUCTIONS (ATMs)					
June 16, 2010	ATM	$ 150.00			
June 21, 2010	ATM	300.00			

Cooperative Learning

1. Form a group of three or four students. As a group, examine the Cash Flow Manager and Collection Manager features of Peachtree. These features can be located by accessing Analysis on the main menu. Discuss how these features can be used to help a business meet its financial obligations and increase its collection of accounts receivable.
2. As a group, select a local business that you are familiar with, such as a fast-food restaurant, a supermarket, or a department store. What type of cash control problems might this business have? What procedures could this business use to protect its cash?

Writing and Decision Making

Assume that you work for a small company that has a substantial volume of cash receipts from credit customers and cash payments to vendors. The owner, Jesse Ramirez, is thinking about buying Peachtree for her accounting system. Because you have had experience with Peachtree in a college course, she asks you to provide her with information about the Peachtree procedures for the tasks listed below. Write a memo that provides information on the following tasks:

1. Setting up customer accounts and vendor accounts
2. Recording credit sales and credit purchases
3. Recording cash receipts and cash payments on account

CHAPTER 7

Preparing the Financial Statements

Learning Objectives

1. Journalize the adjusting entries

2. Prepare and print the financial statements

3. Change the accounting period

Software Features

- Print and Filter feature

- Copying Financial Statement Format feature

- Designing Reports feature, including text formatting

- Changing the Accounting Period feature

Every accounting system must keep a detailed record of the financial transactions that take place within a business. However, the ultimate purpose of an accounting system is to provide timely, reliable information that the owners and managers can use to make decisions. Much of this information comes from financial statements.

How much profit did we earn? Do we have enough cash to meet our operating needs? How much do we owe to vendors? How much can we expect to receive from credit customers? The financial statements provide the answers to questions such as these.

One of the great benefits of a computerized accounting system like Peachtree is the ease with which you can produce financial statements. In manual accounting, the process of taking a trial balance of the general ledger accounts, recording adjustments, calculating the adjusted account balances, and then preparing the financial statements can be difficult and time consuming. In Peachtree, much of this work is done by the system itself.

Once adjusting entries have been recorded, Peachtree can automatically produce an income statement, a balance sheet, a statement of changes in financial position, and a statement of cash flow.

OBJECTIVE 1 — Journalize the Adjusting Entries

> **adjusting entries**
> Entries that are used to bring the general ledger accounts up to date so that they include previously unrecorded items that relate to the period.

Before the financial statements are prepared at the end of a period, it is necessary to make **adjusting entries**. These types of entries are used to bring the general ledger accounts up to date so that they include previously unrecorded items that relate to the period.

In accrual accounting, all revenue must be recorded when earned and all expenses must be recorded when incurred. However, in most businesses, certain items are not recorded during a period. For example, as of January 31, 2010, Superior Carpet and Tile has not yet recorded the expenses for supplies used, depreciation of equipment, and unpaid salaries. Adjusting entries must be made for these items. Adjusting entries affect one balance sheet account and one income statement account.

Recording the Adjusting Entry for Supplies Used

During any accounting period, the employees of a firm constantly use paper clips, computer paper, staples, and other office supplies. Obviously, it is not practical to record the expense for supplies used on a day-to-day basis. Instead, businesses make an adjusting entry for supplies used at the end of the period.

Remember that when Superior Carpet and Tile purchases office supplies, it records their cost in the asset account Office Supplies. On January 31, 2010, this account has a balance of $1,962. However, when the firm takes an inventory of the office supplies on hand, it finds that they total $1,062. Thus, the firm has used $900 of office supplies during January.

On January 31, 2010, Superior must make an adjusting entry to record the expense for the $900 of office supplies used in January. This entry appears in the general journal. It consists of a debit of $900 to Office Supplies Expense and a credit of $900 to Office Supplies.

One effect of this adjusting entry is to establish the expense for office supplies for the period. The other effect is to reduce the balance of the asset account Office Supplies to $1,062, the amount of supplies actually on hand.

Recording the Adjusting Entry for Depreciation

depreciation The process of allocating the cost of a fixed asset to operations during its useful life.

Every fixed asset except land is subject to depreciation. Remember that **depreciation** is the process of allocating the cost of a fixed asset to operations during its useful life. An adjusting entry must be made to record the depreciation expense for each type of fixed asset that a business owns. Various methods are available for calculating depreciation. Some of these methods will be discussed in a later chapter.

Superior Carpet and Tile owns one type of fixed asset—equipment. It depreciates the equipment at the rate of $1,000 a month. Therefore, on January 31, 2010, Superior makes an adjusting entry to record $1,000 of depreciation expense for January. This entry consists of a debit to Depreciation Expense–Equipment and a credit to Accumulated Depreciation–Equipment.

Remember that Accumulated Depreciation–Equipment is a contra asset account. It has a credit balance, which is contrary to the normal debit balance of an asset account. Accumulated Depreciation–Equipment is used to show the total amount of depreciation taken on the equipment during its useful life.

Recording the Adjusting Entry for Unpaid Salaries

Often, when an accounting period ends, a business owes salaries to its employees. This situation occurs because the end of the accounting period falls in the midst of a payroll period. For example, suppose that a firm has a weekly payroll period that extends from Monday to Friday, and the employees receive their paychecks on Friday. If the accounting period ends on a Wednesday, the firm will owe unpaid salaries for three days—Monday, Tuesday, and Wednesday.

On January 31, 2010, Superior Carpet and Tile owes $800 of unpaid salaries. An adjusting entry must be made to record the expense for unpaid salaries. This entry consists of a debit of $800 to Wages and Salaries Expense and a credit of $800 to Wages and Salaries Payable.

The firm has a liability for the salaries owed to its employees. Therefore, the account credited in the adjusting entry is the liability account Wages and Salaries Payable.

Using Peachtree to Record Sample Adjusting Entries

Follow the steps outlined below to make adjusting entries for Superior Carpet and Tile as of January 31, 2010. All of these entries should appear in the general journal.

Step 1:
Open Superior Carpet and Tile (Chp. 7 – Superior Carpet and Tile if student disk is used). Close the Action Items log.

Step 2:

The first adjusting entry is for $900 of office supplies used during January. Click *General Journal Entry* from the Shortcuts section at the side of the basic Peachtree window, as shown in figure 7–1.

FIGURE 7–1
General Journal Entry from the Shortcuts Section

Step 3:

The General Journal Entry window will appear. Change the date to *Jan 31, 2010.*

Step 4:

Key **506** (Office Supplies Expense) in the *GL Account* field.

Step 5:

Key **Adjusting Entry** in the *Description* field.

Step 6:

Key **900.00** as the amount in the *Debit* field, and tab to the next row.

Step 7:

Key **108** (Office Supplies) in the *GL Account* field.

Step 8:

Key **900.00** in the *Credit* field.

Step 9:

Compare your work with the completed entry shown in figure 7–2. Make any necessary changes.

FIGURE 7–2
Completed Adjusting
Entry for Office Supplies
Used

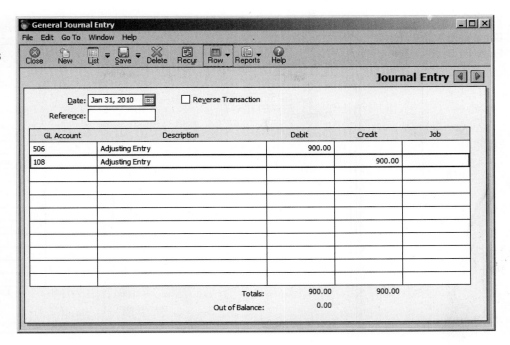

Step 10:
Click Save. **Note:** Although there are additional blank lines on which to record other adjusting entries, it is good practice to enter them separately.

Step 11:
The second adjusting entry is for $1,000 of depreciation on Superior's equipment during January. Key **510** (Depreciation Expense–Equipment) in the *GL Account* field.

Step 12:
Key **Adjusting Entry** in the *Description* field.

Step 13:
Key **1,000.00** in the *Debit* field, and tab to the next row.

Step 14:
Key **112.5** (Accum. Depreciation–Equipment) in the *GL Account* field.

Step 15:
Key **1,000.00** as the amount in the *Credit* field.

Step 16:
Check your work for accuracy by comparing it with figure 7–3. Then click Save.

FIGURE 7–3
Completed Adjusting
Entry for Depreciation

General Journal Entry

File Edit Go To Window Help

Close New List Save Delete Recur Row Reports Help

Journal Entry

Date: Jan 31, 2010   ☐ Reverse Transaction
Reference:

GL Account	Description	Debit	Credit	Job
510	Adjusting Entry	1,000.00		
112.5	Adjusting Entry		1,000.00	

Totals:	1,000.00	1,000.00	
Out of Balance:	0.00		

Step 17:
The third adjusting entry is for $800 of unpaid salaries. Key **512** (Wages and Salaries Expense) in the *GL Account* field.

Step 18:
Key **Adjusting Entry** in the *Description* field.

Step 19:
Key **800.00** in the *Debit* field, and tab to the next row.

Step 20:
Superior does not have a Wages and Salaries Payable account. Therefore, use the following information to create this account.

Account ID:	**210**
Description:	**Wages and Salaries Payable**
Account Type:	**Other Current Liabilities**

Step 21:
Key **210** in the *GL Account* field.

Step 22:
Key **800.00** in the *Credit* field.

Step 23:
Check your work for accuracy by comparing it with figure 7–4. Then click Save and close the General Journal Entry window.

FIGURE 7–4
Completed Adjusting
Entry for Unpaid Salaries

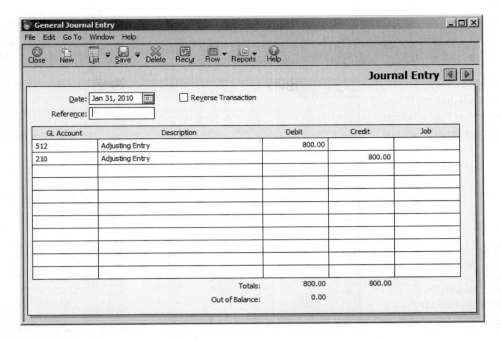

Reviewing the Adjusting Entries

It is a good practice to review the adjusting entries after they have been recorded. To review the adjusting entries made for Superior Carpet and Tile follow these steps:

Step 1:
Click the *Business Status* icon on the Navigation Aids toolbar at the left side of the basic Peachtree window.

Step 2:
Select *General Ledger* from the Find a Report, Category drop-down list, as shown in figure 7–5.

Step 3:
Select *General Journal* from the Find a Report, Report drop-down list, as shown in figure 7–6.

NOTE

Select Reports from the main Menu bar if you wish to narrow the focus of the report.

Step 4:
Click Display.

Step 5:
Compare your adjusting entries with the ones shown in figure 7–7. Make any necessary changes. Note that entries from previous chapters are also included in the *General Journal* report of January 31, 2010.

FIGURE 7–7
Completed Adjusting Entries in General Journal

Chp. 7 - Superior Carpet and Tile
General Journal
For the Period From Jan 1, 2010 to Jan 31, 2010

Page: 1

Filter Criteria includes: Report order is by Date. Report is printed with Accounts having Zero Amounts and with shortened descriptions and in Detail Format.

Date	Account ID	Reference	Trans Description	Debit Amt	Credit Amt
1/1/10	100	BEGBAL		35,900.00	
	102			250.00	
	104			15,000.00	
	106			5,900.00	
	108			590.00	
	110			1,200.00	
	112			21,000.00	
	200				79,840.00
	301				
1/16/10	301.5	Stmnt 1/31	ATM Withdrawals	50.00	
	100		ATM Withdrawals		50.00
1/21/10	301.5	Stmnt 1/31	ATM Withdrawals	100.00	
	100		ATM Withdrawals		100.00
1/31/10	506		Adjusting Entry	900.00	
	108		Adjusting Entry		900.00
	510		Adjusting Entry	1,000.00	
	112.5		Adjusting Entry		1,000.00
	512		Adjusting Entry	800.00	
	210		Adjusting Entry		800.00
1/31/10	100	01/31/10	Service Charge		20.00
	520		Service Charge	20.00	
			Total	**82,710.00**	**82,710.00**

Step 6:
Close the General Journal window.

P r a c t i c e   O b j e c t i v e   1

Step 1:
Open Meadowland Healthcare Services (Chp. 7 – Meadowland Healthcare Services if student data disk is used), and make the following adjusting entries for the firm for January 31, 2010:

1. Record the office supplies used during January. An inventory showed office supplies of $370 on hand on January 31. Subtract this amount from the balance of the Office Supplies account to find the amount of the adjustment. **Hint:** The ledger accounts and the balance sheet will provide the necessary information.
2. Record the unpaid salaries of $3,400 on January 31. There is no account for Wages and Salaries Payable. Create this account, using 21000 as the Account ID. Remember, this account is of type Other Current Liabilities.
3. Record depreciation of $750 on the medical equipment for the month of January.

Step 2:
Compare your adjusting entries with figure 7–8.

FIGURE 7–8
Completed Adjusting Entries in General Journal

Page: 1

Chp. 7 - Meadowland Healthcare Services
General Journal
For the Period From Jan 1, 2010 to Jan 31, 2010
Filter Criteria includes: Report order is by Date. Report is printed with Accounts having Zero Amounts and with shortened descriptions and in Detail Format.

Date	Account ID	Reference	Trans Description	Debit Amt	Credit Amt
1/1/10	10000	BEGBAL		250.00	
	10200			25,000.00	
	10600			1,400.00	
	11200			12,000.00	
	30000				38,650.00
	30100				
1/16/10	30100.5	Stmnt 1/31	ATM	50.00	
	10200		ATM		50.00
1/21/10	30100.5	Stmnt 1/31	ATM	100.00	
	10200		ATM		100.00
1/31/10	50600		Adjusting Entry	502.20	
	10800		Adjusting Entry		502.20
	51200		Adjusting Entry	3,400.00	
	21000		Adjusting Entry		3,400.00
	51000		Adjusting Entry	750.00	
	11200.5		Adjusting Entry		750.00
1/31/10	10200	01/31/10	Service Charge		35.00
	50220		Service Charge	35.00	
		Total		**43,487.20**	**43,487.20**

Step 3:
Close the General Journal window.

OBJECTIVE 2 — Prepare and Print the Financial Statements

After the adjusting entries are journalized and posted, Peachtree can be used to produce the following financial statements: the income statement, the statement of changes in financial position, the balance sheet, and the statement of cash flow. You have already printed some of these reports in chapter 3; in this chapter you will learn more about how these reports are used in business, and will also learn how to customize the reports.

The **income statement** reports the results of operations for a period of time. It shows the revenue, expenses, and net income or net loss for the period. The **net income** or **net loss** is the difference between the revenue and expenses. Some people refer to the income statement as the "profit and loss statement."

The **statement of changes in financial position** reports the sources and uses of a firm's working capital for a period of time. **Working capital** is the excess of current assets over current liabilities. Working capital is a measure of a firm's ability to pay its short-term debts as they become due.

The **balance sheet** shows the financial condition of a business as of a specific date. It lists the assets, liabilities, and owner's equity of a business. The balance sheet is a detailed version of the basic accounting equation: Assets = Liabilities + Owner's Equity.

The **statement of cash flow** reports the inflows and outflows of cash from operating activities, investing activities, and financing activities that a business had during a period of time. This statement also shows the net increase or net decrease in cash for the period.

Income Statement

Step 1:
Open Chp. 7 – Superior Carpet and Tile, which you previously updated, and close the Action Items log.

Step 2:
Click Reports & Forms from the main Menu bar.

Step 3:
Click *Financial Statements* from the Reports & Forms drop-down list, as shown in figure 7–9.

income statement A report of a firm's revenue, expenses, and net income or net loss for a period.

net income or net loss The difference between revenue and expenses.

statement of changes in financial position A report of a firm's sources and uses of working capital for a period.

working capital The excess of current assets over current liabilities.

balance sheet A report of a firm's assets, liabilities, and owner's equity as of a specific date.

statement of cash flow A report of the inflows and outflows of cash from operating activities, investing activities, and financing activities for a period.

FIGURE 7–9
Financial Statements
Selected from the
Reports & Forms
Drop-Down List

Step 4:
The Select a Report or Form dialog box will appear. Click *<Standard>*
Income Stmnt from the Financial Statements: Balance Sheets and Income
Statements section, as shown in figure 7–10.

FIGURE 7–10
<Standard> Income
Stmnt Chosen from
Reports List

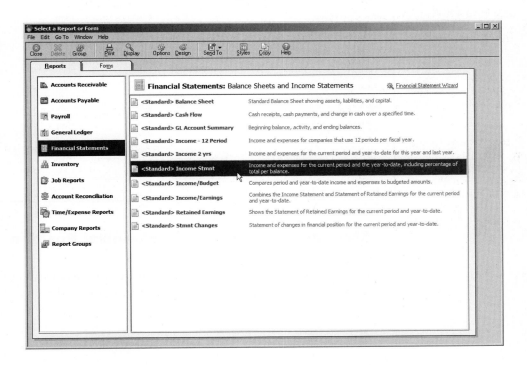

Step 5:
Click the <u>P</u>rint button on the toolbar.

Step 6:
Click *Current Period* at the *Time Frame* field of the Options folder tab.

Step 7:
Click *Show Zero Amounts* to deselect it.

Step 8:
Click OK to print.

Step 9:
Prepare the Print dialog box as needed, and click OK when you are ready to print.

Step 10:
Compare your printout of the income statement with the one shown in figure 7–11.

FIGURE 7–11
Printout of Income Statement

Page: 1

Chp. 7 - Superior Carpet and Tile
Income Statement
For the One Month Ending January 31, 2010

	Current Month			Year to Date	
Revenues					
Installation Services	$	6,250.00	101.63	$ 6,250.00	101.63
Sales Discounts		(100.00)	(1.63)	(100.00)	(1.63)
Total Revenues		6,150.00	100.00	6,150.00	100.00
Cost of Sales					
Total Cost of Sales		0.00	0.00	0.00	0.00
Gross Profit		6,150.00	100.00	6,150.00	100.00
Expenses					
Rent Expense		2,100.00	34.15	2,100.00	34.15
Utilities Expense		226.65	3.69	226.65	3.69
Office Supplies Expense		900.00	14.63	900.00	14.63
Depreciation Expense-Equipment		1,000.00	16.26	1,000.00	16.26
Wages and Salaries Expense		800.00	13.01	800.00	13.01
Miscellaneous Expense		265.89	4.32	265.89	4.32
Uncollectible Accounts Expense		4,000.00	65.04	4,000.00	65.04
Maintenance Expense		250.00	4.07	250.00	4.07
Bank Fee Expense		20.00	0.33	20.00	0.33
Total Expenses		9,562.54	155.49	9,562.54	155.49
Net Income	$	(3,412.54)	(55.49)	$ (3,412.54)	(55.49)

Statement of Changes in Financial Position

Step 1:
Click *<Standard> Stmnt Changes* from the Reports list section of the Select a Report or Form dialog box, as shown in figure 7–12.

FIGURE 7–12
<Standard> Stmnt
Changes Chosen from
Reports List

Step 2:
Click the Print button on the toolbar.

Step 3:
Click *Current Period* at the *Time Frame* field of the Options folder tab.

Step 4:
Click *Show Zero Amounts* to deselect it.

Step 5:
Click OK to print.

Step 6:
Prepare the Print dialog box as needed, and click OK when you are ready to print.

Step 7:
Compare your printout of the statement of changes in financial position with the one shown in figure 7–13.

FIGURE 7–13
Printout of
Statement of
Changes in
Financial Position

Page: 1

Chp. 7 - Superior Carpet and Tile
Statement of Changes in Financial Position
For the one month ended January 31, 2010

	Current Month	Year To Date
Sources of Working Capital		
Net Income	$ (3,412.54)	$ (3,412.54)
Add back items not requiring working capital		
Accum. Depreciation-Equipment	1,000.00	1,000.00
Working capital from operations	(2,412.54)	(2,412.54)
Other sources		
G. Nunez, Capital	79,840.00	79,840.00
Total sources	77,427.46	77,427.46
Uses of working capital		
Equipment	(21,000.00)	(21,000.00)
Total uses	(21,000.00)	(21,000.00)
Net change	$ 56,427.46	$ 56,427.46
Analysis of componants of changes		
Increase <Decrease> in Current Assets		
Cash	$ 34,565.46	$ 34,565.46
Petty Cash	250.00	250.00
Accounts Receivable	12,250.00	12,250.00
Maintenance Supplies	5,900.00	5,900.00
Office Supplies	1,062.00	1,062.00
Prepaid Insurance	1,200.00	1,200.00
<Increase> Decrease in Current Liabilities		
Accounts Payable	1,850.00	1,850.00
Wages abd Salaries Payable	(800.00)	(800.00)
Net change	$ 56,277.46	$ 56,277.46

Balance Sheet

Step 1:

Click *<Standard> Balance Sheet* from the <u>R</u>eports list section in the Select a Report or Form dialog box, as shown in figure 7–14.

FIGURE 7–14
<Standard> Balance
Sheet Chosen from
Reports List

Step 2:

Click the <u>P</u>rint button on the toolbar.

Step 3:
Click *Current Period* at the *Time Frame* field of the Options folder tab.

Step 4:
Click *Show Zero Amounts* to deselect it, if necessary.

Step 5:
Click OK to print.

Step 6:
Prepare the Print dialog box as needed, and click OK when you are ready to print.

Step 7:
Compare your printout of the balance sheet with the one shown in figure 7–15.

FIGURE 7–15
Printout of Balance Sheet

Chp. 7 - Superior Carpet and Tile
Balance Sheet
January 31, 2010

ASSETS

Current Assets		
Cash	$ 34,565.46	
Petty Cash	250.00	
Accounts Receivable	12,250.00	
Maintenance Supplies	5,900.00	
Office Supplies	1,062.00	
Prepaid Insurance	1,200.00	
Total Current Assets		55,227.46
Property and Equipment		
Equipment	21,000.00	
Accum. Depreciation-Equipment	(1,000.00)	
Total Property and Equipment		20,000.00
Other Assets		
Total Other Assets		0.00
Total Assets		$ 75,227.46

LIABILITIES AND CAPITAL

Current Liabilities		
Accounts Payable	$ (1,850.00)	
Wages abd Salaries Payable	800.00	
Total Current Liabilities		(1,050.00)
Long-Term Liabilities		
Total Long-Term Liabilities		0.00
Total Liabilities		(1,050.00)
Capital		
G. Nunez, Capital	79,840.00	
G. Nunez, Drawing	(150.00)	
Net Income	(3,412.54)	
Total Capital		76,277.46
Total Liabilities & Capital		$ 75,227.46

Statement of Cash Flow

Step 1:
Click *<Standard> Cash Flow* from the <u>R</u>eports list section of the Select a Report or Form dialog box, as shown in figure 7–16.

FIGURE 7–16
<Standard> Cash Flow
Chosen from Reports List

Step 2:
Click the <u>P</u>rint button on the toolbar.

Step 3:
Click *Current Period* at the *Time Frame* field of the Options folder tab.

Step 4:
Click *Show Zero Amounts* to deselect it.

Step 5:
Click OK to print.

Step 6:
Prepare the Print dialog box as needed, and click OK when you are ready to print.

Step 7:

Compare your printout of the statement of cash flow with the one shown in figure 7–17.

FIGURE 7–17
Printout of
Statement of
Cash Flow

Page: 1

Chp. 7 - Superior Carpet and Tile
Statement of Cash Flow
For the one Month Ended January 31, 2010

	Current Month	Year to Date
Cash Flows from operating activities		
Net Income	$ (3,412.54)	$ (3,412.54)
Adjustments to reconcile net income to net cash provided by operating activities		
Accum. Depreciation-Equipment	1,000.00	1,000.00
Accounts Receivable	(12,250.00)	(12,250.00)
Maintenance Supplies	(5,900.00)	(5,900.00)
Office Supplies	(1,062.00)	(1,062.00)
Prepaid Insurance	(1,200.00)	(1,200.00)
Accounts Payable	(1,850.00)	(1,850.00)
Wages abd Salaries Payable	800.00	800.00
Total Adjustments	(20,462.00)	(20,462.00)
Net Cash provided by Operations	(23,874.54)	(23,874.54)
Cash Flows from investing activities		
Used For		
Equipment	(21,000.00)	(21,000.00)
Net cash used in investing	(21,000.00)	(21,000.00)
Cash Flows from financing activities		
Proceeds From		
G. Nunez, Capital	79,840.00	79,840.00
Used For		
G. Nunez, Drawing	(150.00)	(150.00)
Net cash used in financing	79,690.00	79,690.00
Net increase <decrease> in cash	$ 34,815.46	$ 34,815.46
Summary		
Cash Balance at End of Period	$ 34,815.46	$ 34,815.46
Cash Balance at Beg of Period	0.00	0.00
Net Increase <Decrease> in Cash	$ 34,815.46	$ 34,815.46

Step 8:

Close the Select a Report or Form dialog box.

Copying One Company's Financial Statement Format for Use by Another

All of the financial statements printed thus far have been selected from the standard list. However, it is possible to use the financial statement format of another company previously set up using Peachtree. For example, suppose a service company likes the format used by another similar company. Peachtree can transfer that format. Follow the steps outlined below to use another company's financial statement format.

Step 1:

Click Reports & Forms from the main Menu bar.

Step 2:

Click *Financial Statements* from the Reports & Forms drop-down list.

PREPARING THE FINANCIAL STATEMENTS **299**

Step 3:

Click *<Standard> Balance Sheet* from the <u>R</u>eports list section of the Select a Report or Form dialog box.

Step 4:

Click the <u>C</u>opy button from the Select a Report or Form toolbar.

Step 5:

The Copy Reports, Financial Statements & Letter Templates dialog box will appear. At the Select a Company to Copy from drop-down list, click the down arrow and then click *Chp 7-Meadowland Healthcare Services*.

Note: You may need to use the Browse feature to locate the company file.

Step 6:

Click the box next to *Include Standard Financial Statements* located at the bottom of the window to select it.

Step 7:

Click *<Standard> Balance Sheet*.

Step 8:

Key **Practice Balance Sheet** in the *New Name* field.

Step 9:

Compare your work with figure 7–18. Then click <u>C</u>opy from the Copy Reports, Financial Statements & Letter Templates toolbar.

FIGURE 7–18
Copy Reports, Financial Statements & Letter Templates Dialog Box

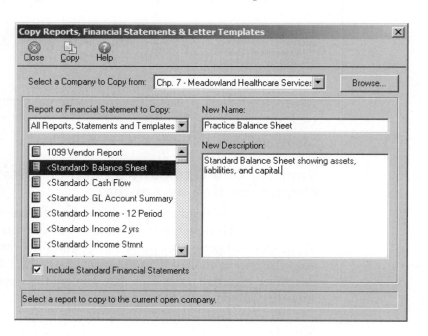

Step 10:

Click Close.

The balance sheet format of Meadowland Healthcare Services is now available for use by Superior Carpet and Tile. The new Practice Balance Sheet is among the financial statement choices appearing in the Reports list section of the Select a Report or Form dialog box, as shown in figure 7–19. Any financial statement can be copied and used in the same manner as the balance sheet discussed here.

FIGURE 7–19
Practice Balance Sheet
Chosen from Report List

Step 11:
Close the Select a Report or Form dialog box.

Designing Financial Statements

Peachtree provides a standard, or default, financial statement format for all statements. However, some companies want to make changes to this format. Such changes may be subtle. For example, a company may want to change the font size or the typeface. The changes in format may also be substantial. Peachtree can accommodate a variety of changes.

You can make changes within each row of the financial statements. A row can have—

- Text Header
- Column Description
- Text Body
- Line Description
- Total Level
- Total Grand Total
- Text Footer

Assume that Superior Carpet and Tile wants to make several changes in the format of its financial statements. Follow the directions given below to make these changes.

Changing the Text Fonts

Step 1:
Click Reports & Forms on the main Menu bar.

Step 2:
Click *Financial Statements* from the drop-down list.

Step 3:
Click *<Standard> Balance Sheet* from the Reports list section of the Select a Report or Form window.

Step 4:
Click the Design button on the Select a Report or Form toolbar.

Step 5:
The <Standard> Balance Sheet window will appear. Click the first Text-Header button, as shown in figure 7–20. This button is aligned with the first line of text of the balance sheet. Notice that each line of text has a corresponding button type.

FIGURE 7–20
Text-Header Button for First Line of Text

Step 6:
Click the *right* mouse button to reveal the drop-down list with text change options, as shown in figure 7–21.

FIGURE 7–21
Drop-Down List with Text
Change Options

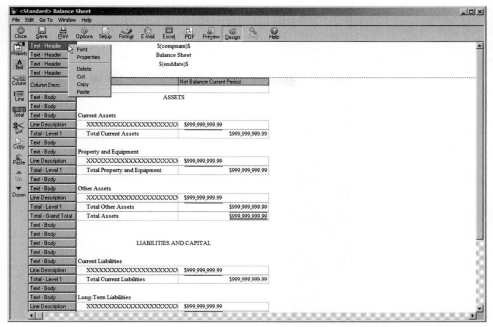

Step 7:
From the drop-down list, click the *left* mouse button to select *Font*.

Step 8:
At the Font dialog box, click *Arial Black* in the Font section.

Step 9:
Click *11* in the Size section, as shown in figure 7–22.

FIGURE 7–22
Font Dialog Box

Step 10:
Click OK and then click No at the Peachtree Query warning. If you click Yes, all fonts on the statement will be changed. If you click No, only the font of the specific line will be changed. Notice the change in the first line of the balance sheet shown in figure 7–23.

FIGURE 7–23

Font Style Change in First Line of Balance Sheet

Changing the Text

Assume that Superior Carpet and Tile would like its balance sheet to have the title of *Special Balance Sheet*. Any change can be made in the wording of the title.

Step 1:
Click the second Text-Header button, which is aligned with the words *Balance Sheet*.

Step 2:
Click the Text button on the left side of the window to reveal the drop-down list with text change options, as shown in figure 7–24.

FIGURE 7–24

Text Drop-Down List with Text Change Options

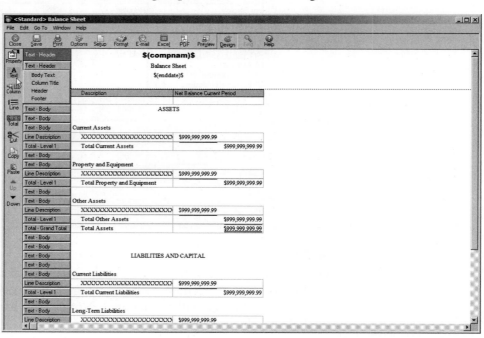

Step 3:
Click *Header*.

Step 4:
The Text dialog box will appear. Key **Special Balance Sheet** in the *Text to Print* box.

Step 5:
Click the down arrow at the *Alignment* field, and then click *Center of Column*, as shown in figure 7–25.

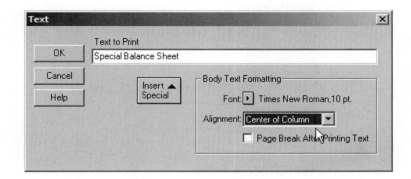

Step 6:
Click OK. Notice that the new text-header *Special Balance Sheet* was inserted above the text-header *Balance Sheet*.

Step 7:
Click the third Text-Header button aligned with the words *Balance Sheet*.

Step 8:
Click the *right* mouse button to reveal the drop-down options for change list.

Step 9:
Click *Delete*.

Step 10:
Review the balance sheet format shown in figure 7–26. Notice the change in the header.

FIGURE 7–26
Balance Sheet Format
with Change in Header

Copying a Line

A line can be copied from one place to another. Copy the header *Special Balance Sheet* to the line below.

Step 1:
Click the second Text-Header button, which is aligned with the words *Special Balance Sheet.*

Step 2:
Click the *right* mouse button to reveal the drop-down list with text change options.

Step 3:
Click *Copy.*

Step 4:
Click the third Text-Header button, and then click the *right* mouse button.

Step 5:
Click *Paste,* and a new line will appear with the words *Special Balance Sheet,* as shown in figure 7–27.

FIGURE 7–27
Copied Line

Deleting a Line

Obviously, Superior does not need two lines that say *Special Balance Sheet*. To delete the second line, follow the steps outlined below.

Step 1:
Click the third Text-Header button, which is aligned with the second *Special Balance Sheet*.

Step 2:
Click the *right* mouse button to reveal the drop-down list with text change options.

Step 3:
Click *Delete*, as shown in figure 7–28.

FIGURE 7–28
Delete Selected from
Text Change Options

Moving rows and changing column titles can be accomplished by using the procedures outlined above.

Step 4:
Close the <Standard> Balance Sheet window.

Step 5:
Save the changes by clicking Yes at the query box.

Step 6:
Key **Modified Balance Sheet** in the *Report name* box of the Save As dialog box.

Step 7:
Key **Font Change** in the *Report description* box, as shown in figure 7–29. Then click Save.

FIGURE 7–29
Modified Balance Sheet
Save As Dialog Box

Step 8:
Close the Select a Report or Form dialog box.

C h e c k   p o i n t

1. What financial statements does Peachtree produce?
2. Which button on the Select a Report or Form toolbar is used to customize financial statements?

Answers
1. *The financial statements produced by Peachtree include the income statement, the statement of changes in financial position, the balance sheet, and the statement of cash flow.*
2. *The Design button is used to customize financial statements.*

P r a c t i c e   O b j e c t i v e   2

Step 1:
Open Chp. 7 – Meadowland Healthcare Services.

Step 2:
Print the following financial statements for the month of January 2010:

- Income statement
- Statement of changes in financial position
- Balance sheet
- Statement of cash flow

Your printouts should look like figures 7–30, 7–31, 7–32, and 7–33.

FIGURE 7–30
Meadowland Healthcare Services Income Statement

Chp. 7 - Meadowland Healthcare Services
Income Statement
For the One Month Ending January 31, 2010

	Current Month			Year to Date	
Revenues					
Revenue	$	21,830.00	100.53	$ 21,830.00	100.53
Sales Discount		(115.20)	(0.53)	(115.20)	(0.53)
Total Revenues		21,714.80	100.00	21,714.80	100.00
Cost of Sales					
Total Cost of Sales		0.00	0.00	0.00	0.00
Gross Profit		21,714.80	100.00	21,714.80	100.00
Expenses					
Rent Expense		1,200.00	5.53	1,200.00	5.53
Utilities Expense		611.87	2.82	611.87	2.82
Bank Fee Expense		35.00	0.16	35.00	0.16
Housekeeping Expense		650.00	2.99	650.00	2.99
Office Supplies Expense		502.20	2.31	502.20	2.31
Depreciation Expense-Medical E		750.00	3.45	750.00	3.45
Wages and Salaries Expenses		3,400.00	15.66	3,400.00	15.66
Uncollectible Accounts Expense		12,000.00	55.26	12,000.00	55.26
Total Expenses		19,149.07	88.18	19,149.07	88.18
Net Income	$	2,565.73	11.82	$ 2,565.73	11.82

FIGURE 7–31
Meadowland Healthcare Services Statement of Changes in Financial Position

Chp. 7 - Meadowland Healthcare Services
Statement of Changes in Financial Position
For the one month ended January 31, 2010

	Current Month		Year To Date
Sources of Working Capital			
Net Income	$	2,565.73 $	2,565.73
Add back items not requiring working capital			
Accum. Depr.-Med Equip		750.00	750.00
Working capital from operations		3,315.73	3,315.73
Other sources			
J. Simon, Capital		38,650.00	38,650.00
Total sources		41,965.73	41,965.73
Uses of working capital			
Medical Equipment		(12,000.00)	(12,000.00)
Total uses		(12,000.00)	(12,000.00)
Net change	$	29,965.73 $	29,965.73
Analysis of componants of changes			
Increase <Decrease> in Current Assets			
Petty Cash	$	250.00 $	250.00
Regular Checking Account		27,950.73	27,950.73
Accounts Recveivable		3,245.00	3,245.00
Medical Supplies		1,400.00	1,400.00
Office Supplies		370.00	370.00
<Increase> Decrease in Current Liabilities			
Wages and Salaries Payable		(3,400.00)	(3,400.00)
Net change	$	29,815.73 $	29,815.73

FIGURE 7–32

Meadowland
Healthcare Services
Balance Sheet

Chp. 7 - Meadowland Healthcare Services
Balance Sheet
January 31, 2010

ASSETS

Current Assets
Petty Cash .... $ 250.00
Regular Checking Account 27,950.73
Accounts Recveivable 3,245.00
Medical Supplies 1,400.00
Office Supplies 370.00

Total Current Assets 33,215.73

Property and Equipment
Medical Equipment 12,000.00
Accum. Depr.-Med Equip .... (750.00)

Total Property and Equipment 11,250.00

Other Assets

Total Other Assets 0.00

Total Assets .... $ 44,465.73

LIABILITIES AND CAPITAL

Current Liabilities
Wages and Salaries Payable .... $ 3,400.00

Total Current Liabilities 3,400.00

Long-Term Liabilities

Total Long-Term Liabilities 0.00

Total Liabilities 3,400.00

Capital
J. Simon, Capital 38,650.00
J. Simon, Drawing .... (150.00)
Net Income 2,565.73

Total Capital 41,065.73

Total Liabilities & Capital .... $ 44,465.73

FIGURE 7–33
Meadowland
Healthcare Services
Statement of Cash
Flow

Chp. 7 - Meadowland Healthcare Services
Statement of Cash Flow
For the one Month Ended January 31, 2010

Page: 1

	Current Month	Year to Date
Cash Flows from operating activities		
Net Income	$ 2,565.73	$ 2,565.73
Adjustments to reconcile net income to net cash provided by operating activities		
Accum. Depr.-Med Equip	750.00	750.00
Accounts Recveivable	(3,245.00)	(3,245.00)
Medical Supplies	(1,400.00)	(1,400.00)
Office Supplies	(370.00)	(370.00)
Wages and Salaries Payable	3,400.00	3,400.00
Total Adjustments	(865.00)	(865.00)
Net Cash provided by Operations	1,700.73	1,700.73
Cash Flows from investing activities Used For		
Medical Equipment	(12,000.00)	(12,000.00)
Net cash used in investing	(12,000.00)	(12,000.00)
Cash Flows from financing activities Proceeds From		
J. Simon, Capital	38,650.00	38,650.00
Used For		
J. Simon, Drawing	(150.00)	(150.00)
Net cash used in financing	38,500.00	38,500.00
Net increase <decrease> in cash	$ 28,200.73	$ 28,200.73
Summary		
Cash Balance at End of Period	$ 28,200.73	$ 28,200.73
Cash Balance at Beg of Period	0.00	0.00
Net Increase <Decrease> in Cash	$ 28,200.73	$ 28,200.73

Step 3:

Make the following changes to the balance sheet:

- Change the font type of the header *Meadowland Healthcare Services* to Arial Black.
- Change the font size of the header *Meadowland Healthcare Services* to 12.
- Add a row below the header *Balance Sheet* that will include the words *Customized Version* centered in the column.
- Save as Customized Balance Sheet.
- Print a new balance sheet with the changes made. Your printout should look like the partial balance sheet in figure 7–34.

Chp. 7 - Meadowland Healthcare Services
Balance Sheet
Customized Version
January 31, 2010

ASSETS

Current Assets
Petty Cash	$ 250.00	
Regular Checking Account	27,950.73	
Accounts Recveivable	3,245.00	
Medical Supplies	1,400.00	
Office Supplies	370.00	
Total Current Assets		33,215.73

Property and Equipment
Medical Equipment	12,000.00	
Accum. Depr.-Med Equip	(750.00)	
Total Property and Equipment		11,250.00

Other Assets

Total Other Assets		0.00
Total Assets	$	44,465.73

LIABILITIES AND CAPITAL

Current Liabilities
Wages and Salaries Payable	$ 3,400.00	
Total Current Liabilities		3,400.00

Long-Term Liabilities

Total Long-Term Liabilities		0.00
Total Liabilities		3,400.00

Capital
J. Simon, Capital	38,650.00	
J. Simon, Drawing	(150.00)	
Net Income	2,565.73	
Total Capital		41,065.73
Total Liabilities & Capital	$	44,465.73

Step 4:
Close the Select a Report or Form dialog box.

OBJECTIVE 3 — Change the Accounting Period

Peachtree allows you to go from month to month without closing the fiscal year by changing the accounting period. This feature makes it possible to produce interim financial statements. You do not have to record the end-of-year closing entries until the fiscal year actually closes. Thus, the balances of the revenue and expense accounts continue to grow after the accounting period is changed. The same is true for the balance of the owner's drawing account.

As you saw, Superior Carpet and Tile has made its adjusting entries and printed its interim financial statements for January 2010. It is now time to get ready for the February entries.

Changing the Accounting Period

Take the following steps to change the accounting period for Superior Carpet and Tile:

Step 1:
Open Chp. 7 – Superior Carpet and Tile and close the Action Items log.

Step 2:
Click Tasks on the main Menu bar, and then *System*, and *Change Accounting Period* from the drop-down lists.

Step 3:
At the Change Accounting Period dialog box, click *02 - Feb 01, 2010 to Feb 28, 2010*, as shown in figure 7–35.

FIGURE 7–35
Feb 01, 2010 to Feb 28, 2010 Selected in Change Accounting Period Dialog Box

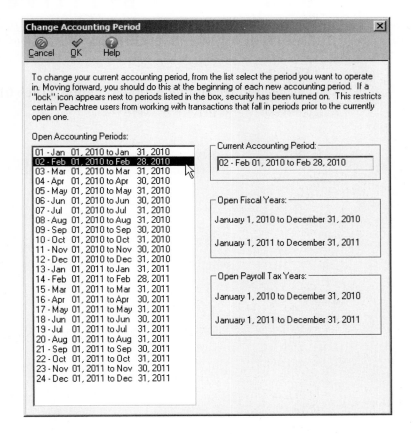

Step 4:
Click OK.

Step 5:
Click No in response to the question "Would you like to print your reports before continuing?" You printed the adjusting entries and the financial statements previously. No further entries or financial statements are needed for January 2010. Click No in response to the question "Would you like to run an Internal Accounting Review?" Superior Carpet and Tile is therefore ready to enter transactions for its second accounting period of the fiscal year—the month of February 2010.

Practice Objective 3

Step 1:
Open Chp. 7 – Meadowland Healthcare Services.

Step 2:
Change the accounting period to Period 2 (Feb 01, 2010 to Feb 28, 2010).
[**Note:** Do not print any reports.]

End of Chapter Review

Software Command Summary

Adjusting Entries	Tasks, General Journal Entry
Customizing Financial Statements	Reports & Forms, Financial Statements, Design
Copying Report Formats	Reports & Forms, Financial Statements, Copy
Changing the Accounting Period	Tasks, System, Change Accounting Period

Projects and Problems

Content Check

Multiple Choice: Choose only one response for each question.

1. Which of the following is the basic accounting equation?
   A. Assets + Liabilities = Owner's Equity
   B. Assets = Liabilities + Owner's Equity
   C. Assets = Liabilities – Owner's Equity
   D. Assets – Owner's Equity = Liabilities
   E. None of the above

2. The financial statement that is a detailed version of the accounting equation is the
   A. income statement.
   B. statement of changes in financial position.
   C. balance sheet.
   D. statement of cash flow.
   E. None of the above

3. If the Office Supplies account has a balance of $2,000 at the beginning of the period and $1,200 at the end of the period, the adjusting entry would include
   A. a debit to Office Supplies and a credit to Office Supplies Expense for $1,200.
   B. a debit to Office Supplies Expense and a credit to Office Supplies for $2,000.
   C. a debit to Office Supplies Expense and a credit to Office Supplies for $800.
   D. a debit to Office Supplies and a credit to Office Supplies Expense for $800.
   E. None of the above

4. The adjusting entry for depreciation expense would include
   A. a debit to Accumulated Depreciation and a credit to Depreciation Expense.
   B. a debit to Depreciation Expense and a credit to Accumulated Depreciation.
   C. a debit to Depreciation Expense and a credit to Revenue.
   D. a debit to Revenue and a credit to Depreciation Expense.
   E. None of the above

5. What are the two types of accounts that appear on the income statement?
   A. expenses and liabilities
   B. expenses and capital
   C. revenue and liabilities
   D. revenue and expenses
   E. None of the above

Short Essay Response: Provide a detailed answer for each question.

1. What information appears on the income statement?
2. What is working capital?
3. Define the balance sheet.
4. Why must businesses depreciate fixed assets such as equipment?
5. Why is it necessary to make an adjustment for supplies used at the end of an accounting period?
6. What information appears on the statement of cash flow?

Case Problems

Problem 1A

Open Premier Management Group, which is located on the student data disk.

1. Make the following adjusting entries for April 30, 2010:
   - Office supplies on hand on April 30, 2010, $180. Use Supplies Expense as the account to be debited.
   - Wages earned, but unpaid, as of April 30, 2010, $1,340. There is no account for Wages Payable. Create the account using 21000 and Other Current Liabilities as the Account ID and Account Type, respectively.
   - Depreciation on the equipment amounted to $100.

2. Print the *General Journal* and *General Ledger Trial Balance* reports.

Problem 2A

Open Professional Accounting Services from the student data disk.

1. Print the following financial statements for the period 2/1/10 to 2/28/10:
   - Income Statement
   - Statement of Changes in Financial Position
   - Balance Sheet
   - Statement of Cash Flow

2. Make the following changes to the Income Statement:
   - Change the Font Type of the first header "Professional Accounting Services" to Arial Black.
   - Change the Font Size of the first and second header to 11.
   - Add a row below the header Income Statement to include the words "For Management Purposes Only" in the center of the column.
   - Delete the Text – Footer.
   - Save as Modified Income Statement.

3. Print a new Income Statement when the changes are complete.

4. Change the accounting period to March 2010.

Problem 1B

Open Cindy's Interior Designs, which is located on the student data disk.

1. Make the following adjusting entries for May 31, 2010:
   - Office supplies on hand on May 31, 2010, $125. Use Supplies Expense as the account to be debited.
   - Wages earned, but unpaid, as of May 31, 2010, $740. There is no account for Wages Payable. Create the account using 21000 and Other Current Liabilities as the Account ID and Account Type, respectively.
   - Depreciation on the equipment amounted to $150.

2. Print the *General Journal* and *General Ledger Trial Balance* reports.

Problem 2B

Open Advanced Graphics from the student data disk.

1. Print the following financial statements for the period 2/1/10 to 2/28/10:
   - Income Statement
   - Statement of Changes in Financial Position
   - Balance Sheet
   - Statement of Cash Flow

2. Make the following changes to the Income Statement:
   - Change the Font Type of the first header "Advanced Graphics" to Arial Black.
   - Change the Font Size of the first and second header to 12.
   - Add a row below the header Income Statement to include the words "For Internal Use Only" in the center of the column.
   - Delete the Text – Footer.
   - Save as Modified Income Statement.

3. Print a new Income Statement when the changes are complete.

4. Change the accounting period to March 2010.

Cooperative Learning

1. Form a group of three or four students. As a group discuss what effects there would be on the income statement and the balance sheet if a business did not make adjustments for supplies used, depreciation, and unpaid salaries. Would expenses be overstated or understated? Net income? Assets? Liabilities?
2. As a group, open any three of the companies you have saved and customize the income statement and balance sheet to the group's liking.

Writing and Decision Making

List the different financial statements that Peachtree produces and state what information each provides. Also explain how these statements can be used to help management make wise financial decisions.

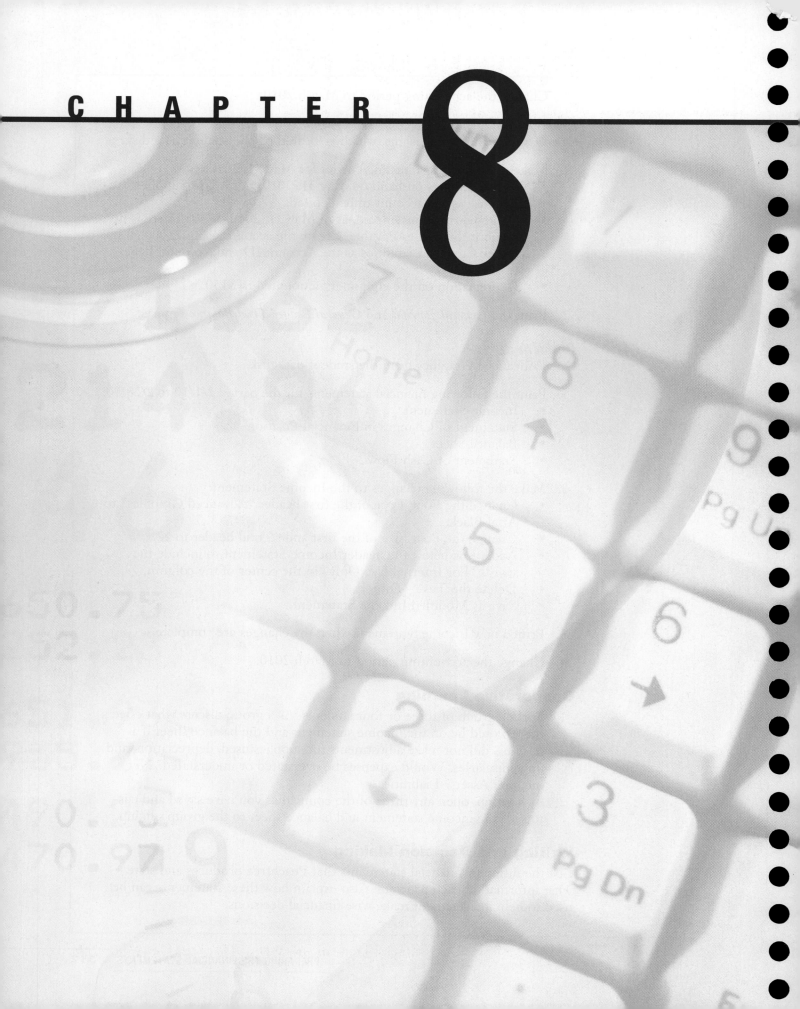

CHAPTER 8

Purchases of Inventory in a Merchandise Business

Learning Objectives

1. Understand the two basic inventory systems

2. Understand the most common inventory costing methods and create the Inventory account

3. Establish subsidiary ledger accounts for inventory items

4. Establish records for sales representatives

5. Process inventory transactions

Software Features

- Maintain inventory items

- Displaying the Item List

- Maintain sales rep records

- Enter purchases/inventory transactions

- Print the *Inventory Valuation* report

Chapters 2 through 7 focused on the accounting procedures of service businesses. In this chapter and succeeding chapters, the focus will be on the accounting procedures of merchandising businesses. Remember that **merchandising businesses** buy goods from manufacturers or wholesalers and resell them for a profit to consumers. Examples of merchandising businesses are department stores, grocery stores, and furniture stores.

One of the assets of a merchandising business is the stock of goods that it has on hand for resale to consumers. This stock of goods is called **inventory** or **merchandise inventory**.

OBJECTIVE 1 — Understand the Two Basic Inventory Systems

Two basic systems are used to keep track of inventory: the periodic inventory system and the perpetual inventory system. In the **periodic inventory system**, a count of all items in a firm's inventory is made at regular intervals, such as at the end of each accounting period, in order to determine ending inventory amounts. In the perpetual inventory system, the firm maintains a running balance for all inventory items.

The **perpetual inventory system** involves the use of inventory records that are updated throughout an accounting period as goods are purchased and sold. The periodic inventory system does not include such records. Peachtree uses the perpetual inventory system. **Note:** Both systems require a physical inventory count in order to determine discrepancies in inventory amounts.

Methods for Costing Inventory

The periodic and perpetual inventory systems keep track of the number of items of each type that a business has in its inventory. In addition to knowing what inventory is on hand, a business also needs to determine the dollar value of its inventory at the end of each accounting period. Various **inventory costing methods** are used for this purpose.

The three most common inventory costing methods are the average cost method, the last-in, first-out (LIFO) method, and the first-in, first-out (FIFO) method. Peachtree supports all of these inventory costing methods.

Processing Sales and Inventory Transactions

Peachtree saves a great deal of time and effort for a merchandising business because it can be used to simultaneously update all records affected by a sale of goods. It increases the Sales, Sales Tax Payable, and Cost of Goods Sold accounts and decreases the Inventory account. Peachtree also adjusts the sales records for individual customers, salespeople, and inventory records for individual items of inventory.

The Relationship between Inventory and Cost of Goods Sold

The income statement of a merchandising business contains a section called Cost of Goods Sold. This section shows the cost of the merchandise that the firm sold during the accounting period. Cost of goods sold is used to determine the gross profit from sales for the period.

When the periodic inventory system is used, the calculation of cost of goods sold on the income statement involves both the beginning and ending inventory, as shown on the following page.

merchandising businesses Firms that buy goods and resell them to consumers.

inventory The stock of goods that a merchandising business has on hand for resale to consumers. Also called *merchandise inventory*.

periodic inventory system A system in which a firm's inventory is counted at regular intervals.

perpetual inventory system A system in which a firm maintains a running balance for all inventory items.

inventory costing methods Methods used to determine the dollar value of the ending inventory.

Beginning Inventory
+ Net Purchases
= Goods Available for Sale
– Ending Inventory
= Cost of Goods Sold

When the perpetual inventory system is used, there is a single Cost of Goods Sold account that includes all merchandise costs.

Inventory Systems

We will now take a closer look at the two basic inventory systems used by merchandising businesses—the periodic inventory system and the perpetual inventory system.

Periodic Inventory System

Traditionally, firms that sell a wide variety of low-cost items have used the periodic inventory system. Drugstores, hardware stores, office supply stores, and grocery stores are examples of such businesses.

With the periodic inventory system, a firm does not keep a continuous record of the changes in its inventory during the accounting period. All purchases of goods are debited to the Purchases account and all sales of goods are credited to the Sales account, but no entries are made in the Inventory account. Therefore, the firm has no precise way of calculating its cost of goods sold during an accounting period.

At the end of the period, a count is made of the goods on hand. The balance of the Inventory account is then updated to show the dollar value of the ending inventory.

The periodic inventory system has several drawbacks. One drawback has already been mentioned—the lack of information about the current dollar value of the inventory during the accounting period. However, an even more serious drawback is the lack of information about the availability of any single inventory item unless a separate tracking system is used.

For example, suppose that an office supply store has a balance of 400 boxes of file folders at the beginning of a period. The store purchases another 700 boxes of file folders during the period, but this amount will not show up in the inventory count until the end of the period. Thus, if a customer orders 500 boxes of file folders, the store will not know for sure whether it has enough stock on hand to fill the order.

Today, the periodic inventory system is less widely used than it was in the past. Modern technology has made the perpetual inventory system feasible and cost efficient for businesses with a large stock of low-priced items. Computerized inventory programs, optical scanners, and the Universal Product Code (UPC) printed on packages allow such firms to maintain a continuous record of inventory transactions.

Perpetual Inventory System

Inventory represents a major investment for a merchandising business. In fact, inventory is often the largest asset that such a firm owns.

The success of a merchandising business depends in part on careful management of its inventory. A firm wants to have an ample supply of fast-selling items available for customers, and it wants to keep its supply of slow-selling items to a minimum. Poor inventory decisions can result in lost sales because of a shortage of needed goods or because of markdowns on surplus goods that customers will only buy at reduced prices.

Because the perpetual inventory system maintains a running balance for all inventory items, it provides the information needed to effectively manage a firm's inventory. In the past, many firms considered the perpetual inventory system too time-consuming and costly. However, computerized accounting programs like Peachtree have made it possible for even very small businesses with limited staff and limited resources to use the perpetual inventory system.

The perpetual inventory system in Peachtree has the following advantages:

- It keeps detailed records for all inventory items and updates these records throughout the accounting period as transactions occur.
- It updates the Inventory and Cost of Goods Sold accounts in the general ledger throughout the accounting period. Thus, there is no need to adjust the Inventory account at the end of the period.
- The costs for inventory items are always known, and selling prices can be changed at any time. The firm can raise selling prices on items with rising costs if it wishes. It can also cut selling prices on items with weak demand.

Check point

1. What are the two basic systems for keeping track of inventory?
2. Which of the two basic inventory systems does Peachtree use?

Answers
1. *The periodic inventory system and the perpetual inventory system are the two basic systems for keeping track of inventory.*
2. *Peachtree uses the perpetual inventory system.*

OBJECTIVE 2 — Understand the Most Common Inventory Costing Methods and Create the Inventory Account

The inventory costing method selected by a business depends on the nature of its merchandise and other factors. Each method will produce a slightly different dollar value for the ending inventory and the cost of goods sold. As noted previously, Peachtree supports three common inventory costing methods: the average cost method; the last-in, first-out (LIFO) method; and the first-in, first-out (FIFO) method.

Average Cost Method

average cost method
Inventory costing method in which the value of the ending inventory is based on a single cost (the average cost) assigned to all units available for sale.

The **average cost method** assigns a single cost (the average cost) to all units of an inventory item. This cost is found by dividing the total cost of the units available for sale during a period by the number of those units. The resulting figure—the average cost—is then multiplied by the number of units in the ending inventory to find the dollar value of the ending inventory.

For example, suppose that a firm had 1,090 units of a certain inventory item available for sale during a period. These units were acquired at three different prices. The total cost of the units available for sale was $12,920. The average cost was $11.85.

Beginning inventory	500 units	@	$11	= $ 5,500
First purchase	250 units	@	$12	= 3,000
Second purchase	340 units	@	$13	= 4,420
	1,090 units			$12,920

Average cost = $12,920 ÷ 1,090 = $11.85

During the period, the firm sold 560 units of this item. Therefore, its ending inventory consists of 530 units (1,090 units – 560 units). The dollar value of the ending inventory is $6,280.50.

Ending inventory: 530 units × $11.85 (average cost) = $6,280.50

The cost of goods sold is $6,639.50.

Cost of goods available for sale	$12,920.00
Less ending inventory	6,280.50
Cost of goods sold	$ 6,639.50

Last-In, First-Out (LIFO) Method

LIFO method
Inventory costing method in which the value of the ending inventory is based on the assumption that the last items purchased are the first ones sold.

The **last-in, first-out (LIFO) method** assumes that the last inventory items purchased are the first ones sold. This pattern may not match the actual flow of inventory items. However, the LIFO method is used for accounting purposes to value the ending inventory and need not be consistent with the physical flow of goods in a business.

Again, suppose that a firm had 1,090 units of a certain inventory item available for sale during a period. It sold 560 units, leaving 530 units in its ending inventory. Also assume the following prices for the beginning inventory and later purchases during the period.

Beginning inventory	500 units	@	$11	= $ 5,500
First purchase	250 units	@	$12	= 3,000
Second purchase	340 units	@	$13	= 4,420
	1,090 units			$12,920

With the LIFO method, the ending inventory consists of the earliest goods because it is assumed that the first goods sold are the last ones purchased. The value of the ending inventory is therefore $5,860, as shown below. The cost of goods sold is $7,060.

Beginning inventory (earliest goods)	500 units	@	$11	= $ 5,500
First purchase (next to earliest goods)	30 units	@	$12	= 360
	530 units			$5,860

Cost of goods available for sale	$12,920
Less ending inventory	5,860
Cost of goods sold	$ 7,060

First-In, First-Out (FIFO) Method

The **first-in, first-out (FIFO) method** assumes that the first inventory items purchased are the first ones sold. This pattern may or may not match the actual flow of inventory items in a business. However, keep in mind that an inventory costing method is selected for accounting purposes to value the ending inventory, not as a means to literally track when particular goods are purchased and sold.

Again, suppose that a firm had 1,090 units of a certain inventory item available for sale during a period, sold 560 units, and had 530 units in its ending inventory. Also assume the following prices for the beginning inventory and later purchases during the period.

Beginning inventory	500 units	@	$11	=	$ 5,500
First purchase	250 units	@	$12	=	3,000
Second purchase	340 units	@	$13	=	4,420
	1,090 units				$12,920

With the FIFO method, the ending inventory consists of the latest goods because it is assumed that the first goods sold are the first ones purchased. The value of the ending inventory is therefore $6,700, as shown below. The cost of goods sold is $6,220.

Second purchase (latest goods)	340 units	@	$13	=	$4,420
First purchase (next to latest goods)	190 units	@	$12	=	2,280
	530 units				$6,700

Cost of goods available for sale	$12,920
Less ending inventory	6,700
Cost of goods sold	$ 6,220

A Comparison of the Inventory Costing Methods

The following table provides a summary of the results of the three inventory costing methods discussed above. In a period of rising prices, the FIFO method will produce the highest dollar value for the ending inventory and the lowest cost of goods sold. The LIFO method will produce the lowest dollar value for the ending inventory and the highest cost of goods sold. The average cost method will produce results that fall between those of FIFO and LIFO.

	FIFO Method	Average Cost Method	LIFO Method
Cost of goods available for sale	$12,920.00	$12,920.00	$12,920.00
Less ending inventory	6,700.00	6,280.50	5,860.00
Cost of goods sold	$ 6,220.00	$ 6,639.50	$ 7,060.00

Keep in mind that the higher the cost of goods sold, the lower the net income. Thus, in a period of rising prices, LIFO provides a tax advantage for a business because it results in less taxable income.

Creating the Inventory Account

To use the inventory features of Peachtree, you must create an Inventory account in the general ledger and also create subsidiary ledger accounts for the various inventory items. For example, suppose that Superior Carpet and Tile, which is a service business, decides to add a merchandising operation. It will sell items such as a carpet cleaning compound, tile and carpet storage racks, and ceramic tile to its customers.

The first step for Superior Carpet and Tile is to create the asset account Inventory and the revenue account Carpet and Tile Sales in its general ledger. The Inventory will serve as the controlling account for subsidiary ledger accounts that will provide detailed records of the various inventory items and the revenue account will keep track of the sales. Remember that a controlling account links the general ledger to a subsidiary ledger. The balance of the controlling account represents the total of all the individual balances in the subsidiary ledger.

Step 1:
Open Superior Carpet and Tile (Chp. 8 – Superior Carpet and Tile if student disk is used) and close the Action Items log.

Step 2:
Click *Company* on the Navigation Aid toolbar at the left side of the basic Peachtree window.

Step 3:
Click *Chart of Accounts* at the *Company Tasks* section and click *New Account*, as shown in figure 8–1.

FIGURE 8–1
Chart of Accounts
Selected from Company
Tasks Section

Step 4:
At the *Account ID* field, key **105**, and then click OK.

Step 5:
Key **Inventory** in the *Description* field.

Step 6:
At the *Account Type* field, click the down arrow key, and then click *Inventory*.

Step 7:
Compare your work with the completed information for the Inventory account as shown in figure 8–2.

FIGURE 8–2
Completed Information for Inventory Account

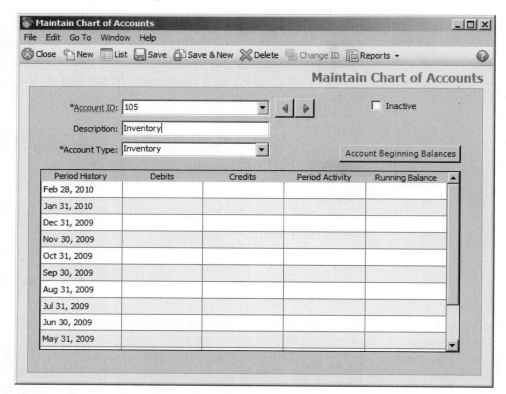

Step 8:
Click Save.

Step 9:
You will also need to create a Cost of Goods Sold account and Carpet and Tile Sales account. According to standard accounting convention, this account should appear before the expense accounts on the chart of accounts. For example, cost of sales account numbers should begin with 500 and expense account numbers should begin with 600. However, keep in mind that this business began strictly as a service business and expense accounts were set up to begin with an account number of 500. Only recently has Superior Carpet and Tile decided to sell merchandise and keep inventory on hand. Therefore, the Cost of Goods Sold account number will be 503, the first available account number within the 500 range. This will have no adverse effect on any of the financial statements as long as Cost of Sales is chosen as the account type.

Create both the Cost of Goods Sold account and the Carpet and Tile Sales account in the general ledger.

Account ID:	**503**
Description:	**Cost of Goods Sold**
Account Type:	**Cost of Sales**
Account ID:	**400.5**
Description:	**Carpet and Tile Sales**
Account Type:	**Income**

Step 10:
After you have entered and checked the information for the two new accounts, click Close.

C h e c k   p o i n t

1. What are the three most common inventory costing methods?
2. What type of account is the Inventory account in the general ledger and what is its function?

Answers
1. *The three most common inventory costing methods are the average cost, LIFO, and FIFO methods.*
2. *The Inventory account in the general ledger is an asset account. It serves as the controlling account for the subsidiary ledger accounts kept for the various inventory items.*

Practice Objective 2

Step 1:
Open Meadowland Healthcare Services (Chp. 8 – Meadowland Healthcare Services if student disk is used).

Step 2:
Create the Inventory account for this firm.

Account ID:	**10500**
Description:	**Inventory**
Account Type:	**Inventory**

Step 3:
Change account 50000 to reflect the following:

Account ID:	**50000**
Description:	**Cost of Goods Sold**
Account Type:	**Cost of Sales**

Step 4:

Create the Rent Expense account for this firm.

Account ID:	**50100**
Description:	**Rent Expense**
Account Type:	**Expense**

Step 5:

Close the Maintain Chart of Accounts window.

OBJECTIVE 3 — Establish Subsidiary Ledger Accounts for Inventory Items

In the perpetual inventory system used by Peachtree, you must set up a subsidiary ledger account for each inventory item. This account contains detailed information about the item and allows the business to keep track of its quantity and cost. Whenever goods are purchased or sold, the subsidiary ledger accounts for the inventory items are updated.

Superior Carpet and Tile will start its merchandising operation with three items: a carpet cleaning compound, tile and carpet storage racks, and ceramic tile. These items will be purchased from two suppliers.

Follow the steps outlined below to establish inventory defaults and to establish subsidiary ledger accounts for the three inventory items that Superior will initially stock.

Step 1:

Open Chp. 8 – Superior Carpet and Tile, which you previously updated in the chapter, and close the Action Items log.

Step 2:

Click Maintain and then click *Default Information* from the drop-down list, as shown in figure 8–3.

FIGURE 8–3

Default Information Drop-Down List

Step 3:
Click *Inventory Items* from the drop-down list and the Inventory Item Defaults window will appear, as shown in figure 8–4.

FIGURE 8–4
Inventory Item Defaults
Window

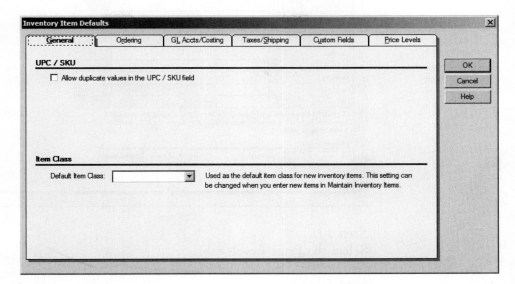

Step 4:
Select the GL Accts/Costing tab from the Inventory Item Defaults window.

Step 5:
Select account *400.5, Carpet and Tile Sales*, in the *GL Sales/Inc* account box aligned with Stock item.

Step 6:
Select account *105, Inventory*, in the *GL Invtry/Wage* account box aligned with Stock item.

Step 7:
Select account *503, Cost of Goods Sold*, in the *GL Cost Sales* account box aligned with Stock item.

Step 8:
Accept the FIFO Costing default.

Step 9:
Enter account *105, Inventory*, in the *GL Freight* account box located at the bottom of the window. Superior adds the freight cost to inventory.

Step 10:
Review figure 8–5 for accuracy, making any necessary changes.

FIGURE 8–5
Completed GL Accts/
Costing Window

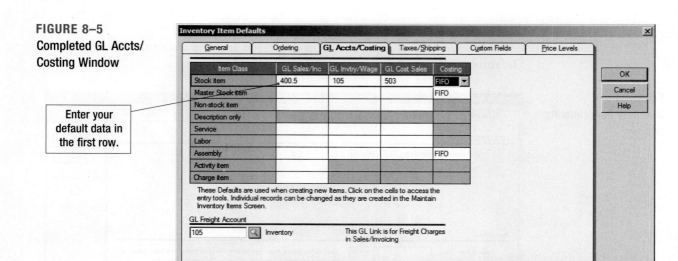

Enter your
default data in
the first row.

Step 11:
Select the Price Levels tab.

Step 12:
Key **Full Price** in the *Level Name* field aligned with Level 1.

Step 13:
Select Check mark Enabled in the cell aligned with Level 1 (if there is not already a check mark). Deselect all other enabled check marks, if present, as shown in figure 8–6.

FIGURE 8–6
Price Levels Completed

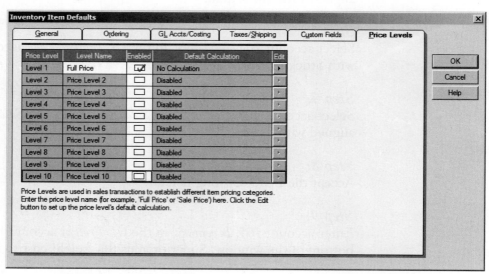

Step 14:
Select the Edit button aligned with Level 1.

Step 15:
Select Last Cost from the Use drop-down list.

Step 16:
Accept the default *Increase by Percent* and leave the (%) *0*.

Step 17:
Select No Rounding at the Round Price drop-down list, if needed.

Step 18:
Review for accuracy, make any necessary changes, and click OK.

Step 19:
Click OK to establish the pricing defaults.

Step 20:
Click Maintain and then click *Inventory Items*. The Maintain Inventory Items window will appear.

Step 21:
Key **CC-1** in the *Item ID* field and then click OK.

Step 22:
Key **Carpet Care** in the *Description* field.

Step 23:
At the *Item Class* field, click the down arrow key, and then click *Stock item*, if needed.

Step 24:
Click the right arrow key to the right of the Full Price box.

Step 25:
Key **22.50** in the *Price* box aligned with Full Price, as shown in figure 8–7.

FIGURE 8–7
Multiple Price Levels Window Completed

Step 26:
Click OK to exit the Multiple Price Levels window.

Step 27:
In the Maintain Inventory Items window, key **10.00** in the *Last Unit Cost* field.

Step 28:

Key **8877665543** in the *UP<u>C</u>/SKU* field and **Retail** in the *Item Type* field. (**Note:** UPC/SKU stands for Universal Product Code/Stock Keeping Units. These numbers are used for bar coding and computerized tracking of inventory items.)

Step 29:

Key **Each** in the *Stocking U/M* field. (**Note:** U/M stands for Units of Measure.)

Step 30:

At the *Preferred <u>V</u>endor ID* field, click the *magnifying glass* icon, and then click *APX-005*.

Step 31:

Compare your completed Maintain Inventory Items window with figure 8–8. Click <u>S</u>ave and then New.

FIGURE 8–8
Completed Maintain
Inventory Items Window

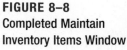
An additional description or comment can be added if desired.

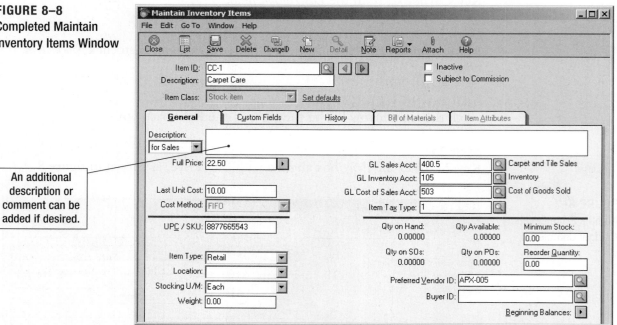

Step 32:

Enter the information for the tile and carpet storage racks:

Item <u>I</u>D:	**SK-2**
Description:	**Storage Rack**
Item Class:	**Stock item**
Description:	**for Sales**
Full Price:	**125.00**
Last Unit Cost:	**52.50**
Cost Method:	**FIFO**
UP<u>C</u>/SKU:	**1234543456**
Item Type:	**Retail**
Stocking U/M:	**Each**

GL Sales Acct:	**400.5**
GL Inventory Acct:	**105**
GL Cost of Sales Acct:	**503**
Item Ta_x_ Type:	**1**
Preferred _V_endor ID:	**None**

Step 33:
Click _S_ave and then New.

Step 34:
Enter the information for the ceramic tile:

Item _I_D:	**CT-3**
Description:	**Ceramic Tile**
Item Class:	**Stock item**
Description:	**for Sales**
Full Price:	**225.00**
Last Unit Cost:	**100.00**
Cost Method:	**FIFO**
UP_C_/SKU:	**9987655645**
Item Type:	**Retail**
Stocking U/M:	**Each**
GL Sales Acct:	**400.5**
GL Inventory Acct:	**105**
GL Cost of Sales Acct:	**503**
Item Ta_x_ Type:	**1**
Preferred _V_endor ID:	**None**

Step 35:
Click _S_ave and then Close.

Displaying the Item List

Peachtree provides a number of different inventory reports. One of these reports—the _Item List_—shows the quantity on hand and other information about all inventory items. Follow the steps outlined below to display the _Item List_.

Step 1:
Click Reports & Forms on the main Menu bar and then click _Inventory_.

Step 2:
At the Inventory: Items and Services You Buy and Sell section, click _Item List_.

Step 3:
Click the _D_isplay button on the Select a Report or Form toolbar, as shown in figure 8–9.

FIGURE 8–9
Select a Report or Form
Display Selected

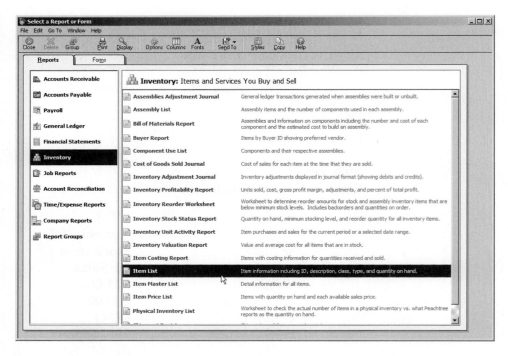

Step 4:

Review the *Item List* report shown in figure 8–10. The *Qty on Hand* field is blank because the firm has not yet received any goods.

FIGURE 8–10
Item List

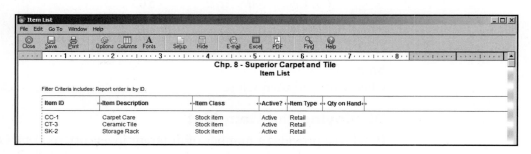

Step 5:

Click Close. Then close the Select a Report or Form dialog box.

Check point

1. What is the purpose of the subsidiary ledger account for each inventory item?
2. What inventory report produced by Peachtree shows the quantity on hand for all inventory items?

Answers
1. *The subsidiary ledger account for each inventory item is used to keep track of the quantity and cost of the item.*
2. *The Item List shows the quantity on hand for all inventory items.*

Practice Objective 3

Meadowland Healthcare Services has decided to sell some goods to patients. It will sell syringes, roller bandages, and medical scales.

Step 1:
Open Chp. 8 – Meadowland Healthcare Services, which you updated previously in the chapter.

Step 2:
Create the Inventory Defaults using the information given below:

GL Accts/Costing

GL Sales/Inc	**40000**
GL Invtry/Wage	**10500**
GL Cost Sales	**50000**
Costing	**FIFO**
GL Freight Account	**10500**

Price Levels

Level Name, Level 1	**Full Price**
Use	**Last Cost**

Step 3:
Create subsidiary ledger accounts for the following inventory items:

Item 1

Item ID:	**SY-1**
Description:	**Syringes**
Item Class:	**Stock item**
Description:	**for Sales**
Full Price:	**12.00**
Last Unit Cost:	**5.00**
Cost Method:	**FIFO**
UPC/SKU:	**3344234564**
Item Type:	**Retail**
Stocking U/M:	**Package**
GL Sales Acct:	**40000**
GL Inventory Acct:	**10500**
GL Cost of Sales Acct:	**50000**
Item Tax Type:	**1**
Preferred Vendor ID:	**None**

Item 2

Item ID:	**RB-2**
Description:	**Roller Bandages**
Item Class:	**Stock item**
Description:	**for Sales**
Full Price:	**75.00**
Last Unit Cost:	**30.00**
Cost Method:	**FIFO**
UPC/SKU:	**4534543457**
Item Type:	**Retail**
Stocking U/M:	**Case**

GL Sales Acct:	**40000**
GL Inventory Acct:	**10500**
GL Cost of Sales Acct:	**50000**
Item Tax Type:	**1**
Preferred Vendor ID:	**None**

Item 3

Item ID:	**MS-3**
Description:	**Medical Scales**
Item Class:	**Stock item**
Description:	**for Sales**
Full Price:	**325.00**
Last Unit Cost:	**130.00**
Cost Method:	**FIFO**
UPC/SKU:	**6234543459**
Item Type:	**Retail**
Stocking U/M:	**Each**
GL Sales Acct:	**40000**
GL Inventory Acct:	**10500**
GL Cost of Sales Acct:	**50000**
Item Tax Type:	**1**
Preferred Vendor ID:	**None**

Step 4:

Preview the *Item List* report and compare it with figure 8–11.

FIGURE 8–11
Item List

Page: 1

Chp. 8 - Meadowland Healthcare Services
Item List

Filter Criteria includes: Report order is by ID.

Item ID	Item Description	Item Class	Active?	Item Type	Qty on Hand
MS-3	Medical Scales	Stock item	Active	Retail	
RB-2	Roller Bandages	Stock item	Active	Retail	
SY-1	Syringes	Stock item	Active	Retail	

Step 5:

Close the Select a Report or Form dialog box.

OBJECTIVE 4 — Establish Records for Sales Representatives

Many merchandising businesses use sales representatives to market their goods. These sales representatives may be employees or independent contractors. Peachtree allows a firm to keep track of the sales made by its sales representatives. However, you must first set up a record for each sales representative.

Superior Carpet and Tile has two sales representatives, Ernesto Garcia and Maria Davis, who are independent contractors. Use the steps outlined below to establish records for these sales representatives. The creation of payroll records for sales representatives who are employees will be discussed in a later chapter.

Step 1:

Open Chp. 8 – Superior Carpet and Tile and close the Action Items log.

Step 2:
Click Maintain, and then click *Employees/Sales Reps*. Click No at the Setup Payroll Wizard query. The Maintain Employees & Sales Reps window will appear. Enter the following information for Ernesto Garcia, a sales representative.

Step 3:
Key **EGA-01** in the *Employee ID* field.

Step 4:
Key **Ernesto J. Garcia** in the *Name* field.

Step 5:
Click the *Sales Rep* option.

Step 6:
Key **2335 Wilson Way** in the *Address* field.

Step 7:
Key **Modesto, CA 95355** in the *City, ST, Zip* fields. Key **USA** in the *Country* field.

Step 8:
Key **209-555-1234** in the *Home phone* field.

Step 9:
Key **887-09-9989** in the *Social Security Number* field.

Step 10:
Key **Independ** for independent contractor in the *Type* field.

Step 11:
Compare your entries with the ones shown in figure 8–12.

FIGURE 8–12
Completed Maintain
Employees & Sales Reps
Window

Step 13:
Click Save & New.

Step 14:
Enter the following information for the second sales representative of
Superior Carpet and Tile.

Employee ID:	**MDA-02**
Name:	**Maria P. Davis**
Address:	**778 Kemp Road**
City, ST, Zip:	**Stockton, CA 95250**
Country:	**USA**
Telephone 1:	**209-555-2468**
Social Security Number:	**662-04-4434**
Type:	**Independ**

Step 15:
Click Save and then Close.

C h e c k   p o i n t

1. Why would a user of Peachtree want to set up records for its sales
   representatives?
2. What are the two types of sales representatives?

Answers
1. *By setting up records for its sales representatives, a user of Peachtree
   can keep track of each representative's sales.*
2. *Some sales representatives are employees, and others are independent
   contractors.*

Practice Objective 4

Meadowland Healthcare Services has hired two sales representatives: Julie Hernandez and Isadora Duncan.

Step 1:
Open Chp. 8 – Meadowland Healthcare Services.

Step 2:
Establish a record for each sales representative.

Employee ID:	**JHE-01**
Name:	**Julie Q. Hernandez**
Address:	**1223 Westin Road**
City, ST, Zip:	**Stockton, CA 95250**
Country:	**USA**
Telephone 1:	**209-555-4556**
Social Security Number:	**533-45-8743**
Type:	**Independ**

Employee ID:	**IDU-02**
Name:	**Isadora X. Duncan**
Address:	**2389 Alexandria Drive**
City, ST, Zip:	**Modesto, CA 95355**
Country:	**USA**
Telephone 1:	**209-555-9008**
Social Security Number:	**332-09-8743**
Type:	**Independ**

OBJECTIVE 5 — Process Inventory Transactions

One of the advantages of using Peachtree for a merchandising business is the ease of processing inventory transactions. Peachtree can be used to quickly and efficiently set up vendor accounts, issue purchase orders, record the receipt of inventory items, pay vendors for the items, and keep track of the quantity and cost of inventory items.

Creating Vendor Accounts with Discounts

The procedure for creating vendor accounts was covered in chapter 5. However, most of the vendors discussed there did not offer discounts. Many vendors who provide goods to merchandising businesses allow discounts for payment within a short period.

For example, Superior Carpet and Tile will buy its storage racks from BMC Supply Company. BMC offers credit terms of 2/10, n/30. This means that Superior can take a 2% discount if it pays within 10 days. Otherwise, it has 30 days to pay the net (full) amount of the invoice.

Use the steps outlined below to create a vendor account for the BMC Supply Company.

Step 1:
Open Chp. 8 – Superior Carpet and Tile.

Step 2:
Click Maintain, and then click *Vendors.*

Step 3:

The Maintain Vendors dialog box will appear. Key **BMC-007** in the *Vendor ID* field.

Step 4:

Key **BMC Supply Company** in the *Name* field.

Step 5:

At the General folder tab, key **Jerome Jones** in the *Contact* field.

Step 6:

Key **00789** in the *Account Number* field.

Step 7:

Key **2150 First Street** in the *Mailing Address* field.

Step 8:

Key **Modesto, CA 95355** in the *City, ST, Zip* field. Key **USA** in the *Country* field.

Step 9:

Key **Supplier** in the *Vendor Type* field and select *None* from the 1099 Type drop-down list (if necessary).

Step 10:

Key **105** (Inventory) in the *Expense Account* field.

Step 11:

Key **209-555-4444** in the *Telephone 1* field. Then check your work for accuracy by comparing it with figure 8–13.

FIGURE 8–13
Completed Entries under General Folder Tab

Step 12:
Click the Purchase Info folder tab.

Step 13:
Key **09-667755** in the *Tax ID Number* field.

Step 14:
Click *UPS Ground* in the *Ship Via* field.

Step 15:
Click the down arrow next to *Terms and Credit* and then select *Customize terms for this vendor*. The dialog box that appears is used to change the credit terms offered by a vendor.

Step 16:
The default terms for vendors were set up when the company was created in Peachtree. Change the standard terms to 2/10, n/30.

Step 17:
Accept the default, *Paper Form*, at the Form Options box.

Step 18:
Compare your work with the completed Purchase Info folder tab shown in figure 8–14.

FIGURE 8–14
Completed Entries under Purchase Info Folder Tab

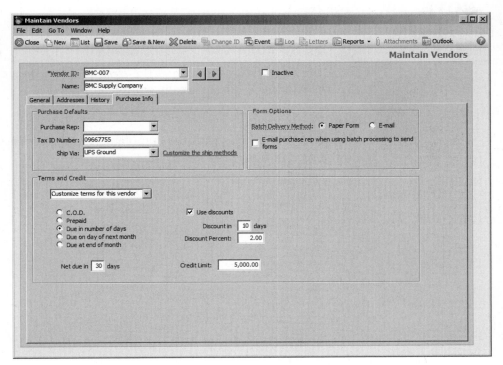

Step 19:
Click Save and then Close.

Purchasing Goods without a Purchase Order

Some businesses issue a purchase order to vendors whenever they want to buy goods. Other businesses buy goods without a purchase order. Peachtree supports either method of purchasing goods.

For example, on February 3, 2010, Superior Carpet and Tile ordered 23 storage racks on credit from the BMC Supply Company. Superior placed the order over the telephone and did not issue a written purchase order. BMC will send Invoice 3244 to bill Superior for the goods.

Follow the steps outlined below to record this purchase without a purchase order.

Step 1:
Click Tasks, and then click *Purchases/Receive Inventory*.

Step 2:
At the Purchases/Receive Inventory window, click the *magnifying glass* icon at the *Vendor ID* field and then click *BMC-007*.

Step 3:
Change the *Date* field to *Feb. 3, 2010*.

Step 4:
Key **3244** in the *Invoice No.* field.

NOTE

Remember to enter a decimal when entering amounts.

Step 5:
Key **23.00** in the *Quantity* field.

Step 6:
Click the *magnifying glass* icon at the *Item* field and then click *SK-2*. Notice that the window is automatically completed.

Step 7:
Compare your entries with the completed Purchases/Receive Inventory window shown in figure 8–15.

FIGURE 8–15
Completed Purchases/
Receive Inventory
Window

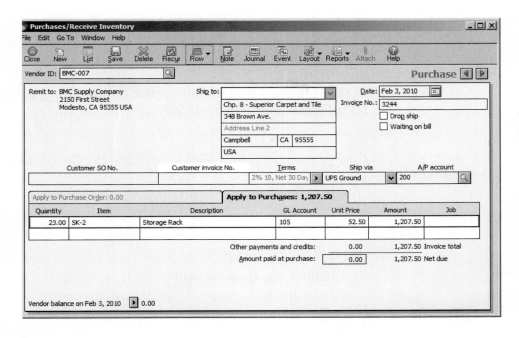

Step 8:
Click Save and then Close.

Purchasing Goods with a Purchase Order

Some businesses have a policy of issuing purchase orders to vendors for all purchases of goods and supplies. This policy helps to guard against unauthorized purchases.

Suppose that Superior Carpet and Tile adopts such a policy. On February 5, 2010, it decides to issue Purchase Order 010500 to the JS West Company for 30 cases of ceramic tile. Follow the steps outlined below to create the necessary purchase order.

Step 1:
Set up a vendor account for the JS West Company.

Vendor ID:	**JSW-008**
Name:	**JS West Company**
Contact:	**Harry West**
Account Number:	**010589**
Mailing Address:	**2121 Third Street**
City, ST, Zip:	**Modesto, CA 95355**
Country:	**USA**
Vendor Type:	**Supplier**
1099 Type:	**None**
Expense Account:	**105**
Telephone 1:	**209-555-2222**
Tax ID Number:	**09-557766**
Ship Via:	**UPS Ground**
Terms and Credit:	**2/10, n/30**
Form Options:	**Default**

Step 2:
Click Tasks, and then click *Purchase Orders*.

Step 3:
At the Purchase Orders window, click the *magnifying glass* icon at the *Vendor ID* field, and then click *JSW-008*.

Step 4:
Change the *Date* field to *Feb. 5, 2010* and the *Good Thru* field to *Mar 6, 2010*.

Step 5:
Key **010500** in the *PO No.* field.

Step 6:
Key **30.00** in the *Quantity* field.

Step 7:
At the *Item* field, click the *magnifying glass* icon, and then click *CT-3*.

Step 8:
Compare your work with figure 8–16.

FIGURE 8–16
Completed Purchase Orders Window

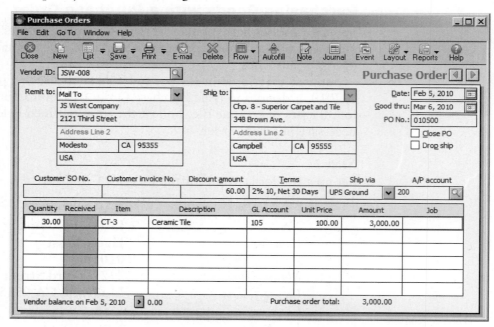

Step 9:
Click Save and then Close.

Receiving Goods Purchased with a Purchase Order

Remember that Superior Carpet and Tile issued Purchase Order 010500 to buy 30 cases of ceramic tile from JS West Company. On February 10, 2010, Superior received the goods along with Invoice 998778. Follow the steps outlined below to record the receipt of these inventory items.

Step 1:
Click Tasks, and then click *Purchases/Receive Inventory*.

Step 2:
At the *Vendor ID* field, click the *magnifying glass* icon, and then click *JSW-008*.

Step 3:
Change the *Date* field to *Feb. 10, 2010*.

Step 4:
Key **998778** in the *Invoice No.* field.

Step 5:
Click the down arrow key to the right of the folder tab label *Apply to Purchase Order No.*, and then click *010500*, as shown in figure 8–17.

FIGURE 8–17
Purchase Order Selected

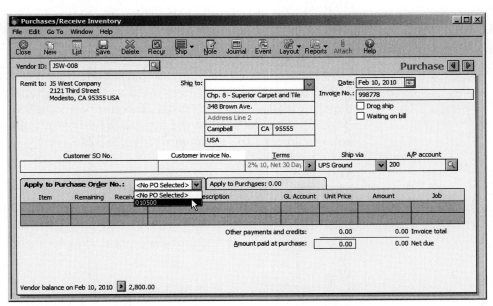

Step 6:
Key **30.00** in the *Received* field. This indicates that all the ceramic tile that the business ordered were received.

Step 7:

Compare your completed Purchases/Receive Inventory window with figure 8–18.

FIGURE 8–18
Completed Purchases/
Receive Inventory
Window

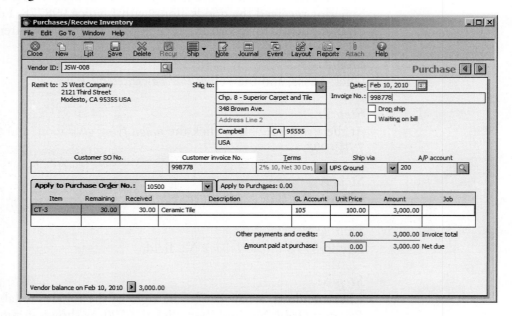

Step 8:
Click $\underline{S}$ave and then Close.

Paying an Invoice with a Discount

On February 10, 2010, Superior Carpet and Tile issued a check for $1,183.35 to pay Invoice 3244 owed to the BMC Supply Company. Because Superior paid within the 10-day discount period, it took a 2% discount ($24.15) from the total of the invoice ($1,207.50). Follow the steps outlined below to record the payment of Invoice 3244.

Step 1:
Click Tasks, and then click *Payments*.

Step 2:
At the Select a Cash Account dialog box, click *Cash Account, 100*, if needed.

Step 3:
At the Payments window, click the *magnifying glass* icon in the box to the right of the *Vendor ID* field box, and then click *BMC-007*.

Step 4:
Key **105** in the *Check Number* field.

Step 5:
Change the *Date* field to *Feb. 10, 2010*.

Step 6:
Click the *Apply to Invoices* folder tab, if needed.

Step 2:
At the Select a Report or Form dialog box, in the Inventory: Items and Services You Buy and Sell section, click *Inventory Valuation Report*.

Step 3:
Click Print on the Select a Report or Form toolbar.

Step 4:
Click OK at the Modify Report – Inventory Valuation Report, and then OK again at the Print dialog box.

Step 5:
Compare your printout to the *Inventory Valuation Report* shown in figure 8–21.

FIGURE 8–21
Inventory Valuation
Report

Chp. 8 - Superior Carpet and Tile
Inventory Valuation Report
As of Feb 28, 2010

Filter Criteria includes: 1) Stock/Assembly. Report order is by ID. Report is printed with shortened descriptions.

Item ID Item Class	Item Descriptio	Stocking U/M	Cost Method	Qty on Han	Item Value	Avg Cos	% of Inv Valu
CC-1 Stock item	Carpet Care	Each	FIFO				
CT-3 Stock item	Ceramic Tile	Each	FIFO	28.00	2,800.00		69.87
SK-2 Stock item	Storage Rack	Each	FIFO	23.00	1,207.50		30.13
					4,007.50		100.00

Step 6:
Click Close.

Check point

1. What do the terms 2/10, n/30 on an invoice mean?
2. What does the *Inventory Valuation* report show?

Answers
1. *A 2% discount can be taken if the invoice is paid within 10 days. If not, the entire net amount is due within 30 days of the invoice date.*
2. *The Inventory Valuation Report shows the quantity on hand, the cost of each inventory item, and the total cost of the firm's inventory.*

Practice Objective 5

Meadowland Healthcare Services buys its roller bandages from General Medical Services and its syringes from LK Surgical Supply Co.

Step 1:
Open Chp. 8 – Meadowland Healthcare Services.

Step 2:

Create the following vendor accounts using the information provided below. Be careful to adjust vendor terms as given.

Vendor ID:	**GMS-006**
Name:	**General Medical Services**
Contact:	**Stan Sherman**
Account Number:	**09088676**
Mailing Address:	**3450 Orangeburg Drive**
City, ST, Zip:	**Modesto, CA 95357**
Country:	**USA**
Vendor Type:	**Supplier**
1099 Type:	**None**
Expense Acct:	**10500**
Telephone 1:	**209-555-8894**
Tax ID Number:	**09-754345**
Ship Via:	**UPS Ground**
Terms and Credit:	**1/10, n/45**
Form Options:	**Default**

Vendor ID:	**LKS-007**
Name:	**LK Surgical Supply Co.**
Contact:	**Lou Kim**
Account Number:	**1000345**
Mailing Address:	**1245 Arrow Smith Road**
City, ST, Zip:	**Modesto, CA 95353**
Country:	**USA**
Vendor Type:	**Supplier**
1099 Type:	**None**
Expense Acct:	**10500**
Telephone 1:	**209-555-8445**
Tax ID Number:	**09-777998**
Ship Via:	**UPS Ground**
Terms and Credit:	**3/15, n/60**
Form Options:	**Default**

Step 3:

Record the following transactions:

- On February 2, 2010, Meadowland Healthcare Services purchased 230 roller bandages (RB-2) on credit from General Medical Services. Meadowland received Invoice 4556.
- On February 4, 2010, Meadowland ordered 100 packages of syringes (SY-1) on credit from LK Surgical Supply Co. Meadowland issued Purchase Order 010402.
- On February 10, 2010, Meadowland received 100 packages of syringes ordered on Purchase Order 010402 from LK Surgical Supply Co. Enclosed with the syringes was Invoice 558990.
- On February 11, 2010, Meadowland returned 10 cases of roller bandages purchased from General Medical Services. Meadowland received Vendor Credit Memo 890 (CM890). The original invoice was 4556.

- On February 11, 2010, Meadowland paid Invoice 558990, less discount, to LK Surgical Supply Co., Check No. 705. **Note:** The *Discount Account* field should read **10500**.

Step 4:

Print the *Inventory Valuation Report*. Your printout should look like figure 8–22.

FIGURE 8–22
Inventory
Valuation Report
for Meadowland
Healthcare Services

Page: 1

Chp. 8 - Meadowland Healthcare Services
Inventory Valuation Report
As of Feb 28, 2010

Filter Criteria includes: 1) Stock/Assembly. Report order is by ID. Report is printed with shortened descriptions.

Item ID Item Class	Item Descriptio	Stocking U/M	Cost Method	Qty on Han	Item Value	Avg Cos	% of Inv Valu
MS-3 Stock item	Medical Scales	Each	FIFO				
RB-2 Stock item	Roller Bandages	Case	FIFO	220.00	6,600.00		92.96
SY-1 Stock item	Syringes	Package	FIFO	100.00	500.00		7.04
					7,100.00		100.00

End of Chapter Review

Software Command Summary

Create Inventory Item	Maintain, Inventory Items
Display Item List	Reports & Forms, Inventory, Select Item List
Create Salesperson Record	Maintain, Employees/Sales Reps
Create Vendor Account	Maintain, Vendors
Enter Purchase without Purchase Order	Tasks, Purchases/Receive Inventory
Create Purchase Order	Tasks, Purchase Orders
Pay Invoice	Tasks, Payments
Return Goods	Tasks, Vendor Credit Memos

Projects and Problems

Content Check

Multiple Choice: Choose only one response for each question.

1. Peachtree supports which of the following inventory costing methods?
   A. average cost
   B. LIFO
   C. FIFO
   D. All of the above

2. Credit terms of 1/10, n/30 mean
   A. a 1% discount is allowed if the invoice is paid within 10 days, or the entire net amount is due within 30 days.
   B. a 1% discount is allowed if the invoice is paid within 30 days.
   C. a 10% discount is allowed if the bill is paid within 1 day of receipt, or the entire amount is due within 30 days.
   D. None of the above

3. The perpetual inventory system involves
   A. counting goods at regular intervals.
   B. estimating the number of goods on hand.
   C. maintaining a running balance for all inventory items.
   D. estimating the cost of the goods on hand.

4. In a period of rising prices, which inventory costing method will result in the highest cost of goods sold?
   A. average cost
   B. LIFO
   C. FIFO
   D. perpetual

5. What function of Peachtree will a firm use to record the return of damaged goods to a vendor?
   A. Sales/Invoicing
   B. Receipts
   C. Vendor Credit Memos
   D. Payments

Short Essay Response: Provide a detailed answer for each question.

1. What is the difference between the perpetual inventory system and the periodic inventory system?
2. Explain each of the three most common inventory costing methods: average cost, LIFO, and FIFO.
3. Peachtree will automatically update which accounts when an inventory item is sold? Will these accounts increase or decrease?
4. Explain the steps necessary to create a new vendor account.
5. List two inventory reports that Peachtree produces. What information does each of these reports contain?
6. What advantages might a business gain by switching from the periodic inventory system to the perpetual inventory system?

Case Problems

Problem 1A

Open Kathleen's Designs, an interior decorating business, which is located on the student data disk.

1. Create the Inventory account for this firm.

Account ID:	**105**
Description:	**Inventory**
Account Type:	**Inventory**

2. Create the Cost of Sales account.

Account ID:	**503**
Description:	**Cost of Goods Sold**
Account Type:	**Cost of Sales**

3. Create the following vendor accounts:

Vendor ID:	**SHGS-01**
Name:	**Sanders Home and Garden Supply**
Contact:	**Robert Sanders**
Account Number:	**169135**
Mailing Address:	**23451 Main Street**
City, ST, Zip:	**Modesto, CA 95355**
Country:	**USA**
Vendor Type:	**Supplier**
1099 Type:	**None**
Expense Acct:	**105**
Telephone 1:	**209-555-9756**
Tax ID Number:	**09-999378**
Ship Via:	**Fed-Ex**
Terms and Credit:	**2/10, n/30**

Vendor ID:	**MHS-02**
Name:	**Martin's Hobby Store**
Contact:	**Luke Martin**
Account Number:	**1239437**
Mailing Address:	**2348 West Lane**
City, ST, Zip:	**Modesto, CA 95355**
Country:	**USA**
Vendor Type:	**Supplier**
1099 Type:	**None**
Expense Acct:	**105**
Telephone 1:	**209-555-5623**
Tax ID Number:	**09-999465**
Ship Via:	**Fed-Ex**
Terms and Credit:	**5/10, n/30**

4. Create the following subsidiary ledger accounts for inventory items:

Item ID:	**STENCILS-01**
Description:	**Flower Stencils**
Item Class:	**Stock item**
Description:	**for Sales**
Full Price:	**15.00**
Last Unit Cost:	**5.50**
Cost Method:	**FIFO**
UPC/SKU:	**1722839894**
Item Type:	**Retail**
Stocking U/M:	**Each**
GL Sales Acct:	**401**
GL Inventory Acct:	**105**
GL Cost of Sales Acct:	**503**
Item Tax Type:	**1**
Preferred Vendor ID:	**MHS-02**

Item *ID*:	**PILLOWS-02**
Description:	**12-inch Pillows**
Item Class:	**Stock item**
Description:	**for Sales**
Full Price:	**35.00**
Last Unit Cost:	**12.50**
Cost Method:	**FIFO**
UP*C*/SKU:	**7930093271**
Item Type:	**Retail**
Stocking U/M:	**Each**
GL Sales Acct:	**401**
GL Inventory Acct:	**105**
GL Cost of Sales Acct:	**503**
Item Ta*x* Type:	**1**
Preferred *V*endor ID:	**SHGS-01**

5. Record the following transactions, which occurred in January 2010.

Jan. 6   Ordered 15 flower stencils from Martin's Hobby Store, using Purchase Order 100.

8   Ordered 20 pillows from Sanders Home and Garden Supply, using Purchase Order 101.

10   Received the stencils ordered, Invoice 3264.

11   Received 16 of the pillows ordered, Invoice 16425.

11   Returned 2 of the stencils, and received CM15 from the vendor.

20   Paid the balance owed to Sanders Home and Garden Supply, less discount, Check 125. (Use 105 as the Discount Account.)

20   Paid the balance owed to Martin's Hobby Store, less discount, Check 126.

> **HINT**
>
> Enter the return of inventory using the Apply to Purchases tab of the Vendor Credit Memos screen.

6. Print the *Inventory Valuation Report*, *Vendor Ledgers*, and *Cash Disbursements Journal* reports.

Problem 2A

Open Kathleen's Designs, which you updated in 1A.
Create records for the following sales representatives:

Employee ID:	**ACHANG-01**
Name:	**Annette Chang**
Address:	**2984 Monte Vista Lane**
City, ST, Zip:	**Modesto, CA 95355**
Country:	**USA**
Telephone 1:	**209-555-6565**
Social Security Number:	**888-55-5555**
Type:	**Independ**

Employee ID:	**TWILSON-02**
Name:	**Thomas Wilson**
Address:	**21543 Holly Drive**
City, ST, Zip:	**Modesto, CA 95355**
Country:	**USA**
Telephone 1:	**209-555-9564**
Social Security Number:	**555-88-8888**
Type:	**Independ**

Problem 1B

Open Ana's Creations, a beauty salon, which is located on the student data disk.

1. Create the Inventory account for this firm.

Account ID:	**105**
Description:	**Inventory**
Account Type:	**Inventory**

2. Create the Cost of Sales account.

Account ID:	**503**
Description:	**Cost of Goods Sold**
Account Type:	**Cost of Sales**

3. Create the following vendor account:

Vendor ID:	**BP-01**
Name:	**Beauty Products**
Contact:	**Maxine Williams**
Account Number:	**16531**
Mailing Address:	**2951 Corral Hollow Road**
City, ST, Zip:	**Tracy, CA 95376**
Country:	**USA**
Vendor Type:	**Supplier**
1099 Type:	**None**
Expense Acct:	**105**
Telephone 1:	**209-555-4612**
Tax ID Number:	**09-912348**
Ship Via:	**Fed-Ex**
Terms and Credit:	**2/10, n/30**

4. Create the following ledger accounts for inventory items:

Item ID:	**EXSHAMPOO-01**
Description:	**Ecstasy Shampoo**
Item Class:	**Stock item**
Description:	**for Sales**
Full Price:	**22.00**
Last Unit Cost:	**13.50**
Cost Method:	**FIFO**
UPC/SKU:	**1209234291**
Item Type:	**Retail**
Stocking U/M:	**Each**
GL Sales Acct:	**401**
GL Inventory Acct:	**105**
GL Cost of Sales Acct:	**503**
Item Tax Type:	**1**
Preferred Vendor ID:	**BP-01**

Item ID:	**EXCONDITIONER-02**
Description:	**Ecstasy Conditioner**
Item Class:	**Stock item**
Description:	**for Sales**
Full Price:	**18.00**
Last Unit Cost:	**9.50**
Cost Method:	**FIFO**
UPC/SKU:	**3948909812**
Item Type:	**Retail**
Stocking U/M:	**Each**
GL Sales Acct:	**401**
GL Inventory Acct:	**105**
GL Cost of Sales Acct:	**503**
Item Tax Type:	**1**
Preferred Vendor ID:	**BP-01**

Item ID:	**HAIRGEL-03**
Description:	**Ecstasy Hair Gel**
Item Class:	**Stock item**
Description:	**for Sales**
Full Price:	**12.00**
Last Unit Cost:	**5.50**
Cost Method:	**FIFO**
UPC/SKU:	**8127673219**
Item Type:	**Retail**
Stocking U/M:	**Each**
GL Sales Acct:	**401**
GL Inventory Acct:	**105**
GL Cost of Sales Acct:	**503**
Item Tax Type:	**1**
Preferred Vendor ID:	**BP-01**

5. Record the following transactions, which occurred in June 2010.

June 10   Ordered 22 bottles of shampoo and 8 bottles of conditioner, using Purchase Order 200.

13   Ordered 15 bottles of hair gel, using Purchase Order 201.

13   Received 22 bottles of shampoo and 6 of the bottles of conditioner that were ordered, Invoice 1864.

15   Received 15 bottles of hair gel, Invoice 1925.

23   Paid Invoices 1864 and 1925, less discounts, Check 450. (Use 105 as the Discount Account.)

6. Print the *Inventory Valuation Report*, *Vendor Ledgers*, and *Cash Disbursements Journal* reports.

Problem 2B

Open Ana's Creations, which you updated in Problem 2A.

Create records for the following hairstylists who are independent contractors:

Employee ID: **MANDERSON-01**
Name: **Melody Anderson**
Address: **19974 West Pershing Avenue**
City, ST, Zip: **Tracy, CA 95376**
Country: **USA**
Telephone 1:   **209-555-6936**
Social Security Number: **645-55-5555**
Type: **Independ**

Employee ID: **WKINCAID-02**
Name: **William Kincaid**
Address: **6543 Angelica Court**
City, ST, Zip: **Modesto, CA 95355**
Country: **USA**
Telephone 1:   **209-555-9564**
Social Security Number: **544-55-9999**
Type: **Independ**

Cooperative Learning

1. Form groups of three or four students, and discuss how each of the inventory costing methods will affect taxable income in periods when prices are rising.
2. As a group, choose a local business such as a clothing store, a sporting goods store, or a drugstore. What inventory control problems might this business have?

Writing and Decision Making

Assume that you work for a small merchandising business that does not yet use computerized inventory procedures. The owner, Marie Ramirez, has asked you to provide information on how Peachtree can help her to manage the firm's inventory. She has specifically asked you to explain the steps necessary to set up Peachtree's inventory system, what tasks the system can handle, and what records and reports it produces. Prepare a memo providing the information that has been requested.

CHAPTER 9

Sales of Inventory in a Merchandise Business

Learning Objectives

1. Understand inventory sales concepts

2. Create sales tax accounts and codes

3. Process sales transactions and create invoices

4. Create sales orders and invoices from quotations

5. Record finance charges on overdue customer balances

6. Print inventory and sales reports

Software Features

- Sales Invoices

- Credit Memos

- Sales Quotations and Orders

- Sales Taxes

- Finance Charges

Chapter 8 focused on establishing a perpetual inventory system for a merchandising business and recording the initial purchases of goods. In this chapter, you will see how a merchandising business processes sales of inventory, sales tax, sales returns and allowances, sales discounts, and finance charges on overdue customer balances.

OBJECTIVE 1 — Understand Inventory Sales Concepts

Some merchandising businesses sell goods "over the counter" and record their sales transactions on a cash register. Examples of such businesses are supermarkets, drugstores, and department stores. Increasingly, these businesses are using optical scanners and electronic cash registers that transfer information about their sales to a computerized accounting system and a computerized inventory system.

Other merchandising businesses sell their goods through sales representatives who visit customers, through catalogs sent to customers, over the telephone, or through Web sites. When businesses sell through these types of channels, they usually issue invoices to their customers. Remember that an invoice is a bill for goods or services. It lists the items sold, the prices, the total owed, the credit terms, and other information about the sale. The invoice is sent to the customer with the goods or mailed after the goods are shipped.

These businesses may also issue sales quotations, sales orders, and credit memos—

- Sometimes a potential customer will ask a business to provide a form showing the prices it will charge for specified goods. In response, the business will issue a **sales quotation**.
- When a customer orders goods, a business may prepare a form that shows the items involved, the quantities, the name of the sales representative, and other information about the order. This form is called a **sales order**.
- If a customer returns damaged or incorrect goods, the business provides credit for the return. It issues a **credit memo** to the customer to show the amount of credit granted.

Peachtree allows a merchandising business to quickly and efficiently prepare invoices, sales quotations, sales orders, and credit memos. It also helps a merchandising business by automatically calculating sales tax, sales discount, and finance charges.

Accounting for Sales under the Perpetual Inventory System

Suppose that a business sells goods for $500 on credit to a customer. The business must collect a 7% sales tax on all of its sales. The cost of the items sold was $300. Because the business uses the perpetual inventory system, it must make two sets of entries to record this sale.

- The business must debit Accounts Receivable for $535 (the total amount owed by the customer), credit the appropriate revenue account for $500 (the amount of revenue earned by the business), and credit Sales Tax Payable for $35 (the amount of sales tax owed).

sales quotation A form that shows the prices a business will charge for specified goods.

sales order A form that a business may prepare to record the details of a customer's order.

credit memo A form issued to a customer to show the credit granted for a return of goods.

- The business must debit Cost of Goods Sold for $300 and credit Inventory for $300. This amount is the cost of the items sold to the customer.

One of the advantages of Peachtree is that it can update all of these general ledger accounts simultaneously when you enter a sale on credit. It can also update the subsidiary ledger accounts for the customer and for the inventory items sold.

Check point

1. Name four types of forms that many merchandising businesses prepare when they sell their goods.
2. A merchandising business that uses the perpetual inventory system makes a sale for $1,000. The goods have a cost of $600. What entry is made in the Cost of Goods Sold account and the Inventory account?

Answers
1. *The four types of forms that many merchandising businesses prepare are the invoice, sales quotation, sales order, and credit memo.*
2. *The Cost of Goods Sold account is debited for $600 and the Inventory account is credited for $600.*

OBJECTIVE 2 — Create Sales Tax Accounts and Codes

Most states and some cities and counties impose a sales tax on goods that are sold to consumers. The retail businesses that make the sales are responsible for collecting the tax and sending it to the sales tax authority at regular intervals—usually monthly or quarterly.

When a sale is recorded, the amount of sales tax owed is credited to a liability account called Sales Tax Payable. Later, when the business remits the sales tax owed for a period to the sales tax authority, it debits the Sales Tax Payable account.

Sales Tax Payable is a current liability (a short-term debt) for a business. In the Peachtree system of account classification, this account appears after Accounts Payable and is part of the group of accounts called Other Current Liabilities.

Superior Carpet and Tile must charge a 7% sales tax on the inventory that it sells. In California, where Superior is located, there are several local sales tax authorities and a state sales tax authority. Superior is under the jurisdiction of an agency called the Board of Equalization and will send the amounts of sales tax it owes to this agency.

Superior must now create the Sales Tax Payable account in its general ledger and a vendor account for the Board of Equalization in its accounts payable ledger. Follow the steps outlined on the next page to accomplish these tasks.

Step 1:
Open Superior Carpet and Tile (Chp. 9 – Superior Carpet and Tile if student data disk is used).

Step 2:
Create the Sales Tax Payable account in the general ledger. Use the following information:

Account ID:	**212**
Description:	**Sales Tax Payable**
Account Type:	**Other Current Liabilities**

Step 3:
Compare your work with figure 9–1, then click Save and Close.

FIGURE 9–1
Completed Entries
for Sales Tax Payable
Account

Step 4:
Create a vendor account for the Board of Equalization.

Vendor ID:	**BRE-006**
Name:	**Board of Equalization**
Expense Account:	**212**
Tax ID Number:	**None**
Ship Via:	**US Mail**
Terms and Credit:	**Net due in 30 days, 0.00 Discount**
Form Options:	**Default**

Step 5:
Compare your work with figure 9–2, then click Save and Close.

FIGURE 9–2
Completed Vendor
Account for Board of
Equalization

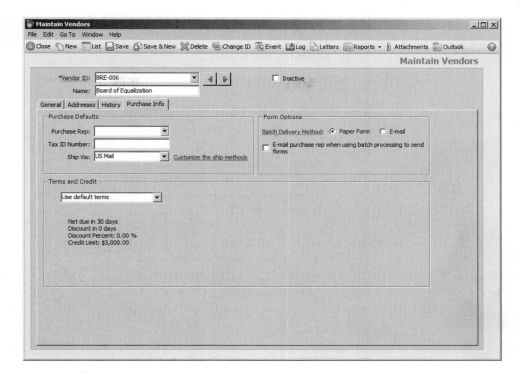

Step 6:
Click Maintain, then *Sales Taxes*, and then click the radio button next to *Set up a new sales tax* from the Sales Taxes window.

Step 7:
Click Next to continue setting up the new sales tax.

Step 8:
Key **7.00** in the What is the total rate that you will charge? box.

Step 9:
Select *1* from the How many individual rates make up this total rate? drop-down list. Then click Next to continue.

Step 10:
Key **CA** in the *Sales tax agency ID* field and key **Board of Equalization** in the *Sales tax agency name* field.

Step 11:
Select *BRE-006 (Board of Equalization)* from the Which vendor do you send the taxes you've collected to? drop-down list.

Step 12:
Select *by single rate* in the next drop-down list, if necessary.

Step 13:
Key **7.00** in the *Rate* field, and select *212 (Sales Tax Payable)* from the Select an account to track sales taxes drop-down list. Compare your entries with figure 9–3. Click Next.

FIGURE 9–3
Completed Add Sales Tax
Agency Window

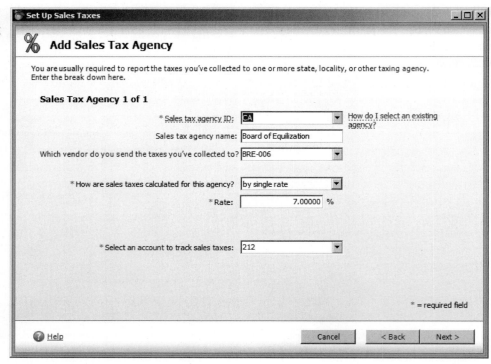

Step 14:
Key **CAL** in the *Sales tax ID* field of the Sales Tax Entered window.

Step 15:
Key **California Sales Tax** in the *Sales tax name* field, and select *No* from the Do you charge sales tax on freight? drop-down list. Compare your work with figure 9–4.

FIGURE 9–4
Completed Sales Tax
Entered Window

Step 16:
Click Finish. Click the radio button next to *Close the sale tax wizard* and then
Finish.

C h e c k   p o i n t

1. Who is responsible for collecting sales tax from consumers?
2. What type of account is Sales Tax Payable?

Answers
1. *The businesses that sell goods to consumers are responsible for collecting sales tax from them.*
2. *Sales Tax Payable is a current liability account.*

P r a c t i c e   O b j e c t i v e   2

Meadowland Healthcare Services must revise its general ledger accounts so
that it can record sales of goods and sales tax.

Step 1:
Open Meadowland Healthcare Services (Chp. 9 – Meadowland Healthcare
Services if student data disk is used).

Step 2:
Create the new income account needed to record sales of goods.

Account ID:	**40000.5**
Account Description:	**Medical Sales Revenue**
Account Type:	**Income**

Step 3:
Because you now have two separate income accounts, change the *GL Sales
Acct* field for each of your current inventory items from *40000 (Revenue)* to
40000.5 (Medical Sales Revenue).

Step 4:
Create the Sales Tax Payable account.

Account ID:	**21200**
Description:	**Sales Tax Payable**
Account Type:	**Other Current Liabilities**

Step 5:
Create a new vendor account for the Board of Equalization.

Vendor ID:	**BRE-008**
Name:	**Board of Equalization**
Expense Account:	**21200**
Tax ID Number:	**None**
Ship Via:	**US Mail**
Terms and Credit:	**Net due in 30 days, 0.00 Discount**
Form Options:	**Default**

Step 6:

Enter the information about the sales tax agency.

Total Tax Rate:	**7.00**
Sales Tax Agency ID:	**CA**
Sales Tax Agency Name:	**Board of Equalization**
Vendor:	**BRE-008**
Taxes Calculated:	**by single rate**
Tax Rate:	**7.00**
Account to Track Sales Tax:	**21200**
Sales Tax ID:	**CATAX**
Sales Tax Name:	**California Sales Tax**
Sales Tax on Freight:	**No**

Step 7:

To view the Sales Tax Payable account, display the chart of accounts and compare it to figure 9–5.

FIGURE 9–5
Chart of Accounts for Meadowland Healthcare Services

Page: 1

Chp. 9 - Meadowland Healthcare Services
Chart of Accounts
As of Feb 28, 2010

Filter Criteria includes: Report order is by ID. Report is printed with Accounts having Zero Amounts and in Detail Format.

Account ID	Account Description	Active?	Account Type
10000	Petty Cash	Yes	Cash
10200	Regular Checking Account	Yes	Cash
10400	Accounts Recveivable	Yes	Accounts Receivable
10500	Inventory	Yes	Inventory
10600	Medical Supplies	Yes	Other Current Assets
10800	Office Supplies	Yes	Other Current Assets
11000	Prepaid Insurance	Yes	Other Current Assets
11200	Medical Equipment	Yes	Fixed Assets
11200.5	Accum. Depr.-Med Equip	Yes	Accumulated Depreciation
20000	Accounts Payable	Yes	Accounts Payable
21000	Wages and Salaries Payab	Yes	Other Current Liabilities
21200	Sales Tax Payable	Yes	Other Current Liabilities
30000	J. Simon, Capital	Yes	Equity-doesn't close
30100	J. Simon, Equity	Yes	Equity-Retained Earnings
30100.5	J. Simon, Drawing	Yes	Equity-gets closed
40000	Revenue	Yes	Income
40000.5	Medical Sales Revenue	Yes	Income
40100	Sales Discount	Yes	Income
50000	Cost of Goods Sold	Yes	Cost of Sales
50100	Rent Expense	Yes	Expenses
50200	Utilities Expense	Yes	Expenses
50220	Bank Fee Expense	Yes	Expenses
50400	Medical Supplies Expense	Yes	Expenses
50520	Housekeeping Expense	Yes	Expenses
50600	Office Supplies Expense	Yes	Expenses
50800	Insurance Expense	Yes	Expenses
51000	Depreciation Expense-Medi	Yes	Expenses
51200	Wages and Salaries Expen	Yes	Expenses
51400	Miscellaneous Expense	Yes	Expenses
52000	Uncollectible Accounts Exp	Yes	Expenses

OBJECTIVE 3 — Process Sales Transactions and Create Invoices

When a merchandising business receives an order from a customer, it selects and packs the necessary goods and issues an invoice to bill the customer. The invoice may be enclosed with the goods when they are shipped to the customer, or it may be mailed separately.

Occasionally, a merchandising business will send incorrect goods to a customer or the goods will arrive in damaged condition. The customer will then return the goods and request credit or agree to keep the goods if an allowance is offered. (An allowance is a reduction in the selling price of goods.) To provide evidence of the credit granted for a return or allowance, the business issues a credit memo to the customer.

Peachtree allows a merchandising business to efficiently make accounting entries for sales on credit and sales returns and allowances and also generate the necessary invoices and credit memos.

Recording a Sale on Credit and Creating the Invoice

Suppose that on February 7, 2010, Superior Carpet and Tile sells storage racks on credit to Jim Green, who operates his own business. The terms of the sale are 2/10, n/30.

Because Green is a new customer, it is necessary to create a customer account for him before recording the sale and issuing Invoice 1003.

Step 1:
Open Chp. 9 – Superior Carpet and Tile, which you updated previously in the chapter.

Step 2:
Create a new customer account for Jim Green. Use the following information.

Customer
Customer ID:	**Green-11**
Name:	**Jim Green**

General Tab
Account Number:	**1821**
Billing Address:	**12 Onyx Road**
City, ST, Zip:	**Modesto, CA 95355**
Country:	**USA**
Sales Tax:	**CAL**
Customer Type:	**Retail**
Telephone 1:	**209-555-4845**

Contact Tab
Contact:	**Jim Green**

Sales Info Tab
GL Sales Account:	**400.5**
Ship Via:	**UPS Ground**
Pricing Level:	**Full Price**
Form Options:	**Default**

Payment & Credit Tab
Terms and Credit:	**2% 10 Days, Net 30 Days**

History Tab
Beginning Balance:	**0**

Now record the credit sale to Jim Green and create Invoice 1003.

Step 3:
Click Tasks, and then click *Sales/Invoicing*.

Step 4:
The Sales/Invoicing window now appears. At the *Customer ID* field click the *magnifying glass* icon and then click *Green-11*.

Step 5:
Key **02/07/09** in the *Date* field.

Step 6:
Key **1003** in the *Invoice No.* field.

Step 7:
Key **6.00** in the *Quantity* field.

Step 8:
In the *Item* field click the *magnifying glass* icon, and then click *SK-2*.

Step 9:
Compare your completed work with figure 9–6.

FIGURE 9–6
Completed Sales/
Invoicing Window

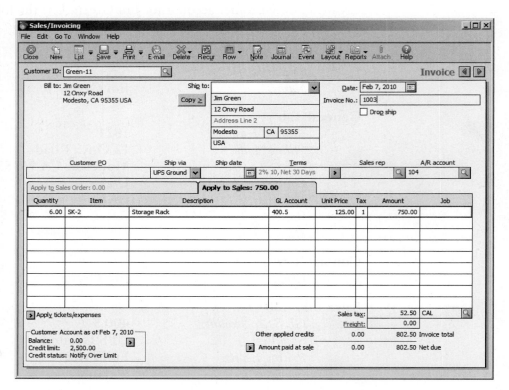

Step 10:
Click Save and then click Close.

Printing the Invoice

The sale on credit made to Jim Green has now been posted to the general ledger and the appropriate subsidiary ledgers. In the general ledger, Accounts Receivable has been debited for $802.50, Sales Revenue has been credited for $750, and Sales Tax Payable has been credited for $52.50. Also in the general ledger, Cost of Goods Sold has been debited for $315 and

Inventory has been credited for $315. This amount is the cost of the six storage racks. Finally, the account for Jim Green in the accounts receivable subsidiary ledger has been debited for $802.50 and the account for the storage racks in the inventory subsidiary ledger has been credited for $315.

The next task for Superior Carpet and Tile is to print Invoice 1003 and send it to Jim Green. Superior has a policy of mailing an invoice on the day the goods are shipped to the customer. Follow the steps outlined below to print Invoice 1003.

Step 1:
Click Tasks, and then click *Sales/Invoicing*.

Step 2:
Click the List button at the top of the Sales/Invoicing window.

Step 3:
The Sales Invoice List window will appear. Click the sale to Jim Green (Invoice 1003), as shown in figure 9–7.

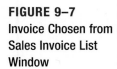
FIGURE 9–7
Invoice Chosen from
Sales Invoice List
Window

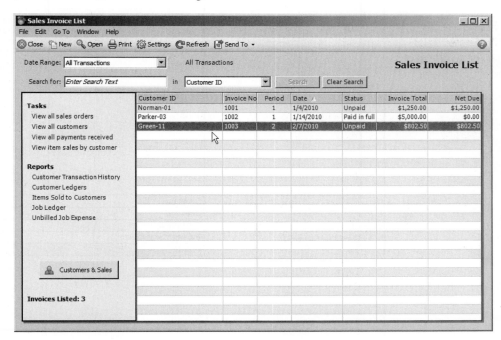

Step 4:
Click Open.

Step 5:
Click the Print button on the Sales/Invoicing toolbar.

Step 6:
Click Print at the Print Forms: Invoices dialog box. Compare your completed invoice with figure 9–8.

FIGURE 9–8
Invoice 1003

INVOICE

Chp. 9 - Superior Carpet and Tile
348 Brown Ave.
Campbell, CA 95555
USA

Voice: 916-655-2222
Fax: 916-655-2222

Invoice Number: 1003
Invoice Date: Feb 7, 2010
Page: 1
Duplicate

Bill To:	Ship to:
Jim Green 12 Onxy Road Modesto, CA 95355 USA	Jim Green 12 Onxy Road Modesto, CA 95355 USA

Customer ID	Customer PO	Payment Terms	
Green-11		2% 10, Net 30 Days	
Sales Rep ID	Shipping Method	Ship Date	Due Date
	UPS Ground		3/9/10

Quantity	Item	Description	Unit Price	Amount
6.00	SK-2	Storage Rack	125.00	750.00
		Subtotal		750.00
		Sales Tax		52.50
		Total Invoice Amount		802.50
Check/Credit Memo No:		Payment/Credit Applied		
		TOTAL		802.50

Step 7:

Close the Sales/Invoicing window and the Sales Invoice List window.

Recording a Sales Return and Creating the Credit Memo

Suppose that on February 8, 2010, Jim Green receives the six storage racks shipped by Superior Carpet and Tile on February 7. Green finds that one storage rack is damaged and notifies Superior that he intends to return the storage rack. Superior agrees to give him a credit of $133.75 for the return. This amount includes the selling price of $125 and sales tax of $8.75.

Superior must now record the sales return and create a credit memo. The return requires a debit of $125 to Sales Returns and Allowances, a debit of $8.75 to Sales Tax Payable, and a credit of $133.75 to Accounts Receivable. It is also necessary to record a credit of $133.75 in the subsidiary ledger account for Jim Green.

Sales returns and allowances reduce the revenue of a business. These transactions can be recorded by debiting them to the Sales Revenue account if desired. Most businesses, however, prefer to have a separate record of these transactions and therefore use a Sales Returns and Allowances account.

Follow the steps outlined below to record the storage rack returned by Jim Green and create the necessary credit memo.

Step 1:
Click Tasks, and then click *Credit Memos*.

Step 2:
At the *Customer ID* field, click the *magnifying glass* icon, and then click *Green-11*.

Step 3:
At the *Date* field, click the *calendar* icon, and choose *Feb 8, 2010*.

Step 4:
Key **CM012** (the credit memo number) in the *Credit No.* field.

Step 5:
Select Invoice *1003* from the drop-down list next to the *Apply to Invoice No.* tab.

Step 6:
Key **1.00** in the *Returned* field.

Step 7:
Key **Storage Rack** in the *Description* field, if needed.

Step 8:
Click the Journal button on the Credit Memos toolbar. The Accounting Behind the Screens window will appear, as shown in figure 9–9.

FIGURE 9–9
Accounting Behind the Screens Window

Account No.	Description	Debit	Credit
212	CA: Board of Equilization	8.75	
400.5	Storage Rack	125.00	
503	Cost of sales	To be calculated	
105	Cost of sales	To be calculated	
104	Accounts Receivable		133.75
	Totals:	133.75	133.75

Date: Feb 8, 2010
Credit #: CM012

Sales Journal / Cash Receipts Journal

Because Superior does not yet have a Sales Returns and Allowances account, this window shows that the Sales Revenue account (400.5) is being decreased to record the return. It is therefore necessary to create a Sales Returns and Allowances account in Superior's general ledger.

Step 9:
Click the *magnifying glass* icon in the second row of the *Account No.* field, and then click the New button at the bottom of the window.

Step 10:
Use the following information to create the Sales Returns and Allowances account:

Account ID:	**404**
Description:	**Sales Returns and Allowances**
Account Type:	**Income**

Step 11:
Compare your work with figure 9–10. Click Save and then Close.

FIGURE 9–10
Account 404 Added
to Maintain Chart of
Accounts Window

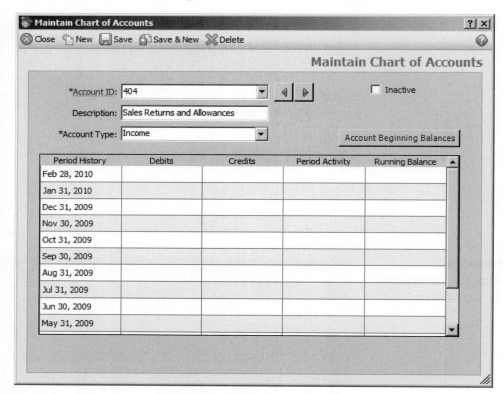

Notice that account 404 will now appear in the *Account No.* field.

Note: Peachtree automatically updates Cost of Goods Sold and Inventory for returned items. However, you may still need to manually adjust for the cost of damaged or defective inventory that cannot be placed back in stock.

Step 12:
Click OK to close the Accounting Behind the Screens window.

Printing the Credit Memo

Follow the steps outlined below to print the credit memo that Superior Carpet and Tile must send to Jim Green.

Step 1:
Click the Print button on the Credit Memos toolbar.

Step 2:
At the Print Forms: Credit Memos dialog box, click Print, as shown in figure 9–11.

FIGURE 9–11
Print Forms: Credit Memos Window

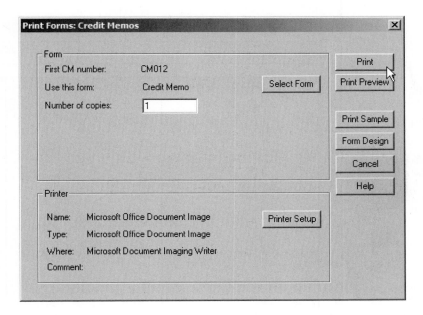

Step 3:
Compare your completed credit memo with figure 9–12.

FIGURE 9–12
Credit Memo 012

Chp. 9 - Superior Carpet and Tile
348 Brown Ave.
Campbell, CA 95555
USA

Voice: 916-555-2222
Fax: 916-555-2222

CREDIT MEMO

Credit Memo Number: CM012
Credit Date: Feb 8, 2010
Page: 1
Duplicate

Credit To:

Jim Green
12 Onyx Road
Modesto, CA 95355
USA

Customer ID	Customer PO	Sales Rep ID
Green-11		

Quantity	Item	Description	Unit Price	Amount
-1.00	SK-2	Storage Rack	125.00	-125.00
		Subtotal		-125.00
		Sales Tax		-8.75
		Freight		
		TOTAL		-133.75

Invoice No: 1003

Step 4:

Click Close to close the Credit Memos window.

Recording a Cash Receipt When a Customer Pays an Invoice

Suppose that on February 20, 2010, Superior Carpet and Tile receives a check for $668.75 from Jim Green. This check is in payment of Invoice 1003 ($802.50) less Credit Memo 012 ($133.75).

When Superior Carpet and Tile receives the check from Jim Green, it must debit Cash for $668.75 (the amount received), and credit Accounts Receivable for $668.75 (the total amount owed by the customer).

Follow the steps outlined below to record the payment Superior has received from Jim Green for Invoice 1003 less Credit Memo 012.

Step 1:
Click Tasks, and then click *Receipts*.

Step 2:
Select *Check* from the Payment Method drop-down list and *100 (Cash)* from the Cash Account drop-down list.

Step 3:
At the *Deposit Ticket ID* field, key **02/20/10**.

Step 4:
At the *Customer ID* field of the Receipts window, click the *magnifying glass* icon, and then click *Green-11*, as shown in figure 9–13.

FIGURE 9–13
Green-11 (Jim Green) Selected from Drop-Down List

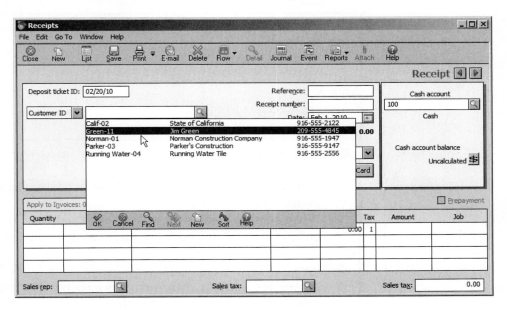

Step 5:
Key **1328** (the check number) in the *Reference* field.

Step 6:
At the *Date* field, click the *calendar* icon and choose *Feb 20, 2010*.

Step 7:
Click the box in the *Pay* field for the invoice as shown in figure 9–14. Notice that the *Receipt Amount* field indicates that the amount paid is $668.75.

FIGURE 9–14
Pay Boxes Selected

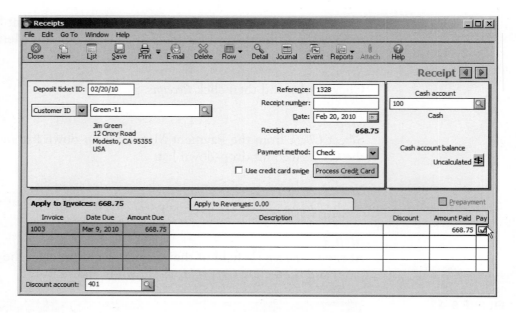

Step 8:
Click Save.

Step 9:
Close the Receipts window.

C h e c k   p o i n t

1. What document does a business issue in connection with a sales return or allowance?
2. When entering a sales return using the Credit Memo, is the number entered in the *Returned* field as a positive or negative number?

Answers
1. *A business issues a credit memo as evidence that it is granting credit to a customer for a return or allowance.*
2. *You must enter a positive number in the Returned field for a sales return.*

P r a c t i c e   O b j e c t i v e   3

On February 11, 2010, Meadowland Healthcare Services sold 20 packages of syringes on credit to Dr. George Johnson, a new customer. Meadowland issued Invoice 1105 with credit terms of 3/10, n/30.

Step 1:
Open Chp. 9 – Meadowland Healthcare Services, which you updated previously in the chapter.

Step 2:

Create a new customer account for George Johnson. Use the following information.

Customer

Customer ID:	**Johnson-50**
Name:	**Dr. George Johnson**

General Tab

Account Number:	**1290**
Billing Address:	**1342 Rose Marie Lane**
City, ST, Zip:	**Modesto, CA 95355**
Country:	**USA**
Sales Tax:	**CATAX**
Customer Type:	**Retail**
Telephone 1:	**209-555-4982**

Contact Tab

Contact:	**Dr. George Johnson**

Sales Info Tab

GL Sales Account:	**40000.5**
Ship Via:	**UPS Ground**
Pricing Level:	**Full Price**
Form Options:	**Default**

Payment & Credit Tab

Terms and Credit:	**3% 10 Days, Net 30 Days**

History Tab

Beginning Balance:	**0**

Step 3:

Use the Sales/Invoicing feature to record the sale and create Invoice 1105.

Step 4:

Print the invoice. Your invoice should look like figure 9–15.

FIGURE 9–15
Invoice 1105

Chp. 9 - Meadowland Healthcare Services
3456 Highland Ave.
Sacramento, CA 95655
USA

Voice: 916-555-3455
Fax: 916-555-4434

INVOICE

Invoice Number: 1105
Invoice Date: Feb 11, 2010
Page: 1

Duplicate

Bill To:	Ship to:
Dr. George Johnson	Dr. George Johnson
1342 Rose Marie Lane	1342 Rose Marie Lane
Modesto, CA 95355	Modesto, CA 95355
USA	USA

Customer ID	Customer PO	Payment Terms	
Johnson-60		3% 10, Net 30 Days	
Sales Rep ID	Shipping Method	Ship Date	Due Date
	UPS Ground		3/13/10

Quantity	Item	Description	Unit Price	Amount
20.00	SY-1	Syringes	12.00	240.00

Subtotal		240.00
Sales Tax		16.80
Total Invoice Amount		256.80
Payment/Credit Applied		
TOTAL		256.80

Check/Credit Memo No:

Step 5:

On February 12, 2010, Dr. Johnson returned two packages of syringes. Meadowland issued Credit Memo 201 (CM201).

Create the Sales Returns and Allowances account. Use the following information:

Account ID:	**40400**
Description:	**Sales Returns and Allowances**
Account Type:	**Income**

Step 6:

Create the credit memo, and then print the credit memo. Your credit memo should look like figure 9–16.

FIGURE 9–16
Credit Memo CM201

CREDIT MEMO

Chp. 9 - Meadowland Healthcare
3455 Highland Ave.
Sacramento, CA 95655
USA

Voice: 916-555-3455
Fax: 916-555-4434

Credit Memo Number: CM201
Credit Date: Feb 12, 2010
Page: 1

Credit To:
Dr. George Johnson
1342 Rose Marie Lane
Modesto, CA 95355
USA

Customer ID	Customer PO	Sales Rep ID
Johnson-50		

Quantity	Item	Description	Unit Price	Amount
-2.00	SY-1	Syringes	12.00	-24.00

Subtotal		-24.00
Sales Tax		-1.68
Freight		
TOTAL		-25.68

Invoice No: 1105

OBJECTIVE 4 — Create Sales Orders and Invoices from Quotations

Some businesses have a policy of requesting a price quotation or bid before they buy goods from a new supplier. Usually, these businesses obtain quotations from several competing suppliers and then compare the prices and credit terms offered.

Peachtree allows you to easily create quotations for potential customers. It also permits you to maintain a list of potential customers who have requested quotations and to convert quotations into sales orders or invoices if the potential customers end up placing orders.

Creating the Quotation

Suppose that Maria Davis, one of the sales representatives for Superior Carpet and Tile, visits Parker's Construction. She finds that the management of this firm is interested in buying 10 cases of ceramic tile but wants a price quotation. Thus, on February 10, 2010, Superior issues Quotation 2345. The prices quoted are good until February 25, 2010.

Follow the steps outlined below to create the quotation for Parker's Construction.

Step 1:
Open Chp. 9 – Superior Carpet and Tile and close the Action Items log.

Step 2:
Click Tasks, click *Quotes/Sales Orders*, and then click *Quotes*.

Step 3:
At the Quotes window, in the *Customer ID* field, click the *magnifying glass* icon, and then click *Parker-03*.

Step 4:
At the *Date* field, click the *calendar* icon, and then choose *Feb 10, 2010*.

Step 5:
At the *Good Thru* field, click the *calendar* icon, and choose *Mar 25, 2010*.

Step 6:
Key **2345** in the *Quote No.* field.

Step 7:
At the *Sales Rep* field, click the *magnifying glass* icon, and then click *MDA-02*.

Step 8:
Key **10.00** in the *Quantity* field.

Step 9:
Click in the *Item* field, click the *magnifying glass* icon, and then click *CT-3*.

Step 10:
At the *Sales Tax* field at the bottom of the Quotes screen, click the *magnifying glass* icon, and then click *CAL*. Compare your work with figure 9–17.

FIGURE 9–17
Completed Quotes
Dialog Box

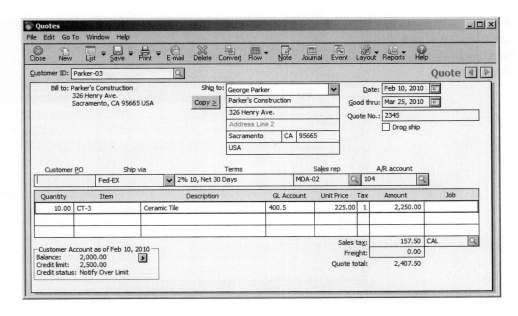

Step 11:
Click Save and then click Close.

Converting a Quotation into a Sales Order or an Invoice

If a customer places an order after a quotation is issued, Peachtree makes it possible to quickly convert the quotation into a sales order or an invoice. Some firms need a sales order because they use it for the internal processing of the customer's order—the removal of the necessary goods from inventory and the packing and shipping of the goods. When the goods are sent to the customer, the sales order is converted into an invoice.

Other firms do not use a sales order and immediately convert the quotation into an invoice. Superior Carpet and Tile follows this policy.

Suppose that on February 15, 2010, Parker's Construction accepts Quotation 2345. Superior must now use the quotation to create an invoice. Follow the steps outlined below to accomplish this task.

Step 1:
Click Tasks, click *Quotes/Sales Orders*, and then click *Quotes*.

Step 2:
The Quotes window appears. Click the List button on the Quotes toolbar.

Step 3:
The Quote List dialog box will appear. Click the quotation *2345* issued to Parker's Construction, as shown in figure 9–18.

FIGURE 9–18

Quotation 2345 Chosen
from the Quote List
Dialog Box

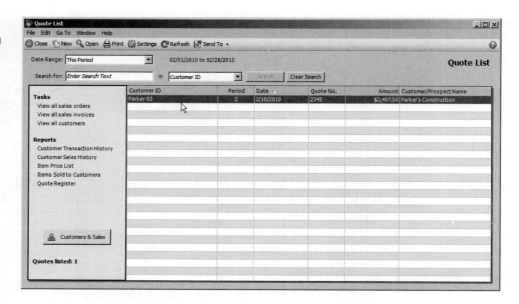

Step 4:
Click Open and Quotation 2345 will appear in the active Quotes window.

Step 5:
At the _Date_ field, click the _calendar_ icon, and choose _Feb 15, 2010_.

Step 6:
Click the Conver**t** button on the Quotes toolbar.

Step 7:
Click the Sale/Invoice button in the Convert Quote dialog box.

Step 8:
Key **1004** in the _Invoice #_ field, as shown in figure 9–19.

FIGURE 9–19
Convert Quote Dialog Box

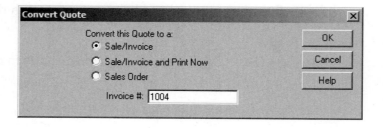

Step 9:
Click OK.

Step 10:
Click Yes to override the customer's credit limit. The quotation has now been converted to an invoice. The invoice can be printed or edited by using the Sales/Invoicing function.

Step 11:
Close the Quotes window.

C h e c k   p o i n t

1. What is the purpose of a quotation?
2. What is the purpose of a sales order?

Answers
1. A quotation shows a potential customer the prices that a firm will charge for specified goods.
2. A sales order is used by a firm in the internal processing of a customer's order.

P r a c t i c e   O b j e c t i v e   4

On February 2, 2010, Isadora Duncan, a sales representative for Meadowland Healthcare Services, gave Quotation 5432 for 120 roller bandages to Rapid Medical Response. This firm intends to use the roller bandages and not resell them. Therefore, sales tax must be collected. The quotation was good until February 15, 2010. Rapid Medical Response accepted the quotation on February 4, 2010.

Step 1:
Open Chp. 9 – Meadowland Healthcare Services.

Step 2:
Create Quotation 5432 for Rapid Medical Response.

Step 3:
Convert the quotation into Invoice 1106 on February 4, 2010.

Step 4:
Print the invoice. Your invoice should look like figure 9–20.

FIGURE 9–20
Invoice 1106

Chp. 9 - Meadowland Healthcare Services
3456 Highland Ave.
Sacramento, CA 95655
USA

Voice: 916-555-3455
Fax: 916-555-4434

INVOICE

Invoice Number: 1106
Invoice Date: Feb 4, 2010
Page: 1
Duplicate

Bill To:	Ship to:
Rapid Medical Response 2516 main Street Sacramento, CA 95671 USA	Rapid Medical Response 2516 main Street Sacramento, CA 95671 USA

Customer ID	Customer PO	Payment Terms	
Rapid-30		2% 10, Net 30 Days	
Sales Rep ID	**Shipping Method**	**Ship Date**	**Due Date**
	Fed-EX		3/6/10

Quantity	Item	Description	Unit Price	Amount
120.00	RB-2	Roller Bandages	75.00	9,000.00

Check/Credit Memo No:

Subtotal	9,000.00
Sales Tax	630.00
Total Invoice Amount	9,630.00
Payment/Credit Applied	
TOTAL	9,630.00

OBJECTIVE 5 — Record Finance Charges on Overdue Customer Balances

In addition to issuing invoices whenever goods are sold to a customer, many firms send a monthly **statement of account** to the customer. This statement lists all transactions with the customer during the period—sales on credit, returns, and cash received on account. Most important, this statement shows the balance owed at the end of the period.

Some businesses have a policy of imposing a finance charge when customers do not pay their bills within a specified period of time. This policy is intended to discourage customers from allowing their balances to become overdue. If the firm has a policy of adding a finance charge to overdue balances, the finance charge appears on the statement of account.

statement of account A form that a business sends each month to show all transactions with a customer and the balance owed by the customer.

Peachtree allows you to set defaults for a finance charge so that the charge is automatically calculated and recorded whenever customer accounts have overdue balances.

Creating the Defaults for Finance Charges

Remember that Superior Carpet and Tile offers credit terms of 2/10, n/30 to its customers. Suppose that Superior decides to add an 8% finance charge to invoices that are more than 30 days overdue. Superior must create the necessary defaults, as outlined below. However, before that, Superior must establish an Interest Income account in its general ledger. This account will be used to record the income received from finance charges. Interest Income will be credited for all finance charges.

Step 1:
Open Chp. 9 – Superior Carpet and Tile, which you updated previously in the chapter.

Step 2:
Create the following account in the general ledger:

Account ID:	**450**
Description:	**Interest Income**
Account Type:	**Income**

Step 3:
Click Maintain, click *Default Information*, and then click *Customers*.

Step 4:
Click the Finance Charges tab from the Customer Defaults dialog box.

Step 5:
Click the box next to *Charge finance charges* in order to insert a check mark.

Step 6:
Key **30** in the *On invoices…days overdue* field.

Step 7:
Key **10,000.00** in the *up to* field.

Step 8:
Key **8.00** in the *Annual interest rate* field.

Step 9:
Click the box next to *Charge interest on finance charges* to insert a check mark. This indicates that the system should calculate interest on any accumulated finance charges.

Step 10:
Key **450** in the *Finance Charge GL Account* field. Compare your work with figure 9–21.

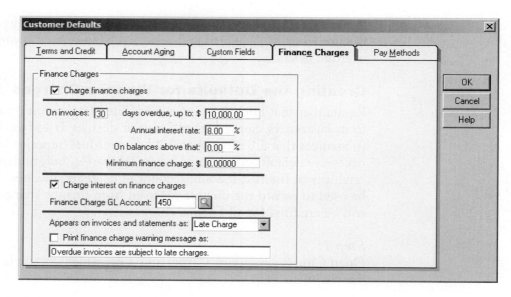

Figure: Customer Defaults dialog box — Finance Charges tab

Step 11:
Click OK to accept the finance charge defaults.

Creating the Finance Charge Report

Suppose that Superior Carpet and Tile has one overdue account on March 31, 2010. A report can be generated showing the finance charges imposed on the customer's account. This report can be printed or viewed on the screen. Follow the steps outlined below to view the finance charge report for Parker's Construction.

Step 1:
Click *Customer/Prospects* from the Maintain drop-down list on the main Menu bar.

Step 2:
Click the *magnifying glass* icon next to the *Customer ID* field, and then click *Parker-03*.

Step 3:
Select the Payment & Credit Tab and click the box next to *Charge Finance Charges* to insert a check mark. Click Save and then Close.

Step 4:
Click Tasks, and then click *Finance Charge*.

Step 5:
The Calculate Finance Charges dialog box appears. At the *Starting Customer* field, click the *magnifying glass* icon, and then click *Parker-03*.

Step 6:
At the *Ending Customer* field, click the *magnifying glass* icon, and then click *Parker-03*.

Step 7:

At the *Date* field, click the *calendar* icon, and then choose *Mar 31, 2010*. Compare your work with figure 9–22.

FIGURE 9–22
Calculate Finance
Charges Window

Step 8:

Click OK.

Step 9:

The Apply Finance Charges dialog box now appears. Click the No button in the Apply Finance Charges section. (You would click Yes if adding finance charges to a statement of account.)

Step 10:

Click the Screen button in the Report Destination section.

Step 11:

Click the No button in the Print Calculation Sheet section. Compare your work with figure 9–23.

FIGURE 9–23
Completed Apply Finance
Charges Window

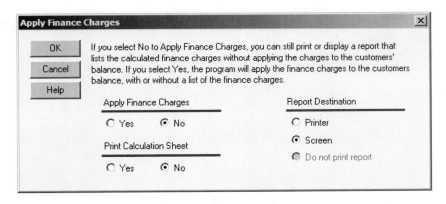

Step 12:

Click OK.

Step 13:

The Finance Charge Report Selection dialog box now appears. Click the Detail button in the Report Style section.

Step 14:

Click the By Id button in the Report Order section. Compare your work with figure 9–24.

FIGURE 9–24
Completed Finance
Charge Report Selection
Window

Step 15:

Click OK.

Step 16:

Compare the report on your screen with figure 9–25.

FIGURE 9–25
Completed Finance
Charges Report

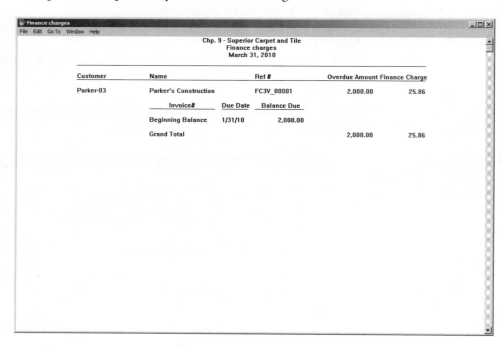

Step 17:

Close the *Finance charges* report.

C h e c k   p o i n t

1. Why do some businesses impose finance charges on customer accounts?
2. What account is used to record finance charges?

Answers

1. Some businesses impose finance charges to discourage customers from allowing their balances to become overdue.
2. The account used to record finance charges is Interest Income.

Practice Objective 5

Meadowland Healthcare Services wants to add a finance charge to all customer balances that are more than 45 days overdue. The interest rate will be 9.5% on invoices up to $15,000. Interest will also be calculated on finance charges.

Step 1:
Open Chp. 9 – Meadowland Healthcare Services, which you updated previously in the chapter.

Step 2:
Create the following account in the general ledger:

Account ID:	**40500**
Description:	**Interest Income**
Account Type:	**Income**

Step 3:
Create the customer finance charge defaults.

Step 4:
Print a report showing the finance charges on the open invoices for Rapid Medical Response as of April 30, 2010. Your report should look like figure 9–26.

FIGURE 9–26
Finance Charges
Report for Rapid
Medical Response

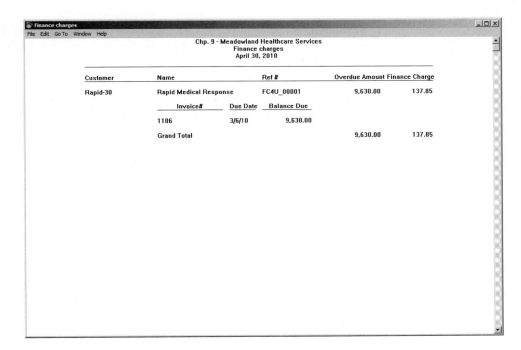

OBJECTIVE 6 — Print Inventory and Sales Reports

Peachtree provides a variety of inventory and sales reports for merchandising businesses. The information from these reports can help management to answer the following types of questions: What items are selling well and what items are selling poorly? Do we have too much stock of the slow-selling items? If we want to close out some of the slow-selling items, how much can we reduce the prices for those items and still make a profit?

Creating Inventory Reports

Peachtree offers the following inventory reports to merchandising businesses. These reports offer a wide range of information that can be used to plan and control inventory.

- The *Inventory Valuation Report* shows the value (cost) of the current inventory.
- The *Inventory Adjustment Journal* lists all inventory adjustments that were made.
- The *Item Costing Report* lists the cost, receipts, and sales for each inventory item.
- The *Cost of Goods Sold Journal* shows the cost of all inventory items sold during a period.
- The *Item Master List* gives detailed information about all inventory items.
- The *Item Price List* gives the various prices and the quantity on hand of all inventory items.
- The *Physical Inventory List* is used to compare the actual inventory on hand with the reported inventory.
- The *Inventory Profitability Report* shows the units sold and profitability of inventory items.

Superior Carpet and Tile wants to see the *Cost of Goods Sold Journal* for the month of February 2010. Follow the steps outlined below to generate this inventory report.

Step 1:
Open Chp. 9 – Superior Carpet and Tile and close the Action Items log.

Step 2:
Click Reports & Forms, and then click *Inventory*.

Step 3:
At the Inventory: Items and Services You Buy and Sell section, select *Cost of Goods Sold Journal*.

Step 4:
Click the <u>D</u>isplay button on the Select a Report or Form toolbar.

Step 5:
Compare your journal with the one shown in figure 9–27.

FIGURE 9–27
Cost of Goods Sold
Journal

Page: 1

Chp. 9 - Superior Carpet and Tile
Cost of Goods Sold Journal
For the Period From Feb 1, 2010 to Feb 28, 2010
Filter Criteria includes: Report order is by Date. Report is printed in Detail Format and with shortened descriptions.

Date	GL Acct ID	Reference	Qty	Line Description	Debit Amount	Credit Amount
2/7/10	105	1003	6.00	Storage Rack		315.00
	503		6.00	Storage Rack	315.00	
2/8/10	105	CM012	-1.00	Storage Rack	52.50	
	503		-1.00	Storage Rack		52.50
2/10/10	105	1004	10.00	Ceramic Tile		1,000.00
	503		10.00	Ceramic Tile	1,000.00	
		Total			**1,367.50**	**1,367.50**

Step 6:
Click Close.

Creating Sales Reports

As we have discussed, Peachtree helps a merchandising business by making it easy to produce a variety of sales-related documents that are needed in the firm's operations:

- Quotations for potential customers
- Sales orders
- Invoices
- Credit memos
- Statements of account
- Collection letters for overdue accounts

Peachtree also provides many different sales reports for merchandising businesses. Some of these reports are described below.

- The *Customer List* shows the names and contact information of all customers.
- The *Prospect List* shows the names and contact information of all prospects.
- The *Invoice Register* is a list of all invoices that have been issued to customers.
- The *Quote Register* is a list of all outstanding price quotations.
- The *Sales Journal* shows all sales on credit made during a period.
- The *Sales Rep Reports* is a list of sales made by each sales representative.
- The *Customer Ledgers* include the accounts for all credit customers.
- The *Sales Taxes* is a list of all sales tax codes used by the business.
- The *Sales Order Register, Journal,* and *Report* show information about all sales orders issued.
- The *Customer Sales History* is a list of the transactions with each customer.

Superior Carpet and Tile wants to see the *Sales Journal* for the month of February 2010. Follow the steps outlined on the following page to create this report.

Step 1:
At the Select a Report or Form dialog box, in the <u>R</u>eports section, click *Accounts Receivable*.

Step 2:
In the Accounts Receivable: Customer and Sales section, select *Sales Journal*.

Step 3:
Click the <u>D</u>isplay button on the Select a Report or Form toolbar.

Step 4:
Compare your journal with the one shown in figure 9–28.

FIGURE 9–28
Sales Journal

Page: 1

Chp. 9 - Superior Carpet and Tile
Sales Journal
For the Period From Feb 1, 2010 to Feb 28, 2010

Filter Criteria includes: Report order is by Invoice/CM Date. Report is printed in Detail Format.

Date	Account ID	Invoice/CM #	Line Description	Debit Amnt	Credit Amnt
2/7/10	212	1003	CA: Board of Equilization		52.50
	400.5		Storage Rack		750.00
	503		Cost of sales	315.00	
	105		Cost of sales		315.00
	104		Jim Green	802.50	
2/8/10	212	CM012	CA: Board of Equilization	8.75	
	400.5		Storage Rack	125.00	
	503		Cost of sales		52.50
	105		Cost of sales	52.50	
	104		Jim Green		133.75
2/15/10	212	1004	CA: Board of Equilization		157.50
	400.5		Ceramic Tile		2,250.00
	503		Cost of sales	1,000.00	
	105		Cost of sales		1,000.00
	104		Parker's Construction	2,407.50	
	Total			**4,711.25**	**4,711.25**

Step 5:
Click Close, then close the Select a Report or Form dialog box.

C h e c k   p o i n t

1. What does the *Cost of Goods Sold Journal* show?
2. What does the *Sales Journal* show?

Answers
1. The Cost of Goods Sold Journal shows the cost of all inventory items sold during a period.
2. The Sales Journal shows all sales on credit made during a period.

Practice Objective 6

Step 1:
Open Chp. 9 – Meadowland Healthcare Services.

Step 2:
Print the following reports for the month of February:

* *Sales Journal*
* *Cost of Goods Sold Journal*

Your printouts should look like figures 9–29 and 9–30, respectively.

FIGURE 9–29
Sales Journal for Meadowland Healthcare Services

Page: 1

Chp. 9 - Meadowland Healthcare Services
Sales Journal
For the Period From Feb 1, 2010 to Feb 28, 2010

Filter Criteria includes: Report order is by Invoice/CM Date. Report is printed in Detail Format.

Date	Account ID	Invoice/CM #	Line Description	Debit Amnt	Credit Amnt
2/4/10	21200	1106	CA: Board of Equalization		630.00
	40000.5		Roller Bandages		9,000.00
	50000		Cost of sales	3,600.00	
	10500		Cost of sales		3,600.00
	10400		Rapid Medical Response	9,630.00	
2/11/10	21200	1105	CA: Board of Equalization		16.80
	40000.5		Syringes		240.00
	50000		Cost of sales	100.00	
	10500		Cost of sales		100.00
	10400		Dr. George Johnson	256.80	
2/12/10	21200	CM201	CA: Board of Equalization	1.68	
	40400		Syringes	24.00	
	50000		Cost of sales		10.00
	10500		Cost of sales	10.00	
	10400		Dr. George Johnson		25.68
		Total		**13,622.48**	**13,622.48**

FIGURE 9–30
Cost of Goods Sold Journal for Meadowland Healthcare Services

Page: 1

Chp. 9 - Meadowland Healthcare Services
Cost of Goods Sold Journal
For the Period From Feb 1, 2010 to Feb 28, 2010

Filter Criteria includes: Report order is by Date. Report is printed in Detail Format and with shortened descriptions.

Date	GL Acct ID	Reference	Qty	Line Description	Debit Amount	Credit Amount
2/4/10	10500	1106	120.00	Roller Bandages		3,600.00
	50000		120.00	Roller Bandages	3,600.00	
2/11/10	10500	1105	20.00	Syringes		100.00
	50000		20.00	Syringes	100.00	
2/12/10	10500	CM201	-2.00	Syringes	10.00	
	50000		-2.00	Syringes		10.00
		Total			**3,710.00**	**3,710.00**

End of Chapter Review

Software Command Summary

Create Sales Tax Agency and Sales Tax	Maintain, Sales Taxes
Create Sales Invoice	Tasks, Sales/Invoicing
Print Sales Invoice	Tasks, Sales/Invoicing, Print
Create a Credit Memo	Tasks, Credit Memos
Collect on an Invoice	Tasks, Receipts, Apply to Invoices
Create a Quotation	Tasks, Quotes/Sales Orders, Quotes
Convert a Quotation to a Sales Order or Invoice	Tasks, Quotes/Sales Orders, Quotes, Convert
Create Finance Charge Defaults	Maintain, Default Information, Customers, Finance Charges
Create a Finance Charge Report	Tasks, Finance Charge
Create Inventory Reports	Reports & Forms, Inventory, Select a Report from the List
Create Sales Reports	Reports & Forms, Accounts Receivable, Select a Report from the List

Projects and Problems

Content Check

Multiple Choice: Choose only one response for each question.

1. The Sales Revenue account is what type of account?
   A. Cost of Sales
   B. Income
   C. Inventory
   D. Asset

2. A business that uses the perpetual inventory system sells goods for $450. The goods cost $200. When recording the sale, the business must
   A. debit Inventory and credit Cost of Goods Sold for $450.
   B. debit Cost of Goods Sold and credit Inventory for $450.
   C. debit Inventory and credit Cost of Goods Sold for $200.
   D. debit Cost of Goods Sold and credit Inventory for $200.

3. When a customer returns damaged goods, what form must be prepared for sales returns and allowances?
   A. Sales Invoice
   B. Sales Order
   C. Credit Memo
   D. Sales Quote

4. Which inventory report lists the quantity on hand and price for each inventory item?
   A. *Inventory Adjustments Journal*
   B. *Inventory Profitability Report*
   C. *Inventory Valuation Report*
   D. *Item Price List*

5. What type of account is Sales Tax Payable?
   A. Inventory
   B. Income
   C. Expense
   D. Liability

Short-Essay Response: Provide a detailed answer for each question.

1. Why would a business want to keep separate accounts for recording sales of services and sales of goods?
2. What is the purpose of each of the following: the sales quotation, the invoice, and the statement of account?
3. Why would a business establish a separate account for recording sales returns and allowances rather than just debiting them to the Sales Revenue account?
4. Why do some businesses impose a finance charge when customers do not pay their invoices on time?
5. How is a finance charge entered in a firm's accounting records?
6. What effect does a sale on credit have on the following accounts: Accounts Receivable, Sales Revenue, Cost of Goods Sold, and Inventory? (Does each account increase or decrease?)

Case Problems

Problem 1A

Open Frederica's Designs, an interior decoration business, which is located on the student data disk.

1. Create the following general ledger accounts:

Account ID:	**212**
Description:	**Sales Tax Payable**
Account Type:	**Other Current Liabilities**

Account ID:	**404**
Description:	**Sales Returns and Allowances**
Account Type:	**Income**

Account ID:	**406**
Description:	**Sales Discount**
Account Type:	**Income**

2. Create a new vendor account for the Board of Equalization.

Vendor ID:	**BE-10**
Name:	**Board of Equalization**
Expense Account:	**212**
Tax ID Number:	**None**
Ship Via:	**US Mail**
Terms and Credit:	**Net due in 30 days, 0.00 Discount**
Form Options:	**Default**

3. Enter the following information about the sales tax authorities:

Total Tax Rate:	**7.00**
Sales Tax Agency ID:	**CA**
Sales Tax Agency Name:	**Board of Equalization**
Vendor:	**BE-10**
Taxes Calculated:	**by single rate**
Tax Rate:	**7.00**
Account to Track Sales Tax:	**212**
Sales Tax ID:	**CATAX**
Sales Tax Name:	**California Sales Tax**
Sales Tax on Freight:	**No**

4. Create the following new customer accounts:

Customer

Customer ID:	**RM-01**
Name:	**Richard Marquez**

General Tab

Account Number:	**1020**
Billing Address:	**1785 Thornton Road**
City, ST, Zip:	**Modesto, CA 95355**
Country:	**USA**
Sales Tax:	**CATAX**
Customer Type:	**Retail**
Telephone 1:	**209-555-3692**

Contact Tab

Contact:	**Richard Marquez**

Sales Info Tab

GL Sales Account:	**401**
Ship Via:	**Fed-Ex**
Pricing Level:	**Full Price**
Form Options:	**Default**

Payment & Credit Tab
    Terms and Credit: **3.5% 10 Days, Net 30 Days**

History Tab
    Beginning Balance: **0**

Customer
    Customer ID: **SM-02**
    Name: **Sandra McGuire**

General Tab
    Account Number: **1030**
    Billing Address: **1495 Lower Stockton Road**
    City, ST, Zip: **Modesto, CA 95355**
    Country: **USA**
    Sales Tax: **CATAX**
    Customer Type: **Retail**
    Telephone 1:   **209-555-8462**

Contact Tab
    Contact: **Sandra McGuire**

Sales Info Tab
    GL Sales Account: **401**
    Ship Via: **Fed-Ex**
    Pricing Level: **Full Price**
    Form Options: **Default**

Payment & Credit Tab
    Terms and Credit: **3% 10 Days, Net 30 Days**

History Tab
    Beginning Balance: **0**

Customer
    Customer ID: **LA-03**
    Name: **Luis Abelar**

General Tab
    Account Number: **1040**
    Billing Address: **2465 Eaton Avenue**
    City, ST, Zip: **Stockton, CA 95210**
    Country: **USA**
    Sales Tax: **CATAX**
    Customer Type: **Retail**
    Telephone 1:   **209-555-5217**

Contact Tab
    Contact: **Luis Abelar**

Sales Info Tab
    GL Sales Account: **401**
    Ship Via: **Fed-Ex**

Pricing Level:	**Full Price**
Form Options:	**Default**

Payment & Credit Tab

Terms and Credit:	**3% 10 Days, Net 30 Days**

History Tab

Beginning Balance:	**0**

5. Record the following transactions for the month of January 2010:

> HINT
>
> Click the Journal button to review the Accounting Behind the Screens window. Make sure Sales Returns and Allowances, account 404, is debited for the return amount.

Jan. 11	Sold 8 flower stencils and 4 pillows on credit to Richard Marquez, Invoice 649.
12	Sold 3 pillows on credit to Sandra McGuire, Invoice 650.
14	Sandra McGuire returned 1 of the pillows. Issued Credit Memo 011 (CM011) to her. (Use the Apply to Sales tab of the Credit Memos screen.)
15	Sold 4 flower stencils and 6 pillows on credit to Luis Abelar, Invoice 651.
18	Richard Marquez paid Invoice 649, less discount, Check No. 1473.
20	Luis Abelar paid Invoice 651, less discount, Check No. 2003.
21	Sandra McGuire paid Invoice 650, less discount, Check No. 1146.

> HINT
>
> Click the Journal button to review the Accounting Behind the Screens window. Make sure Sales Discount, account 406, is debited for the discount amount.

6. Print the *Customer Ledgers* and *Cost of Goods Sold Journal*.

Problem 2A

Executive Consultants, a business consulting company, prepared the following quotations for two prospective clients during the month of June 2010. The prices were negotiated by the firm's sales representatives: Annette Johnson and Thomas Watson.

1. Open Executive Consultants from the student data disk.

2. Create the following general ledger account:

Account ID:	**212**
Description:	**Sales Tax Payable**
Account Type:	**Other Current Liabilities**

3. Create a new vendor account for the Board of Equalization.

Vendor ID:	**BE-30**
Name:	**Board of Equalization**
Expense Account:	**212**
Tax ID Number:	**None**
Ship Via:	**US Mail**
Terms and Credit:	**Net due in 30 days, 0.00 Discount**
Form Options:	**Default**

4. Enter the following information about the sales tax authorities:

Total Tax Rate:	**7.00**
Sales Tax Agency ID:	**CA**
Sales Tax Agency Name:	**Board of Equalization**
Vendor:	**BE-30**
Taxes Calculated:	**by single rate**
Tax Rate:	**7.00**
Account to Track Sales Tax:	**212**
Sales Tax ID:	**CATAX**
Sales Tax Name:	**California Sales Tax**
Sales Tax on Freight:	**No**

5. Create the new following customer accounts:

Customer

Customer ID:	**KD-01**
Name:	**Kathleen's Designs**

General Tab

Account Number:	**10**
Billing Address:	**1748 West Fair Oaks**
City, ST, Zip:	**Modesto, CA 95355**
Country:	**USA**
Sales Tax:	**CATAX**
Customer Type:	**Retail**
Telephone 1:	**209-555-6925**

Contact Tab

Contact:	**Kathleen Rosario**

Sales Info Tab

GL Sales Account:	**401**
Ship Via:	**Fed-Ex**
Pricing Level:	**Full Price**
Form Options:	**Default**

Payment & Credit Tab

Terms and Credit:	**3% 10 Days, Net 30 Days**

History Tab

Beginning Balance:	**0**

Customer

Customer ID:	**HD-02**
Name:	**Hendricks' Construction**

General Tab

Account Number:	**20**
Billing Address:	**2469 Rose Marie Lane**
City, ST, Zip:	**Stockton, CA 95207**
Country:	**USA**
Sales Tax:	**CATAX**

Customer Type:	**Retail**
Telephone 1:	**209-555-6523**

Contact Tab

Contact:	**Randy Hendricks**

Sales Info Tab

GL Sales Account:	**402**
Ship Via:	**Fed-Ex**
Pricing Level:	**Full Price**
Form Options:	**Default**

Payment & Credit Tab

Terms and Credit:	**3% 10 Days, Net 30 Days**

History Tab

Beginning Balance:	**0**

> **HINT**
>
> As these are non-inventory items, enter the number of hours in the *Quantity* field and the hourly rate in the *Unit Price* field.

6. Create the following quotations as of the dates specified:

June 1	Annette Johnson gave Quotation 103 for 7 hours of training at $90 per hour to Kathleen's Designs. The quotation was good until June 10, 2010.
5	Thomas Watson gave Quotation 104 for 5 hours of consulting service at $75 per hour to Hendricks' Construction. The quotation was good until June 18, 2010.

7. Convert both quotations to invoices as of the dates specified:

June 9	Kathleen's Designs has accepted the quotation. Issued Invoice 302.
18	Hendricks' Construction has accepted 4 of the 5 hours for which the quotation was prepared. Issued Invoice 314.

8. Print the *Sales Journal* and *Customer Ledgers*.

Problem 1B

Open Monica's, a beauty salon, which is located on the student data disk.

1. Create the following general ledger accounts:

Account ID:	**212**
Description:	**Sales Tax Payable**
Account Type:	**Other Current Liabilities**

Account ID:	**404**
Description:	**Sales Returns and Allowances**
Account Type:	**Income**

Account ID:	**406**
Description:	**Sales Discount**
Account Type:	**Income**

2. Create a new vendor account for the Board of Equalization.

Vendor ID:	**BE-20**
Name:	**Board of Equalization**
Expense Account:	**212**
Tax ID Number:	**None**
Ship Via:	**US Mail**
Terms and Credit:	**Net due in 30 days, 0.00 Discount**
Form Options:	**Default**

3. Enter the following information about the sales tax authorities:

Total Tax Rate:	**7.00**
Sales Tax Agency ID:	**CA**
Sales Tax Agency Name:	**Board of Equalization**
Vendor:	**BE-20**
Taxes Calculated:	**by single rate**
Tax Rate:	**7.00**
Account to Track Sales Tax:	**212**
Sales Tax ID:	**CATAX**
Sales Tax Name:	**California Sales Tax**
Sales Tax on Freight:	**No**

4. Create the following new customer accounts:

Customer

Customer ID:	**NJ-01**
Name:	**Natalie Jones**

General Tab

Account Number:	**100**
Billing Address:	**1654 Lower Sacramento Road**
City, ST, Zip:	**Stockton, CA 95207**
Country:	**USA**
Sales Tax:	**CATAX**
Customer Type:	**Retail**
Telephone 1:	**209-555-6493**

Contact Tab

Contact:	**Natalie Jones**

Sales Info Tab

GL Sales Account:	**401**
Ship Via:	**Fed-Ex**
Pricing Level:	**Full Price**
Form Options:	**Default**

Payment & Credit Tab

Terms and Credit:	**2% 10 Days, Net 30 Days**

History Tab

Beginning Balance:	**0**

Customer
   Customer ID: **RG-02**
   Name: **Raquel Gannon**

General Tab
   Account Number: **200**
   Billing Address: **2610 Country Club**
   City, ST, Zip: **Modesto, CA 95355**
   Country: **USA**
   Sales Tax: **CATAX**
   Customer Type: **Retail**
   Telephone 1:   **209-555-5915**

Contact Tab
   Contact: **Raquel Gannon**

Sales Info Tab
   GL Sales Account: **401**
   Ship Via: **Fed-Ex**
   Pricing Level: **Full Price**
   Form Options: **Default**

Payment & Credit Tab
   Terms and Credit: **2% 10 Days, Net 30 Days**

History Tab
   Beginning Balance: **0**

Customer
   Customer ID: **RC-03**
   Name: **Richard Chang**

General Tab
   Account Number: **300**
   Billing Address: **1518 West Schulte Road**
   City, ST, Zip: **Modesto, CA 95355**
   Country: **USA**
   Sales Tax: **CATAX**
   Customer Type: **Retail**
   Telephone 1:   **209-555-5639**

Contact Tab
   Contact: **Richard Chang**

Sales Info Tab
   GL Sales Account: **401**
   Ship Via: **Fed-Ex**
   Pricing Level: **Full Price**
   Form Options: **Default**

Payment & Credit Tab
   Terms and Credit: **2% 10 Days, Net 30 Days**

History Tab
Beginning Balance: **0**

5. Record the following transactions for the month of June 2010:

<table>
<tr><td>June 13</td><td>Sold 2 bottles of shampoo and 1 bottle of conditioner on credit to Natalie Jones, Invoice 964.</td></tr>
<tr><td>15 √</td><td>Sold 2 bottles of shampoo and 2 bottles of hair gel on credit to Raquel Gannon, Invoice 965.</td></tr>
<tr><td>17 √</td><td>Natalie Jones paid Invoice 964, less discount, Check No. 7906.</td></tr>
<tr><td>18 √</td><td>Raquel Gannon returned 1 bottle of hair gel. Issued Credit Memo 014 (CM014) to her. (Use the Apply to Sales tab of the Credit Memos screen.)</td></tr>
<tr><td>21 √</td><td>Sold 2 bottles of shampoo and 1 bottle of hair gel on credit to Richard Chang, Invoice 966.</td></tr>
<tr><td>24</td><td>Raquel Gannon paid Invoice 965, less discount, Check No. 1321.</td></tr>
<tr><td>30</td><td>Richard Chang paid Invoice 966, less discount, Check No. 4320.</td></tr>
</table>

6. Print the *Customer Ledgers* and *Cost of Goods Sold Journal*.

Problem 2B

VP Computer Systems, a computer programming services company, prepared the following quotations for two of its prospective clients during the month of April 2010. The prices were negotiated by the firm's sales representatives: Stacy Anderson and William London.

1. Open VP Computer Systems from the student data disk.

2. Create the following general ledger account:

Account ID:	**212**
Description:	**Sales Tax Payable**
Account Type:	**Other Current Liabilities**

3. Create a new vendor account for the Board of Equalization.

Vendor ID:	**BE-40**
Name:	**Board of Equalization**
Expense Account:	**212**
Tax ID Number:	**None**
Ship Via:	**US Mail**
Terms and Credit:	**Net due in 30 days, 0.00 Discount**
Form Options:	**Default**

HINT

Click the Journal button to review the Accounting Behind the Screens window. Make sure Sales Discount, account 406, is debited for the discount amount.

HINT

Click the Journal button to review the Accounting Behind the Screens window. Make sure Sales Returns and Allowances, account 404, is debited for the return amount.

4. Enter the following information about the sales tax authorities:

Total Tax Rate:	**7.00**
Sales Tax Agency ID:	**CA**
Sales Tax Agency Name:	**Board of Equalization**
Vendor:	**BE-40**
Taxes Calculated:	**by single rate**
Tax Rate:	**7.00**
Account to Track Sales Tax:	**212**
Sales Tax ID:	**CATAX**
Sales Tax Name:	**California Sales Tax**
Sales Tax on Freight:	**No**

5. Create the new following customer accounts:

Customer

Customer ID:	**KD-01**
Name:	**Kathleen's Designs**

General Tab

Account Number:	**100**
Billing Address:	**1748 West Fair Oaks**
City, ST, Zip:	**Modesto, CA 95355**
Country:	**USA**
Sales Tax:	**CATAX**
Customer Type:	**Retail**
Telephone 1:	**209-555-6925**

Contact Tab

Contact:	**Kathleen Rosario**

Sales Info Tab

GL Sales Account:	**401**
Ship Via:	**Fed-Ex**
Pricing Level:	**Full Price**
Form Options:	**Default**

Payment & Credit Tab

Terms and Credit:	**3% 10 Days, Net 30 Days**

History Tab

Beginning Balance:	**0**

Customer

Customer ID:	**GJ-02**
Name:	**GJ Marketing Group**

General Tab

Account Number:	**200**
Billing Address:	**1510 East March Lane**
City, ST, Zip:	**Stockton, CA 95207**
Country:	**USA**
Sales Tax:	**CATAX**

Customer Type:	**Retail**
Telephone 1:	**209-555-7685**

Contact Tab
    Contact: **Cynthia Flores**

Sales Info Tab
GL Sales Account:	**402**
Ship Via:	**Fed-Ex**
Pricing Level:	**Full Price**
Form Options:	**Default**

Payment & Credit Tab
Terms and Credit:	**3% 10 Days, Net 30 Days**

History Tab
Beginning Balance:	**0**

HINT

As these are non-inventory items, enter the number of hours in the *Quantity* field and the hourly rate in the *Unit Price* field.

6. Create the quotations as of the dates specified.

   April 10   Stacy Anderson gave Quotation 150 for 12 hours of design services at $65 per hour to Kathleen's Designs. The quotation was good until April 20, 2010.

   15   William London gave Quotation 151 for 6 hours of computer consulting service at $90 per hour to GJ Marketing Group. The quotation was good until April 25, 2010.

7. Convert both quotations to invoices as of the dates specified.

   April 18   Kathleen's Designs has accepted the quotation. Issued Invoice 164.

   25   GJ Marketing Group has accepted the quotation. Issued Invoice 175.

8. Print the *Sales Journal* and *Customer Ledgers*.

Cooperative Learning

1. Form groups of three or four students, and determine the factors to be taken into consideration when establishing credit terms for each customer.
2. As a group, discuss what factors a business should consider when deciding whether to impose a finance charge on customers who do not pay invoices on time.

Writing and Decision Making

Assume that the owner of the company for which you work, Marie Ramirez, is concerned about the increasing level of sales returns that she has noticed on the financial statements during the last six months. She has asked you for reasons why this may be occurring and for ideas about how the level of sales returns can be reduced. She would also like to know how the inventory reports could be used to investigate the problem. Prepare a memo with the information that has been requested.

CHAPTER 10

Payroll

Learning Objectives

1. Understand general payroll concepts

2. Create a payroll system using Peachtree's Payroll Setup Wizard

3. Maintain the payroll system

4. Prepare a payroll and print payroll checks

5. Print payroll reports

Software Features

- Establish a Payroll System

- Set Employee Defaults

- Prepare a Payroll

- Print Payroll Checks

- Print Payroll Reports

People are very aware of payroll because of the checks they receive from their employers. However, issuing payroll checks is just one part of the payroll work that a business must do. For even a small firm with just a few employees, managing a payroll can be difficult and time-consuming.

The payroll activities of a business fall into six basic areas:

- Calculating the earnings and deductions of employees and issuing payroll checks
- Keeping records of the time that employees work and their earnings and deductions
- Calculating the payroll taxes owed by the employer
- Depositing the taxes deducted from employee earnings and the payroll taxes owed by the employer
- Preparing payroll tax returns that must be sent to federal, state, and sometimes local tax agencies
- Making entries for payroll in the accounting records

Obviously, it is important that payroll calculations, records, and tax returns be prepared with great accuracy. It is also important to do all the necessary work on time. Employees expect to receive their payroll checks promptly, and government agencies require that tax deposits and tax returns be submitted according to strict schedules. Failure to meet these schedules can result in financial penalties.

Peachtree allows a business to handle its payroll work quickly and efficiently. Once the payroll system is set up, most operations are done automatically when the information for a payroll period is entered.

OBJECTIVE 1 — Understand General Payroll Concepts

Preparing a payroll can be a complex process because many laws and government regulations affect it. Federal, state, and local tax agencies publish annual guides for employers that specify the requirements for keeping payroll records, withholding taxes from employee earnings, calculating the employer's payroll taxes, depositing all taxes owed, and filing tax returns.

Payroll Periods

payroll period The time period for which earnings and deductions are calculated.

Every business must establish a payroll period. The **payroll period** is the time period for which earnings and deductions are calculated. This period may be weekly, biweekly (every other week), semimonthly (on the 15th and the last day of each month), or monthly. Some large businesses use different payroll periods for different types of employees. For example, they may pay their factory workers on a weekly basis but pay their office staff on a monthly basis.

Pay Plans

pay plan The method used to calculate an employee's earnings.

Employees are paid according to various pay plans. The **pay plan** is the method used to calculate an employee's earnings. The most common pay plans are the hourly rate plan, the salary plan, the commission plan, the salary-commission plan, and the piece-rate plan.

- With the *hourly rate* plan, an employee receives a fixed amount for each hour worked, such as $9 an hour.

- With the *salary* plan, an employee receives a fixed amount for the payroll period, such as $500 a week.
- With the *commission* plan, an employee involved with sales receives a percentage of his or her sales, such as 5% of sales.
- With the *salary-commission* plan, an employee receives a fixed amount for the payroll period plus a percentage of his or her sales, such as $400 a week plus 2% of sales.
- With the *piece-rate* plan, an employee receives a fixed amount for each item produced, such as $2 for each circuit board assembled. This plan is used in some factories.

Payroll Laws and Regulations

Many laws and regulations govern payroll work. The most important of these laws and regulations are briefly described below.

- The *Fair Labor Standards Act* is a federal law that covers many employers. This law requires that employers pay at least the federal minimum wage and pay overtime to most employees when they work more than 40 hours in a workweek. The overtime rate must be at least 1½ times the regular hourly rate. Managerial and supervisory employees may be exempt from the overtime pay requirement.
- Some states and cities have their own *minimum wage laws*, which may set a higher minimum wage than the federal government.
- The *Current Tax Payment Act* requires employers to withhold federal income tax from the earnings of their employees.
- The *Federal Insurance Contributions Act (FICA)* requires employers to withhold Social Security tax and Medicare tax from the earnings of their employees and pay a matching amount themselves.
- The *Federal Unemployment Tax Act (FUTA)* requires employers to pay a tax that is intended to provide jobless benefits to employees who are temporarily out of work.
- Each state has its own *State Unemployment Tax Act (SUTA)*. In most cases, these laws impose a tax on just the employer. However, a few states also require a contribution from employees.
- Many states and some cities and counties have their own *income tax laws* and require employers to withhold this tax from employee earnings.
- Some states have *disability insurance laws*. For example, California requires employers to withhold a state disability insurance (SDI) tax from employee earnings. This tax is used to pay benefits to employees who temporarily cannot work because of illness or injury.

Federal and State Tax Returns

The federal government requires employers to file a variety of tax returns. Some of the most important of these returns are as follows.

- *Form 941*, Employer's Quarterly Federal Tax Return, is prepared after the end of each quarter. It shows the wages paid during the quarter and the federal income tax and FICA taxes owed.
- *Form 940*, Employer's Annual Federal Unemployment Tax Return, is prepared after the end of each year. It shows the wages paid during the year and the FUTA tax liability for the year.

- *Form W-2*, Wage and Tax Statement, is prepared for each employee after the end of each year. This multiple-copy form shows the wages earned by the employee during the year and the federal and state taxes withheld. Copies of this form go to the employee and to federal and state tax agencies.
- *Form W-3*, Transmittal of Wage and Tax Statements, is prepared after the end of each year. This form shows the total wages paid to employees during the year and the federal and state taxes withheld from employee earnings.
- *Form 1099* is prepared for each independent contractor after the end of each year. This multiple-copy form shows the fees paid to the independent contractor during the year. Copies of Form 1099 go to the independent contractor and to federal and some state tax agencies. Remember that an independent contractor does work for a business on a project-by-project basis and is not an employee. As a result, the business does not withhold taxes from the fees paid to an independent contractor. This person is responsible for paying his or her taxes directly to federal and state tax agencies.
- *Form 8109*, Federal Tax Deposit Coupon, is prepared when a deposit of federal taxes is made by check in a bank or other depositary institution. This form shows the amount being deposited. If a business makes deposits by means of electronic funds transfer, Form 8109 is not used. The schedule for making federal tax deposits depends on the amounts owed. (**Note:** This form is not currently included in Peachtree.)

You can prepare and print all of the federal payroll reports and statements mentioned above (except Form 8109) by clicking Reports and then Payroll.

State tax agencies also require employers to file tax returns. These forms vary from state to state, as do the schedules for filing the forms and making tax deposits.

Required and Voluntary Deductions

As you have seen, federal, state, and sometimes local laws require that employers deduct certain taxes from employee earnings. For example, Wardwood Construction Company, which is located in California, must withhold the following taxes from the earnings of its employees: federal income, Social Security, Medicare, state income and State Disability Insurance (SDI).

In addition to these required deductions, some businesses allow voluntary deductions for items such as medical insurance, life insurance, and a retirement savings plan [a 401(k) plan].

Accounting Entries for Payroll

Businesses use a number of liability and expense accounts to record payroll transactions. Taxes withheld from employee earnings and taxes owed by the employer are debts of a business until they are deposited. Therefore, they are recorded in current liability accounts.

- When the payroll is calculated, the total of the employee earnings is debited to Wages and Salaries Expense and the amounts withheld for the various taxes are credited to individual liability accounts such as Federal Income Tax Payable, FICA—Social Security Tax Payable,

FICA—Medicare Tax Payable, State Income Tax Payable, and SDI Tax Payable.
- When the employer's payroll taxes are calculated, the total of the taxes is debited to Payroll Taxes Expense and the amounts of the various taxes owed are credited to individual liability accounts such as FICA—Social Security Tax Payable, FICA—Medicare Tax Payable, FUTA Tax Payable, and SUTA Tax Payable.
- When a business pays the taxes it owes, it debits the appropriate liability accounts and credits Cash.

Features of the Peachtree Payroll System

The Peachtree payroll system allows a business to set up and maintain an earnings record for each employee, calculate earnings and deductions, calculate the employer's payroll taxes, prepare payroll tax returns for government agencies, prepare payroll reports for management, and make the necessary accounting entries for payroll.

Peachtree Complete Accounting 2010 has a special feature called the Payroll Setup Wizard, which will help you to establish the payroll system. Version 2010 also has enhanced Internet access to federal and state tax publications and tax forms. This feature helps employers to stay informed about changes in tax rates, schedules for making deposits, and schedules for filing tax returns.

Check point

1. What are the different types of payroll periods?
2. What three federal taxes must employers withhold from employee earnings?

Answers
1. *Payroll periods may be weekly, biweekly, semimonthly, or monthly.*
2. *The three federal taxes that employers must withhold are federal income tax, Social Security tax, and Medicare tax.*

OBJECTIVE 2 — Create a Payroll System Using Peachtree's Payroll Setup Wizard

The Payroll Setup Wizard in Peachtree Complete Accounting 2010 provides you with step-by-step guidance for establishing your payroll system. At the start of this process, you must select the appropriate payroll tax percentages and create several new general ledger accounts.

Assume that the Wardwood Construction Company decides to establish a payroll system using Peachtree as of February 1, 2010. Follow the steps outlined below to create the new payroll system.

Step 1:
Open Chp. 10 – Wardwood Construction Company and close the Action Items log.

Step 2:

Click Options from the main Menu bar and then *Default Information* and *Payroll Setup Wizard* from the drop-down lists.

Step 3:

Click Next at the *Payroll Setup Wizard* window as shown in figure 10–1.

FIGURE 10–1

Peachtree Payroll Setup Wizard Window

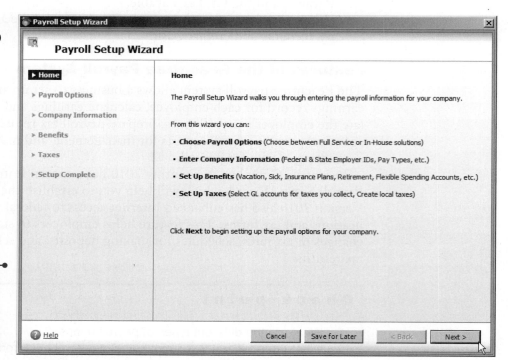

HINT

You can also access the Payroll Setup Wizard by clicking Maintain, *Default Information*, and *Payroll Setup Wizard*.

Step 4:

Click *Do It Yourself In-House* from the Payroll Setup Wizard. Select *Do It Yourself* from the Payroll Setup Wizard screen, as shown in figure 10–2. Click Next to continue and click Next again at the Payroll Setup Wizard *Other Payroll Options* window.

FIGURE 10–2
Payroll Setup Wizard
Screen

Step 5:
Click *CA* from the drop-down list in the *State...* field. (*CA* stands for California, the state where Wardwood is located.) Key **5.00** in the *State Unemployment Rate* field. Your completed work should match figure 10–3.

FIGURE 10–3
Payroll Setup Wizard
Dialog Box – Company
Information

HINT

The tax tables change periodically and must be updated. Contact the Peachtree Web site, www.peachtree.com, for updated information.

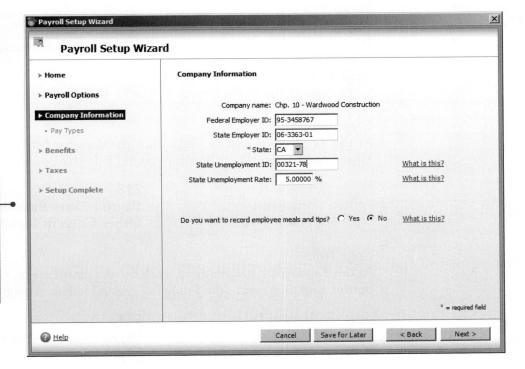

Step 6:
The Payroll Setup Wizard – Pay Types section is on the right side of the screen. At the *Hourly – Regular* field, click the *magnifying glass* icon, and then click *512 - Wages and Salaries Expense*. Repeat this process for the *Hourly – Overtime* and *Salary – Salary 1* sections.

Step 7:
Compare your completed work with figure 10–4 and click Next.

FIGURE 10–4
Completed Payroll
Wizard – Pay Types
Dialog Box

Step 8:
Click Next at the Payroll Setup Wizard – Benefits screen.

Step 9:
At the *Tax liability acct. no.* field, click the *downward arrow*, click the New button, and create the following general ledger account.

Account ID:	**218**
Description:	**Payroll Taxes Payable**
Account Type:	**Other Current Liabilities**

Step 10:
At the *Tax expense acct. no.* field, click the *downward arrow*, click the New button, and then create the following general ledger account.

Account ID:	**513**
Description:	**Payroll Taxes Expense**
Account Type:	**Expenses**

Compare your screen with figure 10–5 and make any necessary corrections. Then click Next to continue.

FIGURE 10–5
Payroll Setup Wizard –
Payroll Taxes Dialog Box

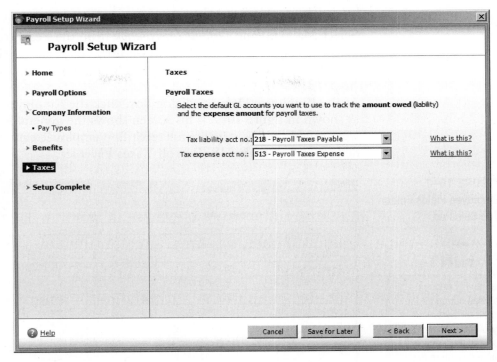

Step 11:
Click Next. At the Payroll Setup Complete screen, click Finish, as shown in figure 10–6.

FIGURE 10–6
Payroll Setup Wizard –
Setup Complete Dialog Box

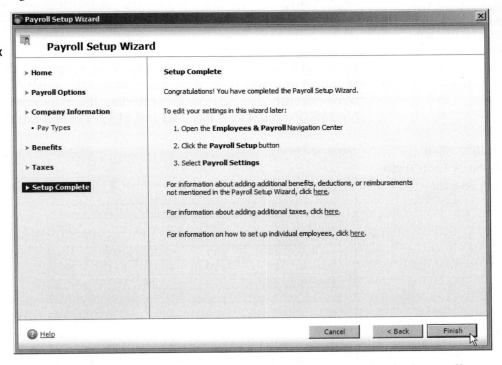

It is necessary to set up the employee and employer individual payroll accounts before Peachtree can be used to complete a payroll. This requires using the general ledger accounts for gross pay and deductions, including required federal and state tax deductions for each individual employee. The same is true for creating the employer general ledger accounts.

Step 12:

Select Maintain and *Default Information* from the Peachtree main Menu bar. Select *Employees* from the drop-down list.

Step 13:

At the Employee Defaults dialog box, click the Employee Fields folder tab, as shown in figure 10–7. This screen shows the general ledger accounts that were established as defaults for recording employee earnings (gross pay) and deductions, notably 218 (Payroll Taxes Payable).

FIGURE 10–7
Employee Fields Folder Tab Selected

HINT

The liability account that was set up as the default for recording payroll taxes owed (Account 218) may be changed to more accurately track the different liabilities. An individual liability account for each type of tax can be established. This process will be demonstrated later in the chapter.

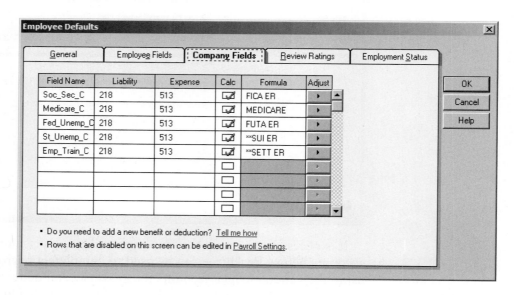

Step 14:

Click the Company Fields folder tab in the Employee Defaults dialog box, as shown in figure 10–8. This screen shows the general ledger accounts that were established as defaults for recording the employer's payroll taxes, notably 218 (Payroll Taxes Payable) and 513 (Payroll Taxes Expense).

FIGURE 10–8
Company Fields Folder Tab Selected

Step 15:
Click OK to accept the Employee Defaults.

This concludes the payroll setup process. Note that changes can be made to the payroll defaults at any time by clicking Maintain on the main Menu bar, clicking *Default Information*, and then clicking *Employees*.

C h e c k   p o i n t

1. Where can Peachtree users find updated tax tables?
2. What account will be used to record gross pay?

Answers
1. *Updated tax tables are available from Peachtree's Web site at www. peachtree.com.*
2. *Wages and Salaries Expense will be used to record gross pay.*

P r a c t i c e   O b j e c t i v e   2

Step 1:
Open Chp. 10 – Bluefrog Maintenance Company.

Step 2:
Use the Payroll Setup Wizard to establish the payroll system for Bluefrog.

Step 3:
Use the following information to set up the payroll system.

State:	**CA**
Unemployment Rate:	**5.00**
Gross Pay Acct:	**512**

Step 4:
Create the following general ledger accounts for recording payroll taxes.

Account ID:	**218**
Description:	**Payroll Taxes Payable**
Account Type:	**Other Current Liabilities**

Account ID:	**513**
Description:	**Payroll Taxes Expense**
Account Type:	**Expenses**

Step 5:
Accept all remaining defaults, and then click Finish.

OBJECTIVE 3 — Maintain the Payroll System

Maintaining the payroll system usually involves updating accounts and updating employee information. Let us look first at the procedures for changing accounts that have been established as defaults.

Creating Additional Default Accounts

Suppose that Wardwood Construction Company is not happy with the default accounts that it established with the Payroll Setup Wizard. Instead of having a single liability account called Payroll Taxes Payable, Wardwood wants to create separate liability accounts to keep track of the different types of employee withholding taxes and employer payroll taxes.

Step 1:
Open Chp. 10 – Wardwood Construction Company, which you updated previously in the chapter, and close the Action Items log.

Step 2:
Click Maintain, click *Default Information*, and then click *Employees*.

Step 3:
At the Employee Defaults window, click the Employee Fields folder tab, as shown in figure 10–9.

FIGURE 10–9
Employee Defaults Window with Employee Fields Folder Tab Selected

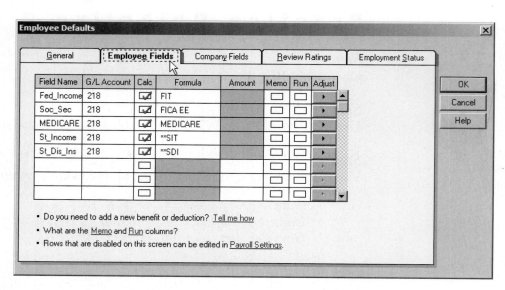

Step 4:
Up to this point, Payroll Taxes Payable (Account 218) was Wardwood's default account for all the employee withholding taxes. Click in the *Fed_Income* row of the *G/L Account* column and then click the *magnifying glass* icon to create new accounts as the defaults in the following fields. Note that all of these accounts are considered "Other Current Liabilities."

a. In the *Fed_Income* field, change Account 218 to:

Account ID:	**220**
Description:	**Federal Income Taxes Payable**
Account Type:	**Other Current Liabilities**

b. In the *Soc_Sec* field, change Account 218 to:

Account ID:	**222**
Description:	**Social Security Taxes Payable**
Account Type:	**Other Current Liabilities**

c. In the *MEDICARE* field change Account 218 to:

Account ID:	**224**
Description:	**Medicare Taxes Payable**
Account Type:	**Other Current Liabilities**

d. In the *St_Income* field, change Account 218 to:

Account ID:	**226**
Description:	**State Income Taxes Payable**
Account Type:	**Other Current Liabilities**

e. In the *St_Dis_Ins* field, change Account 218 to:

Account ID:	**228**
Description:	**SDI Taxes Payable**
Account Type:	**Other Current Liabilities**

Step 5:
Review the new defaults in the Employee Fields folder tab, as shown in figure 10–10. Make any necessary changes.

FIGURE 10–10
New Accounts for
Employee Defaults

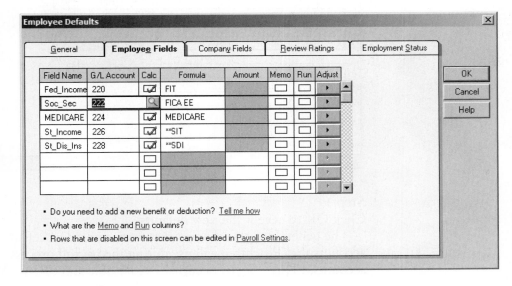

Step 6:
Click the Company Fields folder tab.

Step 7:
Change the defaults for the liability accounts to be used in recording the employer's payroll taxes. Create new accounts as follows.

a. In the *Soc_Sec_C* field, change Account 218 to 222.

b. In the *Medicare_C* field, change Account 218 to 224.

c. In the *Fed_Unemp_C* field, change Account 218 to:

Account ID:	**230**
Description:	**FUTA Taxes Payable**
Account Type:	**Other Current Liabilities**

d. In the *St_Unemp_C* field, change Account 218 to:

Account ID:	**232**
Description:	**SUTA Taxes Payable**
Account Type:	**Other Current Liabilities**

Important Note: The educational version of Peachtree may include the Field Name *Emp_Train_C*. Remove the check mark in the *Calc* field aligned with Emp_Train_C.

Step 8:
Compare your entries with figure 10–11, and make any necessary changes.

FIGURE 10–11
New Accounts for
Company Defaults

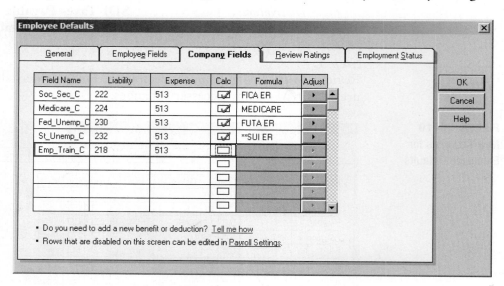

Step 9:
Click OK to accept the new defaults.

The general ledger accounts that were entered as defaults are now the accounts that Peachtree will use during the payroll process. Two of these accounts, FICA—Social Security Tax Payable and FICA—Medicare Tax Payable, are used to record both employee taxes and employer payroll taxes. That is why they were listed in the employee and employer fields. (Remember that the Federal Insurance Contributions Act requires employers to match the Social Security tax and Medicare tax paid by their employees.)

Creating the Employee Records

In the Peachtree payroll system, an individual record must be set up for each employee. This record includes general information, withholding information, and pay information for the employee. The withholding information is needed to calculate the federal, state, and local income tax owed by the employee. The pay information specifies the payroll period (frequency), the pay plan (pay method) used for the employee, and the employee's pay rate.

Follow the steps outlined below to establish employee records for the four employees of Wardwood Construction Company. This firm has a weekly payroll period and uses the hourly rate plan and the salary plan. The hourly employees have a 40-hour workweek.

Step 1:
Click Maintain, and then click *Employees/Sales Reps*.

Step 2:
The Maintain Employees & Sales Reps window will appear, as shown in figure 10–12.

FIGURE 10–12
Maintain Employees & Sales Reps Window

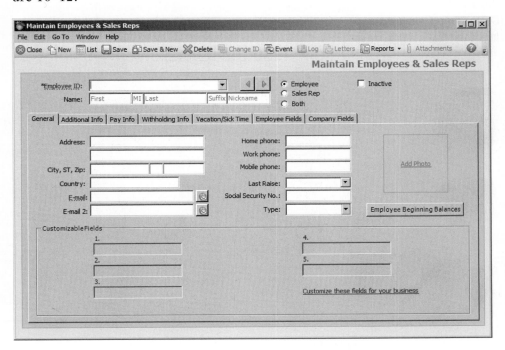

Enter the information for the first employee—George Clark.

Employee ID:	**GCL-03**
Name:	**George Clark**

General Tab

Address:	**126 New Castle Road**
City, ST, Zip:	**Modesto, CA 95355**
Country:	**USA**
Telephone 1:	**209–555-0332**
Last Raise:	**Jan 31, 2009**
Social Security Number:	**559-30-6523**
Type:	**Salaried**

Step 3:
Click the Withholding Info tab and enter the following information:

Withholding Info Tab

Federal Filing Status:	**Single**	*Allow:* **2**	*Additional Withholding:* **0.00**
State Filing Status:	**Single**	*Allow:* **2**	*Additional Withholding:* **0.00**
State:	**CA**		
Local Filing Status:	**Single**		

Step 4:
Compare your completed Maintain Employees & Sales Reps window Withholding Info folder tab to the one shown in figure 10–13, and make any necessary corrections.

FIGURE 10–13
Completed Withholding Info Tab

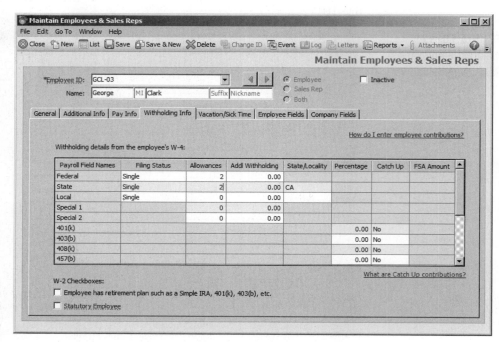

Step 5:
Click the Pay Info folder tab. Then enter the following information:

Pay Info Tab

Pay Method:	**Salary**
Frequency:	**Weekly**
Rate Used to Bill Customer:	**25.00**
Salary Pay Rate:	**1,000.00**

Step 6:
Compare your Pay Info folder tab to the one shown in figure 10–14 and make any necessary corrections. Then click Save to save the new employee information for George Clark.

FIGURE 10–14
Completed Pay
Information

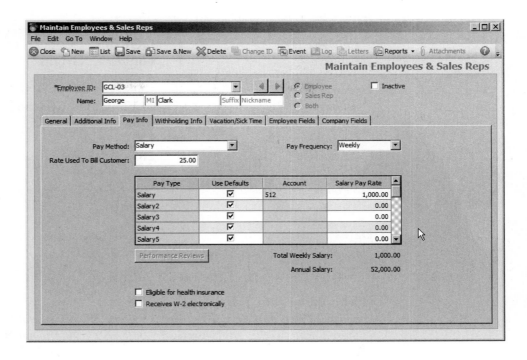

Step 7:

Enter the information for the remaining three employees of Wardwood Construction Company.

Employee

Employee ID:	**SJO-04**
Name:	**Samuel P. Jones**

General Tab

Address:	**413 Mill River Drive**
City, ST, Zip:	**Modesto, CA 95351**
Country:	**USA**
Telephone 1:	**209-555-3032**
Last Raise:	
Social Security Number:	**562-90-9866**
Type:	**Hourly**

Withholding Info Tab

Federal Filing Status:	**Married**	*Allow:* **2**	*Additional Withholding:* **0.00**
State Filing Status:	**Married**	*Allow:* **2**	*Additional Withholding:* **0.00**
State:	**CA**		
Local Filing Status:	**Married**		

Pay Info Tab

Pay Method:	**Hourly—Hours per Pay Period**
Frequency:	**Weekly**
Hours Per Pay Period:	**40.00**
Rate Used to Bill Customer:	**24.00**
Regular:	**15.00**
Overtime:	**22.50**

Employee
Employee ID: **GGR-05**
Name: **Ginger Z. Griggs**

General Tab
Address:	**11121 Ceres Avenue**
City, ST, Zip:	**Modesto, CA 95351**
Country:	**USA**
Telephone 1:	**209-555-2334**
Last Raise:	**Jan 30, 2009**
Social Security Number:	**544-87-9099**
Type:	**Hourly**

Dates
Hired:	**Oct 20, 2005**
Terminated:	

Withholding Info Tab
Federal Filing Status:	**Married**	*Allow:* **2**	*Additional Withholding:* **0.00**
State Filing Status:	**Married**	*Allow:* **2**	*Additional Withholding:* **0.00**
State:	**CA**		
Local Filing Status:	**Married**		

Pay Info Tab
Pay Method:	**Hourly—Hours per Pay Period**
Frequency:	**Weekly**
Hours Per Pay Period:	**40.00**
Rate Used to Bill Customer:	**24.50**
Regular:	**14.50**
Overtime:	**21.75**

Employee
Employee ID: **SBR-06**
Name: **Steven Brown**

General Tab
Address:	**554 Boston Way**
City, ST, Zip:	**Modesto, CA 95351**
Country:	**USA**
Telephone 1:	**209-555-2344**
Last Raise:	**Jan 30, 2009**
Social Security Number:	**545-09-0009**
Type:	**Salaried**

Withholding Info Tab
Federal Filing Status:	**Single**	*Allow:* **2**	*Additional Withholding:* **0.00**
State Filing Status:	**Single**	*Allow:* **2**	*Additional Withholding:* **0.00**
State:	**CA**		
Local Filing Status:	**Single**		

Pay Info Tab

Pay Method:	**Salary**
Frequency:	**Weekly**
Rate Used to Bill Customer:	**60.00**
Salary:	**1,200.00**

Step 8:
Click Save. Then close the Maintain Employees & Sales Reps window.

Practice Objective 3

Check point

1. What three types of information are entered when establishing an employee record?
2. Why does a firm need withholding information for each employee?

Answers
1. *The three types of information used to establish employee records are general information, withholding information, and pay information.*
2. *Withholding information is needed to calculate the income tax owed by each employee.*

Step 1:
Open Chp. 10 – Bluefrog Maintenance Company, which you updated previously in the chapter.

Step 2:
Make the following changes in the employee and employer defaults. Create new accounts as necessary.

Employee Fields
In the *Fed_Income* field, change Account 218 to:

Account ID:	**220**
Description:	**Federal Income Taxes Payable**
Account Type:	**Other Current Liabilities**

In the *Soc_Sec* field, change Account 218 to:

Account ID:	**222**
Description:	**Social Security Taxes Payable**
Account Type:	**Other Current Liabilities**

In the *MEDICARE* field, change Account 218 to:

Account ID:	**224**
Description:	**Medicare Taxes Payable**
Account Type:	**Other Current Liabilities**

In the *St_Income* field, change Account 218 to:

Account ID:	**226**
Description:	**State Income Taxes Payable**
Account Type:	**Other Current Liabilities**

In the *St_Dis_Ins* field, change Account 218 to:

Account ID:	**228**
Description:	**SDI Taxes Payable**
Account Type:	**Other Current Liabilities**

Company Fields

In the *Soc_Sec_C* field, change Account 218 to Account 222.
In the *Medicare_C* field, change Account 218 to Account 224.
In the *Fed_Unemp_C* field, change Account 218 to:

Account ID:	**230**
Description:	**FUTA Taxes Payable**
Account Type:	**Other Current Liabilities**

In the *St_Unemp_C* field, change Account 218 to:

Account ID:	**232**
Description:	**SUTA Taxes Payable**
Account Type:	**Other Current Liabilities**

Important Note: The educational version of Peachtree may include the Field Name *Emp_Train_C*. Remove the check mark in the *Calc* field aligned with Emp_Train_C.

Step 3:

Set up employee records for the following three employees:

Employee

Employee ID:	**HCA-03**
Name:	**Henry Carver**

General Tab

Address:	**2799 Rodeo Drive**
City, ST, Zip:	**Stockton, CA 95501**
Country:	**USA**
Telephone 1:	**209-555-0098**
Last Raise:	
Social Security Number:	**344-58-9088**
Type:	**Hourly**

Withholding Info Tab

Federal Filing Status:	**Single**	*Allow:* **1**	*Additional Withholding:* **0.00**
State Filing Status:	**Single**	*Allow:* **1**	*Additional Withholding:* **0.00**
State:	**CA**		
Local Filing Status:	**Single**		

Pay Info Tab

Pay Method:	**Hourly—Hours per Pay Period**
Frequency:	**Weekly**
Hours Per Pay Period:	**40.00**
Rate Used to Bill Customer:	**20.00**
Regular:	**12.00**
Overtime:	**18.00**

Employee

Employee ID:	**JST-04**
Name:	**James Stewart**

General Tab

Address:	**1221 Grant Avenue**
City, ST, Zip:	**Lodi, CA 95331**
Country:	**USA**
Telephone 1:	**209-555-9867**
Last Raise:	**Jan 30, 2009**
Social Security Number:	**599-09-3343**
Type:	**Hourly**

Withholding Info Tab

Federal Filing Status: **Married** *Allow:* **2** *Additional Withholding:* **0.00**
State Filing Status: **Married** *Allow:* **2** *Additional Withholding:* **0.00**
State: **CA**
Local Filing Status: **Married**

Pay Info Tab

Pay Method:	**Hourly—Hours per Pay Period**
Frequency:	**Weekly**
Hours Per Pay Period:	**40.00**
Rate Used to Bill Customer:	**22.00**
Regular:	**11.50**
Overtime:	**16.75**

Employee

Employee ID:	**SSM-05**
Name:	**Stanley Smith**

General Tab

Address:	**5233 Ireland Way**
City, ST, Zip:	**Galt, CA 95001**
Country:	**USA**
Telephone 1:	**209-555-3422**
Last Raise:	**Jan 30, 2009**
Social Security Number:	**523-88-7654**
Type:	**Salaried**

Withholding Information Tab

Federal Filing Status:	**Single**	*Allow:* **2**	*Additional Withholding:* **0.00**
State Filing Status:	**Single**	*Allow:* **2**	*Additional Withholding:* **0.00**
State:	**CA**		
Local Filing Status:	**Single**		

Pay Info Tab

Pay Method:	**Salary**
Frequency:	**Weekly**
Rate Used to Bill Customer:	**80.00**
Salary Rate:	**1,600.00**

Step 4:
Close the Maintain Employees & Sales Reps window.

OBJECTIVE 4 — Prepare a Payroll and Print Payroll Checks

Once you have set up the Peachtree payroll system and established a record for each employee, it is possible to prepare the payroll. Usually, this process requires entry of the hours worked by employees who are on the hourly rate plan and entry of the overtime earned by any employee.

After you have entered the necessary information about hours worked and overtime, Peachtree will calculate the earnings and deductions of each employee for the payroll period and print a payroll check. The total amount earned by the employee is his or her gross pay. The amount remaining after all deductions is the employee's **net pay**. This is the amount that will appear on the employee's payroll check.

net pay The amount received by employees after deductions are made from their gross pay.

Payroll Tax Tables

When Peachtree is initially installed, a generic tax table is also installed. In most cases, Peachtree will not be able to calculate automatically or accurately federal, state, and most local payroll taxes during the payroll process using this generic table. In order to calculate actual and accurate payroll tax amounts, you should subscribe to the Peachtree Payroll Tax Service and install the most current Tax Service update. Information pertaining to Peachtree Payroll Tax Service can be obtained at www.peachtree.com/taxservice.

For educational purposes a modified tax table has been created that will allow you to complete the payroll process. Remember that this tax table should be used for educational purposes only.

Preparing the Payroll with No Overtime

Suppose that there was no overtime for the employees of Wardwood Construction Company during the weekly payroll period ended February 28, 2010. Follow the steps outlined below to prepare this payroll.

Step 1:
Open Chp. 10 – Wardwood Construction Company and close the Action Items log.

Step 2:
Click the Employees & Payroll tab from the Navigation Aids at the side of the main window.

Step 3:
Click the *Pay Employees* icon and then "Enter Payroll for Multiple Employees," as shown in figure 10–15. Select OK from the Peachtree Payroll query window.

FIGURE 10–15
Enter Payroll for Multiple Employees from Pay Employees Icon

Step 4:
The Select Employees – Filter Selection dialog box will appear. At the *Pay End Date* field, click the *calendar* icon, and then choose the date *Feb 28, 2010.*

Step 5:
In the Include Pay Frequencies section, click *Weekly* only and deselect the other frequency options.

Step 6:
In the Include Pay Methods section, click *Hourly* and *Salary*, if needed.

Step 7:

In the Include Employees section, click All Employees and All Type. Your completed dialog box should look like figure 10–16.

Step 8:

Click OK. (Select *OK* at warning to "update current year's formulae.")

Step 9:

The Select Employees to Pay window will appear. In the *Check Date* field, click the *calendar* icon, and then choose *Mar 1, 2010*. This is the date that will appear on the payroll checks.

Step 10:

At the *Pay End Date* field, click the *calendar* icon, and then choose *Feb 28, 2010*. This is the ending date of the payroll period.

Step 11:

At the *Cash Acct* field, click the *magnifying glass* icon, and then click *100*, if needed.

Step 12:

Review the Select Employees to Pay window to be sure that all employees for Wardwood Construction Company are included in the payroll. Compare your work with figure 10–17.

FIGURE 10–17
Completed Select
Employees to Pay Dialog
Box

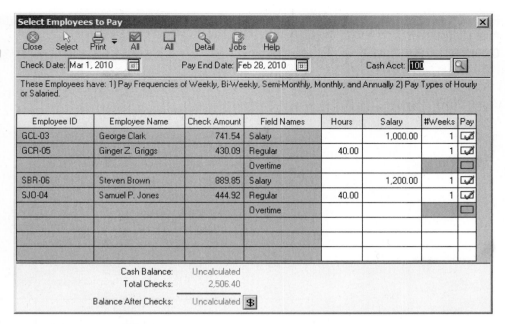

Printing the Payroll Checks

Before you attempt to print the payroll checks, be sure that there are check marks in all the *Pay* boxes at the right of the Select Employees to Pay screen. If a particular individual is not to be paid for the payroll period, no check mark should appear in the *Pay* box for that employee. Follow these steps to print checks.

Step 1:
Click Print on the toolbar at the top of the Select Employees to Pay window.

Step 2:
At the Print Forms: Payroll Checks dialog box, in the *First check number* field, key **2005**, as shown in figure 10–18.

FIGURE 10–18
Print Forms: Payroll
Checks Dialog Box

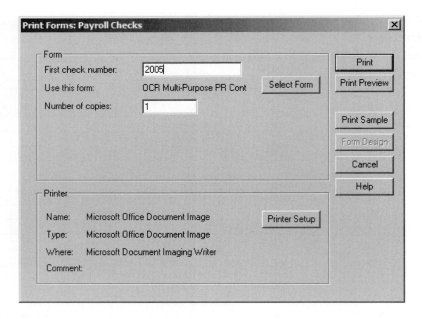

Note: Be sure that the printer is attached and turned on. The checks will print on any plain paper in the printer. Several types of preprinted check forms are available through Peachtree. Refer to the Peachtree Web site (www.peachtree.com) to locate a source for preprinted check forms.

Step 3:
Click Print.

Step 4:
Review your checks. The first one should look like figure 10–19. If there are errors, click No in the Peachtree Accounting query screen and repeat the printing process from step 1 above. Go to step 5 if your checks are correct.

FIGURE 10–19
Check for George Clark of Wardwood Construction Company

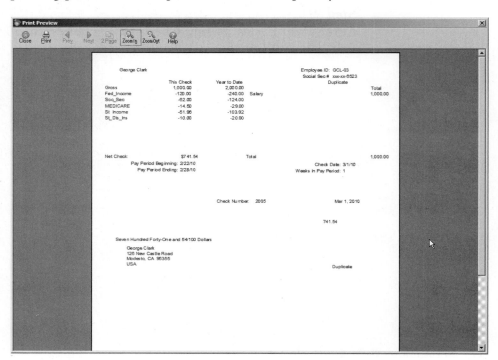

Step 5:

Click Yes in the Peachtree Accounting query screen and the check numbers (2005–2008) will be assigned. The payroll is then posted.

Preparing the Payroll with Overtime

During the weekly payroll period ended February 28, 2010, none of the employees of Wardwood Construction Company worked overtime. However, during the payroll period ended March 7, 2010, Ginger Griggs worked 50 hours rather than the normal 40 hours. She is paid according to the hourly rate plan.

Follow the steps outlined below to prepare the March 7 payroll for Wardwood Construction Company.

Step 1:

Click Employees & Payroll from the Navigation Aids toolbar, if needed.

Step 2:

Click the *Pay Employees* icon and then "Enter Payroll For One Employee" from the Employees & Payroll Tasks section, as shown in figure 10–20.

FIGURE 10–20
Payroll Entry Selected from Pay Employees Icon

Step 3:

Click OK to acknowledge the Peachtree payroll tax registration information, if applicable.

Step 4:

At the Payroll Entry window, at the *Date* field, click the *calendar* icon and choose *Mar 8, 2010.*

Step 5:

At the *Employee ID* field, click the *magnifying glass* icon, and then click *GGR-05.* The *Hours Worked* and *Taxes-Benefits-Liabilities* fields should display their data.

Step 6:

At the *Pay Period Ends* field, click the *calendar* icon, and choose *Mar 7, 2010.*

Step 7:

Key **1** in the *Weeks in Pay Period* field, if needed.

Step 8:

In the Hours Worked section, key **40.00** in the *Regular* field, if needed, and **10.00** in the *Overtime* field. Compare your completed entry with the one shown in figure 10–21. Then click <u>S</u>ave. (Do not print a check unless your instructor tells you to.)

FIGURE 10–21
Completed Payroll Entry for Ginger Z. Griggs

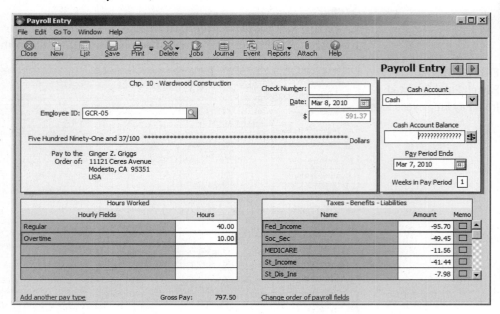

Step 9:

Prepare the payroll for the remainder of the employees listed below for the pay period ending March 7. Use the same steps as you did for Ginger Z. Griggs, excluding overtime (do not print checks).

- George Clark
- Samuel Jones
- Steven Brown

Step 10:

Close the Payroll Entry window.

Printing Payroll Checks at a Later Date

Sometimes payroll checks are printed after the payroll is prepared. Use the following procedure to print the checks for the pay period ending March 8 of Wardwood Construction Company. The date on the checks will be March 8, 2010.

HINT

If you make an error, use the List function on the toolbar to retrieve the entry. Make any necessary corrections and post when it is complete.

Step 1:
Click Tasks from the main Menu toolbar, if needed.

Step 2:
Click *Payroll Entry* from the drop-down list.

Step 3:
Click OK to acknowledge the Peachtree payroll tax registration information, if applicable.

Step 4:
Click List on the Payroll Entry toolbar.

Step 5:
At the Paycheck List window, click the down arrow at the *Date Range* field and then click *Prd 3: 3/1/10 – 3/31/10.*

Step 6:
Click *Ginger Z. Griggs*, as shown in figure 10–22.

FIGURE 10–22
Ginger Z. Griggs Selected from the Paycheck List Window

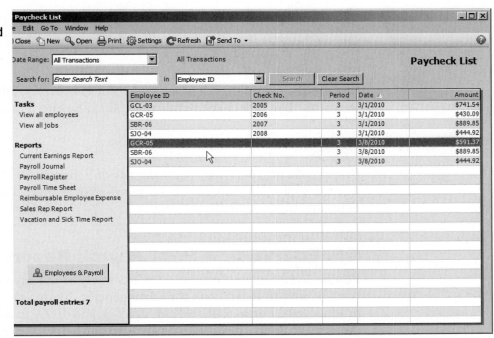

Step 7:
Click Open.

Step 8:
Click Print on the Payroll Entry toolbar.

Step 9:
Click Print in the Print Forms: Payroll Checks dialog box. The first check number should be 2009.

Step 10:
Repeat steps 4 through 9 to print checks for the remaining employees who have not been assigned a check number.

Step 11:
Close the Payroll Entry window.

C h e c k   p o i n t

1. What is net pay?
2. Is it necessary to print payroll checks when the payroll is prepared?

Answers
1. *Net pay is the amount remaining after deductions are made from an employee's gross pay.*
2. *No, payroll checks can be printed at a later date.*

P r a c t i c e   O b j e c t i v e   4

Step 1:
Open Chp. 10 – Bluefrog Maintenance Company.

Step 2:
Prepare the payroll for all employees as of February 8, 2010. There was no overtime. The first check number is 1000. The check date is February 9, 2010.

Step 3:
Prepare the payroll for all employees as of February 15, 2010. Henry Carver worked 45 hours. (This includes 5 hours of overtime). The check date is February 16, 2010. Print the checks.

OBJECTIVE 5 — Print Payroll Reports

Peachtree Complete Accounting prints many of the payroll tax returns that must be sent to federal and state tax agencies. Among the federal tax returns produced are Forms 940, 941, W-2, W-3, and 1099. In addition, Peachtree prepares a variety of payroll reports for management. The following is a partial list of the available payroll reports for management.

- The *Current Earnings Report* lists each employee's earnings and deductions.
- The *Payroll Journal* lists payroll transactions in a journal format.
- The *Payroll Tax Report* lists the payroll deductions.
- The *Quarterly Earnings Report* lists the quarterly earnings of all employees.
- The *Tax Liability Report* lists the employer's liabilities for payroll taxes.
- The *Yearly Earnings Report* lists the annual earnings of all employees.

Follow the steps outlined on the next page to print the *Current Earnings Report*.

Step 1:
Open Chp. 10 – Wardwood Construction Company and close the Action Items log.

Step 2:
Click Reports & Forms, and then click *Payroll*.

Step 3:
At the Payroll: Employee Information and Earnings section, click *Current Earnings Report*.

Step 4:
Click P̲rint on the Select a Report or Form toolbar.

Step 5:
At the Modify Report – Current Earnings Report window, click *Range* in the *Date* field.

Step 6:
At the *From* field, click the drop-down arrow to choose *Feb 1, 2010*. At the *To* field, choose *Mar 31, 2010*, as shown in figure 10–23.

FIGURE 10–23
Modify Report – Current Earnings Report Window

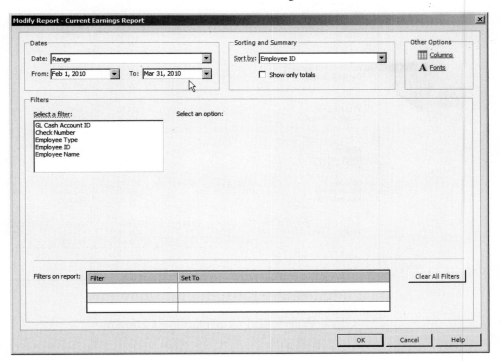

HINT

The tax amounts shown in the *Current Earnings Report* will vary depending on the tax tables that were loaded. This payroll was prepared with the modified tax table that is included on the student data disk.

Step 7:
Click OK and then OK again at the Print dialog box.

Step 8:
Review the *Current Earnings Report* shown in figure 10–24. Notice that this report shows the gross pay, deductions, and net pay for the first three employees as this is a partial view of the report.

PAYROLL **439**

FIGURE 10–24
Current Earnings
Report (Partial View)

Chp. 10 - Wardwood Construction Company
Current Earnings Report
For the Period From Feb 1, 2010 to Mar 31, 2010
Filter Criteria includes: Report order is by Employee ID. Report is printed in Detail Format.

Employee ID Employee Masked SS No	Date Reference	Amount	Gross St_Income Fed_Unemp_	Fed_Income St_Dis_Ins St_Unemp_C	Soc_Sec Soc_Sec_C Emp_Train_C	MEDICARE Medicare_C
GCL-03 George Clark XXX-XX-6523	3/1/10 2005	741.54	1,000.00 -51.96 -16.50	-120.00 -10.00 -50.00	-62.00 -62.00	-14.50 -14.50
GCL-03 George Clark XXX-XX-6523	3/8/10 2012	741.54	1,000.00 -51.96 -16.50	-120.00 -10.00 -50.00	-62.00 -62.00	-14.50 -14.50
Total 2/1/10 thru 3/31/10		1,483.08	2,000.00 -103.92 -33.00	-240.00 -20.00 -100.00	-124.00 -124.00	-29.00 -29.00
Report Date Total for George Clark		1,483.08	2,000.00 -103.92 -33.00	-240.00 -20.00 -100.00	-124.00 -124.00	-29.00 -29.00
YTD Total for George Clark		1,483.08	2,000.00 -103.92 -33.00	-240.00 -20.00 -100.00	-124.00 -124.00	-29.00 -29.00
GCR-05 Ginger Z. Griggs XXX-XX-9099	3/1/10 2006	430.09	580.00 -30.14 -9.57	-69.60 -5.80 -29.00	-35.96 -35.96	-8.41 -8.41
GCR-05 Ginger Z. Griggs XXX-XX-9099	3/8/10 2009	591.37	797.50 -41.44 -13.16	-95.70 -7.98 -39.88	-49.45 -49.45	-11.56 -11.56
Total 2/1/10 thru 3/31/10		1,021.46	1,377.50 -71.58 -22.73	-165.30 -13.78 -68.88	-85.41 -85.41	-19.97 -19.97
Report Date Total for Ginger Z. Griggs		1,021.46	1,377.50 -71.58 -22.73	-165.30 -13.78 -68.88	-85.41 -85.41	-19.97 -19.97
YTD Total for Ginger Z. Griggs		1,021.46	1,377.50 -71.58 -22.73	-165.30 -13.78 -68.88	-85.41 -85.41	-19.97 -19.97
SBR-06 Steven Brown XXX-XX-0009	3/1/10 2007	889.85	1,200.00 -62.35 -19.80	-144.00 -12.00 -60.00	-74.40 -74.40	-17.40 -17.40
SBR-06 Steven Brown XXX-XX-0009	3/8/10 2010	889.85	1,200.00 -62.35 -19.80	-144.00 -12.00 -60.00	-74.40 -74.40	-17.40 -17.40
Total 2/1/10 thru 3/31/10		1,779.70	2,400.00 -124.70 -39.60	-288.00 -24.00 -120.00	-148.80 -148.80	-34.80 -34.80

Step 9:
Close Wardwood Construction Company.

Practice Objective 5

Step 1:

Open Chp. 10 – Bluefrog Maintenance Company.

Step 2:

Print the *Current Earnings Report* for the month of February 2010. Your printout should look like figure 10–25.

FIGURE 10–25
Current Earnings Report – Bluefrog Maintenance Company (Partial View)

Chp. 10 - Bluefrog Maintenance Company
Current Earnings Report
For the Period From Feb 1, 2010 to Mar 31, 2010

Filter Criteria includes: Report order is by Employee ID. Report is printed in Detail Format.

Employee ID Employee Masked SS No	Date Reference	Amount	Gross St_Income Fed_Unemp_	Fed_Income St_Dis_Ins St_Unemp_C	Soc_Sec Soc_Sec_C Emp_Train_C	MEDICARE Medicare_C
HCA-03 Henry Carver XXX-XX-9088	2/9/10 1000	355.94	480.00 -24.94 -7.92	-57.60 -4.80 -24.00	-29.76 -29.76	-6.96 -6.96
HCA-03 Henry Carver XXX-XX-9088	2/16/10 1003	422.67	570.00 -29.62 -9.41	-68.40 -5.70 -28.50	-35.34 -35.34	-8.27 -8.27
Total 2/1/10 thru 3/31/10		778.61	1,050.00 -54.56 -17.33	-126.00 -10.50 -52.50	-65.10 -65.10	-15.23 -15.23
Report Date Total for Henry Carver		778.61	1,050.00 -54.56 -17.33	-126.00 -10.50 -52.50	-65.10 -65.10	-15.23 -15.23
YTD Total for Henry Carver		778.61	1,050.00 -54.56 -17.33	-126.00 -10.50 -52.50	-65.10 -65.10	-15.23 -15.23
JST-04 James Stewart XXX-XX-3343	2/9/10 1001	341.11	460.00 -23.90 -7.59	-55.20 -4.60 -23.00	-28.52 -28.52	-6.67 -6.67
JST-04 James Stewart XXX-XX-3343	2/16/10 1004	341.11	460.00 -23.90 -7.59	-55.20 -4.60 -23.00	-28.52 -28.52	-6.67 -6.67
Total 2/1/10 thru 3/31/10		682.22	920.00 -47.80 -15.18	-110.40 -9.20 -46.00	-57.04 -57.04	-13.34 -13.34
Report Date Total for James Stewart		682.22	920.00 -47.80 -15.18	-110.40 -9.20 -46.00	-57.04 -57.04	-13.34 -13.34
YTD Total for James Stewart		682.22	920.00 -47.80 -15.18	-110.40 -9.20 -46.00	-57.04 -57.04	-13.34 -13.34
SSM-05 Stanley Smith XXX-XX-7654	2/9/10 1002	1,186.46	1,600.00 -83.14 -26.40	-192.00 -16.00 -80.00	-99.20 -99.20	-23.20 -23.20
SSM-05 Stanley Smith XXX-XX-7654	2/16/10 1005	1,186.46	1,600.00 -83.14 -26.40	-192.00 -16.00 -80.00	-99.20 -99.20	-23.20 -23.20
Total 2/1/10 thru 3/31/10		2,372.92	3,200.00 -166.28 -52.80	-384.00 -32.00 -160.00	-198.40 -198.40	-46.40 -46.40

Step 3:
Close Bluefrog Maintenance Company.

End of Chapter Review

Software Command Summary

Establish a Payroll	Maintain, Default Information, Payroll Setup Wizard
Set Employee Defaults	Maintain, Default Information, Employees
Create an Employee Record	Maintain, Employees/Sales Reps
Prepare a Payroll (Group)	Tasks, Select for Payroll Entry
Prepare a Payroll (Individual)	Tasks, Payroll Entry
Preview/Print Payroll Reports	Reports & Forms, Payroll, Select a Report

Projects and Problems

Content Check

Multiple Choice: Choose only one response for each question.

1. The act that requires that employers pay the federal minimum wage and overtime to most employees when they work more than 40 hours a workweek is
   A. Current Tax Payment Act.
   B. Fair Labor Standards Act.
   C. Federal Insurance Contributions Act.
   D. Federal Unemployment Tax Act.

2. Which form is prepared at the end of the year to show the total earnings by independent contractors?
   A. Form 941
   B. Form W-2
   C. Form W-3
   D. Form 1099

3. Payroll taxes deducted from an employee's earnings are recorded in what type of account?
   A. Assets
   B. Accounts Payable
   C. Long Term Liabilities
   D. Other Current Liabilities

4. FICA – Social Security Tax and FICA – Medicare Tax are paid by the
   A. employee.
   B. employer.
   C. both the employee and employer.
   D. local taxing authority.

5. The payroll report which lists each employee's earnings and deductions is the
   A. *Current Earnings Report.*
   B. *Payroll Journal.*
   C. *Payroll Tax Report.*
   D. *Tax Liability Report.*

Short-Essay Response: Provide a detailed answer for each question.

1. What are the six basic areas of payroll activities?
2. List and explain the five various pay plans.
3. List and explain the payroll reports available through Peachtree.
4. What are the six federal tax returns that employers are required to file?
5. What are the various required and voluntary deductions to be withheld from employees' earnings?
6. What is the purpose of the Payroll Setup Wizard?

Case Problems

Problem 1A

Open Rico's Coffee House, a coffee house known for its exotic coffees, from the student data disk.

1. Use the Payroll Setup Wizard to establish the payroll system for Rico's Coffee House.

   Use the following information to set up the payroll system:

Federal Employer ID:	**15-8110392**
State Employer ID:	**123-9567-8**
State:	**CA**
State Unemployment ID:	**123-9567-8**
State Unemployment Rate:	**5.00**
Hourly (Reg. and Over.):	**512**
Salary:	**512**

   Create the following general ledger accounts for recording payroll taxes.

Account ID:	**218**
Description:	**Payroll Taxes Payable**
Account Type:	**Other Current Liabilities**

Account ID:	**513**
Description:	**Payroll Taxes Expense**
Account Type:	**Expenses**

2. Make the following changes in the employee and employer defaults. Create new accounts as necessary.

Employee Fields

In the *Fed_Income* field, change Account 218 to:

Account ID:	**220**
Description:	**Federal Income Taxes Payable**
Account Type:	**Other Current Liabilities**

In the *Soc_Sec* field, change Account 218 to:

Account ID:	**222**
Description:	**Social Security Taxes Payable**
Account Type:	**Other Current Liabilities**

In the *MEDICARE* field, change Account 218 to:

Account ID:	**224**
Description:	**Medicare Taxes Payable**
Account Type:	**Other Current Liabilities**

In the *St_Income* field, change Account 218 to:

Account ID:	**226**
Description:	**State Income Taxes Payable**
Account Type:	**Other Current Liabilities**

In the *St_Dis_Ins* field, change Account 218 to:

Account ID:	**228**
Description:	**SDI Taxes Payable**
Account Type:	**Other Current Liabilities**

Company Fields

In the *Soc_Sec_C* field, change Account 218 to Account 222.
In the *Medicare_C* field, change Account 218 to Account 224.
In the *Fed_Unemp_C* field, change Account 218 to:

Account ID:	**230**
Description:	**FUTA Taxes Payable**
Account Type:	**Other Current Liabilities**

In the *St_Unemp_C* field, change Account 218 to:

Account ID:	**232**
Description:	**SUTA Taxes Payable**
Account Type:	**Other Current Liabilities**

Important Note: The educational version of Peachtree may include the Field Name *Emp_Train_C*. Remove the check mark in the *Calc* field aligned with Emp_Train_C.

3. Set up employee records for the following three employees:

Employee

Employee ID: **BCA-01**
Name: **Benjamin Carter**

General Tab

Address: **2982 West Chrisman Boulevard**
City, ST, Zip: **Stockton, CA 95501**
Country: **USA**
Telephone 1:   **209-555-0251**
Last Raise:
Social Security Number: **654-46-2509**
Type: **Hourly**

Withholding Info Tab

Federal Filing Status: **Single**
     Allow: **1**   *Additional Withholding:* **0.00**
State Filing Status: **Single**
     Allow: **1**   *Additional Withholding:* **0.00**
State: **CA**
Local Filing Status: **Single**

Pay Info Tab

Pay Method: **Hourly—Hours per Pay Period**
Frequency: **Weekly**
Hours Per Pay Period: **40.00**
Rate Used to Bill Customer: **20.00**
Regular Rate: **10.00**
Overtime: **15.00**

Employee

Employee ID: **CSO-02**
Name: **Cynthia Solario**

General Tab

Address: **1651 Central Avenue**
City, ST, Zip: **Tracy, CA 95376**
Country: **USA**
Telephone 1:   **209-555-4852**
Last Raise:
Social Security Number: **568-16-2137**
Type: **Hourly**

Withholding Info Tab

Federal Filing Status:	**Married**
Allow: **2**	*Additional Withholding:* **0.00**
State Filing Status:	**Married**
Allow: **2**	*Additional Withholding:* **0.00**
State:	**CA**
Local Filing Status:	**Married**

Pay Info Tab

Pay Method:	**Hourly—Hours per Pay Period**
Frequency:	**Weekly**
Hours Per Pay Period:	**40.00**
Rate Used to Bill Customers:	**22.50**
Regular Rate:	**12.00**
Overtime:	**18.00**

Employee

Employee ID:	**VMO-03**
Name:	**Victor Moreno**

General Tab

Address:	**5549 Ramona Drive**
City, ST, Zip:	**Tracy, CA 95376**
Country:	**USA**
Telephone 1:	**209-555-4652**
Last Raise:	
Social Security Number:	**558-91-4852**
Type:	**Salary**

Withholding Info Tab

Federal Filing Status:	**Single**
Allow: **1**	*Additional Withholding:* **0.00**
State Filing Status:	**Single**
Allow: **1**	*Additional Withholding:* **0.00**
State:	**CA**
Local Filing Status:	**Single**

Pay Info Tab

Pay Method:	**Salary**
Frequency:	**Weekly**
Rate Used to Bill Customers:	**50.00**
Salary Rate:	**1,600.00**

4. Print the *Chart of Accounts* and *Employee List*.

5. Close Rico's Coffee House.

NOTE

Use Account 100, Regular Checking Account as the payroll cash account.

Problem 2A

Open Rico's Coffee House, which you updated in Problem 1A.

1. Prepare the payroll for all employees as of March 6, 2010. There was no overtime. The first check number is 1500. The check date is March 7, 2010.

2. Prepare the payroll for all employees as of March 13, 2010. Cynthia Solario worked 46 hours (6 hours overtime) this pay period. The check date is March 14, 2010.

3. Print the *Current Earnings Report* and *Payroll Register*.

4. Close Rico's Coffee House.

Problem 1B

Open Barista's, a coffee house known for good friends and great coffee, from the student data disk.

1. Use the Payroll Setup Wizard to establish the payroll system for Barista's.

   Use the following information to set up the payroll system:

Federal Employer ID:	**15-8110478**
State Employer ID:	**123-5734-7**
State:	**CA**
State Unemployment ID:	**123-5734-7**
State Unemployment Rate:	**5.00**
Hourly (Reg. and Over.):	**512**
Salary:	**512**

   Create the following general ledger accounts for recording payroll taxes:

Account ID:	**218**
Description:	**Payroll Taxes Payable**
Account Type:	**Other Current Liabilities**

Account ID:	**513**
Description:	**Payroll Taxes Expense**
Account Type:	**Expenses**

2. Make the following changes in the employee and employer defaults. Create new accounts as necessary.

   Employee Fields
   In the *Fed_Income* field, change Account 218 to:

Account ID:	**220**
Description:	**Federal Income Taxes Payable**
Account Type:	**Other Current Liabilities**

In the *Soc_Sec* field, change Account 218 to:

Account ID:	**222**
Description:	**Social Security Taxes Payable**
Account Type:	**Other Current Liabilities**

In the *MEDICARE* field, change Account 218 to:

Account ID:	**224**
Description:	**Medicare Taxes Payable**
Account Type:	**Other Current Liabilities**

In the *St_Income* field, change Account 218 to:

Account ID:	**226**
Description:	**State Income Taxes Payable**
Account Type:	**Other Current Liabilities**

In the *St_Dis_Ins* field, change Account 218 to:

Account ID:	**228**
Description:	**SDI Taxes Payable**
Account Type:	**Other Current Liabilities**

Company Fields
In the *Soc_Sec_C* field, change Account 218 to Account 222.
In the *Medicare_C* field, change Account 218 to Account 224.
In the *Fed_Unemp_C* field, change Account 218 to:

Account ID:	**230**
Description:	**FUTA Taxes Payable**
Account Type:	**Other Current Liabilities**

In the *St_Unemp_C* field, change Account 218 to:

Account ID:	**232**
Description:	**SUTA Taxes Payable**
Account Type:	**Other Current Liabilities**

Important Note: The educational version of Peachtree may include the Field Name *Emp_Train_C*. Remove the check mark in the *Calc* field aligned with Emp_Train_C.

3. Set up employee records for the following three employees:

Employee
Employee ID:	**MCA-01**
Name:	**Maria Case**

General Tab
Address:	**2256 East Madison Way**
City, ST, Zip:	**Stockton, CA 95210**
Country:	**USA**
Telephone 1:	**209-555-9526**
Last Raise:	
Social Security Number:	**665-58-4259**
Type:	**Hourly**

Withholding Info Tab
Federal Filing Status:	**Single**
Allow: **2** *Additional Withholding:* **0.00**	
State Filing Status:	**Single**
Allow: **2** *Additional Withholding:* **0.00**	
State:	**CA**
Local Filing Status:	**Single**

Pay Info Tab
Pay Method:	**Hourly—Hours per Pay Period**
Frequency:	**Weekly**
Hours Per Pay Period:	**40.00**
Rate Used to Bill Customers:	**30.00**
Regular Rate:	**10.00**
Overtime:	**15.00**

Employee
Employee ID:	**JWH-02**
Name:	**Jonathan White**

General Tab
Address:	**5219 South Grant Line**
City, ST, Zip:	**Stockton, CA 95207**
Country:	**USA**
Telephone 1:	**209-555-9635**
Last Raise:	
Social Security Number:	**559-52-4825**
Type:	**Hourly**

Withholding Info Tab

Federal Filing Status:	**Married**
Allow: **2**	*Additional Withholding:* **0.00**
State Filing Status:	**Married**
Allow: **2**	*Additional Withholding:* **0.00**
State:	**CA**
Local Filing Status:	**Married**

Pay Info Tab

Pay Method:	**Hourly—Hours per Pay Period**
Frequency:	**Weekly**
Hours Per Pay Period:	**40.00**
Rate Used to Bill Customers:	**24.00**
Regular Rate:	**14.00**
Overtime:	**21.00**

Employee

Employee ID:	**ACH-03**
Name:	**Albert Chavez**

General Tab

Address:	**425 East Main Street**
City, ST, Zip:	**Tracy, CA 95376**
Country:	**USA**
Telephone 1:	**209-555-5236**
Last Raise:	
Social Security Number:	**559-64-8745**
Type:	**Salary**

Withholding Info Tab

Federal Filing Status:	**Married**
Allow: **5**	*Additional Withholding:* **0.00**
State Filing Status:	**Married**
Allow: **5**	*Additional Withholding:* **0.00**
State:	**CA**
Local Filing Status:	**Married**

Pay Info Tab

Pay Method:	**Salary**
Frequency:	**Weekly**
Rate Used to Bill Customers:	**50.00**
Salary Rate:	**1,500.00**

4. Print the *Chart of Accounts* and *Employee List*.

5. Close Barista's.

Problem 2B

Open Barista's, which you updated in Problem 1B.

1. Prepare the payroll for all employees as of February 6, 2010. There was no overtime. The first check number is 2200. The check date is February 7, 2010.

2. Prepare the payroll for all employees as of February 13, 2010. Maria Case worked 44 hours (4 hours of overtime) this pay period. The check date is February 14, 2010.

3. Print the *Current Earnings Report* and *Payroll Register*.

4. Close Barista's.

Cooperative Learning

1. Form groups of three or four students, and research the available job market in your area. Determine the factors that are taken into consideration when determining wages and salaries for particular positions.
2. As a group, research jobs that will be in high demand in the future. What skills and training will be required for the jobs of the future? Are you currently acquiring these skills?

Writing and Decision Making

Assume that the owner of the company for which you work, Steve Randolph, is deciding whether to stop outsourcing of payroll and prepare it internally using Peachtree. One of the concerns he has is the time factor that will be required to both initially set up the payroll system, and then prepare the periodic payroll. He also wants to know what are the costs and benefits of using Peachtree to prepare the payroll. Prepare a memo with the information that has been requested.

CHAPTER

11

Job Costing

Learning Objectives

1. Understand the general concepts of job costing

2. Set up a project for job costing

3. Create phase codes and cost codes and enter estimated revenue and expenses

4. Use the job costing system to record purchases, payroll, and sales

5. Create and print job cost reports

Software Features

- Set Up Jobs

- Enter Estimated Expenses and Revenue

- Create Phase Codes and Cost Codes

- Maintain Jobs

- Enter the Costs of Materials and Labor

- Enter Revenue

- Print Job Cost Reports

The work of some manufacturing businesses and service businesses is divided into a series of separate jobs (projects). For example, a printing firm may produce 5,000 catalogs for one customer and 20,000 sales brochures for another customer. A computer-consulting firm may design a Web site for one customer and plan an internal network for another customer.

For businesses such as these, it is important to be able to determine all the costs associated with completing a job. Otherwise, it is difficult to price the job properly and earn a satisfactory profit.

Having detailed information about job costs also helps management to assess the efficiency of the firm's operations. Keeping job costs under control is a necessity if a firm is to be able to offer competitive prices and obtain new business.

OBJECTIVE 1 — Understand the General Concepts of Job Costing

job costs The costs of the materials, labor, and other items required for completion of a job.

job costing Tracking of all costs associated with a job and totaling those costs at the end of the project.

Job costs are the costs of the materials, labor, and other items required for completion of a particular job. The process of **job costing** involves tracking all costs associated with a project and totaling these costs at the end of the project.

Job Costing Procedures

When planning jobs, many businesses break them into a series of phases. Each phase represents a different stage of the project. For example, the first phase of a construction job might be preparing blueprints. The second phase might be excavating the site and putting in the foundation. Often, such jobs are covered by a contract with the customer, and payments are tied to the completion of each phase.

In some cases, however, a job is small and will last for only a short period of time. Therefore, the job is not divided into phases.

If a job does consist of phases, businesses will need to record the costs for each phase. When a phase is completed, the business can bill the customer for any revenue earned.

The Peachtree Job Costing System

Peachtree allows you to assign a job identifier to each project and track the revenue and expenses of many projects at the same time. For example, Wardwood Construction Company usually has several jobs in production simultaneously and must be able to record financial information for each job. In this way, management can evaluate the expenses incurred and the revenue received as each job moves through the production process.

Peachtree supports three methods of job costing:

1. The Jobs Only Method is used for projects that are not divided into phases and do not require cost codes. The jobs that fall into this category are usually small jobs.
2. The Jobs with Phases Method is used for projects that will be completed in phases.
3. The Jobs with Phases and Cost Codes Method is used for projects that are divided into phases and require cost codes.

The method chosen depends on the types of jobs that a business has as well as the amount of information that management wants about each job.

OBJECTIVE 2 — Set Up a Project for Job Costing

Suppose that Smith's Monuments hires Wardwood Construction Company to build a fence around its parking area. Wardwood estimates that its revenue from this project will be $5,240 and its expenses will be $3,150. Because this is a small project, Wardwood will use Peachtree's Jobs Only Method to track the costs of materials and labor and record the revenue. Use the following steps to track the costs of this job.

Step 1:
Open Wardwood Construction Company (Chp. 11 – Wardwood Construction Company if student data disk is used) and close the Action Items log.

Step 2:
Click Maintain, click *Job Costs*, and then *Jobs*.

Step 3:
The Maintain Jobs window will appear. Key **Smith Fence-Job 1** in the *Job ID* field. Then click OK.

Step 4:
Key **Smith Fence Job** in the *Description* field.

Step 5:
Click the General folder tab, and key **George Clark** in the *Supervisor* field.

Step 6:
At the *For Customer* field, click the *magnifying glass* icon, and then click *Smith-01*, as shown in figure 11–1.

FIGURE 11–1
Smith-01 Selected from Customer List

Step 7:
At the *Start Date* field, key **2/20/10**.

Step 8:
At the *End Date* field, key **3/5/10**. (This is the estimated date of completion.)

Step 9:
Key **Fence** in the *Job Type* field.

Step 10:
Key **0** in the *Percent Complete* field, if needed.

Step 11:
Compare your work with figure 11–2. Make any necessary corrections. Then click Save.

FIGURE 11–2
Completed Maintain
Jobs Window

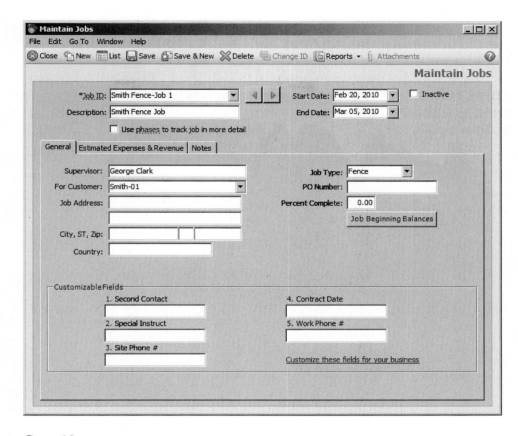

Step 12:
Click the Estimated Expenses & Revenue folder tab, as shown in figure 11–3.

FIGURE 11–3
Estimated Expenses
& Revenue Folder Tab
Selected

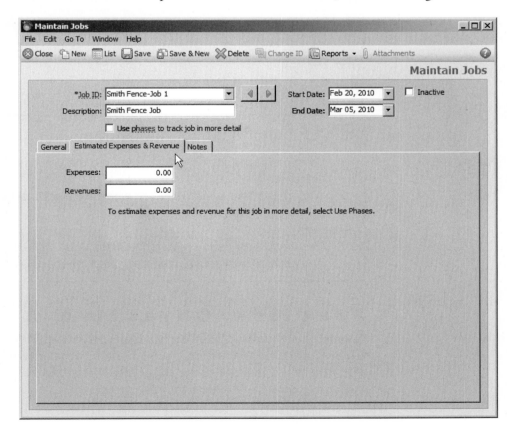

Step 13:
Key **3,150.00** in the *Expenses* field and **5,240.00** in the *Revenues* field, as shown in figure 11–4.

FIGURE 11–4
Entries for Estimated
Expenses and Revenues

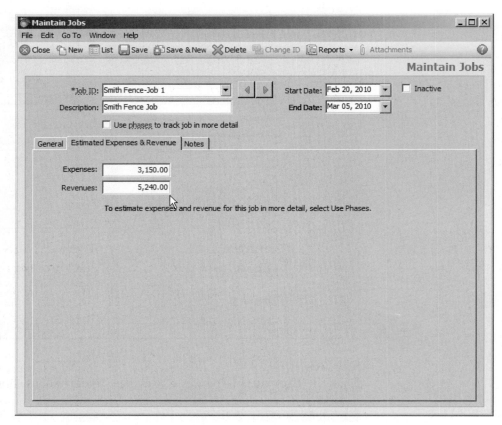

Step 14:
Click Save and then Close.

Check point

1. What menu options do you click to start the process of setting up a project for job costing?
2. What dollar amounts are entered when a project is set up for job costing?

Answers
1. *The menu options to click are Maintain, Job Costs, and Jobs.*
2. *The estimated expenses and estimated revenues are entered.*

Practice Objective 2

Assume that Bluefrog Maintenance Company accepts a job from Tim Conway of Honda Center to clean a building that suffered some fire damage. Bluefrog wants to use the Jobs Only Method to keep track of the revenue and expenses associated with the project.

Step 1:

Open Bluefrog Maintenance Company (Chp. 11 – Bluefrog Maintenance Company if student data disk is used).

Step 2:

Set up the project of Honda Center for job costing. The revenue is expected to be $15,000, and the expenses are expected to be $8,900. The job identifier is Honda Fire-Job 1. The estimated starting date is February 10, 2010, and the estimated ending date is February 28, 2010. The job type is Clean Up and the percentage of completion is zero (0). Stanley Smith will supervise the project.

OBJECTIVE 3 — Create Phase Codes and Cost Codes and Enter Estimated Revenue and Expenses

In many cases, it is not possible to track the costs of a job effectively unless the job is divided into phases. Each phase should represent a significant stage of the project. This approach provides management with useful information throughout the life of a project. If there are cost overruns at any stage, management can take action immediately.

However, in planning the phases of a job, it is important not to create too many small steps. Otherwise, management may be overwhelmed with too much information. Having too many details about a job actually makes it difficult to keep a close watch on its progress.

Suppose that Wardwood Construction Company accepts a job from Barker's Music to build more office space for the firm. Wardwood decides to divide this project into four phases: planning/permits, excavation, building, and landscaping.

The identifier for the job is Barker Office-Job 2. The revenue is expected to be $500,000, and the expenses are expected to be $225,000. The estimated starting date is February 15, 2010, and the estimated ending date is December 30, 2010.

The first task for Wardwood is to set up the project for job costing. Then it must create phase codes and cost codes. Finally, Wardwood must enter the estimated revenue and expenses for each phase of the job.

Setting Up a Project for Job Costing

Follow the steps outlined below to set up the project to build new office space for Barker's Music in the job costing system of Wardwood Construction Company.

Step 1:

Open Chp. 11 – Wardwood Construction Company, which you updated previously in the chapter.

Step 2:

Click Maintain, click *Job Costs*, and then click *Jobs*.

Step 3:

Key **Barker Office-Job 2** in the *Job ID* field. Then click OK.

Step 4:
Key **Barker Office Job** in the *Description* field.

Step 5:
Click the General folder tab, and key **George Clark** in the *Supervisor* field.

Step 6:
At the *For Customer* field, click the *magnifying glass* icon, and then click *Barker-03*.

Step 7:
At the *Start Date* field, click the drop-down arrow and select *Feb 15, 2010*.

Step 8:
At the *End Date* field, click the drop-down arrow and select *Dec 30, 2010*.

Step 9:
Check mark the box next to *Use phases to track...*, as shown in figure 11–5.

FIGURE 11–5
Maintain Jobs
Window with Use
Phases Selected

Step 10:
Key **Const** in the *Job Type* field.

Step 11:
Key **0** in the *Percent Complete* field, if needed.

Step 12:
Click Save and then Close.

Creating the Phase Codes for a Job

The next task for Wardwood Construction Company is to establish the phases and phase codes for the job that it will do for Barker's Music.

Step 1:
Click Maintain, click *Job Costs*, and then *Phases*.

Step 2:
The Maintain Phases window will appear. Key **Plan-01** in the *Phase ID* field. Then click OK.

Step 3:
Key **Planning and Permits** in the *Description* field.

Step 4:
Peachtree supports five different cost types:

- Labor
- Materials
- Equipment
- Subcontractors
- Other

Click the down-arrow key and then click *Other* as the cost type shown for Plan-01, the first phase of the job for Barker's Music. See figure 11–6.

FIGURE 11–6
Other Selected as Cost Type

Step 5:
Click Save.

Step 6:
Create the following additional phases for the job for Barker's Music. (The building phase will be established in the next section.)

Phase ID	Description	Cost Type
Excav–02	Excavation	Subcontractors
Lands–04	Landscaping	Subcontractors

Step 7:
Review your work, make any necessary corrections, then resave each entry. Then click Close.

Creating the Cost Codes for a Job

The cost codes provide additional information for management. These codes help management to track several cost areas for any phase of a job. For example, in the building phase of the project that Wardwood Construction Company is doing for Barker's Music, management wants to track the cost of materials and the cost of labor. Follow the steps outlined below to create the necessary cost codes.

Step 1:
Click Maintain, click *Job Costs*, and then click *Phases*.

Step 2:
Key **Build–03** in the *Phase ID* field. Then click OK.

Step 3:
Key **Building** in the *Description* field.

Step 4:
Click the box next to *This phase uses cost codes*, as shown in figure 11–7.

FIGURE 11–7
Use Cost Codes Selected

Step 5:
Click Save and then Close.

Step 6:
Click Maintain, click *Job Costs*, and then *Cost Codes*.
   Wardwood Construction Company will use Buildlab-10 as the identifier for the labor costs in the building phase and Buildmat-11 as the identifier for the materials costs.

Step 7:
At the Maintain Cost Codes window, key **Buildlab-10** in the *Cost ID* field. Then click OK.

Step 8:
Key **Building Labor** in the *Description* field.

Step 9:
Click the down-arrow at the *Cost Type* field, and then click *Labor* as shown in figure 11–8, if needed.

FIGURE 11–8
Completed Maintain
Cost Codes Window

Step 10:
Click Save.

Step 11:
Create the remaining cost code for the building phase of the job for Barker's Music. Use the following information:

Cost ID	Description	Cost Type
Buildmat-11	Building Materials	Materials

Step 12:
Click Save and then Close.

Entering Estimated Revenue and Expenses for Each Phase

Peachtree allows you to enter the estimated expenses and revenue for a specific phase of a job into the job costing system. For example, Wardwood Construction Company will enter expense and revenue amounts for each phase of the project that it is doing for Barker's Music.

Step 1:
Click Maintain, click *Job Costs*, and then *Jobs*.

Step 2:
The Maintain Jobs window will appear. At the *Job ID* field, click the *magnifying glass* icon, and then click *Barker Office-Job 2*.

Step 3:
Click the Estimated Expenses & Revenue folder tab.

Step 4:

Click in the *Phase ID* field, click the drop-down arrow, and then click *Plan-01*, as shown in figure 11–9.

FIGURE 11–9
Plan-01 Selected in
Phase ID Field

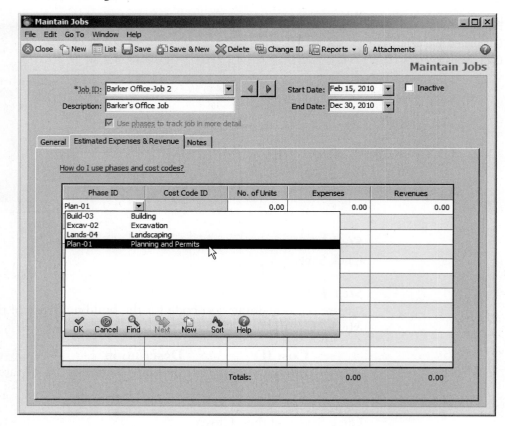

Step 5:

Key **5,000.00** in the *Expenses* field and **12,000.00** in the *Revenues* field.

Step 6:

In the second row of the *Phase ID* field, click the drop-down arrow, and then click *Excav-02.*

HINT

The *Cost Code ID* field is disabled because these phases do not use cost codes.

Step 7:

Key **33,000.00** in the *Expenses* field and **55,000.00** in the *Revenues* field.

Step 8:

In the third row of the *Phase ID* field, click the drop-down arrow, and then click *Lands-04.*

Step 9:

Key **20,000.00** in the *Expenses* field and **40,000.00** in the *Revenues* field.

Step 10:

In the fourth row of the *Phase ID* field, click the drop-down arrow, and then click *Build-03.* Tab to the next field and notice that the *Cost Code ID* field is now enabled.

Step 11:
At the *Cost Code ID* field, click the drop-down arrow, and then click *Buildlab-10*.

Step 12:
Key **100,000.00** in the *Expenses* field and **203,000.00** in the *Revenues* field.

Step 13:
In the fifth row of the *Phase ID* field, click the drop-down arrow and then click *Build-03*.

Step 14:
At the *Cost Code ID* field, click the drop-down arrow, and then click *Buildmat-11*.

Step 15:
Key **70,000.00** in the *Expenses* field and **190,000.00** in the *Revenues* field.

Step 16:
Compare your completed entries with the one shown in figure 11–10. Make any necessary changes.

FIGURE 11–10
Completed Entry for Estimated Expenses and Revenues

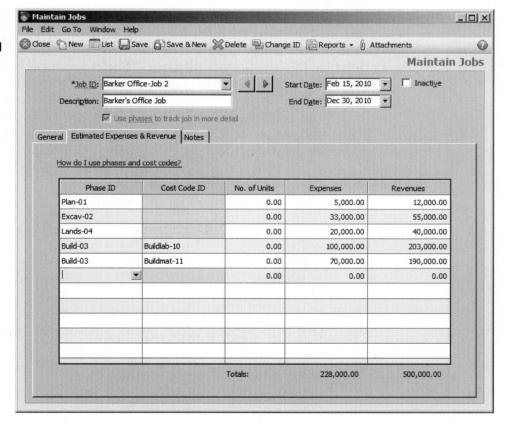

Step 17:
Click Save and then Close.

Step 18:
Close Wardwood Construction Company.

Practice Objective 3

Assume that Bluefrog Maintenance Company accepts a job from Valley Mercedes to develop a maintenance system that can be used at five other Mercedes dealerships throughout the area.

Step 1:
Open Chp. 11 – Bluefrog Maintenance Company, which you updated previously in the chapter.

Step 2:
Set up the project of Valley Mercedes for job costing. The job identifier is Valley System-Job 2, the description is Mercedes Maintenance Job, and the job type is *Maint* (for Maintenance). The estimated starting date is February 20, 2010, and the estimated ending date is April 30, 2010. Stanley Smith will supervise the project.

Bluefrog estimates that this project will generate revenue of $45,500 and have expenses of $22,000. Bluefrog wants to track the costs of the project by using the following three phases: Planning, Implementation, and Feedback.

Step 3:
Create the following phases for the project:

Phase ID	Description	Cost Type
Plan-01	Planning	Other
Impl-02	Implementation	Use cost codes (shown below)
Feed-03	Feedback	Subcontractors

Step 4:
Create the following cost codes for the implementation phase (Impl-02):

Cost ID	Description	Cost Type
Impllab-10	Implementation Labor	Labor
Implmat-11	Implementation Materials	Materials

Step 5:

Enter the estimated revenue and expenses for each phase of the project:

Phase	Expenses	Revenue
Planning	$ 2,000	$ 4,000
Feedback	2,500	5,000
Implementation Labor	8,000	25,000
Implementation Materials	9,500	11,500
Totals	$22,000	$45,500

Step 6:

Compare your work with the Maintain Jobs window shown in figure 11–11. Make any necessary changes. Notice the totals at the bottom of your screen.

FIGURE 11–11
Completed Maintain
Jobs Window

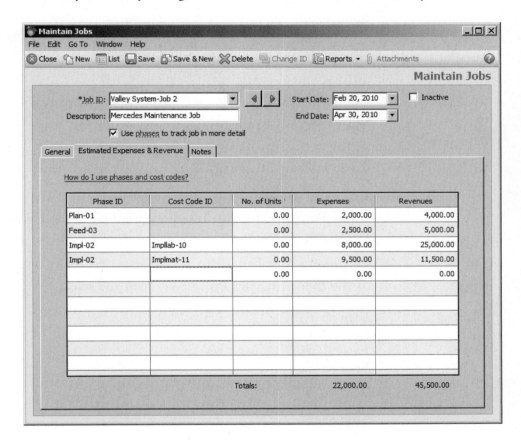

Step 7:

Click Save and Close.

OBJECTIVE 4 — Use the Job Costing System to Record Purchases, Payroll, and Sales

The Peachtree job costing system allows you to record the actual expenses incurred and the actual revenue received as a project moves through production. Remember that the estimated expenses and revenue are entered at the beginning of the project. Management is therefore able to compare estimated and actual amounts for every phase of the project.

Labor costs can easily be allocated to jobs if employees keep track of the hours that they spend on each job. Similarly, the costs of materials and other items purchased specifically for jobs can easily be allocated. However, it is more difficult to allocate the costs of materials and other items that are purchased for the firm's inventory and later used for jobs.

Recording the Cost of Purchases

Suppose that Wardwood Construction Company receives Invoice 1009 from the BMC Supply Company on February 21, 2010. This invoice is for 5,000 feet of lumber to be used in the fence being built for Smith's Monuments and 500 gallons of white paint to be placed in the firm's inventory. The price of the lumber is $0.50 per foot and the price of the paint is $2 per gallon.

The cost of the lumber, which will be used only for the Smith job, is immediately charged to that job. However, the cost of the paint is charged to inventory. Later, when some of the paint is used for the Smith job, the cost of that paint will be allocated to the job.

Step 1:
Open Chp. 11 – Wardwood Construction Company and close the Action Items log.

Step 2:
Click Tasks and then click *Purchases/Receive Inventory*.

Step 3:
At the Purchases/Receive Inventory window, in the *Vendor ID* field, click the *magnifying glass* icon, and then click *BMC-07*.

Step 4:
At the *Date* field, click the *calendar* icon and select *Feb 21, 2010*.

Step 5:
Key **1009** in the *Invoice No.* field.

Step 6:
Key **5,000.00** in the *Quantity* field.

Step 7:
At the *Item* field, click the *magnifying glass* icon, and then click *New* at the bottom of the drop-down list.

Step 8:
Create the following inventory items. Click *Save* after each item is entered.

Non-stock Item (purchased for a job)

Item I*D*:	**BOARD-4**
Description:	**Lumber**
Item Class:	**Non-stock item**
Price Level 1:	**1.50**
Last Unit Cost:	**0.50**
GL Sales Acct:	**400.5**

GL Salary/Wages Acct:	**512**
GL Cost of Sales Acct:	**503**
Item Ta__x_ Type:	**2 (Exempt)**
Stocking U/M:	**Foot**
Preferred _V_endorID:	**BMC-07**

Stock Item (purchased for inventory)

Item _I_D:	**PAINTWH-5**
Descri__p_tion:	**White Paint**
Item Class:	**Stock item**
Price Level 1:	**3.50**
Last Unit Cost:	**2.00**
Cost Method:	**FIFO**
GL Sales Acct:	**400.5**
GL Inventory Acct:	**105**
GL Cost of Sales Acct:	**503**
Item Ta__x_ Type:	**2 (Exempt)**
Stocking U/M:	**Gallon**
Preferred _V_endor ID:	**BMC-07**

Step 9:
Click Close to return to the Purchases/Receive Inventory window.

Step 10:
At the *Item* field of the Purchases/Receive Inventory window, click the *magnifying glass* icon, and then click *BOARD-4*.

Step 11:
At the *GL Account* field, click *105*.

Step 12:
Key **0.50** in the *Unit Price* field.

Step 13:
At the *Job* field, click the *folder* icon, and then click *Smith Fence-Job 1*, as shown in figure 11–12.

FIGURE 11–12
Smith Fence-Job 1
Selected from
Drop-Down List

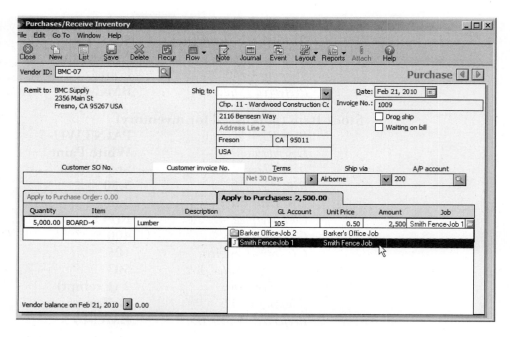

Step 14:
Key **500.00** on the second row in the *Quantity* field.

Step 15:
At the *Item* field, click the *magnifying glass* icon, and then click *PAINTWH-5.*
Compare your entries with those shown in figure 11–13.

FIGURE 11–13
Completed Purchases/
Receive Inventory

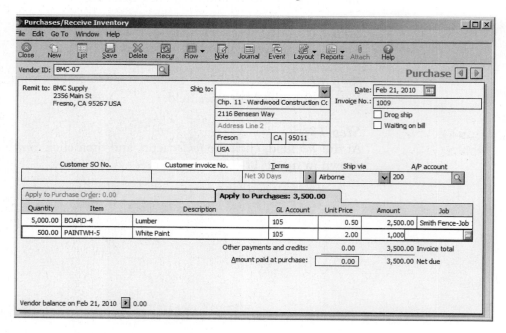

Step 16:
Click Save and then Close.

Allocating the Cost of Inventory Items to Jobs

Assume that Wardwood Construction Company withdraws 40 gallons of white paint from its inventory on February 23, 2010. This paint will be used for the fence that Wardwood is building for Smith's Monuments. Because the purchase of the paint was originally charged to Inventory, Wardwood must now allocate the cost of the 40 gallons to the Smith job. Like the lumber used in the fence, this paint is part of the materials for the job.

Step 1:
Click Tasks, and then click *Inventory Adjustments*.

Step 2:
At the *Item ID* field, click the *magnifying glass* icon, and then click *PAINTWH-5*.

Step 3:
Key **2/23/10** in the *Date* field.

Step 4:
At the *Job* field, click the *folder* icon, and then click *Smith Fence-Job 1*.

Step 5:
At the *GL Source Acct* field, key **105**.

Step 6:
Key **–40.00** in the *Adjust Quantity By* field. (Be sure to key this amount as a negative number.)

Step 7:
Key **Used for Smith Fence Job** in the *Reason to Adjust* field. Compare your completed entries with those shown in figure 11–14.

FIGURE 11–14
Completed Inventory
Adjustments Window

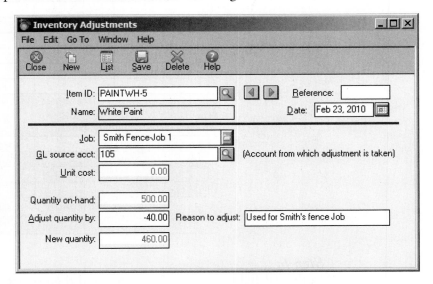

Step 8:
Click Save and then Close.

Allocating Labor Costs to Jobs

On February 28, 2010, Wardwood Construction Company records the labor costs related to the job it is doing for Smith's Monuments. These labor costs consist of one week of salary for George Clark ($1,000) and 40 hours of wages for Samuel Jones at $15 per hour ($15 × 40 = $600). Make note that you had processed the payroll for this period in chapter 10.

Step 1:
Click Tasks and then click *Payroll Entry.*

Step 2:
The Payroll Entry window will now appear. Click the List button on the Payroll Entry toolbar.

Step 3:
Select *All Transactions* at the *Date Range* field of the Paycheck List window.

Step 4:
Double-click *GCL-03, Check 2005.* George Clark's payroll data for the week of Feb 28, 2010 will now appear in the Payroll Entry window.

Step 5:
Click the Jobs button at the top of the Payroll Entry toolbar. A dialog box called Labor Distribution to Jobs will appear, as shown in figure 11–15.

FIGURE 11–15
Labor Distribution to Jobs Dialog Box

Step 6:
In the *Job* field, click the *folder* icon and then select *Smith Fence-Job 1.*

Step 7:

Key **1,000.00** in the *Amount* field and then press Enter. All of George Clark's salary has now been allocated to the Smith job. Compare your completed entries with those shown in figure 11–16.

FIGURE 11–16
Salary Allocated to
Smith Job

Step 8:

Click <u>O</u>K to save, and then <u>S</u>ave again at the Payroll Entry window.

Step 9:

Click the L<u>i</u>st button on the Payroll Entry toolbar.

Step 10:

Double-click *SJO-04, Check 2008*. Samuel Jones' payroll data for the week of Feb 28, 2010 will now appear in the Payroll Entry window.

Step 11:

Click the <u>J</u>obs button at the top of the Payroll Entry toolbar. The Labor Distribution to Jobs dialog box will appear.

Step 12:

In the *Job* field, click the *folder* icon and then select *Smith Fence-Job 1*.

Step 13:

Key **40.00** in the *Hours* field and then press Enter. Note that the total amount of *$600.00* is automatically entered ($15 per hour × 40 hours).

Step 14:

Click <u>O</u>K.

Step 15:

At the Payroll Entry window, click <u>S</u>ave and then Close.

Recording the Revenue Received from Jobs

Suppose that Wardwood Construction Company completes the fence that it is building for Smith's Monuments on February 28, 2010. Wardwood receives a check for $5,240 from Smith.

The effect of this transaction is to increase the revenue earned from construction services and to increase the asset Cash. Therefore, Wardwood must debit Cash and credit Construction Revenue. You make this entry using the Receipts function of Peachtree.

Step 1:
Click Tasks, click *Receipts*, and then after ensuring *Cash* is selected from the drop-down list, click OK at the Select a Cash Account window.

Step 2:
At the Receipts window, key **02/28/10** in the *Deposit Ticket ID* field.

Step 3:
At the *Customer ID* field, click the *magnifying glass* icon, and then click *Smith-01*.

Step 4:
Key **Fence Job** in the *Reference* field.

Step 5:
At the *Date* field, click the *calendar* icon and select *Feb 28, 2010*.

Step 6:
Select *Check* from the Payment Method drop-down list, if needed.

Step 7:
Click the Apply to Revenues folder tab.

Step 8:
Key **Fence Job** in the *Description* field.

Step 9:
At the *GL Account* field, key **400.5**.

Step 10:
Key **5,240.00** in the *Amount* field.

Step 11:
At the *Job* field, click the *folder* icon, and then click *Smith Fence-Job 1*, as shown in figure 11–17.

> **HINT**
>
> If the *GL Account* field does not display on the Apply to Revenues tab, click Options on the main Menu toolbar, and then click *Global*. The Maintain Global Options dialog box will appear. Deselect the box that is checked next to "Accounts Receivable (Quotes, Sales Orders, Invoicing, Credit Memos, Receipts)," then click OK. Close and then reopen the Receipts window.

FIGURE 11–17
Smith Fence-Job 1
Selected

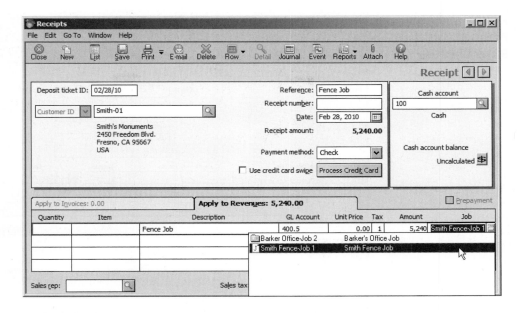

Step 12:
Click Save and then Close.

Tracking Costs and Revenue for Job Phases

The job that Wardwood Construction Company did for Smith's Monuments was a simple one. However, the job for Barker's Music is more complex and was therefore divided into four phases: planning/permits, excavation, building, and landscaping. The building phase was further divided by assigning cost codes for materials and labor.

One of the advantages of the Peachtree job costing system is that you can use it to track costs and revenue for each phase of a project as the project moves through production. The phase codes and cost codes make this possible.

Suppose that Wardwood Construction Company wants to access the phase codes and cost codes for the Barker job. We will use the Purchases function to accomplish this task, but it is also possible to use the Payroll and Sales functions.

Step 1:
Click Tasks, and then click *Purchases/Receive Inventory*.

Step 2:
At the Purchases/Receive Inventory window, click in the *Job* field, and then click the *folder* icon.

Step 3:
Click the *Barker Office-Job 2 folder* icon to view the phases available for cost allocation, as shown in figure 11–18.

FIGURE 11–18
Phases Available for
Barker Office Job

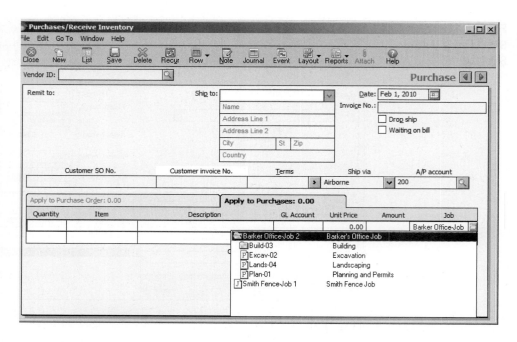

FIGURE 11–19
Cost Codes Available for
Barker Office Job

Step 4:

Click the *Build-03 folder* icon to reveal the cost codes for the building phase
of the Barker job, as shown in figure 11–19.

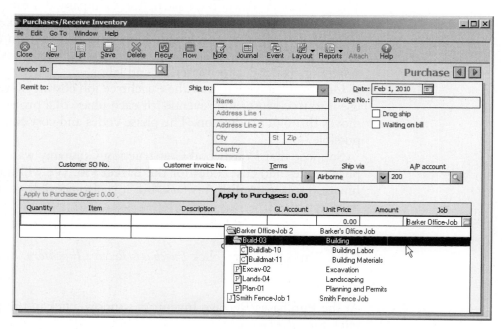

Step 5:

Do *not* click <u>S</u>ave. Click Close to exit the Purchases/Receive Inventory window.

Practice Objective 4

On February 12, 2010, Bluefrog Maintenance Company began the fire cleanup job for Honda Center. It purchased 1,400 gallons of a floor care product on credit from Lou's Janitorial Supply Company at a cost of $4.56 per gallon (Invoice 596781). This product will be used only for the Honda Center job. In addition, Bluefrog will use 20 gallons of carpet shampoo, CPTSHAM-1. The carpet shampoo will be taken from Bluefrog's inventory.

On February 22, 2010, Bluefrog completed the job for Honda Center and recorded the following labor costs: one week's salary for Stanley Smith and 40 hours of wages for James Stewart. On February 28, 2010, Bluefrog received $15,000 from Honda Center for the job.

Step 1:
Open Chp. 11 – Bluefrog Maintenance Company.

Step 2:
Create the following inventory item:

Item ID:	**FLOCARE-4**
Description:	**Floor Care Product**
Item Class:	**Non-stock item**
Price Level 1:	**9.50**
Last Unit Cost:	**4.56**
GL Sales Acct:	**400.5**
GL Salary/Wages Acct:	**512**
GL Cost of Sales Acct:	**503**
Item Tax Type:	**2 (Exempt)**
Stocking U/M:	**Gallon**
Preferred Vendor ID:	**LOU-04**

Step 3:
Enter the purchase of the floor care product. Key **105** at the *GL Account* field and **4.56** at the *Unit Price* field. Compare your entries with figure 11–20.

FIGURE 11–20
Completed
Purchases/Receive
Inventory Window

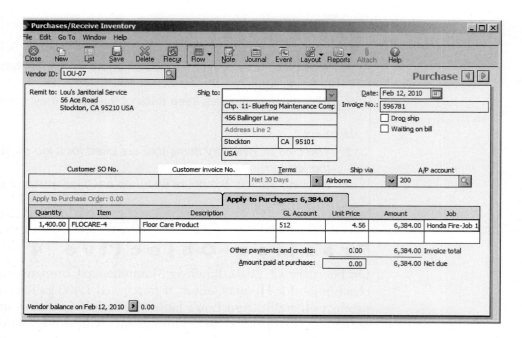

Step 4:

Make the necessary inventory adjustment for the carpet shampoo and allocate its cost to the Honda Center job. Compare your Inventory Adjustments window with figure 11–21.

FIGURE 11–21
Completed
Inventory
Adjustments
Window

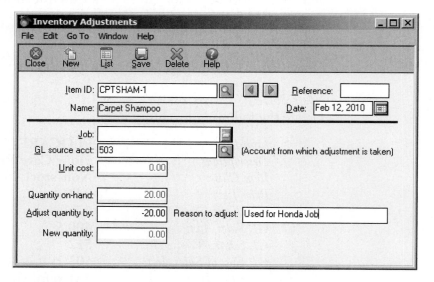

Step 5:

Allocate the labor costs to the Honda Center job. *Note:* The weekly payroll for the week ending February 22, 2010 has not yet been processed; therefore, create the payroll entries for both employees and assign the labor costs to the Honda job. (The pay period ends February 22 and the date of the check is February 23. Do not print the checks.)

Step 6:
Enter the service revenue received from the Honda Center job, Reference Fire Cleanup.

Step 7:
Close the active window.

OBJECTIVE 5 — Create and Print Job Cost Reports

The Peachtree job costing system produces many reports. Management can use the information in these reports to review estimated expenses and revenue for jobs, compare these amounts to the actual expenses and revenue, monitor profitability, and keep track of the progress of each job. Among the reports available from the Peachtree job costing system are the following:

- *Cost Code List*
- *Estimated Job Expenses*
- *Estimated Job Revenue*
- *Job Costs by Type*
- *Job Estimates*
- *Job Ledger*
- *Job List*
- *Job Master File List*
- *Job Profitability Report*
- *Job Register*
- *Phase List*
- *Unbilled Job Expense*

Preparing the Job Profitability Report

Suppose that Wardwood Construction Company wants to create the *Job Profitability Report* for the month of February 2010. This report will show the actual expenses, revenue, and profit for the job that Wardwood completed for Smith's Monuments—building a fence around a parking area.

Step 1:
Open Chp. 11 – Wardwood Construction Company, which you updated previously in the chapter.

Step 2:
Click Reports & Forms, and then click *Jobs.*

Step 3:
The Select a Report or Form dialog box will appear. Click *Job Profitability Report* from the Job Reports: Project Information section.

Step 4:
Click Options on the Select a Report or Form toolbar.

Step 5:

In the *Time Frame* field of the Modify Report – Job Profitability Report window, click *Range*. In the *From* field, select *Feb 1, 2010*, and in the *To* field, select *Mar 31, 2010*.

Step 6:

Click OK at the bottom of the window.

Step 7:

Review the *Job Profitability Report* and compare it to the one shown in figure 11–22.

FIGURE 11–22
Job Profitability
Report

Chp. 11 - Wardwood Construction Company
Job Profitability Report
For the Period From Feb 1, 2010 to Mar 31, 2010

Filter Criteria includes: Report order is by ID. Report is printed including Balance Forward.

Job ID	Phase ID	Cost Code ID	GL Acct ID	Actual Rev.	Actual Exp.	Profit $	Profit
Smith Fence			105		2,500.00		
					80.00		
			400.5	5,240.00			
			512		1,000.00		
					600.00		
				5,240.00	4,180.00		
Smith Fenc	Total			5,240.00	4,180.00	1,060.00	20.23
Report	Total			5,240.00	4,180.00	1,060.00	20.23

Step 8:
Click Close.

Preparing the Estimated Job Expenses Report

Suppose that Wardwood Construction Company now wants to create the *Estimated Job Expenses* report for the month of March 2010. This report will show the estimated expenses for current and completed jobs.

Step 1:

At the Select a Report or Form dialog box, click *Estimated Job Expenses* from the Job Reports: Project Information section.

Step 2:

Click Options on the Select a Report or Form toolbar.

Step 3:

In the *Date* field, click *Exact Date*, and in the *As of* field, select *Mar 31, 2010*.

Step 4:

Click OK in the Modify Report – Estimated Job Expenses window.

Step 5:

Review the *Estimated Job Expenses* report and compare it to the report shown in figure 11–23.

FIGURE 11–23
Estimated Job
Expenses Report

Page: 1

Chp. 11 - Wardwood Construction Company
Estimated Job Expenses
As of Mar 31, 2010

Filter Criteria includes: Report order is by ID.

Job ID	Phase ID	Cost Code ID	Est. Exp. Units	Act. Exp. Units	Diff. Exp. Unit	Est. Expense	Act. Expens	Diff. Expenses
Barker Office-J	Build-03	Buildlab-10				100,000.00		-100,000.00
		Buildmat-11				70,000.00		-70,000.00
	Excav-02					33,000.00		-33,000.00
	Lands-04					20,000.00		-20,000.00
	Plan-01					5,000.00		-5,000.00
Barker Office-	Total					228,000.00		-228,000.00
Smith Fence-J			5,080.00	5,080.00		3,150.00	4,180.00	1,030.00
Smith Fence-	Total		5,080.00	5,080.00		3,150.00	4,180.00	1,030.00
Report	Total		5,080.00	5,080.00		231,150.00	4,180.00	-226,970.00

Step 6:
Close Wardwood Construction Company.

C h e c k   p o i n t

1. Name two reports available from the Peachtree job costing system.
2. What information about a job is shown in the *Job Profitability Report*?

Answers
1. *Answers will vary.*
2. *This report shows the actual expenses, revenue, and profit for a job.*

P r a c t i c e   O b j e c t i v e   5

Bluefrog Maintenance Company wants to prepare two job cost reports for the month of February 2010.

Step 1:
Open Chp. 11 – Bluefrog Maintenance Company, which you updated previously in the chapter.

Step 2:
Prepare and print the *Job Profitability Report* and *Estimated Job Expenses* report. Your printouts should look like figures 11–24 and 11–25, respectively.

FIGURE 11–24
Job Profitability
Report – Bluefrog
Maintenance
Company

Page: 1

Chp. 11- Bluefrog Maintenance Company
Job Profitability Report
For the Period From Feb 1, 2010 to Feb 28, 2010

Filter Criteria includes: Report order is by ID. Report is printed including Balance Forward.

Job ID	Phase ID	Cost Code ID	GL Acct ID	Actual Rev.	Actual Exp.	Profit $	Profit
Honda Fire-			400.5	15,000.00			
			503		100.00		
			512		6,384.00		
					1,600.00		
					460.00		
				15,000.00	8,544.00		
Honda Fire-	Total			15,000.00	8,544.00	6,456.00	43.04
Report	Total			15,000.00	8,544.00	6,456.00	43.04

FIGURE 11–25
Estimated
Job Expenses
Report – Bluefrog
Maintenance
Company

Page: 1

Chp. 11- Bluefrog Maintenance Company
Estimated Job Expenses
As of Feb 28, 2010

Filter Criteria includes: Report order is by ID.

Job ID	Phase ID	Cost Code ID	Est. Exp. Units	Act. Exp. Units	Diff. Exp. Unit	Est. Expense	Act. Expens	Diff. Expenses
Honda Fire-Jo				1,460.00	1,460.00	8,900.00	8,544.00	-356.00
Honda Fire-Jo	**Total**			**1,460.00**	**1,460.00**	**8,900.00**	**8,544.00**	**-356.00**
Valley System-	Feed-03					2,500.00		-2,500.00
	Impl-02	Impllab-10				8,000.00		-8,000.00
		Implmat-11				9,500.00		-9,500.00
	Plan-01					2,000.00		-2,000.00
Valley System	**Total**					**22,000.00**		**-22,000.00**
Report	**Total**			**1,460.00**	**1,460.00**	**30,900.00**	**8,544.00**	**-22,356.00**

End of Chapter Review

Software Command Summary

Set Up a Job for Costing	Maintain, Job Costs, Jobs, Enter Job Information
Estimated Expenses and Revenue	Same as Set Up a Job for Costing, then Estimated Expenses & Revenue Folder Tab and Enter Data
Create Phase Codes	Maintain, Job Costs, Phases, Enter Information, Select the Cost Type
Create Cost Codes	Maintain, Job Costs, Cost Codes, Enter Information, Select the Cost Type
Enter Purchases	Tasks, Purchases/Receive Inventory, Job, Select a Job, a Phase, and a Cost Code
Allocate the Cost of Inventory Items	Tasks, Inventory Adjustments, Item ID, Adjust to Jobs Quantity By
Allocate the Cost of Labor to Jobs	Tasks, Payroll Entry, Employee ID, Jobs, Select a Job, a Phase, and a Cost Code, Enter the Salary/Hourly Information
Enter the Revenue from Jobs	Tasks, Receipts, Job, Select a Job, a Phase, and a Cost Code
Print Job Cost Reports	Reports & Forms, Jobs, Select a Report from the Report List, Print

Projects and Problems

Content Check

Multiple Choice: Choose only one response for each question.

1. Which of the following methods for tracking job costs does Peachtree support?
   A. Jobs Only
   B. Jobs with Phases
   C. Jobs with Phases and Cost Codes
   D. All of the above

2. When managers want maximum detail in their cost reports, they should use
   A. Phases
   B. Cost Types
   C. Cost Codes
   D. All of the above

3. What are job costs?
   A. The costs incurred in operating a business
   B. The revenue and expenses connected with inventory adjustments
   C. The materials, labor, and other items required to complete a job
   D. None of the above

4. The Peachtree job costing system tracks
   A. the estimated revenue and expenses for each job
   B. the actual revenue and expenses for each job
   C. the profit for each job
   D. All of the above

5. Which of the following job cost reports would management consult to see how much profit the business made from a completed job?
   A. *Estimated Job Expenses*
   B. *Job Profitability Report*
   C. *Estimated Job Revenue*
   D. *Job Register*

Short-Essay Response: Provide a detailed answer for each question.

1. What is the purpose of job costing? Why would the information from a job costing system help managers to make decisions?
2. Peachtree supports several levels of detail for job costing. Name two situations in which it would be helpful for management to have cost information for the various phases of a job.
3. Suppose a construction company will complete a job over several months. What factors would management consider when deciding whether to divide this job into phases?
4. Why is the *Job Profitability Report* helpful to a user of Peachtree?
5. What are the steps necessary to set up a project for job costing?
6. List and explain the five different cost types used in Peachtree.

Case Problems

Problem 1A

Robertson Construction Company accepted a job from Jerome Parks of the Parkview Apartments to repair an apartment that had been damaged by renters. Robertson wants to use the Jobs Only Method to keep track of the revenue and expenses associated with the project. The revenue is expected to be $50,000, and the expenses are expected to be $30,000. The job identifier is Park Repair-Job 1. The estimated starting date is January 10, 2010, and the estimated ending date is January 30, 2010. The percentage of completion is zero (0). Barbara Williams will supervise the project.

1. Open Robertson Construction Company from the student data disk.

2. Create a customer account for Parkview Apartments.

Customer ID:	**Park-99**
Name:	**Parkview Apartments**

General Tab

Contact:	**Jerome Parks**
Account Number:	**230**
Billing Address:	**3455 Mission Street**
City, ST, Zip:	**Modesto, CA 95355**
Country:	**USA**
Sales Tax:	**None**
Customer Type:	**Building**
Telephone 1:	**209-555-1234**

Sales Info Tab

GL Sales Account:	**400**
Ship Via:	**Fed-Ex**
Pricing Level:	**Price Level 1**
Form Options:	**Default**

Payment & Credit Tab

Terms and Credit:	**2% 10 Days, Net 30 Days**

History Tab

Beginning Balance:	**0**

3. Set up the project for job costing.

4. On January 10, 2010, Robertson Construction Company purchased the following stock items for its inventory: 1,000 feet of lumber, one sink, and 2,400 feet of vinyl flooring. All items were purchased on credit from Steve's Supply Warehouse (Invoice 1220). Use the following information to create inventory records for the items.

Stock Item

Item ID:	**BOARD-5**
Description:	**Lumber**
Item Class:	**Stock item**
Price Level 1:	**2.50**
Last Unit Cost:	**1.50**
Cost Method:	**Average**
GL Sales Acct:	**400**
GL Inventory Acct:	**105**
GL Cost of Sales Acct:	**503**
Item Tax Type:	**2 (Exempt)**
Stocking U/M:	**Foot**
Preferred Vendor ID:	**STEVES-01**

Stock Item

Item *ID*:	**SINK-12**
Description:	**Sink**
Item Class:	**Stock item**
Price Level 1:	**425.00**
Last Unit Cost:	**250.00**
Cost Method:	**Average**
GL Sales Acct:	**400**
GL Inventory Acct:	**105**
GL Cost of Sales Acct:	**503**
Item Tax Type:	**2 (Exempt)**
Stocking U/M:	**Each**
Preferred Vendor ID:	**STEVES-01**

Stock Item

Item *ID*:	**VFLOOR-15**
Description:	**Vinyl Flooring**
Item Class:	**Stock item**
Price Level 1:	**7.50**
Last Unit Cost:	**4.50**
Cost Method:	**Average**
GL Sales Acct:	**400**
GL Inventory Acct:	**105**
GL Cost of Sales Acct:	**503**
Item Tax Type:	**2 (Exempt)**
Stocking U/M:	**Foot**
Preferred Vendor ID:	**STEVES-01**

5. Enter the purchases.

6. Robertson used 1,000 feet of the lumber, the sink, and 500 square feet of vinyl flooring for the Parkview job. Allocate the cost of these inventory items by making an inventory adjustment as of January 15, 2010. (Use 503 as the GL Source Acct when entering the inventory adjustment.)

7. Barbara Williams worked 40 hours on the Parkview job, and Michael Anderson worked 40 hours. Allocate these employees' labor costs ending January 23, 2010 to the job. The check date is January 24, 2010.

8. Print the following reports for the month of January 2010: *Job Ledger* and *Job Profitability Report*.

Problem 2A

Robertson Construction Company accepted a job from Palmdale Offices to build a new office building. The estimated starting date is February 1, 2010, and the estimated ending date is June 1, 2010. Michael Anderson will supervise the project. The job identifier is Palm Office-Job 2. The percentage complete is zero.

Robertson has decided to create phases and cost codes to better track the revenue and expenses associated with this project. It has decided on the following phases and cost types.

Phases:

Phase ID	Description	Cost Type
Plan-01	Planning	Other
Land-03	Landscaping	Labor
Building-02	Building	Use cost codes shown below

Cost Codes:

Cost ID	Description	Cost Type
BUILDMAT-111	Building Materials	Materials
BUILDLAB-110	Building Labor	Labor

1. Open Robertson Construction Company which you updated in Problem 1A.

2. Create a customer account for Palmdale Offices.

    Customer ID: **Palm-100**
    Name: **Palmdale Offices**

General Tab

    Contact: **Jerome Bromberg**
    Account Number: **250**
    Billing Address: **4315 South First Street**
    City, ST, Zip: **Modesto, CA 95355**
    Country: **USA**
    Sales Tax: **None**
    Customer Type: **Building**
    Telephone 1:   **209-555-2143**

Sales Info Tab

    GL Sales Account: **400**
    Ship Via: **Fed-Ex**
    Pricing Level: **Price Level 1**
    Form Options: **Default**

Payment & Credit Tab

    Terms and Credit: **2% 10 Days, Net 30 Days**

History Tab

    Beginning Balance: **0**

3. Set up the project for job costing.

4. Create the phases and cost codes.

5. Print the following reports: *Phase List*, *Cost Code List*, and General Ledger Trial Balance.

Problem 1B

Abelar Construction Company accepted a job from the City of Lodi to repair a storm drain that had been damaged by heavy rains. Abelar wants to use the Jobs Only Method to keep track of the revenue and expenses associated with the project. The revenue is expected to be $15,000, and the expenses are expected to be $8,000. The job identifier is Lodi Drain-Job 1. The estimated starting date is January 5, 2010, and the estimated ending date is March 31, 2010. The percentage of completion is zero (0). Alfred Martinez will supervise the project.

1. Open Abelar Construction Company from the student data disk.

2. Create a customer account for the City of Lodi.

Customer ID:	**Lodi-89**
Name:	**City of Lodi**

General Tab

Contact:	**James Wright**
Account Number:	**2130**
Billing Address:	**34 Main Street**
City, ST, Zip:	**Lodi, CA 95290**
Country:	**USA**
Sales Tax:	**None**
Customer Type:	**Building**
Telephone 1:	**209-555-3423**

Sales Info Tab

GL Sales Account:	**400**
Ship Via:	**Fed-Ex**
Pricing Level:	**Price Level 1**
Form Options:	**Default**

Payment & Credit Tab

Terms and Credit:	**2% 10 Days, Net 30 Days**

History Tab

Beginning Balance:	**0**

3. Set up the project for job costing.

4. On January 10, 2010, Abelar Construction Company purchased the following stock items for its inventory: 400 feet of 24-inch culvert pipe, one drain assembly, and 400 feet of copper wire. All items were purchased on credit from Construction Supply Warehouse (Invoice 2009). Use the following information to create inventory records for the items.

Stock Item

Item I<u>D</u>:	**CULVERT-9**
Description:	**24-Inch Culvert Pipe**
Item Class:	**Stock item**
Price Level 1:	**25.00**
Last Unit Cost:	**15.00**
Cost Method:	**Average**
GL Sales Acct:	**400**
GL Inventory Acct:	**105**
GL Cost of Sales Acct:	**503**
Item Tax Type:	**2 (Exempt)**
Stocking U/M:	**Foot**
Preferred <u>V</u>endor ID:	**CSW-01**

Stock Item

Item I<u>D</u>:	**DRAIN-16**
Description:	**Drain Assembly**
Item Class:	**Stock item**
Price Level 1:	**950.00**
Last Unit Cost:	**500.00**
Cost Method:	**Average**
GL Sales Acct:	**400**
GL Inventory Acct:	**105**
GL Cost of Sales Acct:	**503**
Item Tax Type:	**2 (Exempt)**
Stocking U/M:	**Each**
Preferred <u>V</u>endor ID:	**CSW-01**

Stock Item

Item I<u>D</u>:	**COPWIRE-20**
Description:	**Copper Wire**
Item Class:	**Stock item**
Price Level 1:	**2.00**
Last Unit Cost:	**0.75**
Cost Method:	**Average**
GL Sales Acct:	**400**
GL Inventory Acct:	**105**
GL Cost of Sales Acct:	**503**
Item Tax Type:	**2 (Exempt)**
Stocking U/M:	**Foot**
Preferred <u>V</u>endor ID:	**CSW-01**

5. Enter the purchases.

6. Abelar used 350 feet of the culvert pipe, the drain assembly, and 200 feet of the copper wire for the Lodi job. Allocate the cost of these inventory items by making an inventory adjustment as of January 15, 2010. (Use 503 as the GL Source Acct when entering the inventory adjustment.)

7. Alfred Martinez worked 40 hours on the Lodi job, and Peter Monroe worked 40 hours. Allocate these employees' labor costs ending January 16, 2010 to the job. The check date is January 17, 2010.

8. Print the following reports for the month of January 2010: *Job Ledger* and *Job Profitability Report*.

Problem 2B

Abelar Construction Company accepted a job from Jeremy Lyons to build a new septic tank for a house he is renovating. The estimated starting date is January 11, 2010, and the estimated ending date is February 28, 2010. Alfred Martinez will supervise the project. The job identifier is Lyons Tank-Job 2. The percentage of the job completed is zero.

   Abelar has decided to create phases and cost codes to better track the revenue and expenses associated with this project. It has decided on the following phases and cost types:

Phases:

Phase ID	Description	Cost Type
Plan-01	Planning/Permits	Other
Excav-02	Excavation	Labor
Build-03	Building	Use the cost codes shown below

Cost Codes:

Cost ID	Description	Cost Type
BUILDMAT-111	Building Materials	Materials
BUILDLAB-110	Building Labor	Labor

1. Open Abelar Construction Company which you updated in Problem 1B.

2. Create a customer account for Lyons Renovation.

Customer ID:	**Lyons-90**
Name:	**Lyons Renovation**

General Tab

Contact:	**Jeremy Lyons**
Account Number:	**2150**
Billing Address:	**1278 Boston Street**
City, ST, Zip:	**Modesto, CA 95357**
Country:	**USA**
Sales Tax:	**None**
Customer Type:	**Building**
Telephone 1:	**209-555-4312**

Sales Info Tab

GL Sales Account:	**400**
Ship Via:	**Fed-Ex**
Pricing Level:	**Price Level 1**
Form Options:	**Default**

Payment & Credit Tab
Terms and Credit: **2% 10 Days, Net 30 Days**

History Tab
Beginning Balance: **0**

3. Set up the project for job costing.

4. Create the phases and cost codes.

5. Print the following reports: *Phase List*, *Cost Code List*, and General Ledger Trial Balance.

Cooperative Learning

1. Form groups of three or four students and visit a local construction company to discuss its use of job costing. If possible, determine the level of detail the managers would like to see in the job cost information. For example, do they want to see the information broken down by phase and cost type?

2. In groups of three or four students, visit a meeting of the local chapter of the Institute of Management Accountants (IMA). Find out what types of jobs are available to management accountants in the area. Also find out what courses are necessary for students who want to become management accountants. Visit the Web site www.imanet.org to gain information about the IMA.

Writing and Decision Making

Assume that you work for a construction company and have been given the job of project manager for a $40,000,000 shopping mall that will take several years to complete. Your supervisor wants some insight about how a job costing system operates. In memo format, briefly explain the possible ways that costs can be broken down so that you can closely monitor them throughout the job, recognize revenue and expenses in a timely manner, and determine the profitability of the project.

CHAPTER 12

Fixed Assets

Learning Objectives

1. Understand fixed assets and depreciation

2. Create subsidiary ledger accounts for individual fixed assets

3. Calculate and record the depreciation of fixed assets

4. Make entries to record the disposal of fixed assets

5. Prepare and modify reports showing fixed assets and depreciation

   Note: The chapter shows how to use Peachtree's Fixed Assets module to perform computerized accounting for fixed assets. Please note that the Educational Version of Peachtree 2010 that is packaged with this textbook does not include the Fixed Assets module. Peachtree's Fixed Assets (FAS) module is available; you will only be able to complete Chapter 12 if you download the FAS program from Peachtree at www.peachtree.com/fas2010download.

Software Features

- Set Up Subsidiary Ledger Records for Fixed Assets

- Select a Depreciation Method

- Calculate and Record Depreciation

- Record the Disposal of Fixed Assets

- Prepare Fixed Asset Reports

Remember that assets are divided into several groups. One group consists of **current assets**: cash, assets that will be turned into cash within one year, and assets that will be used up within one year. Current assets include cash, petty cash, accounts receivable, merchandise inventory, supplies, and prepaid insurance.

Another group consists of **fixed assets**. These assets have the following characteristics:

- They have an expected life of more than one year.
- They are intended for use in the business and not for resale to customers.
- They are tangible, which means that they have a physical substance.

Examples of fixed assets are land, buildings, furniture, office equipment, factory machines, automobiles, and trucks. Fixed assets are also known as *plant assets*, *capital assets*, and *property, plant, and equipment*.

In addition to current assets and fixed assets, some businesses have intangible assets and natural resources. **Intangible assets** are long-term assets that have no physical substance, such as patents, trademarks, copyrights, and franchises. **Natural resources** are long-term assets that are removed from the ground, such as oil, natural gas, coal, and timber.

OBJECTIVE 1 — Understand Fixed Assets and Depreciation

A business must set up a general ledger account for each broad class of fixed assets that it owns. It might have general ledger accounts for land, land improvements, buildings, office furniture, office equipment, factory machines, and trucks. These accounts include all items in a class. For example, the Office Furniture account covers desks, chairs, sofas, file cabinets, and bookshelves. The Office Equipment account covers computers, printers, fax machines, copying machines, and telephone systems.

Because the general ledger accounts for fixed assets involve broad classes, most businesses also maintain records for the individual assets. These records form a subsidiary ledger called the **fixed asset ledger**.

Recording the Cost of Fixed Assets

When a fixed asset is purchased, the cost is debited to the appropriate general ledger account and entered in the appropriate subsidiary record. The cost of a fixed asset may be greater than the price paid for the asset. For example:

- The cost of land includes not only the price but also any amounts paid for real estate commissions, legal fees, taxes, removal of old structures, draining, and grading.
- Newly acquired land may require improvements such as sidewalks, fences, and outdoor lighting. (The cost of these items is debited to an account called Land Improvements rather than to the Land account.)
- The cost of a new building includes not only the amount paid for construction but also any fees paid for the planning work of architects and engineers, for permits and inspections, and for insurance during construction.
- The cost of machinery and equipment includes not only the price of the item but also any amounts paid for freight, taxes, installation, and insurance during delivery and installation.

---

current assets Cash, assets that will be turned into cash within one year, and assets that will be used up within one year.

fixed assets Assets that have an expected life of more than one year, used in the business, and are tangible.

intangible assets Long-term assets that have no physical substance.

natural resources Long-term assets that are removed from the ground.

fixed asset ledger A subsidiary ledger that contains records for individual fixed assets.

Recording Depreciation

depreciation The process of allocating the cost of a fixed asset to operations during its estimated useful life.

Remember that **depreciation** is the process of allocating the cost of a fixed asset to operations during its estimated useful life. Because fixed assets help to produce revenue for a business over time, their cost must gradually be recorded as an expense while they are being used. This procedure allows the business to match its revenue and expenses.

All fixed assets except land are subject to depreciation. Land is not depreciated because it is considered to have an indefinite useful life. The other fixed assets have limited lives.

Because land is not subject to depreciation, when land and a building are purchased together for one price, this amount must be divided. One portion is debited to the Land account, and the other portion is debited to the Building account. Similarly, land improvements, which are subject to depreciation, are recorded in a separate account, not in the Land account.

Depreciation is an operating expense for a business. It is recorded as part of the adjusting entries for each accounting period. The adjustment for each class of fixed assets consists of a debit to a depreciation expense account and a credit to an accumulated depreciation account. For example, the depreciation for office equipment is recorded by debiting Depreciation Expense–Office Equipment and crediting Accumulated Depreciation–Office Equipment.

Notice that the account used for the credit part of the entry is not the asset account Office Equipment. Instead, it is Accumulated Depreciation–Office Equipment, a contra asset account. As long as the business owns the office equipment, the asset account shows the cost and the contra asset account shows all depreciation taken. On the balance sheet, both amounts are reported and the balance of the contra asset account is subtracted from the balance of the asset account. The difference between the two balances is the **book value** of the fixed asset.

book value The difference between the cost of a fixed asset and its accumulated depreciation.

Cost of Fixed Asset – Accumulated Depreciation = Book Value

Each class of fixed assets has its own depreciation expense account and its own accumulated depreciation account.

Calculating Depreciation

Various methods are used to calculate depreciation. Most of these methods base depreciation on three basic factors: the cost of a fixed asset, its estimated salvage value, and its estimated useful life.

estimated salvage value The amount that a business expects a fixed asset to be worth at the end of its useful life; also known as *trade-in value, scrap value*, and *residual value*.

estimated useful life The number of years that a business expects a fixed asset to be used in its operations.

- As noted previously, the cost of a fixed asset is the purchase price plus any amounts that must be spent to prepare the asset for use, such as shipping and installation.
- The **estimated salvage value** is the amount that a business expects a fixed asset to be worth at the end of its useful life. Salvage value is also known as *trade-in value, scrap value*, and *residual value*.
- The **estimated useful life** is the number of years that a business expects a fixed asset to be used in its operations.

Depreciation is calculated on a yearly basis. However, if a business owns a fixed asset for less than a year, it takes depreciation for only the amount of time that the asset was in service during the year. This situation often occurs in the year when a fixed asset was purchased and in the year when it is sold or scrapped.

For financial accounting purposes, the four most commonly used depreciation methods are:

- The straight-line method
- The units-of-production method
- The double declining-balance method
- The sum-of-the-years'-digits method

The Straight-Line Method

straight-line method
A method in which an equal amount of depreciation is taken each year.

The **straight-line method** of depreciation allocates an equal amount of depreciation to each year of an asset's useful life. For example, assume that a business buys a new machine for $42,000 on January 1, 2010. The machine has an estimated salvage value of $2,000 and an estimated useful life of four years. The annual depreciation for the machine is therefore $10,000.

$$\text{Cost} - \text{Salvage Value} = \text{Depreciable Cost}$$
$$\$42,000 - \$2,000 = \$40,000$$

$$\text{Depreciable Cost} \div \text{Useful Life} = \text{Annual Depreciation}$$
$$\$40,000 \div 4 \text{ (years)} = \$10,000$$

Table 12–1 shows the depreciation expense, accumulated depreciation, and book value of the machine throughout its life when the straight-line method is used. Notice that at the end of the fourth year (2013), the book value is equal to the estimated salvage value ($2,000). No fixed asset can be depreciated below its salvage value.

TABLE 12–1
An Example of the Straight-Line Depreciation Method

Year	Cost	Depreciation Expense	Accumulated Depreciation	Book Value End of Year
2010	$42,000	$10,000	$10,000	$32,000
2011	42,000	10,000	20,000	22,000
2012	42,000	10,000	30,000	12,000
2013	42,000	10,000	40,000	2,000

Keep in mind that the book value is simply the depreciated cost of a fixed asset. It does not necessarily represent the market value or even the replacement value of the asset.

The Units-of-Production Method

units-of-production method A method that allocates depreciation on the basis of how much work an asset produces.

The **units-of-production method** allocates depreciation on the basis of how much work the asset produces during each year of its useful life. For a factory machine, the work produced might be expressed in hours of operation. For an automobile or truck, it might be expressed in miles driven.

Consider again the machine purchased for $42,000 on January 1, 2010, which has an estimated salvage value of $2,000. Suppose that management expects the useful life of the machine to be 40,000 hours. The depreciation rate for the machine is $1 per hour.

$$\text{Cost} - \text{Salvage Value} = \text{Depreciable Cost}$$
$$\$42,000 - \$2,000 = \$40,000$$

$$\text{Depreciable Cost} \div \text{Useful Life} = \text{Depreciation Rate}$$
$$\$40,000 \div 40,000 \text{ (hours)} = \$1 \text{ per hour}$$

Assume that the machine is used for 9,000 hours in the first year, 11,000 hours in the second year, 12,000 hours in the third year, and 8,000 hours in the fourth year. The amount of depreciation for the first year will be $9,000.

$$\text{Usage} \times \text{Depreciation Rate} = \text{Depreciation}$$
$$9,000 \text{ hours} \times \$1 \text{ per hour} = \$9,000$$

Table 12–2 shows the depreciation expense, accumulated depreciation, and book value for the machine through its life when the units-of-production method is used. Again, the book value at the end of the asset's life (40,000 hours) is $2,000, which is the salvage value.

TABLE 12–2
An Example of the Units-of-Production Depreciation Method

Year	Cost	Hours	Depreciation Expense	Accumulated Depreciation	Book Value End of Year
2010	$42,000	9,000	$ 9,000	$ 9,000	$33,000
2011	42,000	11,000	11,000	20,000	22,000
2012	42,000	12,000	12,000	32,000	10,000
2013	42,000	8,000	8,000	40,000	2,000

The Double Declining-Balance Method

double declining-balance method A method that allocates depreciation at twice the straight-line rate.

accelerated method A method in which more depreciation is taken in the early years of an asset's useful life and less in the later years.

The **double declining-balance method** allocates depreciation at twice the straight-line rate. The doubled rate is applied to the book value of the asset each year. Because the book value decreases from year to year, more depreciation is taken in the early years of the asset's useful life and less depreciation is taken in the later years. Thus, the double declining-balance method is considered an **accelerated method** of depreciation.

Again, assume that a machine is purchased for $42,000 on January 1, 2010, and has an estimated useful life of four years and an estimated salvage value of $2,000. With the double declining-balance method, the salvage value is ignored. The first step in calculating depreciation is to find the straight-line rate and then double it. In this case, the doubled rate is 50%. (The straight-line rate for an asset with a four-year useful life is 25%.)

$$1/4 = 0.25 \times 2 = 0.50 \text{ or } 50\%$$

When the 50% rate is applied to the first year's book value, the depreciation is $21,000.

$$\text{Book Value} \times \text{Depreciation Rate} = \text{Depreciation}$$
$$\$42,000 \times 0.50 = \$21,000$$

In the second year, the book value is $21,000 and the depreciation is $10,500 ($21,000 × 0.50 = $10,500).

Table 12–3 shows the depreciation expense, accumulated depreciation, and book value for the machine throughout its life when the double declining-balance method is used. Notice that in the fourth year, the remaining book value is $2,625, slightly more than the estimated salvage value of $2,000. (Although salvage value is ignored when calculating depreciation with the double declining-balance method, the asset cannot be depreciated below its salvage value.)

TABLE 12–3
An Example of the Double Declining-Balance Depreciation Method

Year	Cost	Rate	Depreciation Expense	Accumulated Depreciation	Book Value End of Year
2010	$42,000	50%	$21,000	$ 21,000	$21,000
2011	42,000	50	10,500	31,500	10,500
2012	42,000	50	5,250	36,750	5,250
2013	42,000	50	2,625	39,375	2,625

The Sum-of-the-Years'-Digits Method

sum-of-the-years'-digits method A method that allocates depreciation on the basis of a fraction that changes each year.

The **sum-of-the-years'-digits method** allocates depreciation on the basis of a fraction that changes for each year of an asset's useful life. This fraction is applied to the depreciable cost of the asset (the cost less the salvage value). Because the sum-of-the-years'-digits method produces more depreciation in the early years and less depreciation in the later years, it is also considered an accelerated method of depreciation.

The denominator of the fraction (the figure at the bottom of the fraction) remains constant. It is the sum of the digits of the years that make up the useful life of the asset. The numerator of the fraction (the figure at the top of the fraction) changes. It is the number of years that remain in the useful life of the asset.

For example, let us look again at the machine purchased for $42,000 on January 1, 2010. This machine has an estimated useful life of four years and an estimated salvage value of $2,000. The sum of the years' digits for the four years of its useful life is 10 (1 + 2 + 3 + 4 = 10). This is the denominator of the fraction that will be used to calculate depreciation for the asset.

The numerator for the first year will be 4 because there are four years remaining in the useful life of the asset. The numerator for the second year will be 3 because there are only three years remaining in its useful life at that point.

The fraction for the first year is 4/10 while the fraction for the second year is 3/10. Therefore, based on a depreciable cost of $40,000 ($42,000 – $2,000), the depreciation expense for the first two years is calculated as follows:

4/10 of $40,000 = $16,000
3/10 of $40,000 = $12,000

Table 12–4 shows the depreciation expense, accumulated depreciation, and book value for the machine throughout its life when the sum-of-the-years'-digits method is used. The book value remaining at the end of the fourth year is always equal to the estimated salvage value.

TABLE 12–4
An Example of the Sum-of-the-Years'-Digits Method

Year	Cost	Fraction	Depreciation Expense	Accumulated Depreciation	Book Value End of Year
2010	$42,000	4/10	$16,000	$ 16,000	$26,000
2011	42,000	3/10	12,000	28,000	14,000
2012	42,000	2/10	8,000	36,000	6,000
2013	42,000	1/10	4,000	40,000	2,000

Accelerated Cost Recovery Systems

The four depreciation methods that we have discussed so far are used for financial accounting purposes. However, when preparing federal income tax returns, businesses must use either the **accelerated cost recovery system (ACRS)** or the **modified accelerated cost recovery system (MACRS)** to calculate depreciation. The federal government has mandated the use of these two methods to calculate depreciation for most types of fixed assets. ACRS applies to assets placed in service between 1981 and 1986. MACRS applies to assets placed in service after 1986.

The ACRS and MACRS apply to all types of fixed assets. These methods are intended to encourage businesses to purchase new fixed assets by providing quicker depreciation than the other accelerated methods. Both of these methods operate in a similar way, with just the details differing:

- Each method assigns different types of fixed assets to classes. The classes have specified cost recovery periods rather than useful lives. With the MACRS, the cost recovery periods of personal property are 3, 5, 7, 10, 15, and 20 years. For example, automobiles and light trucks have a cost recovery period of 5 years. Office equipment has a cost recovery period of 7 years. Real property (real estate) have cost recovery periods of 27.5 and 39 years.
- Each method ignores salvage value. The cost of the asset is fully depreciated.
- Each method uses accelerated depreciation in the early years of the cost recovery period and then switches to straight-line depreciation in the later years.
- Each method uses an approach called the **half-year convention** for the first year. No matter when the asset is placed in service during the first year, the rate for the first year assumes that the asset has been owned for half a year.
- The federal government publishes a table for each method that shows the year-by-year percentage of the cost of an asset that a business can take as depreciation. A portion of the MACRS table is shown in Table 12–5. (The percentages after year 6 and for the entire 15-year and 20-year classes have been omitted.)

accelerated cost recovery system (ACRS) A depreciation method used for federal income tax purposes that is applied to assets placed in service between 1981 and 1986.

modified accelerated cost recovery system (MACRS) A depreciation method used for federal income tax purposes that is applied to assets placed in service after 1986.

half-year convention An approach used by ACRS and MACRS that allocates depreciation for half a year during the first year an asset is owned.

TABLE 12–5
MACRS Depreciation Percentages

Recovery Year	Recovery Period			
	3-Year	5-Year	7-Year	10-Year
1	33.33%	20.00%	14.29%	10.00%
2	44.45	32.00	24.49	18.00
3	14.81	19.20	17.49	14.40
4	7.41	11.52	12.49	11.52
5		11.52	8.93	9.22
6		5.76	8.92	7.37

To see how MACRS works, assume that the machine purchased for $42,000 on January 1, 2010, falls into the class that has a 5-year cost recovery period. Because of the half-year convention, the machine is actually depreciated for 6 years. The first and last years are considered half years. Table 12–6 provides an example of depreciation using the MACRS method.

TABLE 12-6
An Example of MACRS
Depreciation

Year	Cost	Rate	Depreciation Expense	Accumulated Depreciation	Book Value End of Year
2010	$42,000	20.00%	$ 8,400	$ 8,400	$33,600
2011	42,000	32.00	13,440	21,840	20,160
2012	42,000	19.20	8,064	29,904	12,096
2013	42,000	11.52	4,838	34,742	7,258
2014	42,000	11.52	4,838	39,580	2,420
2015	42,000	5.76	2,420	42,000	—

Check point

1. What is depreciation?
2. Name four financial accounting methods for calculating depreciation.

Answers

1. *Depreciation is the process of allocating the cost of a fixed asset to operations during its estimated useful life.*
2. *Four financial accounting methods for calculating depreciation are the straight-line method, the units-of-production method, the double declining-balance method, and the sum-of-the-years'-digits method.*

OBJECTIVE 2 — Create Subsidiary Ledger Records for Individual Fixed Assets

Wardwood Construction Company currently owns one piece of equipment—a versatile machine that serves as an excavator, backhoe, and bull-dozer. This machine was purchased for $112,000 and recorded in a general ledger account called Equipment. Wardwood's general ledger also contains an Accumulated Depreciation–Equipment account and a Depreciation Expense–Equipment account. These two accounts are used to make adjusting entries for depreciation.

Because of its limited resources, Wardwood currently leases any other fixed assets that it needs such as a pickup truck to transport materials to jobs. Later, as its finances improve, Wardwood plans to purchase additional fixed assets.

As of the current accounting period, Feb 01, 2010 to Feb 28, 2010, Wardwood has decided to use the Peachtree Fixed Assets module that comes with Peachtree Complete Accounting 2010 to maintain asset records and to calculate and record depreciation.

There are three major tasks to using the Peachtree Fixed Assets module:

1. Set up a new company in the Peachtree Fixed Assets module and map (link) it to Peachtree Accounting.
2. Create a new subsidiary ledger record for a fixed asset in the Fixed Assets module.
3. Calculate and record depreciation.

Setting Up the Peachtree Fixed Assets Module

Take the following steps to set up the Peachtree Fixed Assets module.

Step 1:
Download the Peachtree Fixed Assets Module (FAS) from Peachtree at www.peachtree.com/fas2010download.

Step 2:
Open Chp. 12 – Wardwood Construction Company in Peachtree Complete Accounting 2010 and minimize the screen.

HINT

Double-click the *FAS for Peachtree* icon instead if it is on the desktop.

Step 3:
At the Windows desktop, click Start, *All Programs, FAS Solutions, FAS for Peachtree by Sage*, and then click *FAS for Peachtree by Sage*.

Step 4:
Click File from the main Menu bar of the FAS for Peachtree by Sage window.

Step 5:
Click *New Company* from the drop-down list.

Step 6:
Click <u>N</u>ext from the New Company Wizard window as shown in figure 12–1.

FIGURE 12–1
New Company Wizard

Step 7:
Click <u>N</u>ext to accept the default database.

Step 8:
Key **Chp. 12 – Wardwood Construction Co.** in the *Company Name* box, accept the starting system number, and click <u>N</u>ext.

Step 9:
Enter **01/01/09** in the *Start Of Business Date* box and click <u>N</u>ext. (Accept December as the default for Month of Fiscal Year End.) Wardwood began operations in January 2009; however, it switched from a manual accounting system to Peachtree in January 2010. Wardwood has beginning balances.

Step 10:
Click Finish to complete the New Company Setup.

Step 11:
Click the Map to Peachtree button at the bottom of the Edit Company window of the FAS for Peachtree module.

Step 12:
Select Chp. 12 – Wardwood Construction Company from the Link to Peachtree Company window, as shown in figure 12–2.

FIGURE 12–2
Wardwood Construction
Company Selected

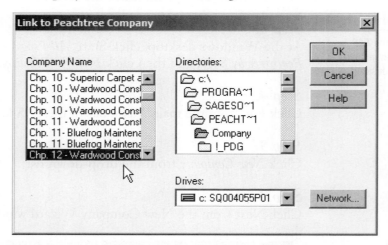

Note: The company folder may be located in a different directory depending on where the student data files were saved.

Step 13:
Click OK to link Chp. 12 – Wardwood Construction Company to FAS for Peachtree.

Step 14:
Click OK at the bottom of the FAS for Peachtree by Sage, Edit Company window to complete the New Company setup process.

Creating a Subsidiary Ledger Record for an Existing Fixed Asset

Take the following steps to create a subsidiary ledger record for an existing fixed asset.

Step 1:
Click File and then *Enable Wizards* from the FAS for Peachtree by Sage main Menu bar.

Step 2:
Check *New Asset Wizard* if a check mark does not appear next to New Asset Wizard.

Step 3:
Click Asset and then *New* from the FAS for Peachtree by Sage main Menu bar.

Step 4:
Click <u>N</u>ext from the New Asset Wizard window.

Step 5:
Click <u>N</u>ext to accept none for the template.

Step 6:
Key **Excavator** in the *Description* field.

Step 7:
Key **001** in the *Co Asset No* field.

Step 8:
Key **EQ** in the *Class* field. (EQ represents Equipment.)

Step 9:
Key **Main Bldg** in the *Location* field.

Step 10:
Key **George Clark** in the *Custodian* field as shown in figure 12–3.

FIGURE 12–3
New Asset Wizard
Completed General
Information Window

Step 11:
Click <u>N</u>ext.

HINT

You may need to close and reopen FAS for Peachtree to synchronize the modules.

Step 12:

At the *G/L Asset Acct No* field, click the arrow, and then click *108 Equipment*, as shown in figure 12–4.

FIGURE 12–4
108 Equipment Selected

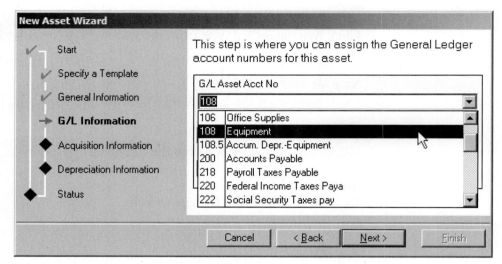

Step 13:

At the *G/L Expense Acct No* field, click the arrow, and then click *510 Depreciation Expense–Equipment*, as shown in figure 12–5.

FIGURE 12–5
510 Depreciation
Expense–Equipment
Selected

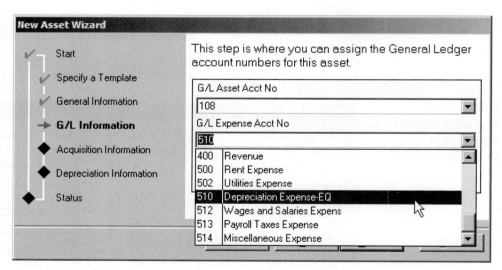

Step 14:

At the *G/L Accum Acct No* field, click the arrow, and then click *108.5 Accum. Depreciation–Equipment*, as shown in figure 12–6. Click Next.

FIGURE 12–6
108.5 Accum.
Depreciation–Equipment
Selected

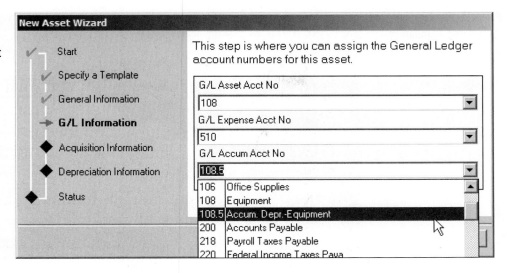

The FAS for Peachtree module automatically calculates depreciation for financial accounting purposes, federal income tax purposes, and other purposes. Wardwood Construction Company wants to keep track of depreciation for financial accounting purposes at this time.

Step 15:
Key **112,000.00** in the *Acquisition Value* field.

Step 16:
At the *Acquisition Date* and the *Placed In Service Date* fields click the drop-down arrow, and then select *01/01/09*.

Step 17:
Key **4323** in the *Purchase Order No* field.

Step 18:
Key **General Dynamics** in the *Vendor/Mfg* field.

Step 19:
Key **GHU7789965** in the *Mfg Serial No* field.

Step 20:
At the *Warranty Date* field click the drop-down arrow, and then enter **01/01/14**, as shown in figure 12–7.

FIGURE 12–7
Completed Acquisition
Information

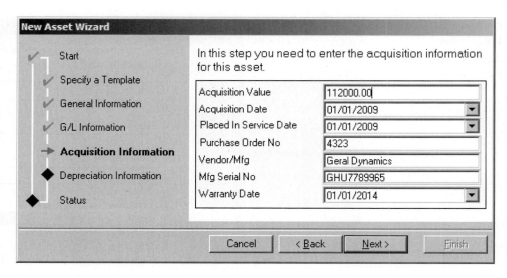

Step 21:
Click Next.

Step 22:
Click *Personal, General* from the Property Type drop-down list.

Step 23:
Click AD (ADS Straight Line) from the *Depreciation Method* field.

Step 24:
Key **05 yrs 00 mos** in the *Estimated Life* field and **05 yrs 00 mos** in the *ADS Life* field, as shown in figure 12–8.

FIGURE 12–8
Completed Depreciation
Information

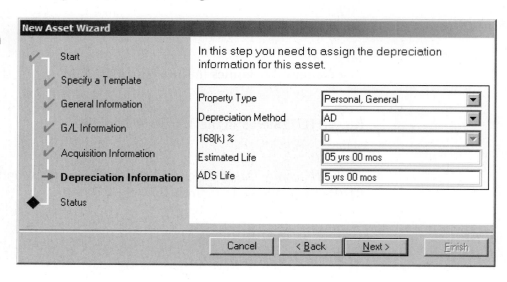

Step 25:
Click <u>N</u>ext and then <u>F</u>inish.

Note: Enter the data for the next five steps under the Internal Column.

Step 26:
Key **100** in the *Bus Use* % field if it is not already entered under the Internal Column.

Step 27:
Key **52,000.00** in the *Salvage* field.

Step 28:
Key **01/2010** in the *Beg Date* field.

Step 29:
Key **1000** in the *Beg YTD* field. This amount represents the depreciation for January 2010. Remember that Wardwood is going to use the Fixed Assets module beginning with February 2010.

Step 30:
Key **13,000** in the *Beg Accm* field. This amount represents the total accumulated depreciation through January 2010 ($12,000 for Fiscal Year 2009, and $1,000 for January 2010). Compare your work with figure 12–9.

FIGURE 12–9
Completed Fixed Asset
Information

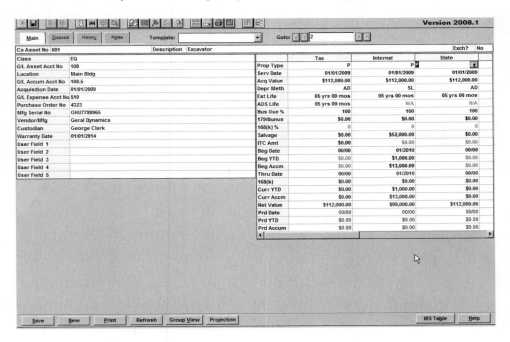

Step 31:
Click <u>S</u>ave at the bottom of the Asset-[1] window.

Step 32:
Exit FAS for Peachtree.

Creating a Subsidiary Ledger Record for a New Fixed Asset

February 1, 2010, Wardwood Construction Company purchased a new pressure washing system for $4,500 on credit from BMC Supply Company (Invoice 33299). Wardwood estimates that the pressure washing system will have a useful life of four years and no salvage value. Record the purchase in Peachtree Complete Accounting.

Step 1:

Open Chp. 12 – Wardwood Construction Company in Peachtree Complete Accounting if it is not already open.

Step 2:

Record the purchase of the pressure washing system using the Purchases/ Receive Inventory window using 108 as the GL Account. Refer to the purchase data information above.

Step 3:

Minimize Peachtree Complete Accounting 2010.

Step 4:

Open the FAS for Peachtree module. Click Asset and then click New.

Step 5:

Click *Don't show me this wizard to create new assets* from the New Asset Wizard window and Cancel to close the wizard window.

Step 6:

Click the *New Asset* icon (the last icon on the left side of the toolbar). The New Asset worksheet appears, as shown in figure 12–10.

FIGURE 12–10
New Asset Worksheet

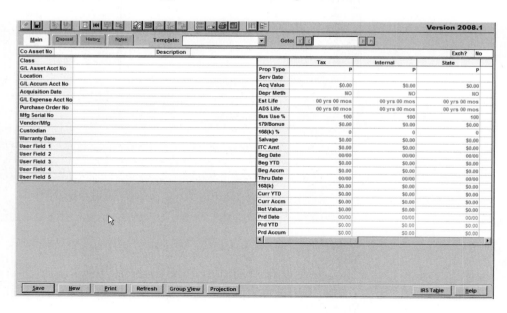

Step 7:

Use the following information to create the record for the new fixed asset:

Co Asset No:	**002**
Description:	**Pressure Washer**
Class:	**EQ**
G/L Asset Acct No:	**108**
Location:	**Main Bldg**
G/L Accum Acct No:	**108.5**
Acquisition Date:	**02/01/10**
G/L Expense Acct No:	**510**
Purchase Order No:	**004569**
Mfg Serial No:	**HHT334**
Vendor/Mfg:	**Honda**
Custodian:	**George Clark**
Warranty Date:	**02/01/14**
Prop Type:	**P** (Use the Internal Column for the remaining entries.)
Serv Date:	**02/01/10**
Acq Value:	**$4,500**
Depr Meth:	**SL**
Est Life:	**04 years 00 mos**
Bus Use %:	**100**
Salvage Value:	
Beg Date:	
Beg YTD:	
Beg Accm:	

Step 8:

Click the *Save Asset* icon (second icon from left) on the main Menu toolbar and exit the FAS module.

C h e c k   p o i n t

1. For what tasks is the Fixed Assets module of Peachtree used?
2. What type of ledger is the fixed asset ledger?

Answers

1. *The Fixed Assets module of Peachtree is used to maintain asset records and to calculate and record depreciation.*
2. *The fixed asset ledger is a subsidiary ledger with records for individual fixed assets.*

Practice Objective 2

Bluefrog Maintenance Company, as of February 2010, wants to use the Fixed Assets module of Peachtree to maintain records of its fixed assets and calculate depreciation. Bluefrog currently owns only one fixed asset, a truck that appears in the Equipment account (108). This truck cost $42,000 and has accumulated depreciation of $8,666.67 through January 31, 2010. Recall that Bluefrog converted from a manual accounting system to Peachtree on January 1, 2010.

Step 1:
Open Chp. 12 – Bluefrog Maintenance Company in Peachtree Complete Accounting 2010 and then minimize the screen.

Step 2:
Start FAS for Peachtree Accounting.

Step 3:
Create Chp. 12 – Bluefrog Maintenance Company as a new company in FAS for Peachtree. Use 01/01/09 as the start date. Remember to map (link) to Peachtree.

Step 4:
Use the following information to set up the asset account:

Co Asset No:	**001**
Description:	**Maintenance Vehicle**
Class:	**EQ**
G/L Asset Acct No:	**112**
Location:	**Garage**
G/L Accum Acct No:	**112.5**
Acquisition Date:	**01/01/09**
G/L Expense Acct No:	**510**
Purchase Order No:	**8569**
Mfg Serial No:	**GM433234**
Vendor/Mfg:	**General Motors**
Custodian:	**Stanley Smith**
Warranty Date:	**01/01/14**
Prop Type:	**T** (Use the Internal Column)
Serv Date:	**01/01/09**
Acq Value:	**$42,000**
Depr Meth:	**SL**
Est Life:	**05 yrs 00 mos**
Bus Use %:	**100**
Salvage Value:	**2000.00**
Beg Date:	**01/2010**
Beg YTD:	**$666.67**
Beg Accm:	**$8,666.67**

Step 5:
Click the *Save* icon.

On February 28, 2010, Bluefrog Maintenance Company purchased a new mailing system for $9,500 on credit from Office Depot (Invoice 47796). Bullfrog estimates that the mailing system will have a salvage value of $2,500 and a useful life of five years.

Step 6:
Open Chp. 12 – Bluefrog Maintenance Company in Peachtree Complete Accounting if it is not already open.

Step 7:
Record the purchase of the mailing system using the Purchases/Receive Inventory window using 112 as the GL Account. Refer to the purchase data information above.

Step 8:
Use the following information to set up the asset record for the mailing system in the FAS for Peachtree module:

Co Asset No:	**002**
Description:	**Mailing System**
Class:	**EQ**
G/L Asset Acct No:	**112**
Location:	**Office**
G/L Accum Acct No:	**112.5**
Acquisition Date:	**02/28/10**
G/L Expense Acct No:	**510**
Purchase Order No:	**6985**
Mfg Serial No:	**M6654**
Vendor/Mfg:	**Motorola**
Custodian:	**Stanley Smith**
Warranty Date:	**02/28/14**
Prop Type:	**P** (Use the Internal Column for the remaining entries.)
Serv Date:	**02/28/10**
Acq Value:	**$9,500**
Depr Meth:	**SL**
Est Life:	**05 yrs 00 mos**
Bus Use %:	**100**
Salvage Value:	**$2,500.00**
Beg Date:	
Beg YTD:	
Beg Accm:	

Step 9:
Click the *Save Asset* (diskette) icon and Exit.

OBJECTIVE 3 — Calculate and Record the Depreciation of Fixed Assets

Wardwood Construction Company wants to calculate and record depreciation for the excavator and the pressure washing system as of March 31, 2010. The FAS for Peachtree Fixed Assets module will make the necessary calculations automatically and transfer the information to the general journal and general ledger.

Calculating Depreciation

Step 1:
Open Chp. 12 – Wardwood Construction Company in both the Peachtree Fixed Assets module and Peachtree Complete Accounting.

Step 2:
In the FAS for Peachtree module, click Depreciation and then *Depreciate* from the main Menu toolbar.

Step 3:
Click Active Assets from the <u>G</u>roup drop-down list if it is not already selected.

Step 4:
Select Internal from the Books list.

Step 5:
Key **03/2010** in the *Calculate depreciation through* field box.

Step 6:
Click *Update current reporting period for selected books* in the Calculation section.

Step 7:
Click Send to *Window*, if needed, as shown in figure 12–11.

FIGURE 12–11
Completed Depreciate
Window

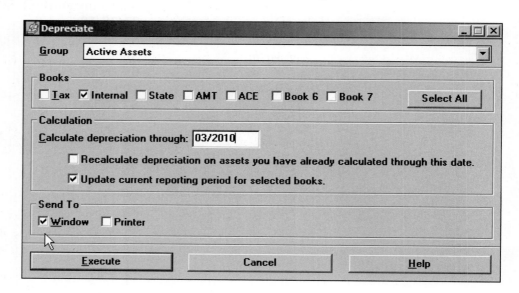

Step 8:

Click Execute and review the report shown in figure 12–12.

FIGURE 12–12
Depreciation Expense
Report

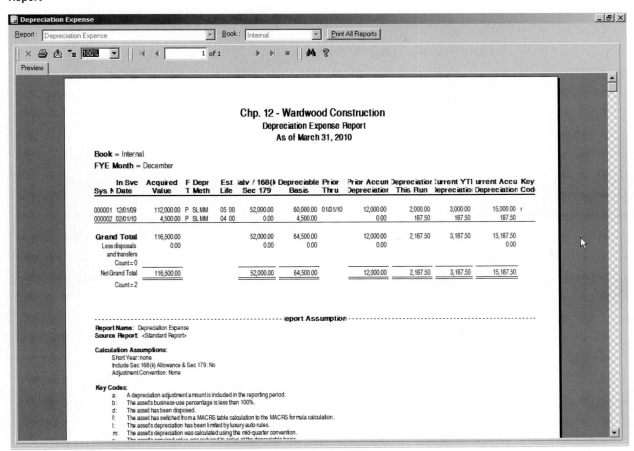

Step 9:

Close the Depreciation Expense Report and Depreciate window.

Transferring Depreciation to the General Journal and General Ledger

HINT

You MUST have Wardwood open before starting Peachtree FAS.

You can use the FAS for Peachtree Fixed Assets module to automatically record depreciation expense in the general journal and post it to the general ledger.

Step 1:

Open Chp. 12 – Wardwood Construction Company in both the Peachtree Fixed Assets module and Peachtree Complete Accounting if it is not already open.

Step 2:
At the FAS for Peachtree window of the Fixed Assets module, click Depreciation and Post Depreciation from the tool bar.

Step 3:
Click *Active Assets* from the <u>G</u>roup drop-down list.

Step 4:
Click *Internal* from the <u>B</u>ook drop-down list.

Step 5:
Key **3/31/2010** in the *P<u>e</u>riod Posting Date* field.

Step 6:
Key **3/31/2010** in the *Journal Entry Date* field, as shown in figure 12–13.

FIGURE 12–13
Completed Post
Depreciation Window

Step 7:
Click Preview from the Post Depreciation window and review the report.

Step 8:
Close the General Ledger Posting Preview report.

Step 9:
At the Post Depreciation window, click Post.

Step 10:
Maximize Chp. 12 – Wardwood Construction Company in Peachtree Complete Accounting 2010.

Step 11:
Click Reports & Forms and then *General Ledger* from the main Menu toolbar.

Step 12:
Select General Journal from the General Ledger: Account Information section and then click Options.

Step 13:
Select the period From: *Mar 1, 2010* To: *Mar 31, 2010* and click OK.

Step 14:

Review the General Journal report you prepared with the one shown in figure 12–14 and close the General Journal window.

FIGURE 12–14
General Journal Entries
for Depreciation Expense

Page: 1

Chp. 12 - Wardwood Construction Company
General Journal
For the Period From Mar 1, 2010 to Mar 31, 2010
Filter Criteria includes: Report order is by Date. Report is printed with Accounts having Zero Amounts and with shortened descriptions and in Detail Format.

Date	Account ID	Reference	Trans Description	Debit Amt	Credit Amt
3/31/10	510	FAS post 03/	Depr Expense: Period Ending 03/10	2,000.00	
	515		Depr Expense: Period Ending 03/10	187.50	
	108.5		Depr Expense: Period Ending 03/10		2,000.00
	110.5		Depr Expense: Period Ending 03/10		187.50
		Total		2,187.50	2,187.50

Step 15:

Close Chp. 12 – Wardwood Construction Company.

Practice Objective 3

Bluefrog Maintenance Company wants to calculate and record depreciation through June 30, 2010.

Check point

1. What journal is used to record depreciation?
2. After the Peachtree Fixed Assets module is opened, what steps are needed to calculate the depreciation of an asset?

Answers
1. *The general journal is used to record depreciation.*
2. *The steps needed are click Depreciation, then Depreciate, complete the Depreciate window, and then click Execute.*

Step 1:

Open Chp. 12 – Bluefrog Maintenance Company in the Peachtree Fixed Assets module and in Peachtree Complete Accounting.

Step 2:

Calculate the internal book depreciation as of June 30, 2010.

Step 3:

Preview the *Depreciation Expense Report* as of June 30, 2010. Your report should look like figure 12–15.

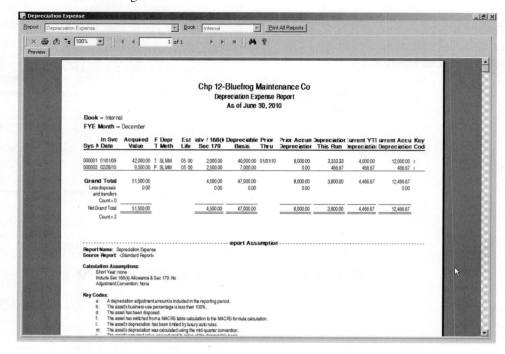

Step 4:

Post the depreciation to the general ledger as of June 30, 2010.

Step 5:

Close Bluefrog Maintenance Company.

OBJECTIVE 4 — Make Entries to Record the Disposal of Fixed Assets

Remember that all fixed assets except land have limited lives. Eventually, they wear out or become obsolete, or their owners want to replace them with newer, more efficient models. When a fixed asset is no longer useful, a business will dispose of the asset by selling it, trading it in for a new asset, or scrapping it if it has no remaining value.

Suppose that Wardwood Construction Company decides to sell the excavator that it owns. On March 31, 2010, it receives $120,000 for the excavator. Wardwood must determine whether there is a gain or loss on this transaction and then record the disposal in its accounting records.

When a firm disposes of a fixed asset, it must bring depreciation on the asset up to date. Then it can find the book value of the asset and determine whether the sale produced a gain or loss.

In the case of the excavator sold by Wardwood Construction Company, the depreciation entry made on March 31, 2010, results in accumulated depreciation of $15,000 and a book value of $97,000. Remember that the book value of a fixed asset is the difference between its cost and its accumulated depreciation. The cost of the excavator was $112,000. The book value is therefore $97,000 ($112,000 − $15,000 = $97,000).

If the selling price of a fixed asset is greater than its book value, there is a gain on the sale. If the selling price of a fixed asset is less than its book value, there is a loss on the sale. Because Wardwood sold its excavator for $120,000 and the book value of the machine is $97,000, the firm has a gain of $23,000.

The gain on the sale of a fixed asset is considered other (non-operating) income because it does not result from the normal operations of a business. It is therefore recorded in an account called Gain on Disposal of Fixed Assets. Similarly, the loss on the sale of a fixed asset is considered other (non-operating) expense. It is recorded in an account called Loss on Disposal of Fixed Assets.

The sale of the excavator by Wardwood Construction Company requires a debit of $120,000 to Cash, a debit of $15,000 to Accumulated Depreciation–Equipment, a credit of $112,000 to Equipment, and a credit of $23,000 to Gain on Disposal of Fixed Assets. The effects of this transaction are as follows:

- The debit to Cash records the amount received for the excavator.
- The debit to Accumulated Depreciation–Equipment removes the accumulated depreciation of the excavator from the accounting records.
- The credit to Equipment removes the cost of the excavator from the accounting records.
- The credit to Gain on Disposal of Fixed Assets records the income earned from the sale of the excavator.

Recording the Disposal of a Fixed Asset at a Gain

Wardwood Construction Company does not yet have a Gain on Disposal of Fixed Assets account in its general ledger. Therefore, it must now create this account.

Step 1:
Open Chp. 12 – Wardwood Construction Company in Peachtree Complete Accounting.

Step 2:
Create the following general ledger account:

Account ID:	**452**
Description:	**Gain on Disposal of Fxd Assets**
Account Type:	**Income**

Step 3:
Minimize the Peachtree window.

Step 4:
Open Chp. 12 – Wardwood Construction Company in the FAS for Peachtree Fixed Assets module.

Step 5:
Double-click on Co Asset 001 and the Asset-[1] window appears.

Step 6:
Click the Disposal tab.

Step 7:
Key **03/31/10** in the *Disposal Date* field.

Step 8:
Click *Sale* from the Disposal Method drop-down list.

Step 9:
Key **120,000.00** in the *Cash Proceeds* field.

Step 10:
Click Save and then review your disposal entries with figure 12–16.

FIGURE 12–16
Partial View of the Asset
Disposal Window

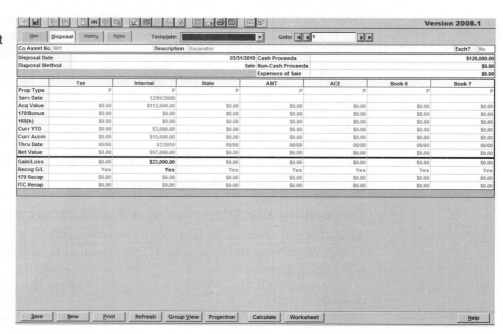

HINT

If you dispose of the wrong asset, you can reinstate it by selecting Reset Depreciation and then entering a date before the disposal date.

Viewing the Disposed Assets Report

The *Disposed Assets Report* shows detailed information about a fixed asset that has been sold, traded in, or scrapped. This information includes the cost, the accumulated depreciation, the net proceeds (the sum received for the asset), the book value, and the amount realized (the gain or loss on the disposal).

Step 1:
In the FAS for Peachtree Fixed Assets module, click Reports, click Standard Reports, and then click Disposal.

Step 2:
Click *Active Assets* from the Group drop-down list.

Step 3:
Click *Internal* from the *Books* field. (Uncheck any other check marks.)

Step 4:
Click *Asset Count* and *Detail, subtotals and totals* from the *Configuration* field.

Step 5:
Select *Send to window* from the *Run Options* field.

Step 6:
Click *Run Report* to view the report in figure 12–17.

FIGURE 12–17
Disposal Report

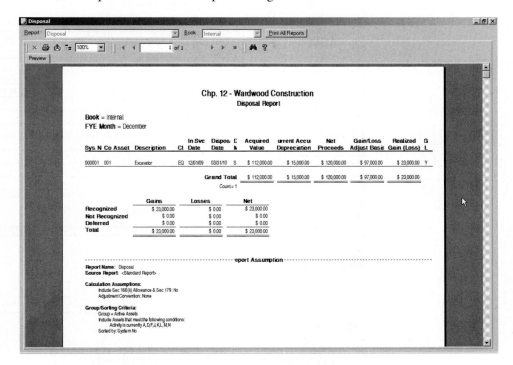

Step 7:
Click Save at the Report Definition window and then minimize or close the Asset window.

Entering the Disposal of a Fixed Asset in the General Journal
You must now enter the disposal of the excavator in Wardwood Construction Company's general journal and post the information to its general ledger.

Step 1:
Open or restore Peachtree Complete Accounting.

Step 2:
Click Tasks and then click *General Journal Entry*.

Step 3:
At the General Journal Entry window, click the *calendar* icon and then select *Mar 31, 2010*.

Step 4:
Key **Asset 001 Disposal** in the *Reference* field.

Step 5:
Record the general journal entry shown in figure 12–18.

FIGURE 12–18
General Journal Entry for
Disposal of Asset 001

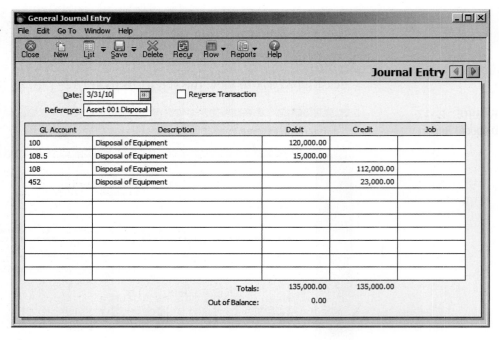

GL Account	Description	Debit	Credit	Job
100	Disposal of Equipment	120,000.00		
108.5	Disposal of Equipment	15,000.00		
108	Disposal of Equipment		112,000.00	
452	Disposal of Equipment		23,000.00	
	Totals:	135,000.00	135,000.00	
	Out of Balance:	0.00		

Step 6:
Click Save and then Close.

C h e c k p o i n t

1. What is the book value of a fixed asset?
2. What type of income is a gain on the disposal of a fixed asset?

Answers
1. *The book value of a fixed asset is the difference between its cost and its accumulated depreciation.*
2. *A gain on the disposal of a fixed asset is considered other (nonoperating) income.*

P r a c t i c e O b j e c t i v e 4

On June 30, 2010, Bluefrog Maintenance Company decides to dispose of the truck that it owns in order to purchase a new model. Bluefrog sells the truck for $40,000 in cash. The current book value is $30,000.

Step 1:
Open Chp. 12 – Bluefrog Maintenance Company in both the Peachtree Fixed Assets module and Peachtree Complete Accounting.

Step 2:
Create the following general ledger account.

Account ID:	**452**
Description:	**Gain on Disposal of Fxd Assets**
Account Type:	**Income**

Step 3:
Enter the disposal in the Fixed Assets module for Asset 001.

Step 4:
Record the disposal of the truck in the general journal and post to the general ledger. Your General Journal Entry window should look like the one shown in figure 12–19.

FIGURE 12–19
Completed General
Journal Entry for
Disposal of Equipment

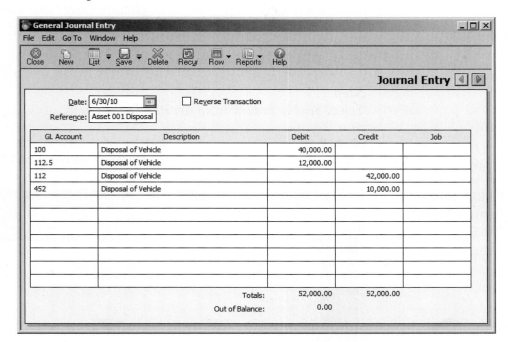

OBJECTIVE 5 — Prepare Reports Showing Fixed Assets and Depreciation

The Peachtree Fixed Assets module produces a variety of reports. Management can use these reports for many purposes. For example, management can periodically review the age of all fixed assets and develop plans to replace the older, less efficient ones. Because fixed assets are costly, many businesses set up long-term budgets for acquiring new fixed assets.

You have already viewed two of the reports available from the Peachtree Fixed Assets module: the *Depreciation Expense Report* and the *Disposal Report*. You will now prepare the *Quarterly Acquisition Report*, which shows information about all fixed assets acquired during the period covered by the report.

On March 31, 2010, Wardwood Construction Company wants to review the fixed assets that it acquired during the first three months of 2010. Follow the steps outlined below to prepare this report.

Step 1:
Open Chp. 12 – Wardwood Construction Company in the FAS for Peachtree Fixed Assets module.

Step 2:
Click Reports and *Standard Reports* from the FAS for Peachtree main menu.

Step 3:
Click *Quarterly Acquisition* from the drop-down list.

Step 4:
Click *Active Assets* from the *Group* field selection list.

Step 5:
Click *Internal* from the *Books* field. (Remove any other checks.)

Step 6:
Enter **3/31/2010** in the *Other Date* field.

Step 7:
Select *Send to window* from the *Run Options* field.

Step 8:
Click *Run* Report and compare your report with figure 12–20.

FIGURE 12–20
Quarterly Acquisition
Report

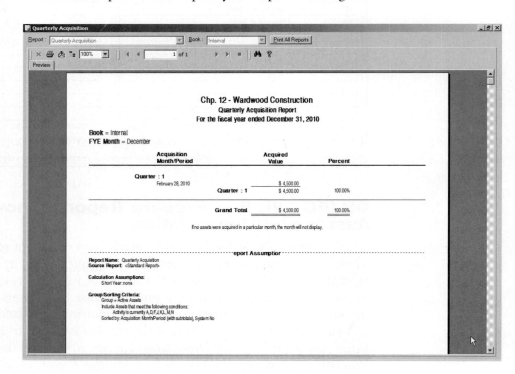

Step 9:
Close the report window.

Check point

1. Name three of the reports produced by the Peachtree Fixed Assets module.
2. What report would management consult to review the cost of recently purchased fixed assets?

Answers
1. *Three reports are the Depreciation Expense Report, the Disposal Report, and the Quarterly Acquisition Report.*
2. *Management would consult the Quarterly Acquisition Report.*

Practice Objective 5

Bluefrog Maintenance Company wants to prepare the *Disposal Report*.

Step 1:
Open Chp. 12 – Bluefrog Maintenance Company in the Peachtree Fixed Assets module and Peachtree Accounting.

Step 2:
Print the report. Your printout should look like figure 12–21.

FIGURE 12–21
Disposal Report for
Bluefrog Maintenance
Company

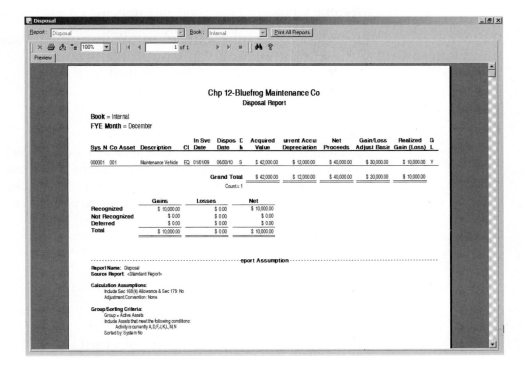

End of Chapter Review

Software Command Summary

Create Subsidiary Ledger Records	Asset, New, Enter the New Asset Information
Calculate Depreciation	Depreciation, Depreciate, Select Book, Select Depreciation Period, Execute
Post Depreciation	Depreciation, Post Depreciation, Post
Record the Disposal of Fixed Assets	Select Co Asset No, Disposal tab, Enter the Disposal Information
Undo the Disposal Entry	Reset Depreciation, Enter a Date Before the Disposal Date
Prepare Reports	Reports, Select Report Type, Select Book and Report Date, Run Report

Projects and Problems
Content Check

Multiple Choice: Choose only one response for each question.

1. Which of the following methods allocates an equal amount of depreciation each year?
   A. Sum-of-the-years'-digits method
   B. Double declining-balance method
   C. Straight-line method
   D. Units-of-production method

2. Which of the following statements about fixed assets is *not* true?
   A. Fixed assets are intended for use in the operations of a business.
   B. Fixed assets have an estimated useful life of more than one year.
   C. Fixed assets are acquired for resale to customers.
   D. Fixed assets are tangible.

3. Depreciation is taken on all fixed assets except
   A. land.
   B. land improvements.
   C. buildings.
   D. equipment and machinery.

4. The difference between the cost of a fixed asset and its accumulated depreciation is the
   A. purchase price.
   B. book value.
   C. salvage value.
   D. selling price.

5. Depreciable cost is
   A. Cost – Depreciation Expense.
   B. Cost – Accumulated Depreciation.
   C. Cost – Salvage Value.
   D. Accumulated Depreciation – Salvage Value.

Short-Essay Response: Provide a detailed answer for each question.

1. What is depreciation? Why must businesses record depreciation?
2. What is accelerated depreciation? Name two financial accounting methods for calculating depreciation that are accelerated.
3. What is the modified accelerated cost recovery system? When is this method used?
4. How is the sale of a fixed asset at a gain recorded? What general ledger accounts are debited and credited?
5. Why does the Fixed Assets module of Peachtree provide for the use of both financial accounting and tax accounting methods of depreciation?

Case Problems

Problem 1A

On January 1, 2010, Flores Construction Company decides to use the Fixed Assets module of Peachtree (FAS for Peachtree) to keep records of its fixed assets. The only fixed asset currently on its books is construction equipment. This construction equipment cost $16,000, has an estimated salvage value of $1,000, and has an estimated useful life of four years. The equipment was purchased on January 1, 2010.

1. Open Flores Construction Company from the student data disk and then create Flores Construction Company in FAS for Peachtree. Remember to map to Peachtree. *Note:* Enter December as the fiscal year ending month and 01/01/10 as the business start date.

2. Use the following information to create a subsidiary ledger record for the construction equipment in FAS.

Co Asset No:	**001**
Description:	**Construction Equipment**
Class:	**EQ**
G/L Asset Acct No:	**108**
Location:	**Storage**
G/L Accum Acct No:	**108.5**
Acquisition Date:	**01/01/10**
G/L Expense Acct No:	**510**
Purchase Order No:	**1482**
Mfg Serial No:	**MHS748392**
Vendor/Mfg:	**Heavy Duty Solutions**
Custodian:	**Michael Anderson**
Warranty Date:	**01/01/14**
Prop Type:	**P** (Use the Internal Column)
Serv Date:	**01/01/10**
Acq Value:	**$16,000**

Depr Meth:	**SL**
Est Life:	**04 yrs 00 mos**
Bus Use %:	**100**
Salvage Value:	**$1,000**
Beg Date:	
Beg YTD:	
Beg Accum:	

HINT

This is the purchase data information.

On January 31, 2010, Flores Construction Company purchases landscaping equipment on credit from Steve's Supply Warehouse. The cost is $13,000, the estimated salvage value is $1,000, and the estimated useful life is four years (Invoice 555).

3. Create the following general ledger accounts.

Account ID:	**109**
Description:	**Landscaping Equipment**
Account Type:	**Fixed Assets**

Account ID:	**109.5**
Description:	**Accum. Depr.-Landscaping Eq.**
Account Type:	**Accumulated Depreciation**

HINT

Change the *GL Account* field to *109*.

4. Use the Purchases/Receive Inventory window to record the purchase. Use the purchase data information above.

5. Use the following information to create a subsidiary ledger record for the landscaping equipment in FAS.

HINT

You may need to close and reopen FAS for Peachtree to synchronize the modules.

Co Asset No:	**002**
Description:	**Landscaping Equipment**
Class:	**EQ**
G/L Asset Acct No:	**109**
Location:	**Storage**
G/L Accum Acct No:	**109.5**
Acquisition Date:	**01/31/10**
G/L Expense Acct No:	**510**
Purchase Order No:	**1489**
Mfg Serial No:	**THH652174**
Vendor/Mfg:	**Heavy Duty Solutions**
Custodian:	**Michael Anderson**
Warranty Date:	**01/31/14**
Prop Type:	**P** (Use the Internal Column)
Serv Date:	**02/01/10**
Acq Value:	**$13,000**
Depr Meth:	**SL**
Est Life:	**04 yrs 00 mos**
Bus Use %:	**100**
Salvage Value:	**$1,000**
Beg Date:	
Beg YTD:	
Beg Accum:	

6. Print the *Quarterly Acquisition Report* for the Internal book.

Problem 2A

On June 30, 2010, Flores Construction Company updates the depreciation expense on its fixed assets. Use Peachtree Complete Accounting 2010 and its Fixed Assets module to do the following:

1. Calculate the depreciation expense as of June 30, 2010.
2. Print the *Depreciation Expense Report* for June 30, 2010.
3. Post to the general ledger.
4. Print the general journal entries for June 30, 2010.

On July 1, 2010, Flores decides to sell the landscaping equipment for $12,900 in cash. Flores wants to purchase a more advanced model.

5. Create the following general ledger account.

Account ID:	**452**
Description:	**Gain on Disposal of Fxd Assets**
Account Type:	**Income**

6. Enter the disposal in the fixed asset record for Asset 002.
7. Print the *Disposal Report*.
8. Record the disposal of the landscaping equipment in the general journal.
9. Print the general journal entries for July 1, 2010.

Problem 1B

On January 1, 2010, NorCal Construction Company decides to use the Fixed Assets module of Peachtree (FAS for Peachtree) to keep records of its fixed assets. The only fixed asset currently on its books is an excavator. This excavator cost $26,000, has an estimated salvage value of $5,000, and has an estimated useful life of seven years. The equipment was purchased on January 1, 2010.

1. Open NorCal Construction Company from the student data disk and then create NorCal Construction Company in FAS for Peachtree. Remember to map to Peachtree. *Note:* Enter December as the fiscal year ending month and 01/01/10 as the business start date.

2. Use the following information to create a subsidiary ledger record for the construction equipment in FAS.

Co Asset No:	**001**
Description:	**Excavator**
Class:	**EQ**
G/L Asset Acct No:	**108**
Location:	**Storage**
G/L Accum Acct No:	**108.5**
Acquisition Date:	**01/01/10**
G/L Expense Acct No:	**510**
Purchase Order No:	**5461**

Mfg Serial No:	**WHS7125123**
Vendor/Mfg:	**Heavy Duty Solutions**
Custodian:	**Juan Abelar**
Warranty Date:	**01/01/16**
Prop Type:	**P** (Use the Internal Column)
Serv Date:	**01/01/10**
Acq Value:	**$26,000**
Depr Meth:	**SL**
Est Life:	**07 yrs 00 mos**
Bus Use %:	**100**
Salvage Value:	**$5,000**
Beg Date:	
Beg YTD:	
Beg Accum:	

> **HINT**
>
> This is the purchase data information.

On January 31, 2010, NorCal Construction Company purchases digging equipment on credit from Construction Supply Warehouse (Invoice 48537). The cost is $18,500, the estimated salvage value is $2,000, and the estimated useful life is five years.

3. Create the following general ledger accounts.

Account ID:	**109**
Description:	**Digging Equipment**
Account Type:	**Fixed Assets**

Account ID:	**109.5**
Description:	**Accum. Depr.-Digging Equipment**
Account Type:	**Accumulated Depreciation**

> **HINT**
>
> Change the *GL Account* field to *109*.

4. Use the Purchases/Receive Inventory window to record the purchase. Use the purchase data information above.

> **HINT**
>
> You may need to close and reopen FAS for Peachtree to synchronize the modules.

5. Use the following information to create a subsidiary ledger record for the digging equipment in FAS.

Co Asset No:	**002**
Description:	**Digging Equipment**
Class:	**EQ**
G/L Asset Acct No:	**109**
Location:	**Storage**
G/L Accum Acct No:	**109.5**
Acquisition Date:	**01/31/10**
G/L Expense Acct No:	**510**
Purchase Order No:	**1254**
Mfg Serial No:	**SW84521**
Vendor/Mfg:	**Heavy Duty Solutions**
Custodian:	**Juan Abelar**
Warranty Date:	**01/31/15**
Prop Type:	**P** (Use the Internal Column)
Serv Date:	**02/01/10**

Acq Value:	**$18,500**
Depr Meth:	**SL**
Est Life:	**05 yrs 00 mos**
Bus Use %:	**100**
Salvage Value:	**$2,000**
Beg Date:	
Beg YTD:	
Beg Accum:	

6. Print the *Quarterly Acquisition Report* for the Internal book.

Problem 2B

On June 30, 2010, NorCal Construction Company updates the depreciation expense on its fixed assets. Use Peachtree Complete Accounting 2010 and its Fixed Assets module to do the following:

1. Calculate the depreciation expense as of June 30, 2010.
2. Print the *Depreciation Expense Report* for June 30, 2010.
3. Post to the general ledger.
4. Print the general journal entries for June 30, 2010.

On July 1, 2010, NorCal decides to sell the digging equipment for $17,550 in cash. NorCal intends to lease a more powerful model.

5. Create the following general ledger account.

Account ID:	**452**
Description:	**Gain on Disposal of Fxd Assets**
Account Type:	**Income**

6. Enter the disposal in the fixed asset record for Asset 002.
7. Print the *Disposal Report*.
8. Record the disposal of the digging equipment in the general journal.
9. Print the general journal entries for July 1, 2010.

Cooperative Learning

1. Form groups of three or four students, and prepare a list of four possible fixed assets that might be found in a doctor's office. Estimate the cost, salvage value, useful life, and depreciable cost for each of the six assets. Calculate the annual straight-line depreciation for each of the assets.
2. Survey a local CPA firm to determine what portion of the firm's clients use the straight-line method of depreciation for financial accounting purposes.

Writing and Decision Making

Gary Stevens, the newly hired manager of an engineering company, does not understand how the cost of the firm's equipment is expensed. In memo format, explain to him how depreciation provides a means of expensing the cost of the equipment.

CHAPTER 13

Partnerships and Corporations

Learning Objectives

1. Understand partnerships and corporations

2. Create partnership accounts and enter partnership transactions

3. Close the fiscal year

4. Create corporate accounts and enter corporate transactions

5. Print partnership and corporate reports

Software Features

- Select or Change Organization Type

- Create General Ledger Accounts

- Edit General Ledger Accounts

- Print Financial Statements

Remember that there are three basic types of business organization: the sole proprietorship, the partnership, and the corporation. A **sole proprietorship** is a business owned by one person. A **partnership** is a business owned by two or more people. A **corporation** is a business owned by stockholders or shareholders. A small corporation may have just a few stockholders, but large corporations have thousands of stockholders.

Up to now, the businesses that we have discussed in this book have all been sole proprietorships. Because sole proprietorships are simple to form and operate, they are the most common type of business organization in the United States. However, the vast majority of sole proprietorships are small firms with limited resources. Larger businesses are usually partnerships or corporations.

The accounting procedures of sole proprietorships, partnerships, and corporations are very similar. The main differences involve owners' equity accounts transactions and financial statements. You can use Peachtree to support all three types of business organization.

OBJECTIVE 1 — Understand Partnerships and Corporations

In this chapter, you will see how Peachtree is used to create owners' equity accounts, record owners' equity transactions, and prepare financial statements for partnerships and corporations. However, it is first necessary to understand the basic characteristics of partnerships and corporations.

Characteristics of Partnerships

A partnership is formed when two or more people enter into a business arrangement for the purpose of making a profit.

Partnerships carry a variety of advantages. Like a sole proprietorship, a partnership is easy to form. In most areas, all that is required to form a partnership is to obtain a business license for the firm. No written contract between the partners is necessary. However, lawyers advise that such a contract, called a **partnership agreement**, be drawn up in order to avoid later disputes. The partnership agreement specifies the beginning investment of each partner, the responsibilities of the partners, the method of dividing profits and losses, the method of admitting new partners, the method of dissolving the partnership, and other important matters. If there is no partnership agreement, by law, all profits and losses are divided equally.

The management of a partnership usually has a greater amount of expertise than the management of a sole proprietorship. Each partner brings additional knowledge, skills, and experience to the business. For example, suppose that a software engineer, a sales manager, and an accountant become partners in a new software company. Each will be able to contribute expertise in a different area of the business: product development, marketing, and financial management. The management contributions of the different partners can have a synergistic effect. Together, the blend of talents may produce more successful results than the individual partners would be able to achieve on their own.

It is difficult to run a business successfully without sufficient capital. This is especially true for new businesses, which may have a weak cash flow in their early years. A partnership has a greater potential for obtaining capital than a sole proprietorship. In a partnership, two or more people are able to pool their resources. If they need additional capital, they may have a better chance of borrowing the required sum than a single individual does.

Partnerships are subject to less government regulation than corporations. Also, unlike corporations, partnerships do not pay an income tax on their earnings. Partnerships file information returns with federal and state tax agencies, but they are not liable for any income tax. Instead, each partner pays income tax on his or her share of the firm's earnings.

There are also disadvantages to organizing a business as a partnership. Like the owner of a sole proprietorship, partners have **unlimited liability** for the debts of the business. If the business is unable to pay its debts, the creditors can sue to obtain the personal assets of the partners in order to satisfy the outstanding debts.

Although the blend of management talent can be very beneficial to a partnership, disputes about management decisions can be harmful. If there are serious, ongoing disagreements about business policy, a partnership may eventually have to dissolve. Because of the divided management control, successful operation of a partnership requires a willingness to consider different viewpoints and make compromises.

Partnerships operate under the **mutual agency rule**. This means that any partner can enter into a contractual agreement on behalf of the partnership. All other partners must honor the agreement, even if they were not consulted in advance and they do not approve of the agreement. The mutual agency rule points out the need to select business partners wisely.

Partnerships have a **limited life**. A partnership ends whenever an existing partner dies or withdraws or when a new partner is admitted. In each of these cases, a new partnership must be formed in order to continue the business.

Accounting for Partnerships

A partnership must have a separate capital account and a separate drawing account for each partner. When a partnership is formed, the investment of each partner is credited to his or her capital account. For example, suppose that Julie Smith and Anna Ramos form a partnership on January 1, 2010. Each invests $75,000 in cash.

January 1, 2010		
Cash	150,000	
J. Smith, Capital		75,000
A. Ramos, Capital		75,000

At the end of each accounting period, the profit or loss of the partnership for the period is calculated. If there was a profit during the period, each capital account is credited for the partner's share. If there was a loss, each capital account is debited for the partner's share. Remember that the division of profits and losses in a partnership is specified in the partnership agreement. If there is no partnership agreement, then, by law, profits and losses must be divided equally among the partners. The following entry is for a year-end profit of $60,000 divided equally.

December 31, 2010		
Income Summary	60,000	
J. Smith, Capital		30,000
A. Ramos, Capital		30,000

unlimited liability Personal responsibility for the debts of a business by a sole proprietor or partner.

mutual agency rule A rule that allows a single partner to enter into a contract that is binding on all other partners with or without their consent.

limited life A partnership ends when an existing partner dies or withdraws or when a new partner is admitted.

When a partner withdraws cash or other assets for personal use, the amounts are debited to the partner's drawing account. Many partners withdraw cash at regular intervals in order to have funds available to pay their personal living expenses. This amount is often referred to as a "salary," but it is actually a withdrawal of expected future profits and is therefore debited to the partner's drawing account rather than to the Salaries Expense account. In a sole proprietorship and a partnership, only the earnings of employees can be recorded in the Salaries Expense account. The following entry is for a monthly withdrawal of $2,000 in cash by each of two partners.

January 31, 2010		
J. Smith, Drawing	2,000	
A. Ramos, Drawing	2,000	
Cash		4,000

At the end of each accounting period, the balances of the partners' drawing accounts are closed into their capital accounts, as shown in the following year-end general journal entry.

December 31, 2010		
J. Smith, Capital	24,000	
A. Ramos, Capital	24,000	
J. Smith, Drawing		24,000
A. Ramos, Drawing		24,000

The balances of the partners' capital accounts are reported on the balance sheet. Some businesses also prepare a separate statement showing all changes in the partners' capital during the accounting period.

	J. Smith	A. Ramos	Total
Capital, Jan. 1, 2010	$ 75,000	$ 75,000	$150,000
Net income for year	30,000	30,000	60,000
Totals	$105,000	$105,000	$210,000
Less: Withdrawals	24,000	24,000	48,000
Capital, Dec. 31, 2010	$ 81,000	$ 81,000	$162,000

Characteristics of Corporations

stockholders or shareholders The owners of a corporation.

The ownership of a corporation is divided into shares of stock. The owners are therefore known as **stockholders** or **shareholders**. Unlike a sole proprietorship or a partnership, a corporation is a legal entity that is separate from its owners.

closely held corporation A corporation owned by just a few stockholders.

A corporation may be small and have just a few stockholders, perhaps family members or a group of managers. This type of corporation is known as a **closely held corporation**. However, the corporations that most of us are familiar with—corporations such as IBM, Microsoft, Dell, Wal-Mart, and General Motors—are very large and have thousands of stockholders. A corporation of this kind is known as a **publicly held corporation** because the public, usually through a stock exchange, can purchase its stock.

publicly held corporation A corporation with stock that can be purchased by the public.

Although there are more sole proprietorships and partnerships than corporations in the United States, corporations produce two-thirds of all business revenue. The reason for this disparity in revenue is that the largest businesses are most often organized as corporations.

Like a sole proprietorship and a partnership, a corporation has both advantages and disadvantages. The ability of a sole proprietorship or partnership to obtain capital depends mostly on the personal resources and personal credit reputation of the owners. A corporation, on the other hand, can raise funds by selling stock or issuing bonds. A corporation that has good prospects for growth can obtain funding from a large pool of potential investors.

Unlike the owners of sole proprietorships and partnerships, the stockholders of a corporation have **limited liability**. They are not personally liable for the debts of the business. If the corporation is unable to pay its debts, creditors cannot sue to obtain the personal assets of the stockholders. Therefore, the maximum amount that stockholders can lose in a failing corporation is the amount of their investment.

Because a corporation is a legal entity that is separate from its owners, it has a **continuous life**. Its life is not affected by changes in ownership, that is, by sales and purchases of shares by stockholders. A corporation can theoretically exist forever unless it is dissolved.

The mutual agency rule mentioned earlier does not apply to corporations. No contractual agreement made by an ordinary stockholder is legally binding on the firm. Only officers of the corporation are able to make binding commitments on its behalf.

When a corporation is formed, the stockholders elect a **board of directors** to look after their interests. The board of directors establishes policies for the firm and hires managers to carry out the policies. This separation of ownership and management allows the corporation to obtain the services of professional managers who have appropriate business training and experience.

Stockholders can vote in periodic elections for the board of directors but do not participate in the day-to-day operations of the corporation unless they are members of management.

The corporation structure has some disadvantages. Corporations require a **charter** from a state in order to operate. The state granting the charter is usually the one in which the corporation will have its headquarters. The process of applying for a charter, organizing the corporation, and issuing stock involves the work of lawyers and accountants. Therefore, the cost of forming a corporation can be substantial.

Organizing a corporation also involves much time and effort. For example, the organizers must establish a set of **bylaws**—the rules by which the corporation will operate. They must also establish corporate records such as the stockholders' ledger.

Corporations are more heavily regulated than sole proprietorships and partnerships. For example, the state and federal governments require that corporations file many different types of reports. Publicly held corporations must also meet accounting and financial reporting standards established by the Securities and Exchange Commission (a federal agency) and by the stock exchange (examples include NASDAQ and NYSE) on which their shares trade. These organizations require that publicly held corporations issue quarterly and annual financial statements.

Because a corporation is a legal entity that is separate from its owners, it pays an income tax on its earnings to the federal and state governments. When it distributes part of its earnings to stockholders in the form of

limited liability The stockholders of a corporation are not personally liable for the debts of the business.

continuous life A corporation can exist forever. Its life is not affected by changes in ownership.

board of directors Individuals elected by stockholders to establish policies for a corporation and hire managers.

charter A legal document issued by a state that permits a corporation to operate.

bylaws A set of rules by which a corporation will operate.

dividends, the individual stockholders must pay income tax on the amounts they receive. This situation is referred to as **double taxation**.

Accounting for Corporations

The corporate charter specifies the types of stock that can be issued and the maximum number of shares of each type. The two basic types of stock are **common stock** and **preferred stock**. Common stock provides various rights such as the right to vote for the board of directors and the right to receive dividends if the board of directors declares them. Preferred stock usually does not carry the right to vote but does provide a fixed dividend. Many corporations issue just one type of stock—common stock.

Some states require that stock be issued with a par value. The **par value** is an arbitrary amount that a corporation assigns to each share of its stock for legal and accounting purposes. This amount is printed on the stock certificate. The par value of a stock has nothing to do with its **market value**—the amount that a buyer is willing to pay for the stock at any given time.

The maximum number of shares of stock permitted by the corporate charter is known as the **authorized stock**. However, the number of shares actually sold is called **issued stock**. As the corporation sells more shares to investors, the amount of issued stock changes. Sometimes, a corporation will buy back shares from investors in the form of **treasury stock**. When treasury stock exists, **outstanding stock** refers to the number of shares that are actually held by investors. For example, if a corporation issues 100,000 shares and then buys back 10,000 shares, the number of issued shares is still 100,000; however, the number of outstanding shares is now 90,000. Dividends are only paid on outstanding shares. The earnings per share (EPS) ratio is also based on the number of outstanding shares.

Recording Paid-in Capital and Retained Earnings

When a corporation issues common stock at par value for cash, it debits the amount received to Cash and credits a stockholders' equity account called Common Stock. If the stock is issued above par value, the corporation still credits the par-value amount to the Common Stock account. However, it must credit the amount that is above par value to another stockholders' equity account called Paid-in Capital in Excess of Par—Common. For example, suppose that a corporation sells 1,000 shares of $10 par-value common stock at $15 per share. It receives $15,000 in cash. The journal entry appears below.

January 6, 2010

Cash	15,000	
Common Stock		10,000
Paid-in Capital in Excess of Par—Common		5,000

If a corporation has par-value preferred stock, it will use stockholders' equity accounts called Preferred Stock and Paid-in Capital in Excess of Par—Preferred to record transactions involving the preferred stock.

At the end of each accounting period, the corporation's profit or loss for the period is transferred from the Income Summary account to a stockholders' equity account called Retained Earnings. This account shows the accumulated earnings of the corporation that have not been distributed to

---

double taxation As a legal entity, a corporation pays income tax on its earnings. When the stockholders receive part of the earnings in the form of dividends, they also pay income tax.

common stock Stock that provides the right to vote and to receive dividends if the board of directors declares them.

preferred stock Stock that usually does not carry the right to vote but provides a fixed dividend.

par value An arbitrary amount that some states require corporations to assign to each share of stock for legal and accounting purposes.

market value The amount that a buyer is willing to pay for stock.

authorized stock The maximum number of shares of stock permitted by the corporate charter.

issued stock The number of shares of stock actually sold by a corporation.

treasury stock The shares a corporation buys back from its investors.

outstanding stock The number of shares that are actually held by investors.

stockholders in the form of dividends. For example, suppose that a corporation has a profit (net income) of $130,000 for the year 2010. This amount is credited to Retained Earnings.

December 31, 2010
    Income Summary   130,000
         Retained Earnings   130,000

The Stockholders' Equity Section of the Balance Sheet

The balance sheet of a corporation has a Stockholders' Equity section, which contains the type of information shown below. Notice that the total stockholders' equity consists of paid-in capital and retained earnings.

Paid-in capital is the amount of capital received from stockholders through their purchases of stock. **Retained earnings** are accumulated profits less dividends from past operations. The term **earned capital** is often used to describe retained earnings.

paid-in capital The amount of capital received from stockholders through their purchases of stock.

retained earnings The accumulated profits of a corporation less dividends from past operations.

earned capital A term often used to describe retained earnings.

Stockholders' Equity

Paid-in Capital:		
Preferred Stock	$200,000	
Paid-in Capital in Excess of Par—Preferred	40,000	$240,000
Common Stock	$450,000	
Paid-in Capital in Excess of Par—Common	80,000	530,000
Total Paid-in Capital		$770,000
Retained Earnings		180,000
Total Stockholders' Equity		$950,000

Recording Dividends

Stockholders expect to receive a return on their investments. This return can come from an increase in the market value of their stock and/or from dividends paid by the corporation to its stockholders. When the market value of a stock increases, stockholders can sell their shares and realize the monetary gain if they wish.

dividend A distribution of part of a corporation's earnings to stockholders.

A **dividend** is a distribution of part of a corporation's earnings to stockholders. Some corporations have a policy of paying dividends on a regular basis, such as every quarter. Other corporations, especially newer corporations in high-growth industries such as software and computers, might not pay dividends because they want to use their accumulated earnings to expand operations.

The board of directors is responsible for declaring dividends. For example, suppose that on January 31, 2010, the board of directors of a corporation declares a dividend of $1 per share to be paid on February 28 to "stockholders of record" (stockholders whose names appear in the corporation's records) as of February 15.

Dividends are usually paid in cash, but they may be paid in stock. On the date when a cash dividend is declared, the total amount is debited to Cash Dividends and credited to Cash Dividends Payable. Cash Dividends is a contra stockholders' equity account—a stockholders' equity account with a debit balance. Cash Dividends Payable is a liability account. On the date when the dividend is paid, Cash Dividends Payable is debited and Cash is credited. (Note that no journal entry is made on the date of record.)

January 31, 2010
    Cash Dividends   20,000
        Cash Dividends Payable   20,000

February 28, 2010
    Cash Dividends Payable   20,000
        Cash   20,000

Cash Dividends is a temporary account. When closing entries are made at the end of an accounting period, its balance is transferred to Retained Earnings. For example, suppose that the corporation discussed in this section pays only $20,000 in cash dividends during 2010. On December 31, it makes the entry shown below. The effects of this entry are to close the Cash Dividends account and to decrease the Retained Earnings account by $20,000, the amount paid out of retained earnings for the dividends.

December 31, 2010
    Retained Earnings   20,000
        Cash Dividends   20,000

The Statement of Retained Earnings

statement of retained earnings
A financial statement that shows the changes in a corporation's retained earnings during an accounting period.

Many corporations prepare a **statement of retained earnings** at the end of each accounting period. This statement shows the beginning balances of the Retained Earnings account, an addition for net income or a deduction for a net loss, a deduction for dividends paid, and the ending balance of the Retained Earnings account. An example is shown below.

Retained Earnings, Jan. 1, 2010	$ 70,000
Add: Net Income	130,000
	$200,000
Less: Dividends	20,000
Retained Earnings, Dec. 31, 2010	$180,000

Check point

1. What is a partnership?
2. Name five advantages of a corporation.

Answers
1. *A partnership is a business owned by two or more people.*
2. *Five advantages of a corporation are ease of raising capital, limited liability, continuous life, no mutual agency rule, and professional management.*

OBJECTIVE 2 — Create Partnership Accounts and Enter Partnership Transactions

When a partnership is formed, it is necessary to establish a capital account for each partner and a drawing account for each partner. All other general ledger accounts are the same as those used for a sole proprietorship.

Billings Financial Services has operated as a sole proprietorship. However, John Billings, the owner, wants to expand operations and has decided to form a partnership with Molly Stone and Marjorie Brown. Both Stone and Brown have experience as financial managers and will provide additional capital.

According to the partnership agreement, Billings will contribute the assets of his sole proprietorship business as of January 2, 2011. Stone will contribute $20,000 in cash. Brown will contribute $15,000 in cash and $5,000 in office supplies. The partnership will assume the liabilities of Billings' sole proprietorship business. The starting date for the partnership is January 2, 2011.

Because Billings is contributing more capital than the other partners and because they will benefit from his prior work in establishing the business, profits will be shared unequally. The partnership agreement they establish specifies that Billings will receive 80% of the profits, Stone will receive 10%, and Brown will receive 10%. Losses will be shared in the same way.

Follow the steps outlined below to convert Billings Financial Services from a sole proprietorship to a partnership and set up the necessary capital and drawing accounts. Note that the individual (monthly) fiscal year should be closed before converting Billings Financial Services to a partnership.

Closing the Fiscal Year

The closing process is similar to the process for changing the accounting period. However, when the fiscal year is closed, the records are generally purged and the company information must be backed up in order to save the data for future use. Once the fiscal year is closed, it is very difficult to access that information. Although it is not the end of Billings' fiscal year, the closing process will be conducted in order to make a logical progression to the partnership formation.

Step 1:
Open Chp. 13 – Billings Financial Services.

Step 2:
Click Tasks, *System*, and then *Year-End Wizard*.

Step 3:
Click Yes at the opening query, "Do you still want to open the Year-End Wizard?"

Step 4:
At the Year-End Wizard – Welcome window, click Next, as shown in figure 13–1.

FIGURE 13–1
Year-End Wizard
Welcome Window

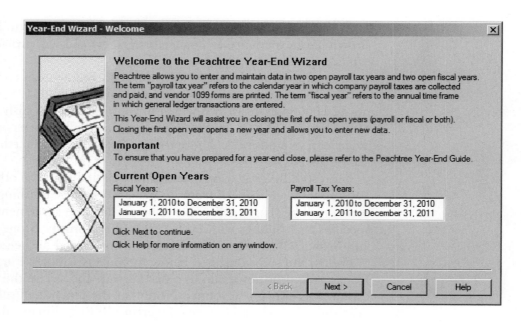

Step 5:

Click Next at the Year-End Wizard – Close Options dialog box to close the Fiscal and Payroll Tax Years as shown in figure 13–2.

FIGURE 13–2
Year-End Wizard-Close
Options Box

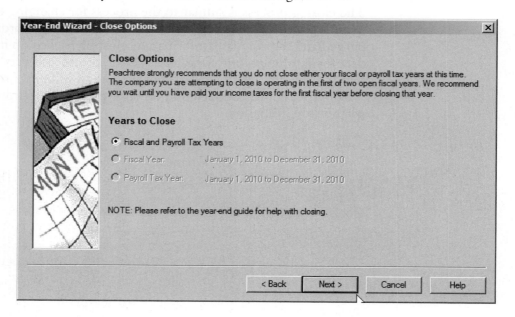

Step 6:

Click Check None and Next at the Year-End Wizard – Reports dialog box.

Step 7:

Click Next at the Year-End Wizard – Internal Accounting Review dialog box.

Step 8:
Click Back Up at the Year-End Wizard – Back Up dialog box and select *Include company name in the backup file name*, as shown in figure 13–3, then click Back Up from the Back Up Company dialog box.

FIGURE 13–3
Back Up Company
Window

Step 9:
Click Save to accept the default file name and location to save the backup file for Billings Financial Services.

Step 10:
Click OK on the Peachtree window indicating the size of the required backup file, and then Next to proceed past the Year-End Wizard Back Up window.

Step 11:
Click Next at the Year-End Wizard – New Open Fiscal Years dialog box, as shown in figure 13–4.

FIGURE 13–4
New Open Fiscal Years
Window

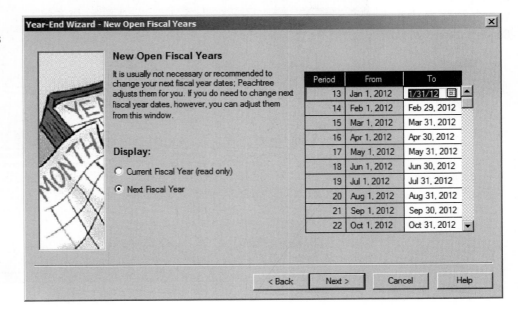

Step 12:

Click Next to confirm the closing of fiscal year 2010 and the opening of fiscal years 2011 and 2012, as shown in figure 13–5.

FIGURE 13–5
Year-End Wizard –
Confirm Close Window

Step 13:

Click Begin Close from the Year-End Wizard – Begin Close dialog box to begin the closing process.

Step 14:

Finally, click Finish from the Year-End Wizard – Congratulations! dialog box, as shown in figure 13–6.

FIGURE 13–6
Year-End Wizard
Congratulations! Window

Converting to a Partnership and Creating the Partnership Accounts

Step 1:
Open Chp. 13 – Billings Financial Services, if needed.

Step 2:
Click Maintain and then *Company Information*.

Step 3:
At the Maintain Company Information window, click the down arrow at the *Form of Business* field, and then click *Partnership*, as shown in figure 13–7.

FIGURE 13–7
Partnership Selected as the Form of Business

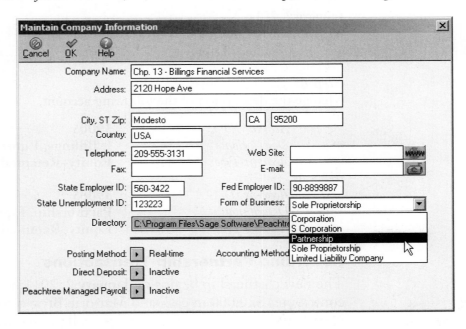

Step 4:
Click <u>O</u>K. The form of business has now been changed from a sole proprietorship to a partnership.

Step 5:
It is necessary to establish a capital account and a drawing account for each of the new partners. Create the following general ledger accounts:

Account ID:	**39026**
Description:	**M. Stone, Capital**
Account Type:	**Equity–doesn't close**
Account ID:	**39027**
Description:	**M. Stone, Drawing**
Account Type:	**Equity–gets closed**
Account ID:	**39046**
Description:	**M. Brown, Capital**
Account Type:	**Equity–doesn't close**

Account ID:	**39047**
Description:	**M. Brown, Drawing**
Account Type:	**Equity–gets closed**

Note: A balance of $16,546.34 in the J. Billings, Equity Account (39005) has been transferred to the J. Billings, Capital Account (39006) using the general journal entry below. The $16,546.34 is his beginning capital at the formation of the partnership. This is standard procedure because John Billings had earned this before he admitted partners into the business. It is not necessary to make the journal entry as it has already been made.

The general journal entry to make the transfer was:

January 2, 2011

| J. Billings, Equity | 16,546.34 | |
| J. Billings, Capital | | 16,546.34 |

Step 6:

Change the description of the following account:

Account ID:	**39005**
Description:	**J. Billings, Equity**
Account Type:	**Equity–Retained Earnings**

to:

Account ID:	**39005**
Description:	**Partnership, Equity**
Account Type:	**Equity–Retained Earnings**

Recording Partnership Transactions

The new partnership begins on January 2, 2011, when Molly Stone contributes $20,000 in cash and Marjorie Brown contributes $15,000 in cash and $5,000 in office supplies. Follow the steps outlined below to enter these partnership transactions.

Step 1:

Click Tasks and then *Receipts*.

Step 2:

Select *Regular Checking Account* from the drop-down list at the Select a Cash Account dialog box. Then click OK.

Step 3:

At the Receipts window, key **Cash** in the *Name* field.

Step 4:

Key **Partner** in the *Reference* field.

Step 5:

At the *Date* field, click the *calendar* icon, and then select *Jan 2, 2011*.

Step 6:
Key **Partner Contribution** in the first row of the *Description* field.

Step 7:
Key **20,000.00** in the *Amount* field, as shown in figure 13–8.

FIGURE 13–8
Completed Receipts Window

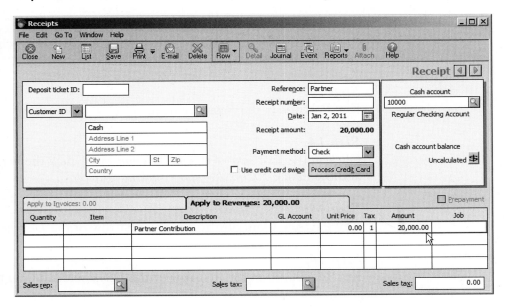

Step 8:
Click Journal on the Receipts toolbar. The Accounting Behind the Screens window will appear. At the *Account No.* field in the first row, click the *magnifying glass* icon, and then select *39026, M. Stone, Capital.* Compare your screen with figure 13–9.

FIGURE 13–9
Accounting Behind the Screens Window

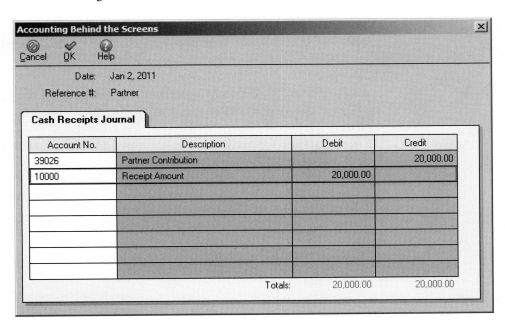

Step 9:
Click <u>OK</u> to close the Accounting Behind the Screens window.

Step 10:
Click Save to save the entry, and then click Close.

Step 11:
Click Tasks, and then click *General Journal Entry*.

Step 12:
At the General Journal Entry window in the *Date* field, click the *calendar* icon, and then select *Jan 2, 2011*.

Step 13:
Key **Partner** in the *Reference* field.

Step 14:
Click in the first row of the *GL Account* field, click the *magnifying glass* icon, and then click *10200, Regular Checking Account*.

Step 15:
Key **Partner Contribution** in the first row of the *Description* field.

Step 16:
Key **15,000.00** in the first row of the *Debit* field, and tab to the next line.

Step 17:
Key **14000** (Prepaid Expenses) in the second row of the *GL Account* field.

Step 18:
Key **Partner Contribution** in the second row of the *Description* field, if needed.

Step 19:
Key **5,000.00** in the second row of the *Debit* field, and tab to the next line.

Step 20:
Key **39046** (M. Brown, Capital) in the third row of the *GL Account* field.

Step 21:
Key **Partner Contribution** in the third row of the *Description* field.

Step 22:
Key **20,000.00** in the third row of the *Credit* field. Compare your completed entry with the one shown in figure 13–10.

FIGURE 13–10
Completed General
Journal Entry for
Partner's Investment

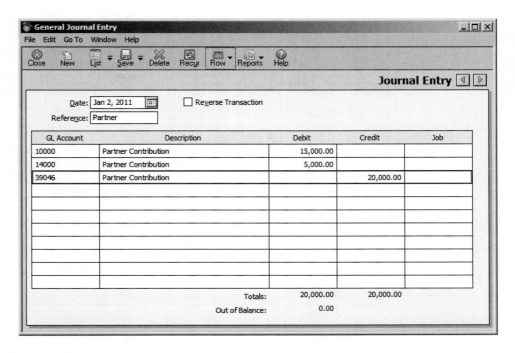

Step 23:
Click Save, and then click Close.

Allocating Partnership Profits and Losses

Billings Financial Services will allocate profits and losses to the partners in the following proportions: 80% to Billings, 10% to Stone, and 10% to Brown. Peachtree does not automatically distribute profits and losses to the capital accounts of partners. You must make the distribution prior to the closing process.

Before we can look at how profits and losses are allocated at Billings Financial Services, we have to record the transactions for the month of January 2011.

Step 1:
Record the following transactions for January 2011 in the general journal using Account 10000 for all cash transactions. Then compare your completed entries with the ones shown on the General Journal report in figure 13–11.

Jan. 10	Received $25,000 for brokerage services provided to customers. (Use Account 40200, Brokerage Fees Earned.)
12	Paid $1,400 for rent.
14	Paid $2,600 for utilities.
20	Molly Stone withdrew $1,500 for personal use.
21	Marjorie Brown withdrew $1,600 for personal use.

FIGURE 13-11
Completed General
Journal Entries
January 2011

Page: 1

Chp. 13 - Billings Financial Services
General Journal
For the Period From Jan 1, 2011 to Jan 31, 2011

Filter Criteria includes: Report order is by Date. Report is printed with Accounts having Zero Amounts and with shortened descriptions and in Detail Format.

Date	Account ID	Reference	Trans Description	Debit Amt	Credit Amt
1/2/11	10000	Partner	Partner Contribution	15,000.00	
	14000		Partner Contribution	5,000.00	
	39046		Partner Contribution		20,000.00
1/10/11	10000		Provided brokerages services	25,000.00	
	40200		Provided brokerages services		25,000.00
1/12/11	50000		Paid monthly rent	1,400.00	
	10000		Paid monthly rent		1,400.00
1/14/11	50400		Paid monthly utilities	2,600.00	
	10000		Paid monthly utilities		2,600.00
1/20/11	39027		Partner draw	1,500.00	
	10000		Partner draw		1,500.00
1/21/11	39047		Partner draw	1,600.00	
	10000		Partner draw		1,600.00
		Total		52,100.00	52,100.00

Step 2:

Use the Report feature to review the income statement for the month of January 2011. Your income statement should look like the one shown in figure 13–12.

FIGURE 13-12
Income Statement
for January 2011

Page: 1

Chp. 13 - Billings Financial Services
Income Statement
For the One Month Ending January 31, 2011

	Current Month		Year to Date	
Revenues				
Brokerage Fees Earned	$ 25,000.00	100.00	$ 25,000.00	100.00
Total Revenues	25,000.00	100.00	25,000.00	100.00
Cost of Sales				
Total Cost of Sales	0.00	0.00	0.00	0.00
Gross Profit	25,000.00	100.00	25,000.00	100.00
Expenses				
Rent Expense	1,400.00	5.60	1,400.00	5.60
Utilities Expense	2,600.00	10.40	2,600.00	10.40
Total Expenses	4,000.00	16.00	4,000.00	16.00
Net Income	$ 21,000.00	84.00	$ 21,000.00	84.00

Although the allocation of profit or loss from the Partnership Equity Account does not usually occur until the fiscal year is closed, it will be done at the end of January for educational purposes.

Notice that the income statement shows a net income (profit) of $21,000 for the month of January 2011. This net income must be distributed to the capital accounts of the partners as follows: $16,800 (80%) to Billings, $2,100 (10%) to Stone, and $2,100 (10%) to Brown. The entry to distribute the net income involves a debit of $21,000 to Partnership Equity (Account 39005) and a credit to each of the capital accounts for the appropriate amount. Partnership Equity takes the place of Income Summary in Billings' accounting system. Its balance at the end of the accounting period represents the firm's net income or net loss for the period.

Step 3:
Click Tasks, and then click *General Journal Entry*.

Step 4:
Record the entry needed to distribute the net income to the capital accounts of each of the partners. Compare your completed entry with the one shown in figure 13–13.

FIGURE 13–13
Completed Entry for Distribution of Net Income to Partners

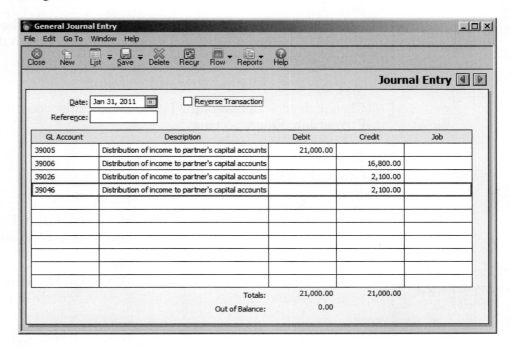

Step 5:
Click Save and then Close.

Check point

1. What two general ledger accounts are required for each partner?
2. What accounts are credited when net income is distributed to partners?

Answers
1. *A capital account and a drawing account are required for each partner.*
2. *The capital accounts of the partners are credited (increased) when net income is distributed.*

Practice Objective 2

On January 1, 2011, James Overland of Overland Management Services will form a partnership with Michael Green and Mitchell Norris. Overland will contribute the assets of his business, Green will contribute $30,000 in cash, and Norris will contribute $20,000 in cash and $10,000 in office equipment. The partnership will assume the liabilities of Overland's business. Profits and losses will be allocated in the following proportions: 70% to Overland, 15% to Green, and 15% to Norris.

Step 1:
Open Chp. 13 – Overland Management Services.

Step 2:
Close the current fiscal year. (Do not print any reports.) Change the form of business to a partnership.

Step 3:
Create a journal entry as of January 2, 2011 to transfer the balance of $10,629.06 in the J. Overland, Equity account (39005) to the J. Overland, Capital account (39006).

Step 4:
Change the description of the J. Overland, Equity account (39005) to the Partnership, Equity account.

Step 5:
Create the following accounts:

Account ID:	**39026**
Description:	**M. Green, Capital**
Account Type:	**Equity–doesn't close**
Account ID:	**39027**
Description:	**M. Green, Drawing**
Account Type:	**Equity–gets closed**
Account ID:	**39046**
Description:	**M. Norris, Capital**
Account Type:	**Equity–doesn't close**
Account ID:	**39047**
Description:	**M. Norris, Drawing**
Account Type:	**Equity–gets closed**

Step 6:
Journalize the contributions of Green and Norris as of January 2, 2011.

Step 7:
Journalize the following transactions that occurred in January 2011 using Account 10200 for all cash transactions.

Jan. 10	Received $50,000 for management services provided to customers. (Credit Account 40200, Management Fees.)
12	Paid $3,400 for rent.
14	Paid $4,600 for utilities.

Step 8:
Review the Income Statement for the period.

Step 9:
Journalize the distribution of $42,000 of net income on January 31, 2011. Transfer the partnership equity balance to the capital accounts of the partners according to the allocation agreement regarding profits and losses.

OBJECTIVE 3 — Create Corporate Accounts and Enter Corporate Transactions

Legaleze Law Firm, Inc. has obtained a corporate charter from the State of California and is now ready to begin operations. It will do research and prepare documents for law firms and the legal departments of large companies.

The corporate charter authorizes Legaleze to issue 1,000,000 shares of $1 par-value common stock and 25,000 shares of $100 par value, 5% noncumulative preferred stock. The preferred stock pays an annual dividend of $5 per share (5% of $100). This stock is called "noncumulative" because unpaid dividends do not accumulate from year to year. If the corporation is not able to pay the dividend one year, it does not have to add the unpaid amount to the next year's dividend.

Legaleze plans to use Peachtree to keep its accounting records. Therefore, its first task is to complete the new company setup procedure of Peachtree.

Setting Up a Corporation in Peachtree

Step 1:
Set up a new company in Peachtree using the company information found in figure 13–14.

FIGURE 13–14
Create a New Company – Company Information Dialog Box

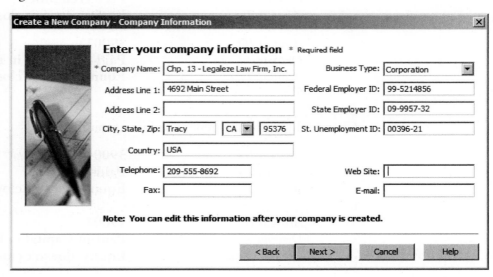

Step 2:
Select Legal Firm as the business type to create a chart of accounts.

Step 3:
Select Accrual as the Accounting Method.

Step 4:
Select Real Time as the Posting Method.

Step 5:
Select 12 Monthly Accounting Periods.

Step 6:
Select January 2010 as the date of the first monthly accounting period.

Step 7:
Accept all other defaults.

Creating Corporate Accounts

Legaleze will make use of a sample corporate chart of accounts for a legal firm provided by Peachtree. This chart of accounts includes general ledger accounts for common stock. However, because Legaleze plans to issue preferred stock as well as common stock, it must add the following accounts: Preferred Stock and Paid-in Capital in Excess of Par—Preferred.

Remember that when preferred stock is issued for more than its par value, two stockholders' equity accounts are affected. Preferred Stock is used to record the par-value amount of the shares issued. Paid-in Capital in Excess of Par—Preferred is used to record the amount received that is above par value.

Step 1:
Create the following general ledger accounts:

Account ID:	**39000**
Description:	**Preferred Stock**
Account Type:	**Equity–doesn't close**

Account ID:	**39001**
Description:	**Paid-in Capital in Excess-PS**
Account Type:	**Equity–doesn't close**

Step 2:
Change the following general ledger account:

Account ID:	**39004**
Description:	**Paid-In Capital**
Account Type:	**Equity–doesn't close**

to:

Account ID:	**39004**
Description:	**Paid-in Capital in Excess-CS**
Account Type:	**Equity–doesn't close**

Step 3:
View the newly created stock accounts on the firm's chart of accounts. Compare them with the stockholders' equity accounts shown in figure 13–15. Make any necessary corrections.

FIGURE 13–15
Partial Chart of
Accounts with Newly
Created Accounts

Chp. 13 - Legaleze Law Firm, Inc.
Chart of Accounts
As of Jan 31, 2010

Page: 1

Filter Criteria includes: Report order is by ID. Report is printed with Accounts having Zero Amounts and in Detail Format.

Account ID	Account Description	Active?	Account Type
10000	Petty Cash	Yes	Cash
10100	Cash on Hand	Yes	Cash
10200	Regular Checking Account	Yes	Cash
10300	Payroll Checking Account	Yes	Cash
10400	Savings Account	Yes	Cash
10500	Special Account	Yes	Cash
10600	Trust Account	Yes	Cash
10700	Money Market Savings	Yes	Cash
10800	Certificates of Deposit	Yes	Cash
11000	Client Fees Receivable	Yes	Accounts Receivable
11400	Other Receivables	Yes	Accounts Receivable
11500	Allowance for Doubtful Acc	Yes	Accounts Receivable
12000	Inventory	Yes	Inventory
14000	Prepaid Expenses	Yes	Other Current Assets
14100	Employee Advances	Yes	Other Current Assets
14200	Notes Receivable-Current	Yes	Other Current Assets
14700	Other Current Assets	Yes	Other Current Assets
15000	Furniture and Fixtures	Yes	Fixed Assets
15100	Equipment	Yes	Fixed Assets
15200	Automobiles	Yes	Fixed Assets
15300	Other Depreciable Property	Yes	Fixed Assets
15400	Leasehold Improvements	Yes	Fixed Assets
15500	Building	Yes	Fixed Assets
15600	Building Improvements	Yes	Fixed Assets
16900	Land	Yes	Fixed Assets
17000	Accum. Depreciation - Furn	Yes	Accumulated Depreciation
17100	Accum. Depreciation - Equi	Yes	Accumulated Depreciation
17200	Accum. Depreciation - Auto	Yes	Accumulated Depreciation
17300	Accum. Depreciation - Oth	Yes	Accumulated Depreciation
17400	Accum. Depreciation - Lea	Yes	Accumulated Depreciation
17500	Accum. Depreciation - Buil	Yes	Accumulated Depreciation
17600	Accum. Depreciation - Bldg	Yes	Accumulated Depreciation
19000	Deposits	Yes	Other Assets
19100	Organization Costs	Yes	Other Assets
19150	Accum. Amortiz. - Org. Co	Yes	Other Assets
19200	Note Receivable-Noncurren	Yes	Other Assets
19900	Other Noncurrent Assets	Yes	Other Assets
20000	Accounts Payable	Yes	Accounts Payable
23000	Accrued Expenses	Yes	Other Current Liabilities
23100	Sales Tax Payable	Yes	Other Current Liabilities
23200	Wages Payable	Yes	Other Current Liabilities

Entering Corporate Transactions—Issuing Common Stock

On January 2, 2010, Legaleze issued 50,000 shares of its $1 par-value common stock for $10 per share. It received $500,000 in cash. The entry for this transaction requires a debit of $500,000 to Cash, a credit of $50,000 to Common Stock (50,000 shares × $1 par value), and a credit of $450,000 to Paid-in Capital in Excess of Par—Common Stock (50,000 shares × $9).

Step 1:
Click Tasks, and then click *General Journal Entry.*

HINT

This entry can also be made in the cash receipts journal by using the Accounting Behind the Screens feature.

Step 2:
At the General Journal Entry window, at the *Date* field, click the *calendar* icon, and then select *Jan 2, 2010.*

Step 3:
At the *GL Account* field, click the *magnifying glass* icon, and then click *Regular Checking Account (10200)* as the account to be debited. (Legaleze uses Regular Checking Account as its main cash account.)

Step 4:
Key **Issued 50,000 shares of common stock** in the *Description* field.

Step 5:
Key **500,000.00** in the *Debit* field.

Step 6:
Tab to the next row, and click *Common Stock (39003)* as the first account to be credited.

Step 7:
Key **50,000.00** in the *Credit* field. This amount represents the par value of the 50,000 shares issued (50,000 × $1).

Step 8:
Tab to the next row, and click *Paid-in Capital in Excess – CS (39004)* as the second account to be credited.

Step 9:
Key **450,000.00** in the *Credit* field. This amount represents the difference between the issue price and the par value of the 50,000 shares ($10 – $1 = $9 × 50,000 = $450,000). Compare your completed entry with the one that appears in figure 13–16.

FIGURE 13–16
Journal Entry for the Issuance of Common Stock

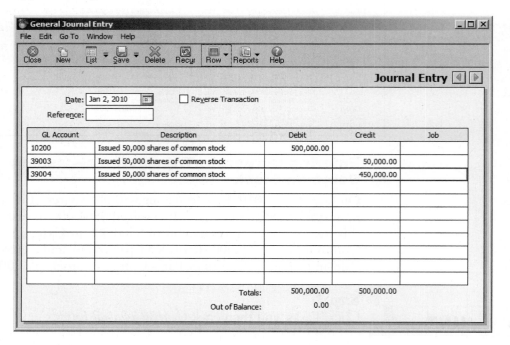

Step 10:
Click Save and Close.

Entering Corporate Transactions—Receiving Donated Capital

Sometimes a state, county, or city will donate an asset such as land or an unused building to a business. This donation is made for the purpose of economic development—so that the business will establish or expand operations in the area and create jobs for local residents.

For example, on January 5, 2010, the City of Tracy donated a parcel of land valued at $150,000 to Legaleze Law Firm, Inc. The firm will use this land to construct a building that will allow it to expand its staff. (The firm is currently renting an office with very limited space.)

To record this transaction, it is necessary to debit Land for $150,000 and credit a stockholders' equity account called Donated Capital for $150,000. Donated capital will appear in the Stockholders' Equity section of the balance sheet along with paid-in capital (the capital supplied by investors through their purchases of stock) and retained earnings (the accumulated profits of the firm less dividends paid).

Step 1:
Create a general ledger account for donated capital. (Replace the account that is currently using 39005 as its ID.)

Account ID:	**39005**
Description:	**Donated Capital**
Account Type:	**Equity–doesn't close**

Create a new account for retained earnings, which was previously Account 39005:

Account ID:	**39006**
Description:	**Retained Earnings**
Account Type:	**Equity–Retained Earnings**

Step 2:
Click Save and Close.

Step 3:
Click Tasks, and then click *General Journal Entry*.

Step 4:
At the General Journal Entry window, in the *Date* field, click the *calendar* icon and then select *Jan 5, 2010*.

Step 5:
Click in the *GL Account* field, click the *magnifying glass* icon, and then click *Land (16900)*.

Step 6:
Key **Received donation of land** in the *Description* field.

Step 7:
Key **150,000.00** in the *Debit* field and tab down to the next row.

Step 8:
Click the *magnifying glass* icon and then *Donated Capital (39005)* in the *GL Account* field.

Step 9:
Key **150,000.00** in the *Credit* field. Compare your completed entry with the one that appears in figure 13–17.

FIGURE 13–17
Journal Entry for a
Donation of Land

FIGURE 13–17 Journal Entry for a Donation of Land

Step 10:
Click Save and Close to save the entry.

Entering Corporate Transactions—General Transactions

Legaleze had the following revenue and expense transactions during the month of January 2010.

Jan. 10	Received fees of $10,000 in cash for corporate legal services performed.
15	Paid $2,500 for rent.
16	Paid $565 for utilities.
20	Paid $1,200 for professional development costs.

Step 1:
Record the transactions in the general journal. Then compare your entries with figure 13–18.

FIGURE 13–18
Journal Entries
for Revenue
and Expense
Transactions

Chp. 13 - Legaleze Law Firm, Inc.
General Journal
For the Period From Jan 1, 2010 to Jan 31, 2010

Page: 1

Filter Criteria includes: Report order is by Date. Report is printed with Accounts having Zero Amounts and with shortened descriptions and in Detail Format.

Date	Account ID	Reference	Trans Description	Debit Amt	Credit Amt
1/2/10	10200		Issued 50,000 shares of common st	500,000.00	
	39003		Issued 50,000 shares of common st		50,000.00
	39004		Issued 50,000 shares of common st		450,000.00
1/5/10	16900		Received a donation of land	150,000.00	
	39005		Received a donation of land		150,000.00
1/15/10	10200		Performed corporate legal services	10,000.00	
	40000		Performed corporate legal services		10,000.00
	76000		Paid monthly rent	2,500.00	
	10200		Paid monthly rent		2,500.00
1/16/10	79000		Paid monthly utilities	565.00	
	10200		Paid monthly utilities		565.00
1/20/10	74500		Paid professional development cost	1,200.00	
	10200		Paid professional development cost		1,200.00
		Total		664,265.00	664,265.00

Step 2:
Click Close.

Declaring a Cash Dividend

On January 30, 2010, Legaleze declares a cash dividend of $0.10 per share of common stock outstanding. The dividend is payable on February 20, 2010. Because there are 50,000 shares of common stock outstanding, the total amount of the dividend will be $5,000 (50,000 × $0.10 = $5,000).

The declaration of the dividend creates a liability for Legaleze to its stockholders. To record this transaction, the firm must debit Cash Dividends for $5,000 and credit Dividends Payable for $5,000. Remember that Cash Dividends is a contra stockholders' equity account and Dividends Payable is a liability account.

When the dividend is paid, Legaleze will debit Dividends Payable for $5,000 and credit Cash for $5,000. This entry eliminates the liability.

Step 1:
Create the following general ledger account:

Account ID:	**24300**
Description:	**Dividends Payable**
Account Type:	**Other Current Liabilities**

Change the following general ledger account from:

Account ID:	**39007**
Description:	**Dividends Paid**
Account Type:	**Equity–gets closed**

to:

Account ID:	**39007**
Description:	**Cash Dividends**
Account Type:	**Equity–gets closed**

Step 2:
Record the declaration of the cash dividend in the general journal. Then compare your entry with figure 13–19.

FIGURE 13–19
Journal Entry for
Declaration of a Cash
Dividend

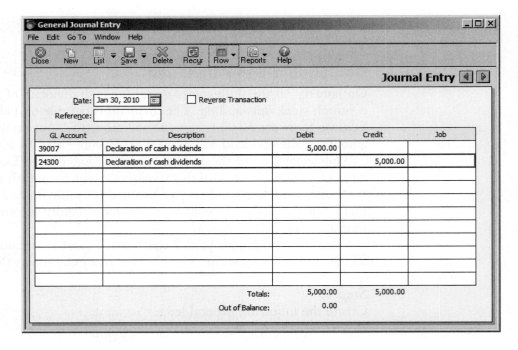

Step 3:
Click Save and Close to save the entry.

C h e c k   p o i n t

1. What two types of stock can a corporation issue?
2. What account is credited when a cash dividend is declared?

Answers
1. *A corporation can issue common stock and preferred stock.*
2. *The account credited is Dividends Payable.*

P r a c t i c e   O b j e c t i v e   3

Abacus Executive Search, Inc., is a new corporation that will use Peachtree Complete Accounting 2010. On January 2, 2010, Abacus received its corporate charter. This charter authorizes the firm to issue 450,000 shares of $2 par-value common stock and 20,000 shares of $50 par value, 6% preferred stock.

Step 1:
Complete the new company setup procedure for Abacus. Use the information provided in figure 13–20.

FIGURE 13–20

Create a New Company
Setup – Company
Information for Abacus
Executive Search, Inc.

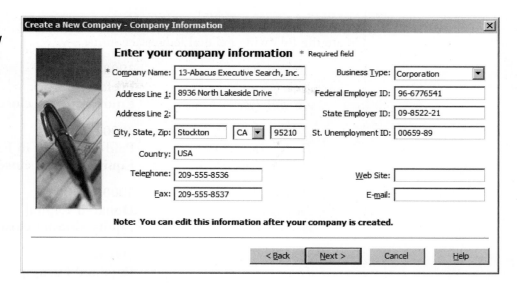

Step 2:
Use a sample company Chart of Accounts, and click *Employment Agency* as the type of business.

Step 3:
Use accrual accounting and real-time posting.

Step 4:
Use a fiscal year of 12 monthly accounting periods. Set up the monthly periods as shown in figure 13–21.

FIGURE 13–21

Create a New
Company – Fiscal
Year

Step 5:
Accept all other defaults.

Step 6:

Create the following general ledger accounts:

Account ID:	**39001**
Description:	**Preferred Stock**
Account Type:	**Equity–doesn't close**
Account ID:	**39002**
Description:	**Paid-in Capital in Excess-PS**
Account Type:	**Equity–doesn't close**
Account ID:	**39005**
Description:	**Donated Capital**
Account Type:	**Equity–doesn't close**
Account ID:	**39006**
Description:	**Retained Earnings**
Account Type:	**Equity–Retained Earnings**
Account ID:	**24300**
Description:	**Dividends Payable**
Account Type:	**Other Current Liabilities**

Change the following general ledger account from:

Account ID	**39004**
Description	**Paid-in Capital**
Account Type	**Equity–doesn't close**

to:

Account ID	**39004**
Description	**Paid-in Capital in Excess-CS**
Account Type	**Equity–doesn't close**

Change the following general ledger account from:

Account ID:	**39007**
Description:	**Dividends Paid**
Account Type:	**Equity–gets closed**

to:

Account ID:	**39007**
Description:	**Cash Dividends**
Account Type:	**Equity–gets closed**

Step 7:

Abacus had the following transactions during the month of January 2010. Record these transactions in the general journal using Account 10200 for all cash transactions.

Jan. 3	Issued 45,000 shares of common stock for $300,000 in cash.
4	Issued 3,000 shares of preferred stock for $200,000 in cash.
5	Received land valued at $54,000 as a donation from the City of Stockton.

10	Received fees of $20,000 in cash for professional placement services performed.
15	Paid rent of $4,500.
16	Paid utilities of $1,565.
20	Paid professional dues of $1,200 (Account 64500, Dues and Subscriptions Exp).
21	Paid license fees of $1,345.
31	Declared a $4,500 cash dividend to all common stockholders. This dividend is payable on Feb. 15 at a rate of $0.10 per share. (The preferred stockholders do not receive a dividend until year-end.)

Step 8:
Review your work, and make any necessary corrections. Then save the entries.

OBJECTIVE 4 — Print Partnership and Corporate Reports

Every business—sole proprietorship, partnership, and corporation—prepares an income statement and a balance sheet at the end of the accounting period. Remember that the **income statement** reports the results of operations for the accounting period—the revenue, expenses, and net income or net loss. The **balance sheet** reports the financial condition of the business as of a specific day of the accounting period—the assets, liabilities, and owner's equity.

These statements are essentially the same for all types of business organization. The one major difference is the treatment of owner's equity on the balance sheet, as will be seen on the next few pages.

Partnerships and corporations may also prepare certain supplemental statements. For example, a corporation may prepare a statement of retained earnings that shows the changes in its retained earnings during the accounting period.

Preparing a Partnership Report

The balance sheet of a partnership shows the capital and cash withdrawals of each partner. A separate statement that explains the changes that took place in the partnership's equity during the accounting period may supplement this information. Such a statement usually includes the beginning balance of each partner's capital account, each partner's share of the net income or net loss for the period, each partner's withdrawals for this period, and the ending balance of each partner's capital account. This report is usually known as a statement of partners' equity.

Follow the steps outlined below to prepare a balance sheet for the partnership of Billings Financial Services. (The income statement for this partnership appeared earlier in figure 13–12.)

Step 1:
Open Chp. 13 – Billings Financial Services, which you updated previously in the chapter.

Step 2:
Click Reports & Forms, and then click *Financial Statements*.

income statement A report of a firm's revenue, expenses, and net income or net loss for an accounting period.

balance sheet A report of a firm's assets, liabilities, and owner's equity as of a specific date.

Step 3:
In the Financial Statements: Balance Sheets and Income Statements section, click *<Standard> Balance Sheet*.

Step 4:
Display the balance sheet with a date of January 31, 2011. Examine the Capital section of the balance sheet, which shows the partners' equity. There is a separate capital account for each partner, as shown in figure 13–22.

FIGURE 13–22
Partners' Equity on the Balance Sheet

Chp. 13 - Billings Financial Services
Balance Sheet
January 31, 2011

ASSETS

Current Assets		
Regular Checking Account	$ 69,446.34	
Prepaid Expenses	5,000.00	
Total Current Assets		74,446.34
Property and Equipment		
Total Property and Equipment		0.00
Other Assets		
Total Other Assets		0.00
Total Assets		$ 74,446.34

LIABILITIES AND CAPITAL

Current Liabilities		
Total Current Liabilities		0.00
Long-Term Liabilities		
Total Long-Term Liabilities		0.00
Total Liabilities		0.00
Capital		
Partnership, Equity	$ (21,000.00)	
J. Billings, Capital	33,346.34	
M. Stone, Capital	22,100.00	
M. Stone, Drawing	(1,500.00)	
M. Brown, Capital	22,100.00	
M. Brown, Drawing	(1,600.00)	
Net Income	21,000.00	
Total Capital		74,446.34
Total Liabilities & Capital		$ 74,446.34

Step 5:
Print the report, if desired. Then close the display window.

Preparing a Corporate Report

As noted previously, the balance sheet of a corporation contains a Stockholders' Equity section. This section shows the various types and amounts of capital that the corporation has as of a specific date. The three basic types of corporate capital are paid-in capital, earned capital, and donated capital.

Remember that paid-in capital is the capital received from stockholders through their purchases of common and preferred stock. Earned capital consists of accumulated earnings from the firm's operations. Donated capital comes from assets that are donated to a corporation by a state, county, or city.

The statement of retained earnings reports the changes that took place in retained earnings during the accounting period. It shows the beginning balance of the Retained Earnings account, an addition for net income or a deduction for a net loss, a deduction for dividends paid, and the ending balance of the Retained Earnings account.

Follow the steps outlined below to prepare a balance sheet for Legaleze Law Firm, Inc.

Step 1:
Open Chp. 13 – Legaleze Law Firm, Inc. which you created previously in the chapter.

Step 2:
Click Reports & Forms, and then click *Financial Statements*.

Step 3:
In the Financial Statements: Balance Sheets and Income Statements section, click *<Standard> Balance Sheet*.

Step 4:
Display the balance sheet with a date of January 31, 2010. Examine the Capital section of the balance sheet, which shows the stockholders' equity. It should resemble figure 13–23.

FIGURE 13–23
Stockholders' Equity on the Balance Sheet

Chp. 13 - Legaleze Law Firm, Inc.
Balance Sheet
January 31, 2010

ASSETS

Current Assets		
Regular Checking Account	$ 505,735.00	
Total Current Assets		505,735.00
Property and Equipment		
Land	150,000.00	
Total Property and Equipment		150,000.00
Other Assets		
Total Other Assets		0.00
Total Assets		$ 655,735.00

LIABILITIES AND CAPITAL

Current Liabilities		
Dividends Payable	$ 5,000.00	
Total Current Liabilities		5,000.00
Long-Term Liabilities		
Total Long-Term Liabilities		0.00
Total Liabilities		5,000.00
Capital		
Common Stock	50,000.00	
Paid-in Capital in Excess-CS	450,000.00	
Donated Capital	150,000.00	
Cash Dividends	(5,000.00)	
Net Income	5,735.00	
Total Capital		650,735.00
Total Liabilities & Capital		$ 655,735.00

Step 5:
Close the display window.

Practice Objective 4

Step 1:

Open Chp. 13 – Abacus Executive Search, Inc. which you created previously in the chapter.

Step 2:

Print the income statement, the balance sheet, and the statement of retained earnings for the month of January 2010. Your printouts should look like figures 13–24, 13–25, and 13–26, respectively.

FIGURE 13–24
Income Statement for Abacus Executive Search, Inc.

Page: 1

Chp. 13 - Abacus Executive Search, Inc.
Income Statement
For the One Month Ending January 31, 2010

	Current Month		Year to Date	
Revenues				
Professional placement fees/co	$ 20,000.00	100.00	$ 20,000.00	100.00
Total Revenues	20,000.00	100.00	20,000.00	100.00
Cost of Sales				
Total Cost of Sales	0.00	0.00	0.00	0.00
Gross Profit	20,000.00	100.00	20,000.00	100.00
Expenses				
Dues and Subscriptions Exp	1,200.00	6.00	1,200.00	6.00
Licenses Expense	1,345.00	6.73	1,345.00	6.73
Rent or Lease Expense	4,500.00	22.50	4,500.00	22.50
Utilities Expense	1,565.00	7.83	1,565.00	7.83
Total Expenses	8,610.00	43.05	8,610.00	43.05
Net Income	$ 11,390.00	56.95	$ 11,390.00	56.95

FIGURE 13–25
Balance Sheet for
Abacus Executive
Search, Inc.

Chp. 13 - Abacus Executive Search, Inc.
Balance Sheet
January 31, 2010

ASSETS

Current Assets		
Regular Checking Account	$ 511,390.00	
Total Current Assets		511,390.00
Property and Equipment		
Land	54,000.00	
Total Property and Equipment		54,000.00
Other Assets		
Total Other Assets		0.00
Total Assets		$ 565,390.00

LIABILITIES AND CAPITAL

Current Liabilities		
Dividends Payable	$ 4,500.00	
Total Current Liabilities		4,500.00
Long-Term Liabilities		
Total Long-Term Liabilities		0.00
Total Liabilities		4,500.00
Capital		
Preferred Stock	150,000.00	
Paid-in Capital in Excess-PS	50,000.00	
Common Stock	90,000.00	
Paid-in Capital in Excess-CS	210,000.00	
Donated Capital	54,000.00	
Cash Dividends	(4,500.00)	
Net Income	11,390.00	
Total Capital		560,890.00
Total Liabilities & Capital		$ 565,390.00

FIGURE 13–26
Statement of
Retained Earnings
for Abacus Executive
Search, Inc.

Page: 1

Chp. 13 - Abacus Executive Search, Inc.
Statement of Retained Earnings
For the One Month Ending January 31, 2010

Beginning Retained Earnings	$ 0.00
Adjustments To Date	0.00
Net Income	11,390.00
Subtotal	11,390.00
Cash Dividends	(4,500.00)
Ending Retained Earnings	$ 6,890.00

End of Chapter Review

Software Command Summary

Change Organization Type	Maintain, Company Information, Change the Business Form
Edit Account Information	Maintain, Chart of Accounts, Enter the Changes, Save
Print Financial Statements	Reports & Forms, Financial Statements, Select the Report Type

Projects and Problems

Content Check

Multiple Choice: Choose only one response for each question.

1. The equity section of the balance sheet for a partnership must show the
   A. liabilities.
   B. assets.
   C. capital of each partner.
   D. expenses.

2. Unless otherwise stated, partners share profits and losses
   A. according to their capital balances.
   B. according to the amount of time spent at the firm by each partner.
   C. based on the amount of business each partner generates.
   D. equally.

3. Which of the following is a disadvantage of the partnership form of organization?
   A. ease of formation
   B. greater management expertise than a sole proprietorship
   C. mutual agency rule
   D. less regulation and taxation than a corporation

4. Which of the following is a disadvantage of a corporation?
   A. limited liability
   B. ease of raising capital
   C. continuous life
   D. double taxation

5. Which of the following accounts would *not* be found in the equity section of a corporation's balance sheet?
   A. Common Stock
   B. Donated Capital
   C. Preferred Stock
   D. Dividends Payable

Short-Essay Response: Provide a detailed answer for each question.

1. What is the par value of stock? What is the market value?
2. What is a partnership? What are the advantages and disadvantages of this type of business organization?
3. What is the difference between authorized and outstanding stock?
4. What is a dividend?
5. What is the paid-in capital of a corporation? What is the earned capital?
6. What information appears on the statement of retained earnings for a corporation?

Case Problems

Problem 1A

On January 2, 2010, Jim Mathews and Gary Corbett formed a partnership. They will operate a business called ABC Collection Service. Each will contribute $30,000 in cash. Profits and losses will be divided equally.

1. Use the information in figure 13–27 and the information given below to set up the business in Peachtree.

FIGURE 13–27
Setup Information for
ABC Collection Service

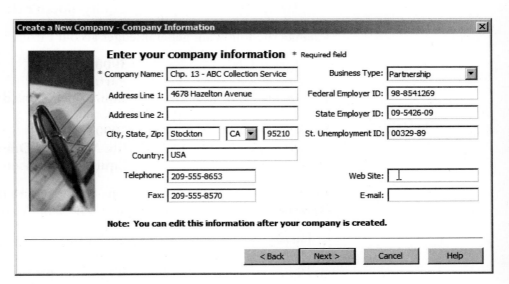

Chart of Accounts:	**Service Company (Detailed Type)**
Accounting Method:	**Accrual**
Posting Method:	**Real Time**
Accounting Periods:	**12 Monthly Accounting Periods**
Fiscal Year to Start:	**January 2010**

2. Establish the capital and drawing accounts needed by the partnership.

Create the following general ledger accounts:

Account ID:	**39008**
Description:	**Gary Corbett, Capital**
Account Type:	**Equity–doesn't close**

Account ID:	**39009**
Description:	**Gary Corbett, Drawing**
Account Type:	**Equity–gets closed**

Change the following general ledger account from:

Account ID:	**39006**
Description:	**Partners Contribution**
Account Type:	**Equity–gets closed**

to:

Account ID:	**39006**
Description:	**Jim Mathews, Capital**
Account Type:	**Equity–doesn't close**

Change the following general ledger account from:

Account ID:	**39007**
Description:	**Partners Draw**
Account Type:	**Equity–gets closed**

to:

Account ID:	**39007**
Description:	**Jim Mathews, Drawing**
Account Type:	**Equity–gets closed**

3. Journalize the following transactions for the month of January 2010. (Use the general journal and Regular Checking Account.)

Jan. 2	Mathews contributed $30,000 in cash, and Corbett contributed $30,000 in cash.
10	Had cash sales of $23,000 for professional fees from customers.
11	Paid rent of $4,500.
15	Paid utilities of $1,500.
20	Mathews withdrew $1,000 in cash, and Corbett withdrew $1,000 in cash.

4. Print the following financial statements as of January 31, 2010: the income statement, balance sheet, and statement of retained earnings.

Problem 2A

On January 2, 2010, General Consulting, Inc., received its corporate charter, which authorizes it to issue up to 2,000,000 shares of $1 par-value common stock and 50,000 shares of $100 par value, 6% cumulative preferred stock.

1. Open General Consulting, Inc. from the student data disk.

2. Journalize the following transactions for the month of January 2010. (Use the general journal and Regular Checking Account.)

Jan. 3	Issued 30,000 shares of common stock for $300,000 in cash.
10	Had cash sales of $43,000 for consulting services provided to customers.
11	Paid rent of $6,000.
15	Paid utilities of $1,600.
31	Declared a cash dividend of $0.20 for each share of common stock outstanding. (Create the Dividends Payable account. Change the Dividends Paid account into the Cash Dividends account.)

3. Print the following financial statements as of January 31, 2010: the income statement, balance sheet, and statement of retained earnings.

Problem 1B

On January 2, 2010, Terry Jones and Carol Smith formed a partnership. They will operate a business called CBA Résumé Service. Each will contribute $25,000 in cash. Profits and losses will be divided equally.

1. Use the information in figure 13–28 and the information given below to set up the business in Peachtree.

FIGURE 13–28
Setup Information for
CBA Résumé Service

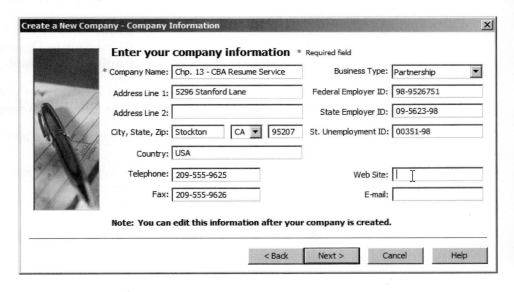

Chart of Accounts:	**Service Company (Detailed Type)**
Accounting Method:	**Accrual**
Posting Method:	**Real Time**
Accounting Periods:	**12 Monthly Accounting Periods**
Fiscal Year to Start:	**January 2010**

2. Establish the capital and drawing accounts needed by the partnership.

   Create the following general ledger accounts:

Account ID:	**39008**
Description:	**Terry Jones, Capital**
Account Type:	**Equity–doesn't close**

Account ID:	**39009**
Description:	**Terry Jones, Drawing**
Account Type:	**Equity–gets closed**

   Change the following general ledger account from:

Account ID:	**39006**
Description:	**Partners Contribution**
Account Type:	**Equity–gets closed**

   to:

Account ID:	**39006**
Description:	**Carol Smith, Capital**
Account Type:	**Equity–doesn't close**

   Change the following general ledger account from:

Account ID:	**39007**
Description:	**Partners Draw**
Account Type:	**Equity–gets closed**

   to:

Account ID:	**39007**
Description:	**Carol Smith, Drawing**
Account Type:	**Equity–gets closed**

3. Journalize the following transactions for the month of January 2010. (Use the general journal and Regular Checking Account.)

Jan. 2	Jones contributed $25,000 in cash, and Smith contributed $25,000 in cash.
5	Had cash sales of $13,000 for professional services provided to customers.
11	Paid rent of $2,500.
15	Paid utilities of $1,500.
20	Jones withdrew $1,500 in cash, and Smith withdrew $1,500 in cash.

4. Print the following financial statements as of January 31, 2010: the income statement, balance sheet, and statement of retained earnings.

Problem 2B

Barker Architectural Services, Inc. received its corporate charter, which authorizes it to issue up to 1,000,000 shares of $2 par-value common stock and 100,000 shares of $50 par value, 5% cumulative preferred stock.

1. Open Barker Architectural Services, Inc. from the student data disk.

2. Journalize the following transactions for the month of January 2010. (Use the general journal and Regular Checking Account.)

Jan. 3	Issued 20,000 shares of common stock for $200,000 in cash.
10	Had cash sales of $56,000 for design services provided to customers.
11	Paid rent of $11,000.
15	Paid utilities of $4,700.
31	Declared a cash dividend of $0.60 for each share of common stock outstanding. (Create the Dividends Payable account. Change the Dividends Paid account into the Cash Dividends account.)

3. Print the following financial statements as of January 31, 2010: the income statement, balance sheet, and statement of retained earnings.

Cooperative Learning

1. In groups of three or four students, visit two different partnerships in your area. (Accounting and law firms are often partnerships.) Speak with a partner about the advantages and disadvantages of this type of organization. Ask how disagreements among partners are resolved. Prepare a brief report with your findings.
2. In groups of three or four students, research the requirements for obtaining a corporate charter in your state. Check the Web site of your state or the office of your Secretary of State. Prepare a list of the requirements.

Writing and Decision Making

Bruce Cho, the owner of a sole proprietorship software business, would like to expand operations. He needs additional capital to develop new products. He is thinking of forming a corporation. In memo form, briefly explain the advantages and disadvantages of a corporation to Bruce Cho.

Index

Select a Report or Form toolbar, 333, 392
Display in Action Items check box, 158
Disposal, of fixed asset at a gain, recording, 518-522
Disposal Date field, Asset window, 520
Disposal Report, 523
Disposal tab, Asset window, 519
Disposed Assets Report, viewing, 520-521
Dividends, 539, 559-560
    definition, 539
    recording, 539-540
Dollar ($) icon, 347
Dollars field, Write Checks window, 236
Donated capital, 556-558, 564
Double declining-balance method of depreciation, 499-500
Double-entry accounting, 82
Double taxation, 39, 538
Drop-down list, use of, 18

E

Earned capital, 539, 564
Earnings, retained, 538-539, 540, 564
Edit button, 330
Edit command, Menu bar, 14
Editing
    accounts, 57
    accounts payable transactions, 203-204
    memorized transaction, 107
    transactions in general journal, 100-101
Electronic cash registers, 362
E-mail Address field, Maintain Customers/Prospects window, 132
E-mail field, Maintain Vendors window, 187
Employee Defaults dialog box, 418
Employee ID field
    Maintain Employees & Sales Reps window, 337, 423, 425, 426
    Payroll Entry window, 435
Employees, creating payroll records for, 422-427
Employees & Payroll tab, 431
    Peachtree opening window, 7
End Date field, Maintain Jobs window, 458, 462
Ending bank statement balance, 253, 254
Equal to radio button, 255

Equipment cost type, 463
Equity, account classification, 52-53
Equity - Doesn't Close account, 54
Equity - Gets Closed account, 54
Equity - Retained Earnings account, 54
Errors, bank, 254
Estimated Expenses & Revenue folder tab, 459, 465
Estimated Job Expenses Report, 481, 483, 484
Estimated Job Revenue Report, 481
Estimated Life field, New Asset Wizard, 508
Estimated salvage value, 497
Estimated useful life, 497
Event logs, 153
Events
    adding to action list, 157-159
    displaying, 159-160
    recording on action list, 157-159
    recording on the To Do list, 156-157
    setting up as defaults, 155
Events tab, Action Items window, 158
Event Type field, Create Event window, 158
Exit command, File menu, 10, 11
Expense account, 54-55
Expense Account field
    Maintain Vendors window, 186, 235, 340
    Write Checks window, 237
Expenses, account classification, 52-53
Expenses account, 412
    account ID numeric ranges, 52
Expenses field, Maintain Jobs window, 460, 466, 467
Explore a sample company command, 6
Explore a Sample Company window, 7

F

Fair Labor Standards Act, 411
FAS for Peachtree
    accessing, 503
    calculation of depreciation, 514-515
    New Asset Wizard, 505-509
    Reports menu, 523-524
    setting up, 503-504
    tasks related to, 502
    transferring depreciation to general journal and general ledger, 515-517

FAS for Peachtree by Sage window, 503, 504
Fax field, Maintain Vendors window, 235
Federal income taxes, 412
Federal Income Tax Payable (FICA) account, 412
Federal Insurance Contributions Act (FICA), 411, 422
Federal tax returns, 411-412
Federal Unemployment Tax Act (FUTA), 411
Fed_Income field, Employee Defaults window, 420
FICA-Medicare Tax Payable account, 413
FICA-Social Security Tax Payable account, 413
File command, Menu bar, 14
File menu
    Back Up command, 26
    drop-down list, 15
    Exit command, 10
    Open Company command, 26
    options, 15
    Restore command, 28
File name text box, 27
Finance Charge GL Account field, Finance Charges tab, 387
Finance Charge report, creating, 388-390
Finance Charge Report Selection dialog box, 389, 390
Finance charges
    creating defaults for, 387-388
    Finance Charge report, 388-390
    recording on overdue customer balances, 386
Financial statements. *See also Balance sheet; Income statement; Statement of cash flow; Statement of changes in financial position*
    changing text, 304-306
    changing text fonts, 302-303
    copying a company's format, 299-301
    copying a line, 306-307
    deleting a line, 307-308
    designing, 301
    interim, 312
    printing, 112-117, 292
Find a Report, Category drop-down list, General Ledger command, 289
Find a Report menu
    Account Reconciliation command, 264
    Accounts Receivable command, 150, 170